The
Encyclopedia
of
CRAFTS

The
Encyclopedia
of
CRAFTS

CHANCELLOR
PRESS

Previously published in 1982 by
The Hamlyn Publishing Group Limited
part of Reed International Books.

This edition published in 1992 by
Chancellor Press
Michelin House
81 Fulham Road
London SW3 6RB

The material used in this book formed part of a
series of cards published by Odhams Mail Order,
a Division of The Hamlyn Publishing Group Limited.

Copyright © this arrangement 1982 by Reed International
Books Limited.

ISBN 1 85152 168 2

Printed in Czechoslovakia
52056/02

Contents

Detailed contents are shown on pages 6 and 7

The technique of patchwork

Hand-sewn patchwork is not only an economical way of using up odd scraps of material, it is also a soothing and relaxing pastime, since you can pick it up and do a little whenever you feel like it.

Beginners may like to start by buying a kit, which will contain everything needed, including a design to work. Many of those on the market are good value, but if you save old clothes and scraps from dressmaking, the materials needed for patchwork are easily come by, and anyway it is more interesting making up your own designs.

Materials and tools
Since the patches must be sewn together very neatly, you need fine needles and thread which will blend unobtrusively with the materials being used. You also need fine pins, sharp scissors, and paper for patterns. Use two pairs of scissors, one for cutting fabrics and another for cutting paper patterns, as cutting paper will blunt a pair of scissors quickly.

Fabrics should be non-stretch and should not fray too easily. If the work is to receive hard wear, such as some clothes and furnishings, choose firmly woven cottons, which will wash. If the finished patchwork is simply decorative you can mix fabrics. However, remember that some fabrics wear out more quickly than others. When mixing old and new fabrics, wash both before using them and always iron fabrics before cutting out.

Cutting patterns and patches
In hand-sewn patchwork, each patch is made over a paper shape and is tacked to the paper. This holds the patch firmly in shape. The paper shapes are cut from templates, made of plastic or metal, which can be bought from craft shops in different geometric shapes, such as hexagons, diamonds, triangles etc. The most popular shape is the hexagon (6-sided) because the angles are wide and it is easy to turn hems and join patches neatly. Hexagons used alone will make all kinds of interesting patterns.

The paper used to back patches should be fairly heavy, such as stiff brown paper or old gift cards. The fabric must be able to be folded sharply on edges and corners, and if the paper is too soft, the edges will not be sharp.

Cut as many paper shapes as you need (one for each patch), cutting from the template. Accurate cutting is essential. Lay the paper pattern on the wrong side of the material with parallel sides on the straight grain. Pin, and cut out patches, allowing a 6mm. (¼in.) turning all round.

Turn over all the edges and tack them to the paper, as shown in the diagram. Take out the pins. On very fine fabrics, stick the edges to the paper patch with a scrap of cellophane tape catching the pleats at the corners only with a stitch. This prevents pins marking the fine fabric.

With the right sides of two patches held together, oversew the edges with tiny upright stitches starting at the right. Do not tie a knot in the thread. Lay the end of the thread along the top of the patches and work the first stitches over it. When joining dark patches to light ones, dark thread will show less than light thread. When the whole patchwork is finished, snip the tacking stitches and then press on the right side. Shake out the papers. Patchwork is usually lined to preserve its shape.

Planning patchwork
Plan your design carefully before starting, making sure that you have enough patches of the right colour, as it may be difficult to find substitutes. It is a good idea to make something small and quick to begin with, perhaps a hexagon rosette (see photograph) which could be appliquéd to a cushion, or a tea cosy.

If you are uncertain of the design, place the ready-to-sew patches on a flat surface and move them about until you reach a pattern which suits the colours you have. You can then make a note of the arrangement to guide you as you work.

Too many printed fabrics together will look muddled, so link prints with a plain fabric. Patches in strong colours grouped together will stand out better than single strong-coloured patches among paler ones.

Contrast dark colours in groups with light, or make a related design by choosing colours, toning and matching yellows with oranges and greens, or blues shading to greens, or reds shading to purples, rather than choosing colours at random.

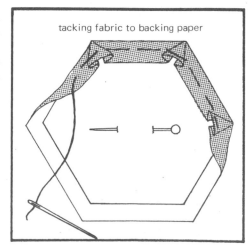
tacking fabric to backing paper

Patchwork cot quilt

This pretty and economical patchwork quilt was quickly made by machine-sewing squares of material together, one of the easiest ways of doing patchwork.

Materials required
Cotton fabrics, sufficient for 104 9cm. (3½in.) squares (unstitched)
Striped cotton backing fabric, 1 metre (39in.) square
Polyester wadding 1 metre (39in.) square
Piece of cardboard for template 9cm. (3½in.) square
Craft knife
Ruler
Set square
Sewing cotton

Note
The best fabrics for the patchwork panels are those which do not stretch or fray, so good quality cotton is ideal and it has the added advantage of washing well. You could also use polyester and cotton mixtures, but do not mix fabrics, and do not mix old and new fabrics, as the weaker ones will wear out more quickly than the stronger ones. Make sure all materials are colour-fast before using them, and wash and press new fabric before using it in case of shrinkage.

To make the quilt
Cut an accurate cardboard template, 9cm. (3½in.) square, using the following method. Draw a straight line, 9cm. (3½in.) long. Place your set square on the line so that the corner of the set square is on one end (Fig. 1). Mark a point about half way up the set square and draw another line from the end of the first line through the point (Fig. 2). Repeat the process for 3rd and 4th sides. Cut out carefully with a craft knife.

Iron all the materials. Placing the template on the straight grain of the wrong side of the material, draw round it with a soft but sharp pencil. Use a sharp, light crayon for dark fabrics. Cut out all the patches with sharp scissors.

Lay the patches out on a table, arranging them in a pleasing design.

With the right side of the fabric facing, and allowing 1cm. (⅜in.) for seam allowance, machine stitch the patches into 8 strips, each strip containing 13 patches. Press open all the seams.

Now the strips have to be stitched together. It is easy to make an error in seam allowances, so tack the strips together, allowing 1cm. (⅜in.) seam allowance, and making sure that the corners of the patches match up. If they do not, either ease the fabric a little, or if necessary, unpick the faulty seam and re-stitch it.

Machine stitch the strips together.

The centre panel will now measure 58cm. by 93cm. (approximately 22¾in. by 36½in.).

Cut 2 strips of striped material measuring 68cm. by 7.5cm. (27in. by 3in.) for foot and top border, and 2 strips of striped material measuring 93cm. by 7cm. (36½in. by 2¾in. approximately) for the side borders.

Sew these strips all round the centre panel so as to frame it, taking in the usual 1cm. (⅜in.) seam allowance at the sides, but a 1.5cm. (⅝in.) seam allowance at the foot and the top of the panel. This extra seam allowance top and bottom enables you to get the backing material out of a 1 metre (39in.) length of material.

When stitched, with borders, the quilt should now measure 68cm. by 105cm. (27in. by 42in. approximately). Press open all seams.

Cut a backing of striped material measuring 68cm. by 105cm. (27in. by 42in. approximately) and a piece of polyester wadding the same size.

With the right sides of the fabrics facing, tack 3 sides and the wadding together, leaving one narrow end open for turning. Machine-stitch the 3 sides, taking in 1cm. (⅜in.) seam allowance. Trim off surplus

wadding from the seam edges and turn right side out. Oversew the open end by hand, using small stitches.

Tack and then machine-stitch all round the centre panel, to give the edges a quilted look.

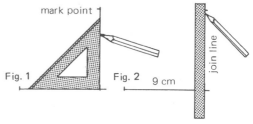

mark point

join line

Fig. 1   Fig. 2   9 cm

PLAN OF QUILT

top edge 68 cm x 7.5 cm (unsewn)

side edges 93 cm x 7 cm

patchwork (sewn) 58 cm x 93 cm

bottom edge 68 cm x 7.5 cm (unsewn)

seam allowances 1 cm **except** for top and bottom

Quilting

Quilting, one of the oldest forms of embroidery, originally served an entirely practical purpose – it was a way of making bedcovers and garments warmer by sewing an interlining between two layers of fabric. As the stitches themselves formed an attractive relief pattern in conjunction with the padding, more elaborate designs were created, many of them very beautiful.

Types of quilting

There are three main types, English, Italian and trapunto. The commonest is English in which the design or motif is stitched right through all three layers, usually in running or back stitch. This is the most suitable type for quilting by machine.

Italian quilting differs from English in that the two layers of fabric are sewn together first and then stuffed. The designs are outlined with parallel lines which are worked in running stitch. The lines are close together and various kinds of threads are drawn through the channels created by the lines, to give the raised look. The stuffing is always done from the back: sometimes thick wool is used, and sometimes cord or piping.

Trapunto is in some ways a mixture of the two previous methods. The design is sewn through two layers of material, as in Italian quilting, but the design is sewn with only one line, not two, as in English quilting. The work is then padded from the back. Various stuffings are used, such as kapok or cotton wool. A slit is made in the backing fabric, in the middle of the shape. Stuffing is pushed in through this slit to fill the shape and the slit is then sewn up with oversewing.

Materials

The top layer of a piece of quilting can be a thin, firm fabric such as cotton, organdie or fine linen. The backing should be a fairly loosely woven fabric such as cotton cheese cloth, which will prevent the stitches from sinking through into the padding. You can, of course, use the same fabric for top and backing if you want the article to be reversible.

The thinner the top fabric, the 'higher' it will quilt. If a bottom fabric of calico was used and the top layer was of fine cotton, the pattern would be more defined on the cotton.

The middle filling can be a variety of fabrics. Polyester wadding is very useful and available in different weights, which enables you to choose the thickness of

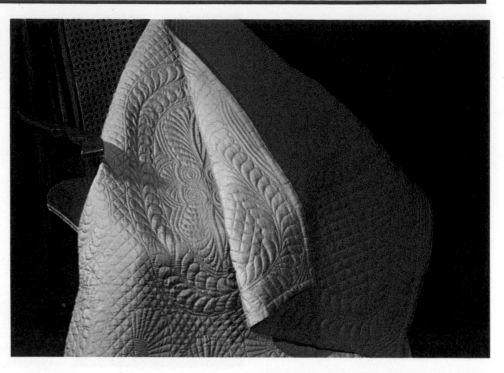

the finished work. For quilting between fine fabrics such as silk, soft woollens or even felt can be used to give a gentler effect. (Felt cannot of course be washed.)

It is advisable to use needles instead of pins for fastening the work as they leave no mark even on delicate fabrics, but if you do use pins, make sure they are the steel dressmaker's type. The ones with coloured, glass heads are best.

Working the quilting

To mark designs on to the fabric, either use a commercial transfer or the dressmaker's carbon method explained on page 108. You can transfer the design either on to the top surface or the under surface of the work. If you are making something which will be frequently washed it does not matter if the design shows between the quilting stitches at first, and it is more interesting to quilt on the top surface. However, if it is a delicate piece of work which will not be much used and will be occasionally dry-cleaned, it is safer to mark the design on the under surface, as this will show less.

When you have ironed off the transfer, place the three thicknesses together with the padding in the middle and tack them very firmly together, as they must not be allowed to move while you are working. It is safest to tack all round the edges of the work through all three thicknesses, then tack close together in all directions across the work (vertically, horizontally and diagonally). If you are going to do a

lot of traditional quilting it is worth investing in a frame. If you are working a large item without a frame, the best way is to quilt each block separately and join them together afterwards.

Quilting can be done by machine, but traditionally it is done by hand, in either running stitch, backstitch or chain stitch (see page 103). Only one type of stitch should be used in any one piece of work. Of the three stitches, backstitch is the strongest and firmest. Chain stitch is the least used nowadays but is found in old work.

If you are working on a thick piece of quilting, it is better to stab the stitches through individually from back to front because, if you take two or three running stitches at once, there is a risk that they may not go through all the layers in some places.

You can achieve various effects by the colour of the sewing thread you use, which should be a strong cotton or, if you are working on a silk material, a strong sewing silk. Choose a thread the same colour as the top surface, but a shade or two darker if you want to add emphasis. In fact, if the wadding is thick the stitching will not show very much, the effect being obtained by the design.

Quilted evening bag

This evening bag is quilted in the trapunto style with a simple geometric pattern based on oblongs. The silver handle is bought, and its size determines how much fabric is needed (you can make the bag larger or smaller).

You will need

A bought silver clasp handle 20cm. (7¾in.) long

Piece of fine cotton lawn or silk 30cm. by 22cm. (11¾in. by 8½in.)

Piece of heavier cotton fabric 30cm. by 22cm. (11¾in. by 8½in.) for backing

Silk or cotton the same size for lining

Crewel needle No.8

Small amount of kapok or wadding

1 skein blue stranded cotton

40cm. (15¾in.) dark blue silken cord

You may find it helpful to read page 10 before starting to make the bag.

Working the embroidery

Traditionally this type of embroidery is worked by hand in a small even running stitch, but you can sew this by machine if you prefer. The design is a simple pattern of oblongs, and the quilting is sewn through both layers of fabric.

Tack the two layers together with a vertical line up the centre and a horizontal line crossing it. If you wish, you can transfer the design on to the cloth before you start the work, but it is quite simple to work without transferring, just by following the diagram. First sew the horizontal lines of the pattern which form the basis of the design, and then work the small lines that cross the main ones. Work both sides of the bag in the same way.

Once the sewing is complete you are ready to insert the padding. This is done from the back. Using a very sharp pair of pointed scissors, cut a small slit in the back of each shape created by the sewn lines, taking great care only to cut through one layer.

You can now stuff the shape through this slit, pushing the stuffing into place with a round-ended knitting needle or some similar implement. Fill each shape evenly and firmly. If you are using wadding rather than kapok you will need to tear it into small pieces first. Do not stuff the narrow shapes at the top and bottom of the oblong, as these parts of the fabric are sewn into the handle. When all the shapes are stuffed, slip stitch slits up by hand.

Lay the lining fabric on the right side of the work and sew it down each of the long sides 1cm. (⅜in.) from the edge. Turn this 'envelope' right side out so that the seams are on the inside.

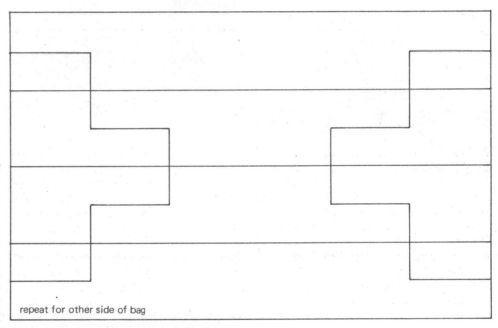

repeat for other side of bag

Making up

You will find that the handle has holes in it for sewing through. Carefully fit the top of the oblong into the handle, and sew the fabric into it, using three strands of the stranded cotton. Go through the holes in a running stitch and back again, to give a solid effect. When you have sewn in both tops, slip stitch the sides of the bag together.

Cut the silken cord in half. Take the top of the cord through the underneath of the clasp at the hinge and stitch it down along the inside seam. Then sew it in place along the outside edge, finishing at the end with a binding stitch over the cord. Fray the spare end of the cord up to the binding stitch and tease the fibres out with a needle or a metal comb.

Designs in patchwork

Tumbling block

Spool

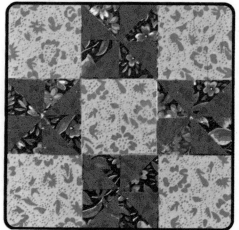
Pinwheel

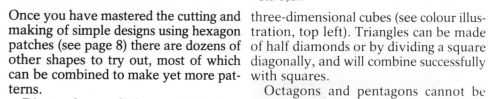
Bear's paw

furnishings. These old American designs are enjoying a revival today.

The significant point of American patchwork is that it is pieced without inner papers or cardboard shapes. Individual patches are joined with fine running stitches. The process is much faster than English patchwork.

The 'Spool' design, based on a cotton reel pattern, is a combination of the trapezium and squares; Bear's Paw is based on triangles, squares and strips, while the 'Pinwheel' pattern is again triangles and squares (see colour illustrations) **All these designs demonstrate how, with a little ingenuity, it is possible to create exciting and different patterns from relatively simple basic shapes.**

'Log Cabin' is another American patchwork design, slightly different from the others in that it is made up in blocks of patches, which are then joined together to make a quilt or a large piece of patchwork. It differs also from simple patchwork in that the blocks are made by sewing strips of fabric to a foundation fabric, each strip being built out from a central square, with the edges overlapping (Figs. 2a, b, c, d). This technique is especially suitable for quilts because the resultant fabric is both strong and warm.

Once you have mastered the cutting and making of simple designs using hexagon patches (see page 8) there are dozens of other shapes to try out, most of which can be combined to make yet more patterns.

Diamonds are a little more difficult to work than hexagons because of their sharp points. Cutting these accurately needs a great deal of care in the folding, trimming and tacking. When working with diamonds, it is a good idea to use thin card rather than paper shapes, as the card is stronger and the fabric can be folded around it more accurately. If you find it too difficult to tack through the cardboard, turn the edges under by sticking them to the cardboard with masking tape. Catch the corners firmly with the thread and then remove tape and cardboard.

You can create some lovely designs with diamonds, such as the starburst pattern known as 'Star of Bethlehem', or the famous 'Tumbling Blocks' design, when three diamonds in dark, medium and light shades of different colours are joined in hexagon shapes to give the effect of

three-dimensional cubes (see colour illustration, top left). Triangles can be made of half diamonds or by dividing a square diagonally, and will combine successfully with squares.

Octagons and pentagons cannot be used on their own but have to be combined with squares and diamond shapes.

Other shapes to experiment with are the trapezium, stripes and long rectangles, and the clamshell pattern (Fig. 1) in which the curved edges overlap each other. This attractive design is made by turning the curved edge on to a card template, taking tiny pleats in the material so that it lies flat, then hemming down the patches in straight rows, each row overlapping the previous one. **If you are thinking of embarking on this it might be as well to buy a template as the shape is quite difficult to cut accurately.**

American patchwork
There is a long tradition of patchwork in America, dating back to the days of the early settlers, when every available scrap of material that came to hand had to be used to make bed quilts and other home

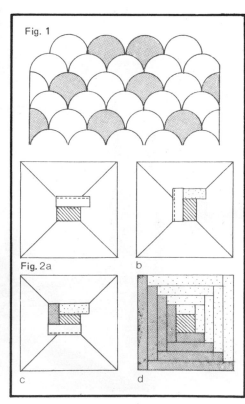

Patchwork tray set

They look as if they came from an exclusive craft shop, but you can make them for next to nothing. The patchwork tea cosy, egg cosy and oven mitt can be assembled from any scraps of finely woven fabrics, sewn together on a machine.

You will need

Scraps of at least 4 different patterned fabrics
About 20cm. (8in.) of one other patterned fabric 90cm. (36in.) wide
Piece of 40cm. (16in.) of lightweight polyester wadding
Oddments of toning fabric to use for the lining
Graph paper marked in 1cm. squares
Sheet of cartridge paper

The tea cosy

Copy the outline of the tea cosy shown in Fig. 1 on to the graph paper, square by square. Trace this shape on to folded cartridge paper, placing the fold along the dotted line as indicated. Cut out the paper template.

From the patterned fabrics cut out 33 7cm. (2¾in.) squares. Lay them down touching each other in 4 horizontal rows of 7 squares each, and one top row of 5 squares, centrally positioned over the other rows. Swop the squares around until you are satisfied with the arrangement.

Pick up the 7 squares which form the bottom row, and pin them together with right sides facing and taking 1cm. (⅛in.) seams. Machine them to form a long strip. Join the squares in each horizontal row in the same way. Trim seams and press them open. Finally pin and machine together all 5 strips, taking care to match seams each time.

Make the other side of the cosy in the same way and trim both sides to the size of the template.

Again using the template, cut 2 pieces of lining fabric and 2 of wadding. For binding, cut several crossways strips 2cm. (¾in.) wide from the largest piece of patterned fabric, joining the strips as necessary.

Sandwich each piece of wadding between the patchwork piece and the lining, with right sides outwards. Tack each triple thickness together round the edges. With right sides facing and taking a very small turning, pin and machine one long edge of a binding strip to the straight edge of each cosy half. Hand-stitch outer long edge of binding to lining, enclosing raw edges. With the patchwork outside, and taking 1cm. (⅜in.) seam, machine together the two cosy halves round the curved raw edges. Trim seam. Use another crossways strip of fabric to bind the round curved raw edges, turning in the ends of the binding and finishing neatly by hand at the base of the cosy.

The oven mitt

Make the template for the oven mitt as before.

Make in the same way as the tea cosy, using 12 fabric squares for each half of cover, arranged in 4 horizontal rows of 3 squares.

When binding curved edges, extend the binding to make a hanging loop.

The egg cosy

Make the template as before.

Cut 6 10cm. (4in.) by 2.5cm. (1in.) strips from each of 2 different patterned fabrics. With right sides facing, join matching strips in pairs, short to long edge, taking a narrow seam (Fig. 2). Trim and press seams open. The strips now form a V-shape.

Arrange the V-shapes to form a parquet design (Fig. 3). With right sides facing, join the V-shapes with narrow seams. Trim and press open seams.

Make another patchwork piece in the same way for the second side of the cosy cover. Trim both pieces to the size of your template making sure that the points of the V-shape fall in the centre of each cosy piece.

Complete as for the tea cosy.

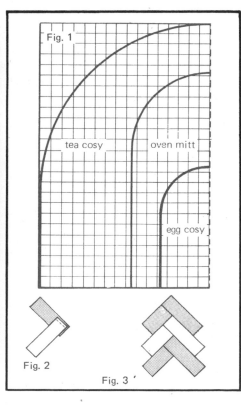

Fig. 1
tea cosy   oven mitt
egg cosy

Fig. 2
Fig. 3

The art of appliqué

Appliqué is the technique of applying one fabric to another. There are different methods but the finished effect is always of a pattern or shape on a foundation fabric of a different kind. Appliqué is one of the oldest forms of embroidery. It was certainly known in the Middle Ages and was probably introduced into the West from the Middle East where the Crusaders saw appliquéd flags in the Holy Wars.

If the item is to be washed, only colour-fast cottons should be used for appliqué. If it can be dry cleaned, then you can mix fabrics of different types, but they should be closely woven and non-pile. However, non-fray and non-stretch fabrics are best. Background fabrics should always be new and closely woven.

Appliqué can be used with embroidery stitches and in conjunction with patchwork and quilting, as in the making of American quilts.

There are different methods of working appliqué but the basic method for preparing the shapes is the same.

Preparing fabric

Appliqué designs can be made from embroidery patterns or book and magazine illustrations. Trace the design on to thin card or thick interfacing and cut out for a template. Lay the template on the fabric, making sure that the shape is on the straight grain.

Blind appliqué

Lay the template on the wrong side of the fabric and pencil round the shape. Cut out with 6mm. (¼in.) seam allowance all round. Using the template, turn the raw edges of the shape to the wrong side. Snip into curves to make a neat turn (Fig. 1). Press. Pin the prepared shape on the background fabric and slip stitch the edges neatly. The stitches should be almost invisible.

If you are making up a picture by this method, lay the largest areas of the design first and then add the small areas.

Machine-stitched appliqué

Both of the following techniques are best used on fabrics which do not stretch and are non-fray.

Lay the template on the right side of the fabric and pencil round lightly. Without cutting out, work a line of machine stitching on the pencilled line. Cut out the shape, 3mm. (⅛in.) away from the machined line. Pin and tack to the background fabric. Set your sewing machine to a zigzag stitch so that you are working satin stitch. Work satin stitch over the raw edges of the shape (Fig. 2). If you prefer, you can work buttonhole stitch over the edges, by hand.

The alternative method involves cutting out the shape without a seam allowance, tacking it to the background fabric and satin stitching the edges. This technique is ideal for working appliqué on denim and is very quick. If used on thinner fabrics, however, it is inclined to pucker.

Felt appliqué

Felt, being a non-fray fabric, is ideal for appliqué. Simply cut out the shapes, pin them to the background, or hold them in position with a touch of fabric adhesive and then work straight machine stitching round the edges (Fig. 4). This is a good technique to use when working large areas of design in felt. It can also be used on other non-fray fabrics such as close-woven cotton when making items such as garden cushions.

San Blas or cut-work appliqué

This method was evolved in the islands of San Blas off the coast of Panama where the Indian women make marvellous brightly coloured panels (molas), using a layering technique. Two to five layers of fabric are laid one on top of another and tacked together. Areas are cut away to reveal the layers beneath (Fig. 5).

The cut edges are turned under and hemmed. If several layers of fabric are used, reversible pieces of San Blas can be made, each side different and fabrics cut away from the middle layer. Sharp scissors are needed for San Blas work and you must be careful to cut through only one layer at a time.

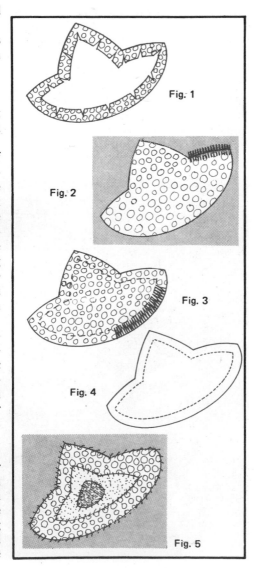

Fig. 1

Fig. 2

Fig. 3

Fig. 4

Fig. 5

Appliqué tablecloth

This bright, bold tablecloth with appliqué flowers will give a feeling of summer even when the sun is not shining. It would look lovely for outdoor teas, and add cheer to festive occasions indoors.

You will need
1.20m. (48in.) of light green cotton fabric 115cm. (48in.) width
½m. (20in.) dark green
½m. (20in.) pink
½m. (20in.) red
1 skein red stranded cotton
Machine thread to match each fabric

Note
Always cut out the shapes to be applied on the straight grain of the fabric, or they may wrinkle when applied.

Fig. 1

Fig. 2

Working the design
The flowers and leaves are very simple shapes and can be drawn freehand, using the diagram (Fig. 1) as a guide. Each one measures about 14cm. (5½in.) across. There are 4 shapes: the flower heads, the centres, the stems and the leaves. Draw all these out on paper, cut them out, and pin the pieces on to the fabric. The flower heads are in red, the middles pink, and the flower stems and leaves dark green. Cut out 3 sets of flowers, middles, stems and leaves for each corner and one set for each side, a total of 16. Pin them in place, with the stems of the flowers tucked under the flower heads at the top, and under the leaves at the bottom. Tack them all very carefully.

All the appliqué is done by machine, using the swing needle. If you wish to work by hand, you can use buttonhole stitch throughout the work. When working by machine, set the swing needle to its widest setting, No.4 or 5, and the stitch length at 0. This gives a close satin stitch effect which will cover all the raw edges.

Sew round the flower heads first, using the matching thread. Sew round the flower centres next, and finally the stems and leaves. When all the appliqué is done, neaten the machine work by taking any spare ends of thread through to the back of the work and fastening them off.

The middle of each flower is decorated with large French knots (Fig. 2), using 4 twists of the thread round the needle. Work several knots in each flower middle, using 2 strands of floss.

When all the embroidery is done, hem the edges of the tablecloth by hand and remove all the tacking threads. Press the work lightly between damp cloths.

Quilted sunflower

Quilting is a fascinating craft because it can be used in so many ways. We have explained the basic technique of quilting and its uses on page 10. Now we show you some of the decorative possibilities. This pages gives instructions for working the sunflower design to make a very striking wall hanging.

Alternatively, you might make two for a brilliant cushion, or combine several flowers to make a bedspread or a door curtain.

You will need

1 sheet tracing paper for pattern for sunflower

Dressmaker's carbon paper

Piece finely woven yellow cotton fabric 61cm. (24in.) long by 38cm. (15in.) wide

Piece finely woven orange cotton fabric 20.5cm. (8¼in.) square

Of stranded cotton: 1 skein each light flame red, dark flame red, yellow

Kapok for filling

Piece soft fibre board 28cm. (11in.) square

Drawing pins

Matching thread

Sharp scissors

To make pattern

Fig. 1 is the sunflower pattern, with each square representing 5cm. (2in.). To enlarge the pattern draw a 20cm. (8in.) square on the tracing paper and then mark it into 16 5cm. (2in.) squares. Copy the design carefully from Fig. 1. (You'll find it easier if you pin the paper to a wooden table top.) You have now made the pattern for the orange areas: the outside edges and the centre circle. With dressmaker's carbon paper under your tracing paper pattern, draw over the outlines on to the orange material, placing the pattern centrally on it. Remove tracing paper and carbon. Machine stitch on the traced line and then carefully cut out from the orange material the large petals (white areas on diagram) and discard. The stitching prevents fraying, but be careful to cut just inside it.

Now cut from the yellow fabric 2 squares, one measuring 22.5cm. (8¾in.) square, and one measuring 38cm. (15in.) square. Cut one circle 9.5cm. (3¾in.) in diameter. Put larger square and circle aside. Place the orange pieces on top of the smaller yellow square, matching edges. Pin, and then tack together round edges and round large petals, inside machine

stitching. Using 2 strands of embroidery cotton, chain stitch round the cut-out edges of the petals, using light flame red round yellow petals and dark flame red round central orange petals.

Turn under 6mm. (¼in.) all round yellow circle, and tack. Using yellow, embroider Jacobean couching (Fig. 2) over circle. Using light flame red, criss-cross the whole design, diagonally in one direction, then the other. Tack and sew embroidered centre centrally over flower.

The flower is now complete, but the quilting has not yet been done. Place the whole flower on the large yellow square, turn under the edges by 1.2cm. (½in.), and sew neatly to the yellow background, leaving an opening at the bottom. Fill the whole flower with kapok, spreading evenly, and sew opening to close. Stab stitch all round the centre and the flower petals, taking the thread through all thicknesses of fabric and kapok. It is this stitching which gives the quilted effect.

Mount the finished work on a board, stretching and securing the background fabric with drawing pins at the back.

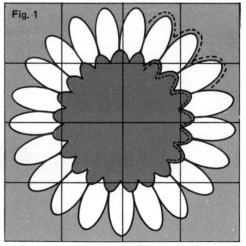

Fig. 1

Machine stitch on dotted line

Fig. 2

Iron and sew patchwork

Appliqué patchwork is one of the iron and sew techniques. Almost no sewing is involved yet the finished result looks very authentic. You can use it to decorate all kinds of home accessories. All you need are some scraps of fabric, a background fabric and iron-on adhesive tape.

The technique
The background fabric and the patches must be able to stand up to the heat of the iron. Test all fabrics before using them because some will melt under heat.

Cut pieces of iron-on adhesive tape to fit the area of fabric to be covered with patchwork. Lay it on the right side. Following the instructions on the pack, press the adhesive tape on to the fabric. Peel off the paper backing. Cut the patches to shape with no turnings allowance. Arrange them on the prepared fabric, right side up, edges butting exactly so that no background fabric shows. Cover with a piece of muslin or thin cotton and press as described on the adhesive tape pack. Leave work to cool off. Test, and if any of the patches are not securely adhering, press again.

Finishing the patchwork
If you are applying a fabric such as felt to a felt background, you might decide to leave the appliqué just as it is. Cotton, wool and similar close-weave fabrics look better if the cut edges are covered with embroidery; this also helps to give the effect of real patchwork.

You can finish the edges with stitches such as buttonhole stitch, blanket stitch, Cretan stitch, feather stitch and chain stitch. Use stranded embroidery cotton or pearl cotton if the item is going to be washed. If your piece can be dry cleaned, you can use a whole range of decorative threads.

Machine finishing
Satin-stitch edging can only be worked on a swing-needle sewing machine. Set the machine to a narrow zigzag for a satin stitch effect of about 3mm. (⅛in.) wide. Work all along the cut edges of the patches. If you are using non-fray fabrics, straight stitching can be worked about 3mm. (⅛in.) from the edge.

Uses for iron and sew patchwork
This is a quick decorative technique so you can use it for quite large projects. You could make a bed cover, combining patchwork shapes and large areas of a single colour fabric. Cushions look effective, or you might work a strip of patches as a trim for plain curtains. Bed sheets and pillow cases can be personalised with a group of patches. Hexagons, applied in a rosette pattern, would look pretty in pastel shades or in a small, contrasting print.

Small, home accessories – cosies, tray-cloths, place mats, oven mitts and so on, can be matched to a colour scheme with a group or trim of patches.

Patchwork designs are simple to apply to children's clothes and sports clothes using the iron and sew method. Keep patches simple and fairly large and work out your designs on squared paper before applying them to the garment (Fig. 1).

Dressmaking with iron and sew
Patchwork projects which you might not otherwise attempt are easier with the iron and sew technique. Patchwork skirts or jackets, where a large area of fabric is required, are quick to make up and you have the advantage that the patchwork is already backed and ready to use. Make up your pieces of patchwork and then use it as ordinary fabric, pinning the paper pattern to it and cutting out. Take extra care if you are making an item such as a jacket where the fronts should match. Work two pieces of patchwork side by side so that patches align and match when the garment is made up (Fig. 2).

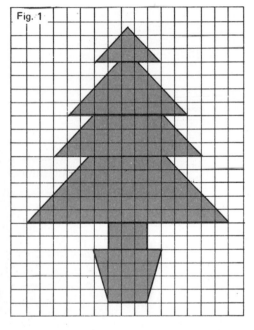

Fig. 1

Fig. 2

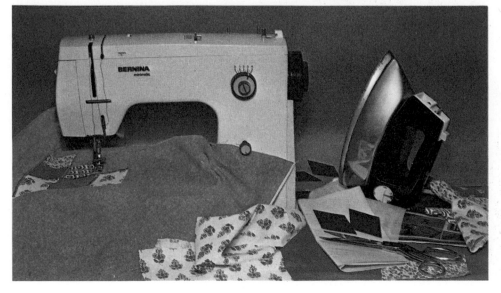

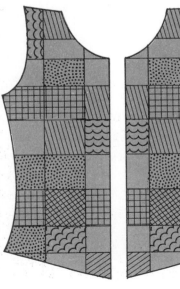

Animal cushions

There's no special skill required to make these appliqué nursery cushions and you can use a sewing machine throughout.

You will need

For each cushion
50cm. (½yd.) 90cm. (36in.) wide sailcloth or strong cotton: yellow, purple and pink.
Matching thread. Cushion pad 40cm. (16in.) square. Graph paper, pencil

Squirrel cushion
Piece brown felt 30cm. by 60cm. (12in. by 24in.); scraps of black and white felt

Owl cushion
18cm. (7in.) squares of mauve, coral and pink felt; scraps of pale pink and orange felt

Cat cushion
30cm. (12in.) square black felt; 18cm. (7cm.) square fawn felt; scrap pink felt
Fabric adhesive

Patterns

Copy outlines and details from diagram on to graph paper (each square on the diagram represents 2.5cm. (1in.). Cut out complete patterns from the graph paper and then cut the component parts, following diagram and colour illustration. The squirrel has 2 parts; the owl 9; the cat 7. Do not cut out the details of the faces; these are used as a guide later. Cut out the felt pieces. Cut 2 43cm. (17in.) square pieces of sailcloth for each cushion.

Arrange the felt pieces on the right side of each sailcloth square, stick them down lightly with adhesive, and machine each piece in place 3mm. (⅛in.) from edges. For the squirrel's eyes, cut 1 circle 6mm. (¼in.) in diameter from black felt. Stick in place, following your pattern. For the cat's nose, cut a triangle 1.2cm. (½in.) wide in pink, stick in place. The other details of the faces are made with machine stitching. You will find it easier if you mark the curved lines for the owl's eyes, and the whiskers, mouth and eyes for the cat in pencil or chalk before stitching. Follow your pattern for position, or make a tracing of the pattern pieces and transfer on to the felt.

Finishing

Make up each cushion as follows. With right sides facing, machine the two squares together, leaving a 1.2cm. (½in.) seam allowance. Leave one side open. Clip seam at corners and press on wrong side. Turn covers right side out and insert cushion pads. Turn in remaining raw edges 1.2cm. (½in.) and oversew together.

Quilted picnic set

This picnic set has everything – a place mat, pockets for knife, spoon and fork, a napkin in a ring – and the whole thing rolls and ties up to go in the picnic basket.

You will need
For one set
Cotton fabric with 5cm. (2in.) squares, size 45cm. by 30cm. (18in. by 12in.)
Plain fabric to tone for napkins, ties and trim, approximately 45cm. by 90cm. (18in. by 36in.)
Piece cotton fabric in small checks, size about 25cm. by 90cm. (10in. by 36in.)
Sew-in interfacing

Note
If you can't get checked fabric, use two contrasting fabrics of your own choice. A small floral design in two different colours would look attractive, and so would plain, strongly coloured fabrics in two shades.

Place mat
Cut a piece 45cm. by 30cm. (18in. by 12in.) from the plain fabric. Cut a piece of the interfacing to the same size. Tack it to the wrong side of the fabric. Tack the large-square fabric on top of the interfacing right side up. Tack first round the edges then horizontally and vertically several times to hold the layers firmly. Quilt diagonally as shown in the illustration, using machine stitching.

Pockets
Cut the small-check fabric to make pockets, 1 piece 15cm. by 5cm. (6in. by 2in.) for the spoon pocket and 15cm. by 6.2cm. (6in. by 2½in.) for the knife and fork. Turn in the edges once 6mm. (¼in.) and machine stitch. Press and slip stitch the pockets to the place mat. Work back stitch down the middle of the knife and fork pocket to make 2 pockets. Make sure that slip stitches go through the top fabric of the place mat only.

Napkin and ring
Cut a 25cm. (10in.) square from the plain fabric. Machine hem the edges. Cut a strip of the small check fabric 18.5cm. (7in.) square. Fold it and machine stitch round on 3 sides leaving a gap to turn through. Turn right side out and press, sew up the gap. Sew press fasteners and wrap the napkin ring round the folded napkin.

Finishing
Cut bias strips from the remaining plain fabric. Cut strips on the straight 5cm.

(2in.) wide. Fold and machine stitch to make a tie. Bind the edges of the place mat with bias strips. Hand stitch the fold of the tie to the outside of the place mat abut 2.5cm. (1in.) from the left edge.

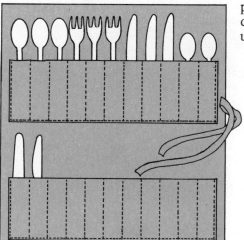

Other ideas
Fabric rolls like this make very good cases for your best silver cutlery. After making the basic mat, cut 2 strips of fabric to just under half the depth. Neaten the top edges. Press a turning on 3 sides. Stitch pockets to slip forks and spoons into (see drawing). Roll up and tie. This could be used for knitting needles if you prefer.

Ribbon appliqué

Decorating clothes and accessories with ribbons and braids is a popular technique, and very pretty, but had you thought of using it for home furnishings? Plain fabric curtains can have two or three bands of contrasting ribbon along the hems or down the sides. Tablecloths can look very special with a wide band of a patterned ribbon appliquéd round the hem. You might decorate a set of napkins to match, stitching the ribbon strip down the side of the napkin or round the edges. Cushions present lots of opportunities for decorating with ribbons. Stitch them flat on the fabric to make patterns or geometric designs or use some of the techniques illustrated to make flowers or leaf designs.

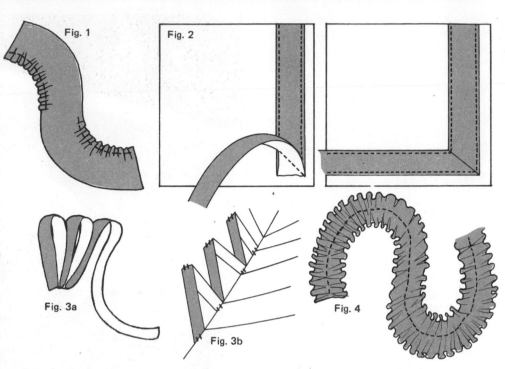

Flat appliqué
Ribbons and braids should be machine stitched to the background fabric, using a closely matching thread or one that contrasts strongly. If the ribbon and the background fabric will stand the heat of an iron (test a scrap first) apply the ribbon with iron-on adhesive tape first then machine stitch along both edges on the right side. Alternatively, you will have to tack the ribbon in position along both edges using small stitches, then machine stitch. Turn the ends under neatly and stitch across.

Curved shapes
Run a gathering thread along one edge. Pin the ribbon to the fabric (Fig. 1). Hand hemstitch the gathered edge. Machine stitch the plain edge.

Turning corners and mitres
Pin and tack in position. Topstitch to the place where the ribbon will be turned for the corner. Fold the ribbon back and press the fold (Fig. 2). Fold forward again in the direction intended and make a diagonal crease. Stitch on the crease, through both the ribbon and the background fabric. Cut away the triangle of ribbon, then continue applying the ribbon and topstitching.

Petals and leaves
Mark the fabric with chalk lines. Turn and press under the end of the ribbon. Lay the ribbon on the chalk line and pin. Fold and pin the ribbon to make petals (Fig. 3a). Catch the loops down with two small stitches (Fig. 3b).

Ruched appliqué
Run a gathering thread along the middle of the ribbon. Pull up the thread. Pin and tack the ribbon to the fabric. Machine stitch along the gathering line (Fig. 4). This effect looks pretty worked in scrolled patterns for a bed cover.

Clamshell patchwork

Clamshell patchwork is much more like appliqué than the other patchwork techniques. The template is non-geometric and cannot be combined with any other shape. It is mostly used for working areas of colourful edging or for a motif on a garment, such as the panel on the cotton dress illustrated. However, clamshell patchwork is also used for making small accessories – bags, cushions, teacosies, pincushions and so on. The patchwork is worked first and then is cut into the shape required for the item.

The technique for working clamshell patchwork is slow and time-consuming and you should practise a small piece before attempting a large project.

Fabrics, needles and thread
The clamshells are hemmed together by hand and thus only smooth, fine fabrics are suitable. The example illustrated is worked in polyester satin ribbon, which is ideal as you can buy quite short lengths of wide ribbon and thus get a good range of colours quite cheaply. Woven cotton and cotton mixtures, lawn, silk, satin and similar fabrics are used for this patchwork. If you are using semi-transparent fabrics, baste the fabric to muslin first and then work both layers together to prevent the turnings showing through.

Use fine sewing needles and closely matching, good-quality sewing threads. If possible, use tacking thread or real silk thread for tacking – sewing thread is inclined to leave holes in fine fabrics. Use only glass-headed dressmaker pins, which are fine and slim.

Templates
Clamshell templates can be bought in most needlework shops and haberdashery counters. If you have difficulty in obtaining one, you can make your own from the shape shown here (Fig. 1). Trace it off carefully and transfer it onto a piece of stiff cardboard. Make sure that

the curve is smooth because this is the most important part of the template. Cut out the template with a pair of sharp scissors and, if necessary, smooth off the curved edge with sandpaper.

Use the template to cut out the backing papers for each patch, as for other types of patchwork (see page 8). To cut the fabric patches, lay the template on the wrong side of the fabric, on the true grain and draw round it with a soft, sharp pencil, on the curved edge only, 8mm. (5/16in.) away from the template. Draw round the stem close to the template, as this has no turnings (Fig. 2).

Preparing patches
Pin fabric patches to papers and tack the turning on the curved edge onto the paper (Fig. 2). This is the most important part of the work. You must get an absolutely smooth curve without 'pokes' because a bad shape cannot be corrected later. Work slowly and carefully, pleating the fabric on the back as you tack, taking stitches right through the backing paper (Fig. 2).

When all the patches are mounted, dry-press them on the wrong side, under tissue paper.

Mounting and sewing patches
The illustration shows how the shapes are overlapped, so that the stems are covered up and only the curved top shows. Begin with the top row. Work on a padded board so that you can hold your work steady with pins. Lay a ruler on the board and place the first patch so that the curved edge touches the straight edge of the ruler (Fig. 3). Put two pins in to hold it. If you want more than one patch on the top row, continue placing them, side edges just touching, until the row is complete. Tack with one row of tacking, just inside curved edge. Arrange the second row of patches on top of the first in the same way (Fig. 3), and tack to

the first row with two rows of tacking. When the second row is complete, sew the patches together with tiny hemming stitches, leaving all tacking stitches in (Fig. 4). Arrange and tack the patches of the third row, and hem to second row. Use a closely matching thread each time, choosing the colour which matches the darker-toned fabric. Sew all the patches together and finally dry press. Snip the tacking stitches and remove the backing papers. Hem the finished patchwork down onto its ground fabric or prepare it for making up.

Making up items
If you are using clamshell patchwork for items such as a teacosy, you will need to add one more clamshell all round your designated area for seams. Fig. 5 shows you how much extra patchwork you would need for instance, for a teacosy. When papers are removed, mount the patchwork on a plain fabric and then cut out and make up as though you were using ordinary fabric.

Polyester satin ribbon 76mm. (3in.) wide was used for the clamshell patchwork illustrated.

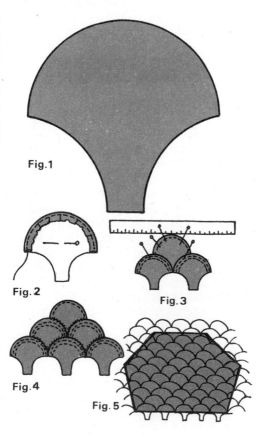

Fig.1

Fig. 2

Fig. 3

Fig. 4

Fig. 5

Appliqué shoulder bag

This brightly coloured shoulder bag is decorated with San Blas appliqué in a design inspired by the traditional work of Panama's San Blas Indians, whose patterns are often based on plants and animals.

San Blas appliqué is sometimes called reverse appliqué because it is done in the opposite way to traditional appliqué. Instead of applying material, you start with several different-coloured layers then cut away the fabric to reveal the design. You should never use more than five layers, nor should you use heavy or loosely woven fabric. Felt, however, is very good because you don't have to turn under any raw edges.

You will need

A shoulder bag at least 28cm. (11in.) square, in a lightweight, closely woven fabric
3 28cm. (11in.) squares of plain, lightweight, closely woven fabric such as cotton, polycotton or lawn, in colours of your choice, cut on the straight grain
Matching sewing cotton, fine needle
Tacking cotton, pins
Small sharp scissors
3 sheets of tracing paper, at least 25cm. (10in.) square
Pencil, chalk

A pattern for the applique appears on the opposite page.

Note

You can decorate your shoulder bag in whatever colours you choose, though the traditional garments made by the San Blas Indians are always in bright primary colours like those used here. Our shoulder bag is green, and we used yellow on top of the green, followed by purple, with red on top. The instructions refer to these colours, but if you use different colours simply substitute them in the instructions as necessary.

Preparing the fabric

1. Lay the shoulder bag right side up on a table. Place the square of yellow fabric on top of it, with the purple square on top of that, and the red square on top of the purple.
2. Pin the three squares and the front of the bag together at the corners. (If your bag has a thin lining, treat it as part of the bag, catching the front of the lining in with the front of the bag. If the lining is thick, however, you must remove it first.)

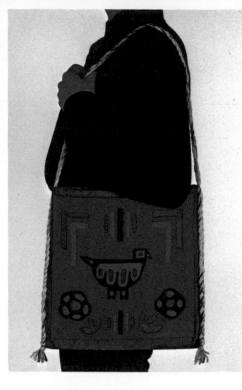

3. Starting from the centre, using 6mm. (¼in.) tacking stitches, tack through all layers, including the front of the bag. Tack all round the square, 1.5cm. (½in.) in from the edges, and remove the pins.

Tracing the patterns

1. Using the pattern provided, trace all the broken-line outlines on to a sheet of tracing paper. (You can draw the outlines as solid lines on the tracing paper.) This will be the pattern for the red layer.
2. Trace all the solid lines on to another sheet, which will be the pattern for the purple layer.
3. Trace the dotted lines from the pattern for the yellow layer.
4. Cut out the shapes you have traced, starting from the centre of each shape. Discard the cut-out pieces and keep the sheets of tracing paper to use as the patterns.

Working the design

1. With the pattern for the red fabric positioned exactly over the square, draw round the cut-out design on to the fabric with a pencil.
2. Pick up the layer of red fabric, holding the centre of the shape you are about to cut, and making sure you have not picked up any other layers at the same time. With the scissors, cut around the lines you have drawn, revealing the purple layer beneath. (Some of the

shapes you are working are so thin that they can only be drawn and then cut as lines, with little diagonal clips into the corners.) Don't worry if you cut through some of the tacking thread; enough should remain to keep the layers in place.
3. Now look at the photograph. Wherever the shape underneath the red should be yellow instead of purple, you have to cut away exactly the same shape from the purple layer. And wherever the colour should be green, you have to cut away the same shape from both the purple and the yellow layers.
4. After you have cut away all the layers you need to from the shapes on the red pattern, turn under the edges 3mm. (⅛in.), clipping curves and corners. Where you have cut away more than one layer for one shape, it isn't necessary to turn under the edges of each layer. Simply cut away the excess material from the underneath layer, then turn under 3mm. (⅛in.) on the top layer only. This will cover up the raw edges underneath.
5. Using invisible slip stitches or running stitches, sew the turned-under edges of the red layer in place. Stitch through all layers, working into the corners with an extra stitch. Don't worry if the stitches show a little; this gives the work the traditional San Blas look.
6. Now start the shapes on the purple layer. Trace around the shapes from the appropriate pattern on to the purple fabric. (For darker colours chalk will show up better than pencil.) Cut away, and turn under 3mm. (⅛in.). As before, where you have to cut away the same shape from the yellow layer beneath in order to reveal the green, cut away the excess yellow and turn under only the purple. Stitch in place invisibly.
7. Finally, cut away the remaining shapes in the yellow layer, turn under and stitch.
8. If you make a mistake and cut away a layer you didn't intend to, you can repair it by inserting a small piece of the right fabric in the hole. When you stitch down the turned-under edges from the above layer, it will catch the new fabrics as well – and the mistake won't show at all. This method can also be used if you want to add new colours.
9. To finish off, remove all tacking thread, turn under outer edges by 1.5cm. (½in.) and hem.

Appliqué shoulder bag

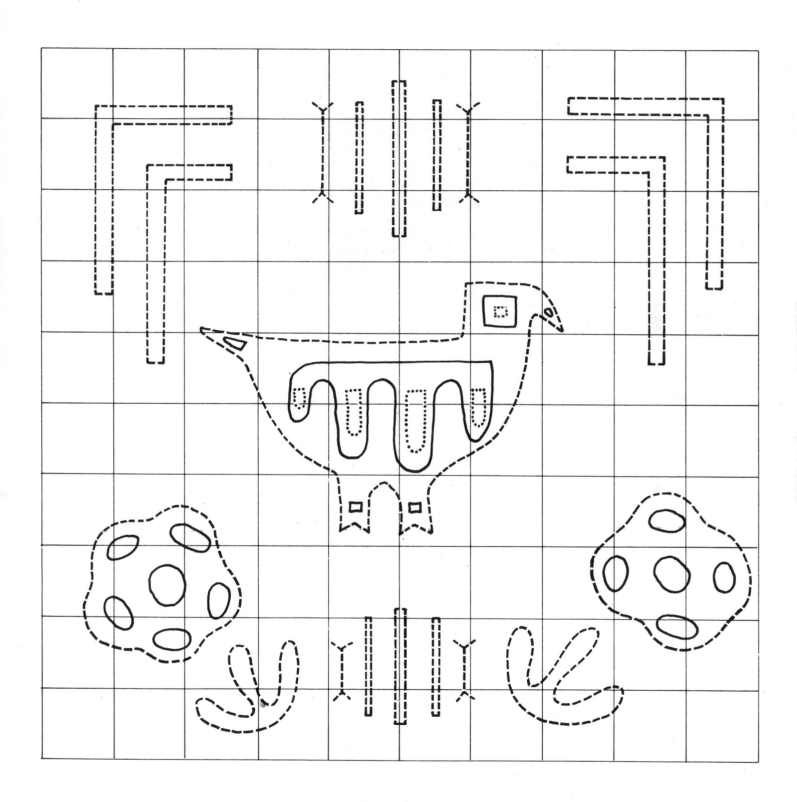

Striped quilt

9. Turn work to right side. Tack round 1cm. (¾in.) from edge. Press.
10. Turn over open end and tack down.
11. Using either a plain stitch or decorative scallop, and allowing 1cm. (¾in.) seam allowance, machine round quilt (Fig. 3). Remove all tacking.

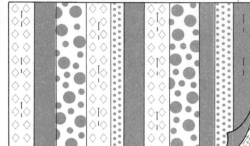

Fig. 1

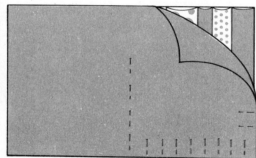

Fig. 2

Here is something rather special for a baby – a light but warm cot quilt worked in a quick, easy technique combining patchwork and machine quilting.

The cot quilt measures 70cm. by 97cm. (27in. by 38in.). If you want to make it larger or smaller, either cut each strip wider or make more of them.

You will need
1 metre plain fabric 90cm. (36in.) wide
½ metre each of 3 different co-ordinated printed fabrics 90cm. (36in.) wide
Washable wadding 70cm. by 97cm. (27in. by 38in.) (If wadding is lightweight 2 layers are required.)
Sewing equipment and matching threads

To make the quilt
1. Trim 15cm. (6in.) from the width of each of the fabrics – all lengths are now 75cm. 30in. wide.
2. Cut the printed fabrics into horizontal strips. The widths of the strips may vary, but should not be narrower than 5cm. (2in.).

3. Lay the strips on a table in a pleasant arrangement.
4. With the right side of the fabric facing, and allowing 1cm. (⅜in.) seam allowance, pin, tack and machine stitch the strips together. Press open all the seams and the right side of the completed patchwork. The work should now measure 70cm. by 97cm. (27in. by 38in.).
5. Place wadding on a table and position patchwork face upwards over wadding.
6. Pin together down the centre of the strips and, allowing 1cm. (⅜in.) seam allowance, machine stitch each fabric join to produce a quilted effect (Fig. 1).
7. Place patchwork and plain fabric together, right sides facing. Pin together, working from the centre outwards to ease the fullness out of the quilting and avoid puckers (Fig. 2). Tack round edge on three sides, leaving one end open. Machine stitch, allowing 1cm. (¾in.) seam allowance.
8. Trim off surplus wadding and material to reduce bulk and cut diagonally across the corners.

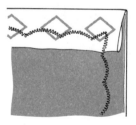

Fig. 3

24

Quilted satin cushion

1 Square = 10cm

This lovely cushion has been made in a machine quilting technique to imitate trapunto quilting. Two layers of polyester wadding are sandwiched between fabric and backing.

You will need

For a cushion 45cm. (18in.) square
Of acetate satin fabric:
    2 squares 48.5cm. (19in.) square
    4 strips 48.5cm. (19in.) long by 2.5cm. (1in.)
1 square butter muslin 48.5cm. (19in.)
2 squares polyester wadding 48.5cm. (19in.)
Matching sewing thread; pins; blunt needle
Squared dressmaker's paper
Dressmaker's carbon paper (choose a colour that will show on the satin but is not too dark)

To prepare the fabric and pattern

1. Draw up the design from the diagram.
2. Iron the satin smooth.
3. Lay the piece of butter muslin on a firm, hard surface and put the two squares of wadding on top. Lay one square of satin on the wadding, right side up. Pin all four thicknesses of fabric together round the edges, keeping the satin smooth.
4. Lay the dressmaker's carbon paper on the satin, carbon side down. (You will need to use two pieces to cover the area of the design.
5. Lay the pattern on top and pin to the satin round the edges. Try not to use pins on the area of the design because pin marks show in satin.
6. Now, using the blunt needle, stab through the paper pattern into the satin along the lines of the design. Make each stab fairly close together, about 9mm. (3/16in.) apart.
7. Unpin the pattern and remove the carbon paper. You should be able to see coloured dots marking out the design. If you feel a bit doubtful about being able to machine stitch along the lines, make them clearer by painting along them in watercolour paint using a fine brush. But keep the painted line very fine and use a colour you can just see on the satin.

Stitching the design

1. Set your sewing machine to a medium to large stitch. If you have a machine with a speed setting, set it to slow because you need quite a lot of control.
2. Lift the machine foot and the needle to their highest points. Start with the circle in the middle of the flower, and set the padded satin under the foot. Lower the foot and start machine-stitching along the design line. You will find that if you gently turn the fabric under both hands as you slowly stitch, you will be able to follow the broad curves fairly easily. Complete all the lines of the design in this way.

To make up the cushion

1. Make a flat piping from the strips of satin as follows. Fold the strips along the length and pin and tack them along the edges of the unused square of satin (cushion back), raw edges matching.
2. Stitch the piping to the fabric about 3mm. (1/8in.) from the fold.
3. Then pin and tack the cushion front to the cushion back, right sides together, and machine stitch again along the same stitching line on three sides.
4. Turn to right side. Insert zip if required, or insert the cushion pad and close the seam with slip stitches.

25

Reverse appliqué wallhanging

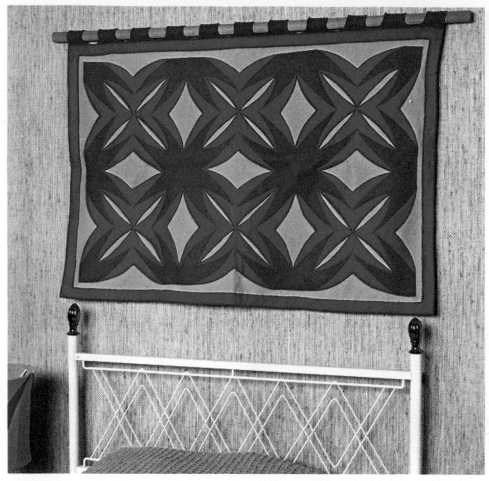

This striking reverse appliqué hanging is made in felt which, because it is easy to cut and sew, is particularly suitable for this kind of work.

You will need
1m. (40in.) each of beige, red berry and plum felt
1m. (40in.) hessian or other lining
Matching sewing threads
Large scissors and small blunt-ended embroidery scissors
Pins, needles, pencil, ruler
2.5cm. (1in.) squared paper, tracing paper, dressmaker's carbon paper, plain paper or card

Making the wallhanging
The diagram represents half of the finished wallhanging. Make a scale drawing of this on the graph paper, then make a tracing of the drawing. To ensure the motifs are identical make a template of a complete motif (see diagram) by placing carbon paper and thin card under the graph paper. Cut out the card template and draw round this for the other motifs.
Cut a piece of felt 95cm. by 79cm.

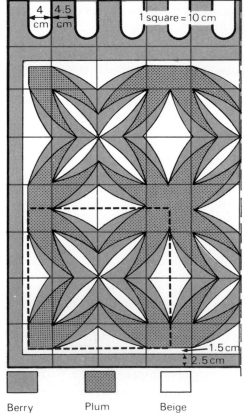

Berry   Plum   Beige

(37½in. by 31in.) in each colour. Press with a warm iron (do not steam).
Place the pieces of felt in the following sequence on top of each other: beige, plum, cherry (beige at the bottom). Pin and tack the pieces together, radiating tacking from the centre to avoid any bulges when sewing.
Place carbon paper face down on the felt and position the tracing on top over one half of the felt, aligning the outer border lines with the edge of the felt.
Pin all layers together to ensure that the carbon paper does not move. Trace over the complete design. Turn the pattern over to the other half of felt and pin together, making sure to match the centre points, and trace over the design again. Remove tracing and carbon paper.
Starting from the centre of the hanging and using the berry thread and a straight machine stitch, sew round the motifs, working outwards to prevent a build-up of felt.
Machine stitch along both edges of the outer border (berry colour). Trim away the berry felt which does not appear in the motif or the outer border.
Replace the tracing paper and carbon and re-mark the right angles in the corners and the lines which join the motifs as these will have been cut away with the berry felt. Machine stitch these with plum thread. Cut away plum felt from the inner border and then cut away the four leaves in the centre of the motifs to reveal beige felt.
Cut away beige and berry felt from the top edge of the hanging – there is a thin piece of plum felt left for the scallops.
Cut eleven scallops each measuring 4.5cm. (1¾in.) wide, with 4cm. (1⅝in.) wide gaps between.
Fold top edges in half to the back and hem to the machine line.
Pin and tack hessian to the back of the hanging and hem stitch all round.

Within broken line – complete motif for hanging

Matching patchwork motifs

Making motifs that can be applied to a wide variety of room accessories is simple to do and looks very effective as it gives a thought-out, co-ordinated appearance. A basic motif made, for instance, for a cushion cover, can be scaled down to a size suitable for a dressing table runner or a make-up bag. If you felt really adventurous, you could even make a felt rug using the same motif scaled up. You can make your own designs for a patchwork motif or copy the one illustrated.

You will need
A swing needle sewing machine
Thread to match motif
Iron-on interfacing (soft iron-on for a soft handle, firm iron-on for a firmer finish)
Fabrics in a selection of colours and designs to co-ordinate with existing room scheme (cotton fabrics are best for patchwork)
Iron-on adhesive tape
Paper, pencil, ruler

To make the motif
1. Work out the design to be used on paper and then cut out. You now have a pattern for the main shape.
2. Place the paper motif on the interfacing (with adhesive side uppermost).
3. Cut the interfacing to the exact size of the motif. To ensure complete accuracy, you can mark the layout for the fabric itself on the interfacing.
4. Remove paper motif and cut it into individual sections.
5. Pin each section to chosen fabric and cut out.
6. Place cut-out fabric shapes on the adhesive side of the interfacing.
7. When the interfacing is completely covered with fabric shapes, pin the fabrics carefully in place.
8. Press with a medium-hot iron. Once the shapes have stuck, remove pins and press thoroughly. Use steam or a damp cloth for a really good bond.
9. Using a fine zig-zag stitch, machine along the edges of all the fabric sections. You will find the interfacing gives support to the fabric so that the machining lies flat, as well as holding the shapes in place and giving a smooth, flat backing.
10. Machine around the outside of the motif using a fine zig-zag stitch and sew in all the loose ends of thread by hand.
11. Cut out adhesive tape to the exact size of the motif.
12. Iron the adhesive side of the adhesive tape to the wrong side of the motif. Leave to cool.
13. Peel off the paper backing.
14. The motif is now ready to iron on to your article. Use a damp cloth and a pressing action for a permanent bond.

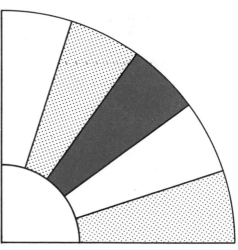

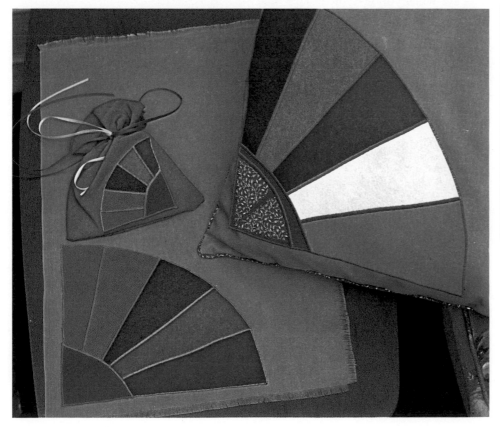

Paper patchwork boxes

If you don't like sewing, but love the look of patchwork, you can have the pleasure but less of the work by doing paper patchwork. These small boxes are decorated with tiny hexagons or diamonds of paper in different patterns. It's good practice for real patchwork, as you learn to design with these shapes, and the finished boxes make lovely gift containers or trinket boxes.

Collect together lots of different papers with tiny patterns on them. These can come from home-making magazines, which often show advertisements for curtains and carpets, or you can sometimes buy wrapping papers with actual patchwork designs and cut out the colours you want from them. Or you can just use several different wrapping papers.

Boxes to decorate can come from a junk shop or a craft shop, or you can use discarded cigar boxes or chocolate boxes.

You will need
A variety of papers with small patterns
Small box
Scissors; craft knife
Small piece thin card
Ruler; protractor; pencil
White PVA adhesive; clear varnish

How to work
All the designs here are based on the hexagon, so make a template for this (Fig. 1). Make the hexagon the right size in proportion to the box you are covering, as huge hexagons will look meaningless and small ones will look confused.

To make a hexagon, draw a circle on a piece of thin cardboard and, keeping the span of the compasses the same (i.e. at the radius of the circle you have drawn) place the pin on the circumference and draw an arc. Repeat this round the circumference of the circle to give six points of the hexagon. Join up the arcs in straight lines, cut out cleanly, and you have a hexagon. Diamonds are formed by dividing a hexagon into three.

Using the template, cut out plenty of hexagons from different-coloured papers. An effective arrangement is to start each group of hexagons with a plain colour at the centre. If the box is large enough, you could try out a rosette, which is made from seven hexagons, six of them in the same paper, surrounding a central hexagon of a contrasting colour or tone. Add two more hexagons to a rosette and you have something roughly the shape of a diamond (see Fig. 2).

The 'tumbling block' pattern on the smaller box is a traditional American patchwork design in which three diamonds of light, medium and dark tones are joined to construct a hexagon and give the three-dimensional effect of a cube.

Move the hexagons round on the box until you have a pleasing arrangement. Stick them on the box with white adhesive watered down until it is the consistency of thin cream (if you use it too thickly it will stick too quickly and give no time for manoeuvre).

You can take the hexagons over and round corners, as they will continue to match up as long as the cutting has been accurate. Inaccurate cutting can be corrected by cutting a hexagon slightly larger or smaller as the occasion demands. Unless you are a mathematician it is unlikely that you will get a pattern to fit really accurately all the way round a box, so do any filling in with odd shapes at the back, in colours that are not too noticeable.

Close the box and carry the design over the join. When the paper is dry, cut along the join with a sharp knife, so that the box will open.

When the patchwork is complete, seal the whole thing with two thick coats of white adhesive (which dries clear) paying special attention to the join which you have just cut. This sealing is important because when you give the box its final protective coat of varnish, it will seep into the paper and discolour it in places if it has not been sealed properly. When the seal is dry, apply two coats of clear varnish. This will protect the box and keep it in good condition for a long time.

Line the box with paper. To line a deep box, cut out five pieces of paper, one for each of the sides and one for the base. Damp them with water then stick them down one by one. Do the same for the lid. Don't paper the lip of the box, as it will prevent it from closing properly.

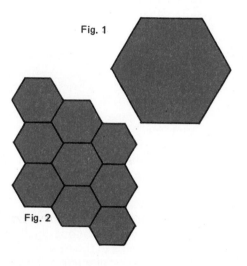

Fig. 1

Fig. 2

Cathedral window patchwork

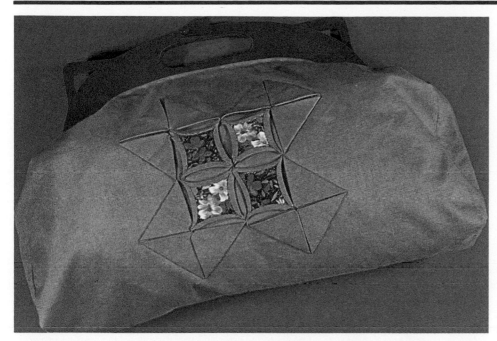

Cathedral window is a modern patchwork type and is worked without a template. In effect colourful patches are mounted on folded squares of a plain, contrasting fabric and then the fabric 'window frame' is folded over the patches. Cathedral window patchwork can be used for large items such as cot quilts or bedcovers, or small pieces can be mounted on another fabric to make decorative panels on everyday items such as the workbag illustrated. If you have not tried this technique before, the bag is a perfect first exercise, as you may lose patience if you start with a large, ambitious project.

Fabrics and threads

Firm, evenweave fabrics should be used – cotton is ideal. If fabric patches are inclined to fray they can be mounted on lightweight iron-on interfacing. Calico is traditionally used for the background fabric but this can be hard to obtain, and good-quality cotton or cotton mixtures will do just as well.

Use a thread closely matching in colour to the background fabric.

Technique

The technique for making cathedral window patchwork is time-consuming, as the key to success is careful measuring and then accurate folding.

1. Cut two squares of the background fabric exactly 15cm. (6in.) square.
2. Thread a needle with soft tacking thread.
3. Press a 3mm. (⅛in.) hem all round each square and then tack it.
4. Working on the ironing board, press the four corners of the squares to the middle, press the fold and pin (Fig. 1).
5. Now press the corners to the centre again. Remove the first pins and repin. The points of the corners should meet exactly in the middle of the square (Fig. 2).
6. Place two prepared squares together with the folded sides touching. Thread a needle with matching thread, and neatly oversew the two squares together, using tiny stitches (Fig. 3).
7. Cut a square of the contrast fabric 4cm. (1¾in.) square. Lay the two joined squares on a table top, folds upwards. Lay the contrast square over the join (Fig. 4), and pin it.
8. Have a threaded needle ready. Turn the folded edge of the background square over the cut edge of the contrast square. As you fold it over you will see that it curves because you are already folding folded fabric on the cross. Fasten the thread end and then stitch the folded edge down over the contrast square, using pick stitch (Fig. 5). Work right on the edge so that the stitches hardly show. Work all round the square. The corners should meet neatly. Make two neat stitches across each corner. Your stitches should go right through all thicknesses of fabric.
9. The two squares and the contrast patch form one single unit. Make up as many units as you need and stitch them together to the area required (Fig. 6).

10. To finish off a complete piece of work, turn over the edges of the outside squares very slightly and oversew. Never press a 'window' after the contrast patch has been mounted and framed.

To make the workbag

The handles of our bag were found in a junk shop, but similar wooden handles can be purchased in needlework shops and department stores.

Fig. 7 gives the shape and measurements of the bag pieces. Cut out a back, a front and two gussets, cutting the same shapes from lining fabric if required. Seam pieces, attach lining, and sew the bag to the handles, taking stitches through the holes along the bottom edge of the handles.

Now you can simply appliqué your patchwork on to the bag, using the smallest possible stitches.

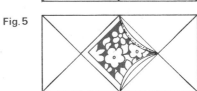

Fig. 1   Fig. 2

Fig. 3

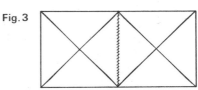

Fig. 4

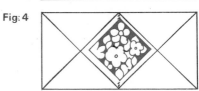

Fig. 5

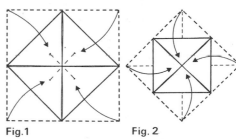

Fig. 6

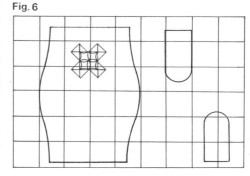

Wall tidy

This attractive wall tidy would make an ideal gift and be well received at any fund raising event. If making it for your own home the theme could, of course, be adjusted to suit the decor of a particular room in the house.

You will need
Hessian 56cm. (22in.) by 72cm. (28in.)
2 pieces sailcloth 20cm. by 56cm. (8in. by 22in.) for top and centre pockets
1 piece sailcloth 22cm. by 56cm. (8½in. by 22in.) for bottom pocket
Ribbon or cotton tape 1.3cm. (½in.) wide as follows: 2.75m. (3yd.) green; 2.5m. (2½yd.) blue; ½m. (18in.) purple; 1m. (3½ft.) pink; 1.5m. (4ft.) light green; 30cm. (1ft.) red
Blue binding 1.5m. long by 5cm. wide (4ft. by 2in.)
Matching sewing threads and other sewing equipment
Bamboo rod 61cm. (24in.) long with a 2.5cm. (1in.) diameter
2 hooks

To work the top pocket
Cut 6-20cm. (8in.) strips of ribbon or cotton tape 1 red, 1 blue, 2 purple, 1 pink and 1 green for stripes. Also cut 2 pieces of blue ribbon to make the cross. One should be 24cm. (9½in.) long and one 12cm. (4½in.). Lay the ribbon on the sailcloth as the coloured photograph shows, then pin and tack in position. Machine close to both edges of the stripes right up to the edges of the sailcloth. Turn a 1.5cm. (½in.) hem on top edge and machine with close satin stitch.

To work the centre pocket
Cut 5 green stalks each 13cm. (5in.) long. Pin first stalk 6cm. (2½in.) from side edge. Space others at 9cm. (3½in.) intervals. Machine. Use a continuous strip for leaves. Begin at side edge, 5cm. (2in.) up and form 'V' shapes with the green ribbon by folding the ribbon at bottom of stalk and between stalks. Machine as Fig. 1. Turn hem on top edge and machine with decorative stitch. Apply pink ribbon as for green (above), but begin at top corner and turn at top of stalk, and top edge of pocket.

To work the bottom pocket
Cut ribbons as follows: 2 pieces blue 56cm. (22in.), 1 piece blue 64cm. (25in.), 1 piece light green 5cm. (2in.), 1 piece light green 65cm. (25in.).
Pin shorter light green ribbon 2.5cm. (1in.) from bottom edge. Pin shorter blue

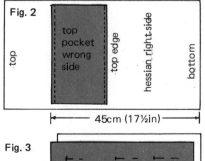

Fig. 1
5cm (2in)
fold
machine stitch

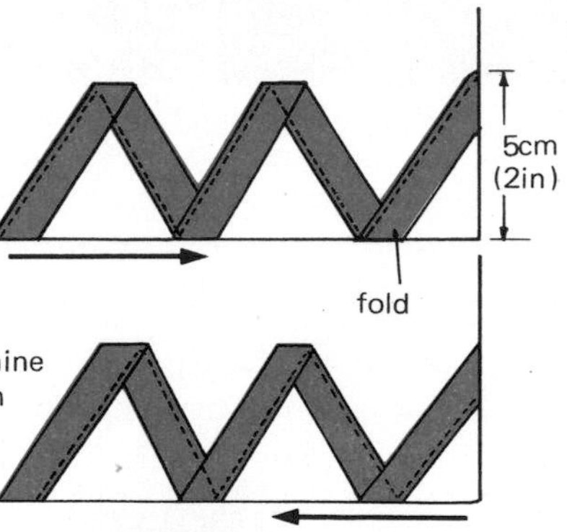

Fig. 2
top pocket wrong side
top
top edge
hessian right side
bottom
45cm (17½in)

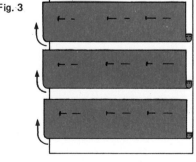

Fig. 3

ribbon 5mm. (¼in.) above light green ribbon. Pin longer blue ribbon above this, making a fold 5cm. (2in.) high, 10cm. (4in.) from end (left side of hanging). Pin blue strip 3cm. (1¼in.) above previous blue strip. Machine all three blue ribbons. Pin last light green strip between blue ribbons, make the first fold 7cm. (3in.) in from edge of hanging. Machine light green strips.

Now turn under the top edge and machine with decorative stitch.

To make up the wall hanging
Lay hessian backing, right side up, with the top pocket face downwards, and turn hem at bottom. The raw edge should measure 45cm. (17½in.) from bottom edge of hessian as in Fig. 2. Machine across making a 1cm. (½in.) seam. Machine the centre pocket as above, the raw edge measuring 23cm. (9in.) from bottom edge of hessian. Machine the bottom pocket 2cm. (¾in.) away from bottom edge. Press all three pockets upwards to conceal raw edges as in Fig. 3 and pin flat to secure position of pockets. Turn a 4cm. (1½in.) hem on top edge of hessian. Sew blue binding to side edges, from back allowing a 1cm. overlap. Fold binding to front and sew on edge. Turn a small hem on bottom of hessian.

Top loops
Mark hessian at 5cm. (2in.) intervals from side edge across top. Begin at corner and secure end of ribbon. Form a loop measuring 4cm. (1½in.) from the top of loop to top edge of hessian. Fold ribbon at 5cm. (2in.) mark on hessian then form another loop (Fig. 4). Machine across all folds to secure loops on top edge. Finally, stitch gussets down pockets. The top pocket has diagonals between pairs of stripes (for holding pencils and thin objects), and one vertical down from blue cross-shape. The centre pocket is divided between tulips. In the bottom pocket, there is one division between the folds of light green ribbon, and another next to the blue fold.

Push the bamboo rod through the green ribbon and hang your wall tidy.

Floral appliqué table linen

This simple but charming design makes clever use of appliquéd shapes, which are enhanced with embroidery. The work is all done by hand, so it is necessary to keep the stitches very small and neat.

The place mat measures 34cm. by 24cm. (13⅜in. by 9⅜in.) and the napkin 38cm. square (15in. square). The materials listed below are for one mat and one napkin, so if you want to make a complete set, just multiply.

You will need

40cm. (15¾in.) of 90cm. (36in.) wide fine white cotton lawn
Small scraps of lilac, grey and pink cotton lawn
Small scraps of iron-on interfacing
1.20cm. (48in.) 2.5cm. (1in.) wide purple bias binding
Sewing threads: white and to match colours
Stranded cottons: olive green, pink and deep mauve
Squared paper
Pencil

To make the napkin

1. Cut a 40cm. (15¾in.) square of white cotton lawn, aligning the sides with the selvedge or the straight grain of the fabric.
2. Turn the edges under twice to make a narrow hem on all four sides, and fold the corners carefully to ensure that they are crisp and neat.
3. Tack, hem and machine in straight stitch with white thread, keeping close to hem edge.

To make the place mat

1. Cut out an oblong 34cm. by 24cm. (13⅜in. by 9⅜in.) from the white lawn.
2. Fold and press the bias binding in half lengthwise.
3. Pin and tack binding along sides of the oblong to neaten and decorate raw edges; carefully fold and turn binding at corners. Tack and machine with purple thread close to edge.

The appliqué

This is the same for napkin and mat.
1. Draw up the motif (Fig. 1) to size on squared paper. Lay the fabric over the design and, using a sharp pencil, draw the stems and positions of petals.
2. Cut out the petals and leaves from interfacing. Iron these on to the fabrics you will use for the appliqué and cut around the shapes, leaving at least 6mm. (¼in.) for turnings.
3. Snip around the curves with sharp-pointed scissors. Fold the turning to the wrong side and tack in position to give a neat fabric leaf or flower-petal (Fig. 2). Repeat for all pieces.
4. Using matching sewing threads, stitch each petal in position with very small, neat slip stitching. Overlap the leaves as shown.
5. Using three strands of embroidery cotton, work the stems in chain stitch (green); the stamen stalks in back stitch (green). The stamen heads are formed by three straight stitches per head (pink and mauve).
6. Remove all tacking threads and press carefully on wrong side to complete.

Note

It is advisable to wash the embroidered linen carefully by hand.

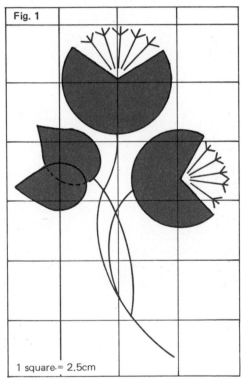

Fig. 1

1 square = 2.5cm

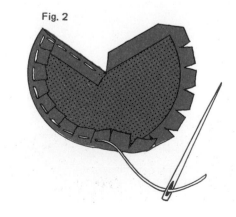

Fig. 2

Petal patchwork tablecloth

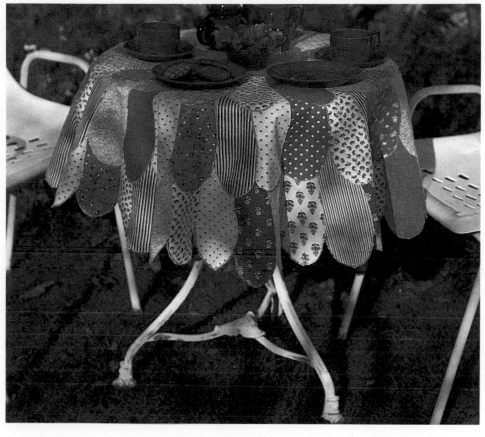

Petal patchwork originated in America and is a piecing technique. Traditionally the edges of the petals are turned and then stitched together with tiny running stitches. This pretty tablecloth is made in a slightly different way which is quicker. The petals are mounted on iron-on interfacing then are handsewn on to a fabric ground with buttonhole stitch. You could use this technique to make warm coverlets using scraps of wool fabrics, tweeds, velvets etc. By drawing the petal shape to a different scale so that it is smaller, you might make a very pretty tray cloth in fine pastel coloured cottons.

You will need

For a round table diameter 60cm. (24in.) 330cm. (10ft. 6in.) of 150cm. (3ft.) wide sheeting fabric for the base fabric
Approximately 160 petal shapes from assorted fabrics
15cm. (6in.) circle of plain coloured fabric
Lightweight iron-on interfacing
Thin card for a template

To make

Fold the sheeting in half and cut two squares. Fold each square in half again. With a pencil and string draw a quarter circle (Fig. 1). Cut out along the pencilled line through both thicknesses. Cut both pieces of fabric out in the same way. You now have two half circles. Seam them together. Press seam open. Neaten raw edges. Turn a tiny narrow doubled hem all round the edges. You will probably find this easier to do by hand – roll the hem in your fingers and make slip stitches through the fold.

Draw up a template to the size as shown on Fig. 2. Mount the patchwork fabrics on interfacing. Lay template on wrong side of the fabric and draw round with a pencil. Cut out petals. Pin the petals round the hem of the tablecloth, the petal tips overhanging the hem by about 5cm. (2in.). Pin so that each petal overlaps the one next to it by about 2.5cm. (1in.). When you have pinned all round the hem, lay the next row of petals on top, the tips of the petals overlapping the first row by about 5cm. (2in.).

Pin the second row and now you are ready to begin stitching. You can use either a matching thread or a contrasting thread. Soft embroidery cotton is best but if you prefer, use three strands of the stranded thread together. Buttonhole stitch has been used for the cloth illustrated but if you prefer to use another embroidery stitch such as chain stitch this is acceptable as long as the raw edges of the patches are caught down to the background fabric.

After embroidering round the first row of petal patches, add the third row and pin it. Then the second row can be embroidered. The table cloth illustrated has five rows of petals but you can have as many as you like depending on how much you want the petals to overlap. When you have worked the last row and you are near the middle of the cloth, cut a circle of plain fabric and turn a neat hem all round the edge. Hem the circle down to cover the edges of the last circle of petals.

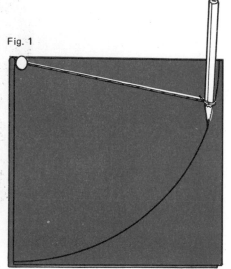

Fig. 1

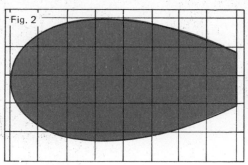

Fig. 2

1 square = 2.5cms

Peacock tea cosy

This attractive tea cosy is made in felt appliqué with details added in embroidery. It is guaranteed to brighten up the tea table on the dullest afternoon.

You will need
2 pieces of felt in dark green 38cm. by 30cm. (15in. by 12in.)
1 piece each of felt 23cm. by 23cm. (9in. by 9in.) in light turquoise and yellow
1 piece of felt in royal blue 15cm. by 15cm. (6in. by 6in.)
1 piece each of felt 10cm. by 10cm. (4in. by 4in.) in the colours bright blue, apple green, cerise, brown and black
1 piece of felt in grey 24cm. by 5cm. (9½in. by 2in.)
2 skeins stranded thread in gold
Small amounts of stranded thread in black and yellow
1 cosy pad
Thread to match each appliqué colour you use

Working the design
Cut the appliqué pieces according to the pattern (which appears on the opposite page) and apply them to the background in numerical order, so that they overlap correctly. All the pieces are stitched in position with tiny stitches round the edges using matching thread.

First assemble the feathers. Fringe the edges of the light turquoise feather pieces and place them in position on the dark green background. Then place the yellow pieces in position and stitch round each one, through the background. Stitch the rounds of royal blue felt in position on the yellow and finish the feathers with a small piece of black felt stitched in the centre of each.

Stitch the grey ground and body pieces in position, then stitch the scalloped tail feathers.

When all the appliqué pieces are fixed, add the embroidery. Outline the pea-cock's front, to the top of the leg, with a line of stem stitch in black. The top of the head and the beak are outlined in yellow stem stitch, and the yellow scallops on the body are also worked in stem stitch. For the yellow markings on the peacock's back, use satin stitch. The crest consists of four lines of chain stitch in black, topped by four small rounds on cerise appliqué or by four green sequins. Embroider the eye in black or use a blue sequin fixed with a bead. All the remaining embroidery is worked in fly stitch with gold thread.

Finishing
With the wrong sides facing, machine together the two parts of the cosy following the sewing line. Then cut all round with pinking shears 12mm. (½in.) outside the stitching. Slip the cosy pad inside, turn up 12mm. (½in.) of the cover at the base and slip stitch to the pad.

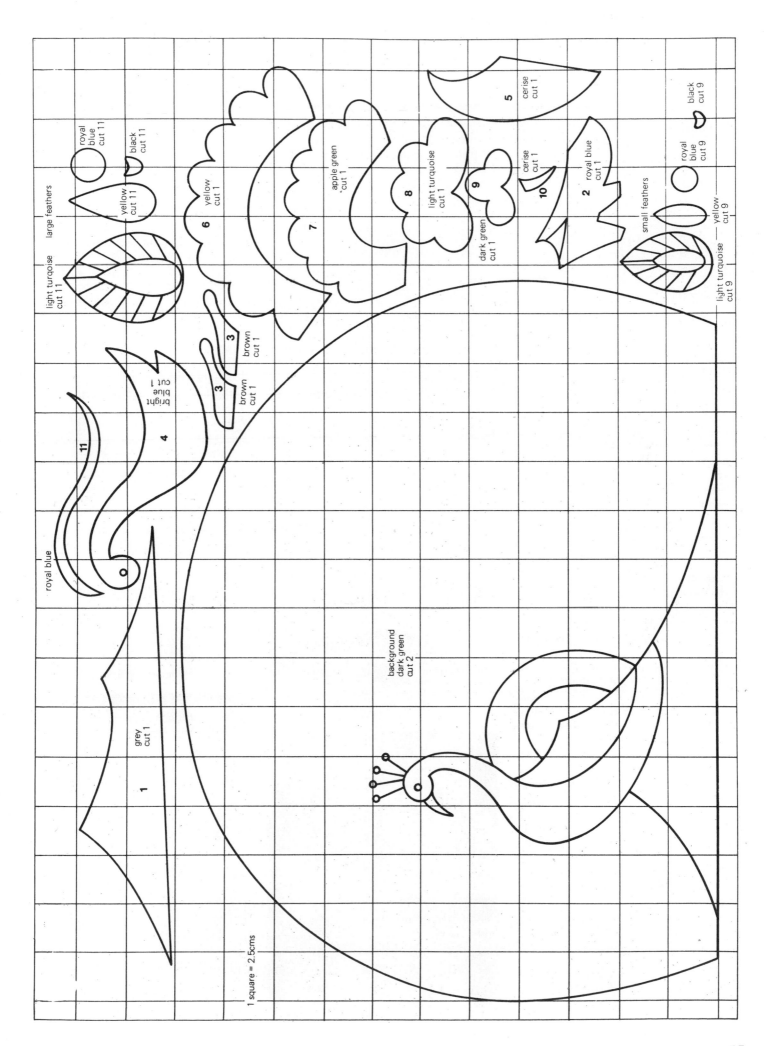

royal blue cut 11

black cut 11

yellow cut 11

large feathers

light turquoise cut 11

yellow cut 1

6

yellow cut 1

7

apple green cut 1

5

cerise cut 1

8

light turquoise cut 1

9

dark green cut 1

cerise cut 1

10

2

royal blue cut 1

royal blue cut 9

black cut 9

small feathers

light turquoise cut 9

yellow cut 9

3

brown cut 1

3

brown cut 1

bright blue cut 1

4

11

royal blue

grey cut 1

1

background dark green cut 2

1 square = 2.5cms

Appliqué baby quilt

This delightful quilt can be used on carry-cot or pram and will keep baby warm and cosy.

You will need

(finished size: 55×40cm. approx).
60cm. (23½in.) 90cm. (35½in.) wide pale green floral print cotton fabric
50cm. (19½in.) 90cm. (35½in.) wide darker floral print cotton fabric to tone
45cm. (17¾in.) 90cm. (35½in.) wide medium-weight interfacing
60cm. (23½in.) 90cm. (35½in.) wide medium-weight terylene wadding
120cm. (47¼in.) 1.3cm. (½in.) satin ribbon in light orchid
2 reels pale mauve sewing thread
Sewing equipment

To make the quilt

1. Cut out two oblongs 57cm. by 42cm. (22½in. by 16½in.) from pale floral fabric, aligning sides of oblongs with straight grain of fabric. There is a 1cm. (⅜in.) seam allowance included.
2. Cut out one oblong 57cm. by 42cm. (22½in. by 16½in.) from interfacing.
3. Cut out one oblong 20cm. by 35cm. (7¾in. by 13¾in.) from contrasting floral fabric, aligning sides with fabric grain.
4. Cut out two strips each 14cm. (5½in.) wide by width of contrasting fabric i.e. 90cm. (35½in.) and on right side mark centre line down each strip with 1cm. (⅜in.) seam join the two pieces to give one long strip. (Fig. 1).
5. Trace off the stork pattern in Fig. 2 on to a thin piece of card and cut it out to give a pattern template. Draw around this with a pencil and cut out four storks from the contrast fabric. Reverse the template when drawing around it on fabric to produce two storks facing to left and two to the right.
6. Place one of the pale fabric oblongs face upwards over the interfacing. Pin and tack the small contrast fabric oblong centrally on to these two layers. Similarly pin and tack the storks in position on to quilt face (Fig. 3).
7. With machine set to satin stitch minimum length, width 2.5cm. (1in.) and a piece of tissue or thin paper under area of stitching, work around raw edge of stork shapes carefully following and covering raw edge to firmly machine appliqué the storks to quilt face. Continue line of stitching between neck and beak to complete.
8. Pin, tack and straight stitch the feather-edge ribbon over raw edge of centre panel. Allow a little extra ribbon at beginning and end to be folded under and neatened. Fold and mitre the ribbon corners taking particular care at the 'last' corner (Fig. 4).
9. With machine set to straight stitch, sew close to both edges of ribbon. Press quilt face on wrong side.
10. If available set your machine to scallop embroidery stitch, (plain satin stitch will suffice). Work scallop line 1cm. (⅜in.) either side of centre line of frill strip (Fig. 5). Cut away centre excess fabric along scalloping to produce two strips, join these with 1cm. (⅜in.) seam to give a continuous band.
11. Work a double line of gathering thread along raw edge of band. Draw up thread to fit around seam line of quilt face. With right sides together pin, tack and stitch frill in position along seam line (Fig. 6). Take care not to catch the fullness of fabric at corners.
12. With right sides together pin, tack and stitch the remaining oblong of pale floral fabric over quilt face keeping frill folded inwards (Fig. 7). Leave 15cm. (6in.) opening along foot of cover. Turn to right side out and press gently.
13. Cut out a double layer of wadding to fit inside cover 39cm. × 54cm. (15¼in. by 21in.). Place layers on top of one another and roll them up lengthways, place inside cover unrolling and pushing the points well into the corners of the quilt.
14. Hand slip stitch edges of opening together to complete baby's quilt cover.

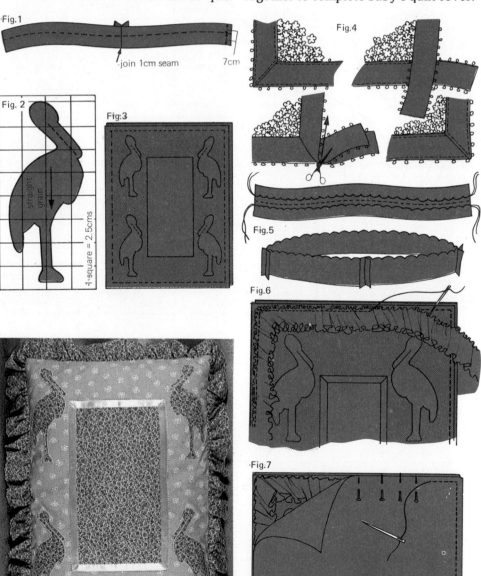

Fig.1 join 1cm seam 7cm
Fig. 2 straight grain 1 square = 2.5cms
Fig:3
Fig.4
Fig.5
Fig.6
Fig.7

Quilted calico holdall

This smart holdall would be ideal for shopping or for the beach – or simply for a summer day accessory. The quilted effect is achieved by inter-lining with heavyweight interfacing.

You will need
70cm. (28in.) of 122cm. (48in.) wide calico fabric
70cm. (28in.) of 122cm. (48in. heavyweight interfacing
Matching sewing thread
Matching (or contrast) embroidery cotton

To prepare fabric
Cut pieces for the bag as follows:
2 backs and 1 lining: 36cm. deep by 30cm. wide (14in. by 12in.)
2 fronts and 1 lining: 36cm. deep by 30cm. wide (14in. by 12in.)
4 sides and 2 linings 36cm. deep by 10cm. wide (14in. by 4in.)
2 bases and 1 lining 30cm. wide by 10cm. deep (12in. wide by 4in. deep)
2 handle pieces (no lining) 46cm. long by 10cm. wide (18in. by 4in.)

To make up
Pin one bag front to bag front lining and then one bag front behind lining, sandwiching it. Pin and then tack all round. Work the back in the same way. Then tack the lines of the 'quilting'. It is better not to pencil or chalk these in because the marks may be difficult to remove. If you find it difficult to tack freehand designs, pencil the lines on the inside of the piece where they will not show when the bag is made up.

Prepare and tack the back and front of the bag pieces ready for quilting. Prepare and tack the two side gusset pieces and the base piece. Work the quilting lines first using a medium length machine stitch and matching colour thread. Remove the quilting line tacking stitches. (If you prefer to hand-quilt, work the quilting lines with back stitches.)

Set the machine for zigzag stitch. Work a close, wide zigzag stitch all round all the pieces through all thicknesses, working about 3mm. (⅛in.) from the edge. Trim close to the zigzag stitches without snipping the stitches.

Assembling the bag
Fold the short ends of the strap pieces in and press. Fold 6mm. (¼in.) hems on both long sides. Press. Fold sides to the middle and press. Machine stitch down outside edges and folds and across ends.

Hand-hem to the inside of the front and back pieces of the bag about 2.5cm. (1in.) down from top edge and 7.5cm. (3in.) from sides. Pin side gussets and base piece to bag front and back wrong sides together and join pieces by working buttonhole stitch or Cretan stitch using embroidery cotton. If you prefer, use a simple oversewing stitch. The effect should be rather rough and homespunlooking. Work the same stitch round top edge of bag.

inside of bag showing strap in position

Simple frame weaving

Weaving can be very complicated, but the principle itself is simple. Try this small project on a home-made loom as an introduction to the art.

You will need
For the loom
2 pieces wood 2.5cm. (1in.) by 5cm. (2in.) by 18cm. (7in.)
2 pieces of wood 2.5cm. (1in.) by 5cm. (2in.) by 23cm. (9in.)
Sheet plastic about 30cm. (12in.) square (a piece of rubbish bag will do)
Woodworking adhesive
1 sheet each coarse and medium sandpaper
4 right-angle braces
8 1.3cm. (½in.) No.7 wood screws
Screwdriver
1 box 1.3cm. (½in.) nails
Panel pins
For the potholder
Large tapestry or darning needle
Crochet hook, size 3.50
Soft unbleached dishcloth cotton and other coloured knitting cottons

To make the loom
Sand corners and ends of wood so that there are no sharp edges to catch the yarns.

Place one of the longer pieces of wood on the floor with the piece of plastic underneath. Push the wood up against the wall lengthways. Abut the two 18cm. (7in.) pieces of wood to this piece so that you have formed 3 sides of a rectangle. When you are sure that the corners are square remove the shorter pieces, glue the ends and replace them. Place the second long piece of wood in position so that the rectangle is complete, and press a weight (a brick, books or anything heavy) up against it while the glue dries. This will take about an hour.

When the glue is dry, put the angle braces on the inside corners and mark where to place the screws. Start the holes for the screws with an awl, gimlet or nail, so it will be easier to get the screws in evenly.

To position the nails proceed as follows. Mark the centre of each piece of wood. Then draw a line along the length of each piece of wood 2.5cm. (1in.) from the edge until they intersect at the corner. On this line mark each 6mm. (¼in.) from the centre putting the marks across the length thus:

Now put the nails in every 6mm. (¼in.) in a zig-zag around the entire loom. This prevents the wood from splitting.

The corner nails appear very close together but don't worry, these are used for tying the threads on when you weave.

To make the potholder
Weaving consists of a warp (threads running lengthways) with interlaced threads at right angles called the weft. First make a knot at the end of the yarn and attach the thread to one of the corner nail heads. Now take your thread over an adjacent nail and start to run it from one side of the loom to the other along the length of the loom until you have used all the nails along these sides. Tie the end to one of the extra nails at the last corner leaving about 7.5cm. (3in.) extra thread. This is now the warp.

The weft can be the same material or a colour, which would allow you to see the weave more clearly. The coloured threads are often finer than the soft dishcloth cotton, so should be used double.

Thread the needle with both cut ends, thus leaving the loop to hook over the first nail along one of the shorter sides of the loom (the weft side). With the needle pick up every second thread of the warp until you have reached the other side of the loom. Now draw the full length of the thread (weft) through so that it is straight but not too tight. If it is not perfectly straight, push the thread along the warp with the tip of the needle until it is. When you have gone around the nail with the

first weft thread, go back and pick up the threads you did not pick up the first time, as though you were darning. Continue in this way until you have completely covered the warp, weaving any ends back into the work and then pushing them to the back. Now remove each corner knot and weave it for about 4 or 5 threads. This will hold all the ends in without knots.

To finish
The tension will be very tight when the weaving is complete, so to remove the weaving from the loom use the point of the needle as a lever to slip each warp or weft thread off. Place the needle under the threads and slide them over the end of each nail. It is important to do this with only 1 or 2 threads at a time. Chain these loops into one another with the crochet hook around the entire potholder. This will not only hold the weaving, but also gives a nice finished edge. When you reach the end there will be an extra loop. With the crochet hook pull this through twice and then you can use it to hang up the potholder.

There is one important final step, that is to soak the finished weaving in very hot water for about 20 minutes. This is to set the woven threads in place.

When you have completed your first potholder you will have a better knowledge of your materials and may decide it is too thick or thin for your liking. This is easily altered by changing the weave, for instance, by picking up 2 or 3 warp threads at a time or not using all the nail heads. Try various designs and see which you like best.

Canvas work

Embroidery on canvas is sometimes known as needlepoint tapestry, but this is incorrect, as true tapestry is woven. It is a popular needlecraft, and can be used for almost any furnishings and clothes, from wall hangings and cushions to belts, bags and covered buttons.

Canvas and yarns

There are two main types of canvas—single thread and double thread, but the mesh varies widely, so that it is possible to produce both very fine and very coarse work. Canvas is measured by the number of threads or holes to 2.5cm. (1in.), and thread counts vary from about 24 to 2.5cm. (1in.) to very coarse canvases with as few as 3 threads to 2.5cm. (1in.)

There is a variety of different yarns on the market, the most common being tapestry wool, stranded tapestry wool, crewel wool, stranded embroidery cotton and embroidery yarns. For very coarse canvas, rug wool can be used.

For furnishings or clothes, the yarns recommended for canvas work give the best results, but for wall hangings and pictures almost anything that gives a pleasing effect can be used – fine ribbons, string, raffia or lurex thread.

Always choose yarns to suit the work you have planned. The yarn should be thin enough to pass easily through the hole but must be thick enough to cover the canvas well so that the background does not show through.

Stitches

As canvas work has a long history, many different stitches have evolved, but it is possible to produce exciting work by using just the simplest of these. The three shown here are tent stitch (Fig. 1) which is also known as *petit point*; half cross stitch (Fig. 2) and cross stitch (Fig. 3). The first two look almost exactly the same, but the working methods are different. In tent stitch the yarn is taken diagonally across at the back so that it covers the canvas at both front and back. This makes it thicker and more hard-wearing than half cross stitch, in which the stitch at the back is a small vertical one. Half cross stitch is ideal for covering large areas with thick wool, and is economical as it uses less yarn. But it is not suitable for anything that has to take a lot of wear, such as a chair cover, and the canvas does tend to show through. Both these stitches can be used in conjunction with tramming, a padding stitch worked over

the canvas before the other stitching (Fig. 4). This can only be done on double thread canvas.

Needles

Use tapestry needles, which are blunt and have large eyes. They are available in various sizes; 18 to 21 are the most often used, but 14 is better for coarse work. The needle should be able to pass comfortably through the mesh of the canvas without pushing it out of shape.

Designs

There are a great many canvas work designs in various forms on the market. Needlework shops and some department stores sell pieces of canvas with designs painted on them in colours approximating to those that are to be used. Designs are also available in chart form, drawn up on squared paper. Obviously, it is more difficult to follow a chart, but it is also more satisfying as you can choose your own colours and even adapt the design.

Cross stitch embroidery designs can be adapted for canvas work, as these are also counted thread.

You can also make your own charted designs. Work out the design on a plain piece of paper, and when you are sure it is right, draw the outlines on to graph paper. Each square represents a stitch in the canvas, so choose a symbol for each of the colours to be used and mark each square with the appropriate symbol.

Frames

Canvas should always be worked in a frame, unless you are doing a small piece which can be held in the hand. Small squares which are to be sewn together for a cushion cover, for example, need not be framed. Frames are sold in most

needlework shops, or you can make one from an old picture frame. Turn the canvas over at the edges, tack to prevent fraying, and then either drawing pin the edges to the frame or lace them firmly to the frame all round.

Stretching the finished work

If you do not work on a frame, the finished work will have a bias to it which will have to be stretched out. Take two or three sheets of clean blotting paper, place them on a board and moisten them thoroughly. Dampen the back of the work with a damp cloth and place it, right side up, on the blotting paper.

Put one of the selvedge edges of the canvas flush with the edge of the board and pin the canvas edges squarely on to the board with non-rusting pins. Begin by pinning in the middle of the four sides. Add pins each side of the middle pin, stretching the work into shape as you pin. Leave to dry for 24 hours.

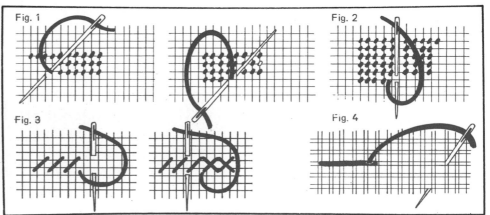

Fig. 1 · Fig. 2 · Fig. 3 · Fig. 4

Canvas work cushion cover

This attractive design is adapted from a traditional American Indian pattern. The cushion cover is quick and easy to work, as it is all done in the straight stitch called upright Gobelin over 4 holes of the canvas. The finished cushion will measure approximately 40.5cm. (16in.) square.

You will need

1 piece single-thread canvas 51cm. (20in.) square, 10 holes to 2.5cm. (1in.)
1 piece plain blue felt or woollen fabric for backing, 51cm. (20in.) square
Of stranded embroidery wool:
   7 skeins white, 2 skeins dark blue,
   2 skeins blue, 2 skeins light blue
No. 18 tapestry needle
Embroidery frame (optional)
Cushion pad
Matching thread

To make up

Find the centre of the canvas by folding it in half lengthways. Mark the fold line with basting stitches. Mount the canvas on the frame if you are using one. It is not strictly necessary in this case, as straight stitch does not distort the canvas, but it is easier to work on a frame. (See page 39 for information about frames.)

Begin working on the centre square of the canvas, as indicated on the chart. Work from the centre of the design out towards the edges, following the chart. Remove the threads marking the centre of the canvas as soon as the centre square has been worked.

To make your first stitch, bring yarn forward from back to front of canvas, leaving about 5cm. (2in.) of yarn at the back of the canvas, and hold it with your left hand. Count 4 holes straight up from where you have brought your yarn through, not counting the hole with yarn already in it. Put needle into 4th hole and bring yarn to back of work. Do not pull the yarn too tightly, as this will cause ugly gaps between rows of stitches, and may even distort the canvas.

Start your next stitch in the hole beside the point at which you first brought your needle through the canvas. Continue making a row of stitches, side by side, working over the loose end.

When you come to the end of a piece of yarn, weave the end in and out across the back of the stitches for about 5cm. (2in.). Trim off any excess yarn. Once you have worked a few rows, you can also begin each new piece of yarn by weaving it in and out along the back of stitches for about 5cm. (2in.).

When working another row of stitches on top of a previous row, bring your yarn up into the same hole as the top of the stitches on the row below.

Continue working, following the chart, until the design is complete.

Finishing and making up

Give the finished work a light 'smoothing' using a well dampened cloth over the canvas and a hot iron. The dampness and heat will help smooth out any wrinkles. Do not press heavily on to the work. Leave the canvas to dry flat.

To make up the cushion, trim canvas to within 2.5cm. (1in.) of embroidery. Trim the plain material to the same size as the canvas and place both pieces right sides together. Sew close to embroidery all round, leaving an opening on one side. Turn to right side. Insert pad, turn in seam allowance and slipstitch opening.

One square = 4 holes and
4 stitches on the canvas
unshaded squares = white
   △ = dark blue
   • = light blue
   ▲ = blue

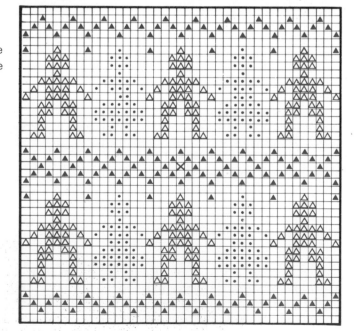

Woven place mats

On page 38 instructions were given for making a small, simple loom as an introduction to weaving. These mats are made on a larger loom, but it is constructed in exactly the same way.

You will need
For the loom
2 pieces of wood 2cm. by 4.5cm. by 40cm. (¾in. by 1¾in. by 15¾in.)
2 pieces of wood 2cm. by 4.5cm. by 60cm. (¾in. by 1¾in. by 23½in.)
Woodworking adhesive
Sandpaper, medium to coarse
4 angle braces
8 1.3cm. (½in.) No.7 screws
1 box 1.3cm. (½in.) panel pins
For the mats:
2 50g. (2oz.) balls rug wool
Large tapestry needle
1 piece cardboard 5cm. (2in.) by 36cm. (14in.)

Note
The amount of rug wool given will make one large mat or two small ones.

The loom
To make the loom, follow the instructions given for the small loom on page 38.

Placement of nails
Mark the centre of the two shorter pieces of wood, and then draw a rectangle of 36cm. (14in.) by 3cm. (1⅛in.) on both ends, making sure they are centred. Mark each length at 3cm. (1⅛in.) intervals, making 12 boxes each 3cm. (1⅛in.) square. Draw three lines along the length of the rectangle at right angles to the existing lines following the measurements given in Fig. 1.

Draw a diagonal line from the top to the bottom of each 3cm. (1⅛in.) box (Fig. 2). The nails should be placed at the intersections of four of the five diagonal and horizontal lines (Fig. 2). This will give you 8 warp ends per 3cm. (1⅛in.).

The weaving
Make a knot at the end of the yarn and place it over the bottom nail of the second square from the end. Now take your thread over the nail above this (Fig. 3) and start to run it from one side of the loom to the other. Use every other nail because of the weight of the rug wool. Continue until you have used the whole of one 50g. (2oz.) ball of wool. Tie the end to one of the extra nails at the other end. This is the warp.

The weft can be of the same wool or a different colour, which would allow you to see the weave more clearly. Before you start to weave insert the piece of cardboard under every other thread. This will give you the spacing for the fringe and help you to weave straight.

Cut off about 50cm. (19½in.) from your ball of wool and put it aside. It is to be used later for finishing. To start the weaving, thread the wool through the warp threads, picking up every other warp thread until you have reached the other side of the loom. Draw the short end through for about 6cm. (2¼in.) beyond the first warp thread, and take it back through the work, picking up the threads you did not pick up the first time. When there is only a short end left (about 3cm. or 1¼in.) left, push it to the back. This will hold the end securely without any knots. For the second row, pick up the threads you did not pick up the first time, passing the wool under them, and repeat for each row of weave until you have used all the weft wool.

When the weaving is complete, thread the tapestry needle with the loose end and weave it back into the second to last row of weave for about 6cm. (2¼in.). This will hold the end.

Before removing the weaving from the loom the last two rows must be secured with an overcast stitch so they do not slide off when the mat is used. Split the spare piece of yarn in half, so that you have two threads, of three strands each, one for each end. Thread the needle, and run the wool into the weaving of the second to the last row, picking up the same threads as this row. Go round the end and under the weft in the last row, also picking up the next to the last row in a diagonal stitch. Repeat, catching both of these rows each time, and finish by running the thread into the weaving. Remove the card from the other side and sew in the same way.

Take the weaving off the loom, cutting all the warp threads to about 5cm. (2in.). Untwist the threads to make the fringe. Wash work in hot soapy water in order to set the weave.

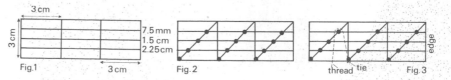

Fig. 1
3 cm
3 cm
3 cm
7.5 mm
1.5 cm
2.25 cm
Fig. 2
thread tie
edge
Fig. 3

Fringed wall hanging

Give your home a real touch of opulence with this vivid, Eastern-looking wall hanging. Don't be daunted – it may look complicated, but in fact most of it is worked in simple cross stitch, and we show you how to do the fringe stitch.

You will need

Of tapestry wool: 5 skeins mauve, 4 skeins magenta, 3 skeins each cyclamen, bright red and deep amber gold, 2 skeins each coral and gold

1 piece dark brown square weave embroidery fabric with approximately 6 squares to 2.5cm. (1in.), 69cm. by 46cm. (27in. by 18in.)

45cm. (½yd.) matching medium weight fabric, 90cm. (36in.) wide

45cm. (½yd.) of bonded fibre interfacing 82cm. (32in.) wide

1 tapestry needle No. 18

Bamboo rod 2.5cm. (1in.) diameter, approximately 51cm. (20in.) long.

6 curtain rings approximately 4.5cm. (1¾in.) in diameter.

Note

A pattern for the wallhanging appears on the opposite page.

To work the embroidery

Mark the centre of the fabric both ways

with a line of tacking stitches along a line of holes. The pattern shows two open arrows which should coincide with the basting stitches. The pattern represents the left half of the design; the right side is exactly the same. The areas with no numbers, at corners and sides, are where the background fabric is left unworked. The parts to be worked in cross stitch are shown as numbers, and those to be worked in fringe stitch as letters. Both are keyed to the tapestry wool colours.

With one short side of fabric facing you, and following the pattern and colour key, start working from the centre at crossed basting stitches. Work the cross stitch areas first, with each stitch worked over one square of fabric. Make sure that all the upper halves of the crosses lie in the same direction.

The fringe stitches are made as follows. Work from left to right, using a double thickness of thread. Bring the thread through at A, insert the needle two holes to the right at B, bring through one hole to the left at C, keeping thread above needle (Fig. 1). Insert needle one hole to the right of B, at D and bring through again at B, one hole to the left, keeping thread below needle (Fig. 2). Hold down the loop of thread to the required length with the left thumb, and continue to end of row, keeping the loops as even as possible (Fig. 3). Work the fringe stitches from the bottom row upwards, making each loop about 3.2cm. (1¼in.) deep, and allow each loop to overlap the one below by about 3mm. (⅛in.).

To make up

Press the embroidery carefully on the wrong side. Cut a piece of lining 69cm. by 46cm. (27in. by 18in.). Cut a piece of interlining 65.5cm. by 42.5cm. (25¾in. by 16¾in.). Place centrally to wrong side of lining, baste and edge-stitch in position. Allowing 1.2cm. (½in.) for seams, baste and then stitch lining to embroidery right sides facing, leaving lower edge open. Press seams, trim to 6mm. (¼in.), cutting corners diagonally. Turn to right side, turn in open edges and slip stitch together. Sew rings to top edge measuring to space them evenly. Insert bamboo rod through rings.

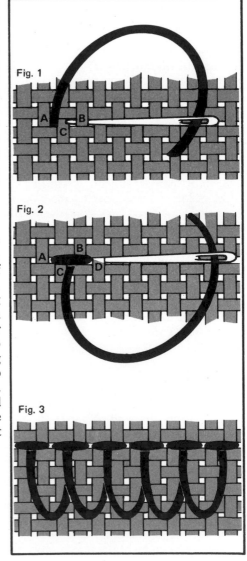

Fig. 1

Fig. 2

Fig. 3

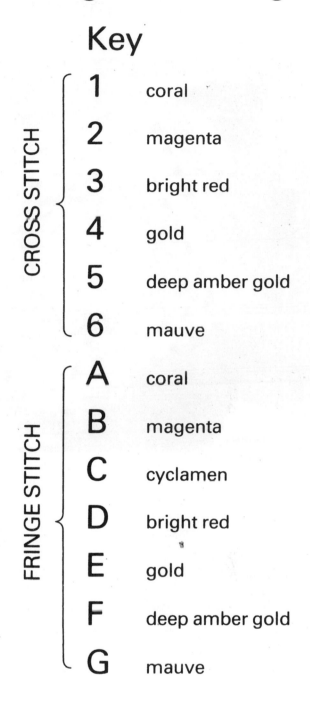

Fringed wall hanging

Key

1	coral
2	magenta
3	bright red
4	gold
5	deep amber gold
6	mauve

A	coral
B	magenta
C	cyclamen
D	bright red
E	gold
F	deep amber gold
G	mauve

43

Geometric cushion

This unusual cushion demonstrates the effectiveness of using a variety of stitches on one piece. The combination of loop stitch (or velvet) with the small flat tent stitch provides a strong surface interest, and the contrast between the areas of cross stitch and the bands of satin stitch create a pattern in which colour is almost unnecessary.

You will need

60cm. (23½ in.) tapestry canvas 68cm. (26¾ in.) wide, 18 holes to 2.5cm. (1in.)
50cm. (19⅝ in.) matching fabric 90cm. (35⅜ in.) wide for backing
Tapestry frames with 68cm. (26¾ in.) tapes (optional)
1 cushion pad to fit
Tapestry needle No. 18
Of tapestry wool: 10 skeins beige, 8 skeins cream, 7 skeins light brown, 3 skeins each violet, terracotta, grey, pink, 2 skeins brown.

Note

A pattern for the cushion appears opposite. The pattern shows one quarter of the design, the centre indicated by an arrow. Each background square represents 2 threads of canvas.

The embroidery

Trim canvas to 60cm. × 60cm. (23½ in.

× 23½ in.). Mark the centre of the canvas lengthwise and widthwise with a line of basting stitches. Mount canvas on frame, if used. The four stitches used are petit point (or tent stitch); cross stitch; satin stitch worked over 4 threads of canvas; and velvet (or loop) stitch. The first two are illustrated on page 39. Satin stitch and velvet stitch are given on this page (Figs. 1 and 2). Start the design two threads down from the crossed basting stitches and work the section given, following the colours. Repeat in reverse from solid arrows to complete one half and work other half to correspond.

To make up

Trim canvas to within 1.3cm. (½ in.) from embroidery. Cut backing fabric to same size. Place back and front pieces right sides together and stitch close to the edge of the embroidery, leaving an opening wide enough for the pad. Turn to right side. Insert pad. Turn in seam allowance on open edges and slipstitch the opening closed.

Fig. 1 Satin Stitch. May be worked from right to left or left to right in horizontal rows over 4 threads of canvas. In this design it will be necessary in some parts to reduce the length of stitches to fit the outline shape.

Fig. 2 Velvet Stitch. Work from left to right in rows, working from the bottom upwards. Fig. 1 Bring the thread through at arrow and insert the needle at A (2 threads up and 2 threads to the right), bring out again at the arrow; re-insert the needle at A leaving a loop of thread at the bottom (the loops may be worked over a thick knitting needle to regulate the length) bring the needle out at B (2 threads down), insert at C (2 threads up and 2 threads to the left), bring out again at B in readiness for the next stitch.

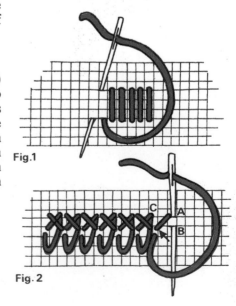

Fig.1

Fig. 2

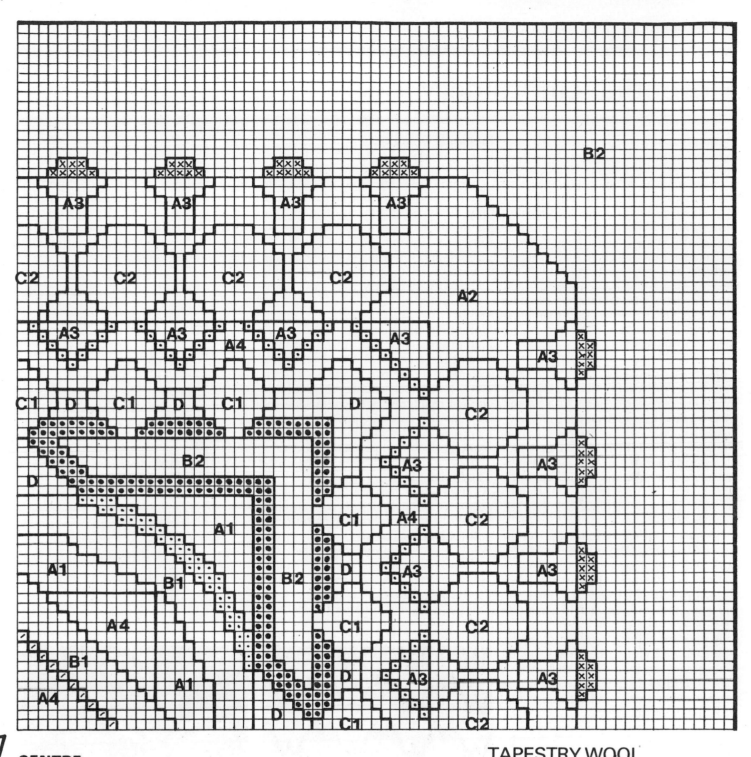

CENTRE

Geometric cushion

TAPESTRY WOOL

A1		brown	
A2	☒	light brown	Cross stitch
A3	⬤	grey	
A4		pink	
B1		light brown	Satin stitch
B2		beige	
C1		violet	Velvet stitch
C2		cream	
D	⊡	terracotta	Petit point stitch
	⧄	brown	

Florentine embroidery

Florentine stitchery, also called bargello or zigzag embroidery, is one of the easiest and most exciting kinds of canvas work. It's very quick to do and as you can cover the canvas in no time at all, you can undertake quite big projects. Basically, Florentine is a zigzag pattern but there are several variations on the pattern.

Charts are usually given for Florentine patterns and show just one row of the design. This is the foundation row and once you have worked this the rest of the pattern is easy to follow. Most Florentine patterns are worked over four or six threads of the canvas.

Colours and canvas

The beauty of Florentine embroidery lies in the use of colour. You can use a range of tones from light to dark with one strong colour or you can use a range of vivid shades in bold contrast. If you are going to enjoy Florentine, it is a good idea to try and obtain a colour card of tapestry yarns. The manufacturers will supply these if you write to them, and they are not very expensive.

Single thread canvas is best for Florentine embroidery. The stitches lie side by side and should cover the canvas completely. For standard tapestry wools, canvas with 16 threads to 2.5cm. (1in.) is the most suitable and you should use a size 18 tapestry needle.

If you are making a small accessory, you can work Florentine using stranded embroidery cottons. With this thread, canvas with 24 threads to 2.5cm. (1in.) is used. Thicker yarns would need a correspondingly coarser canvas.

Preparing canvas

It is a matter of personal preference whether you use an embroidery frame or not. Certainly a frame makes working easier but small pieces and cushion covers can be worked in the hand. You will find it helps if you bind the edges of cut canvas with seam binding or cellophane tape before starting to work to prevent fraying.

Before starting the embroidery, tack vertical and horizontal lines across the centre of the canvas. This will help you to plan your pattern and is helpful when you are making up the piece. It also helps if you work a line of tacking stitches round the edges to show the shape of the finished piece.

Top left, zigzag; top right, flame; bottom left, honeycomb; bottom right, basketweave

Preparing to work

Having marked out the canvas, lay your skeins of yarn out in front of you in the order you are using them. This will help you to keep the colour sequence. Cut only 30-40cm. (12-16in.) of yarn from the skein. If longer pieces are cut, the canvas wears the yarn as it is pulled through and towards the end of a piece of yarn you'll find that it is not covering the canvas adequately.

Stitches

Florentine embroidery is worked using a kind of satin or straight stitch. The stitch is worked over the same number of threads in a pattern and the back of the work looks the same as the front. In curvature patterns, the stitches are worked in 'steps' – as shown in the Ogee or Flame example. Fig. 1 shows the technique for working and interlocking the stitches.

The foundation row

All Florentine patterns depend on an accurate foundation row. In some patterns, such as the zigzag pattern, the embroidery can be worked above and below the foundation row. When you are working more complex designs, such as honeycomb or basketweave (see colour illustrations), a different system is used. For the honeycomb pattern, it helps to work the outline of the honeycomb first and then fill in the central colours. The basketweave pattern is easier to follow if the central diamond is worked first and then the outer lines built up afterwards. Have several needles already threaded in your chosen colour sequence and work a few stitches at a time until you have got one complete pattern worked.

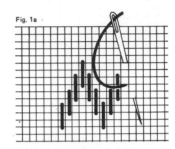
Fig. 1a

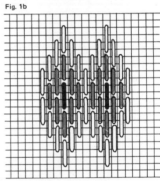
Fig. 1b

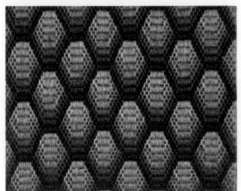

Florentine cushion cover

On page 46 we told you something about the possibilities of this lovely, traditional form of embroidery, and explained the various different patterns you can make. Now we have a project for you, so you can try your hand at it.

You will need
1 piece single thread canvas, 16 holes to 2.5cm. (1in.), 50cm. by 59cm. (½yd. by 23in.)
Of tapestry wool: 3 skeins each amber gold, magenta, light brown, rose, 1 skein bright red, cardinal red
Tapestry needle, No. 18
Furnishing velvet 41cm. by 33cm. (16in. by 13in.)
Matching thread; cushion pad.
Square or rectangular tapestry frame (optional)

Note
If these colours do not match your furnishings, use a combination of your own choice, but remember that you should use a light colour for the centres, and blending, darker colours for the motifs.

To work the design
Overcast the edges of the canvas. If you are working with a frame, mount the canvas on it (you can work the canvas in the hand if you prefer). Mark the centre of the canvas each way with a coloured tacking thread.

The whole design is worked in Florentine stitch, and all the stitches are the same length, worked over 4 holes in the canvas. Start at the centre (which is marked on the diagram with an arrow) with amber gold and complete the outlining of the main motif in the colour, following the diagram. You can fill in the colours of the main motif following the diagram and colour. Having worked the main motif you will find the smaller, filling motif, easy to follow if you again complete the outlining in amber gold. There are 7 complete main motifs across the cushion and 6 motifs down it. (If you have to 'jump' blocks at the back, thread the wool under the stitches already there, and darn ends into the other stitches at the back.)

Finishing and making up
If you have not used a frame, the canvas may be pulled out of shape and will need stretching. Follow the method described on page 39.

To make the cushion, trim the canvas to 43cm. by 36cm. (17in. by 14in.) and overcast the edges again. Cut the cushion backing fabric to the same size. With right sides together, sew embroidery and backing together, being careful to keep the line of sewing just into the edge of the embroidery to prevent any bare thread of canvas showing. Leave one side open, trim corners diagonally. Turn to right side. Insert cushion pad and slipstitch opening to close.

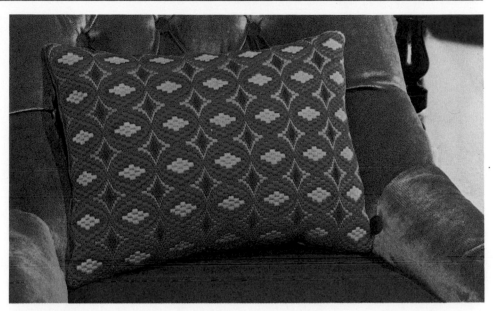

Colour key:

Amber Gold	Bright Red	Magenta
Ecru	Rose	Cardinal Red

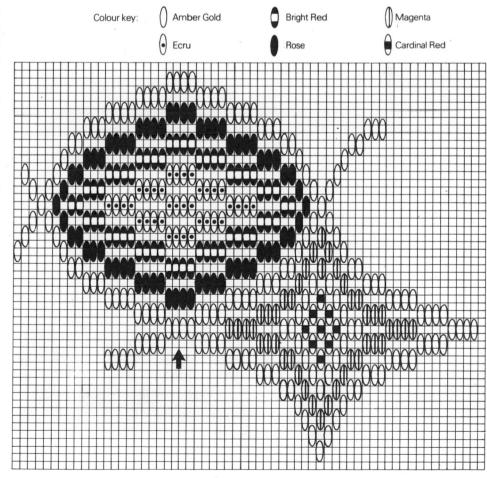

Rag placemats

Remnants of closely woven patterned fabrics can be used to make a set of colourful woven placemats. As long as the colours tone with each other, you can use different fabrics. The simple home-made frame loom on page 41 is used for this project, so first read this page if you have not aleady made the loom. The first page in the same section explains the basic principles of weaving.

You will need
Frame loom
2 pieces stiff card, 5cm. by 36cm. (2in. by 14in.)
Ruler, dressmaker's chalk
1 ball coloured crochet cotton (should be sufficient for making 6 mats)
For each mat: patterned fabric, approximately 1m. by 90cm. (1yd. by 36in.)

Preparing the loom
To put the warp threads on the loom, tie a single knot at the end of the crochet cotton. Attach the thread to the 8th nail from the edge. Take the thread down past the 9th nail and across the loom to the opposite 9th nail. Take the thread round the nail and up to the 11th nail. Go round it and down to the opposite 11th nail. Continue putting on the warp, using every other nail, until you reach the 4th nail from the end. Cut the thread and tie the end to this nail.

Preparing for weaving
To make the fabric suitable for weaving, cut it into strips on the crosswise bias. Chalk a line diagonally. Measure lines 5cm. (2in.) apart from the chalk line. Cut the fabric into strips. Join the strips into one continuous length as follows. Place two strips right sides together, crossing at an angle of 90°. Stitch where they overlap. Trim the ends as shown in Fig. 1. Join all the strips. Press the seams open.

Cut V notches into both ends of one of the card strips. This is used for a bobbin.

The weaving
Slip the un-notched piece of card through the warp threads, weaving it over and under every thread. Slide it up to the top of the loom. This will give you spare warp threads for making the fringe later. Wind some of the cotton warp thread on to the bobbin. Weave about 10 rows to make a selvedge, passing the bobbin under and over every other thread. When you have worked the last row, draw the thread through for about 6cm. (2½in.) and then push the bobbin back, picking up the threads you did not pick up the first time for 6cm. (2½in.). Then push the end through to the back. This will hold the end without knots. Now you are ready to start weaving the actual fabric. Weave the rag fabric in about 6 warp threads before the end of the last end of cotton, going over and under the same threads and continuing across the row. The weave will hold the ends (Fig. 2). This is how you change threads or colours in weaving.

To make working easier, insert a flat smooth piece of wood, such as a ruler, into a row of weft. This will raise every other thread across the warp so that you can get the bobbin through. You can also use the ruler to pack the weft down on the warp. When you insert the weft, do not pull it straight across. Insert it at an angle, making an arch, then push and pack it down. This helps to prevent the warp threads being pulled together. Continue your weaving until you have the length you desire. Work 10 more rows in cotton to make the other selvedge and complete the weaving.

To finish the ends, cut the warp from the loom, leaving at least 5cm. (2in.) of thread. Tie a knot in every 2 threads and slide the knot up the threads to lie against the weaving.

Wash the mat in hot soapy water to set the weave. Rinse well and dry. Press lightly if it seems to need it.

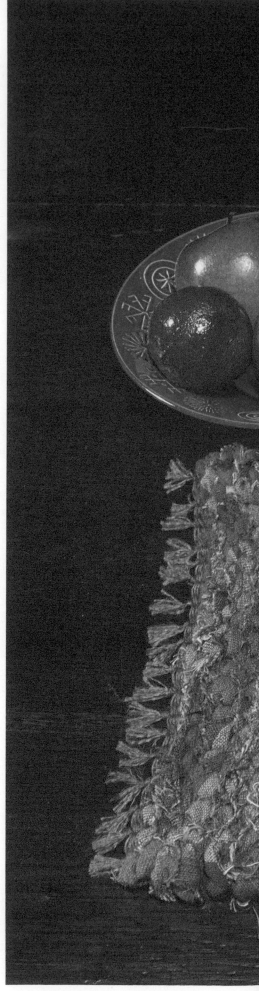

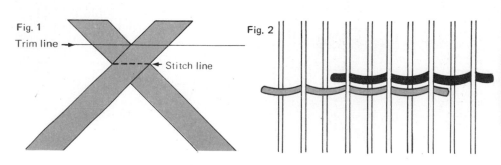

Fig. 1
Trim line →
← Stitch line

Fig. 2

Tapestry

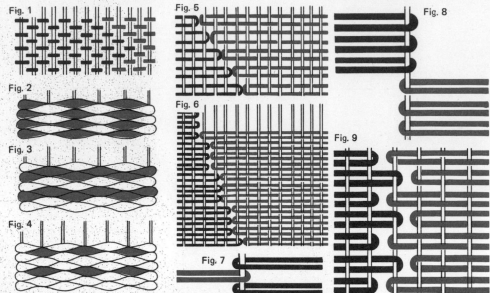

Fig. 1
Fig. 2
Fig. 3
Fig. 4
Fig. 5
Fig. 6
Fig. 7
Fig. 8
Fig. 9

Tapestry is a form of weaving in which the pattern is created by the weft threads, those running horizontally across the loom. The warp threads, those which stretch from top to bottom, are completely hidden. The patterns are made by the colours of the weft threads and the way in which they are placed. The warp and weft threads form a grid, just like darning, so that every shape you decide to make, even a curve, is really a series of straight lines (Fig. 1). Once you have mastered the art of weaving basic shapes, you can start to make up your own designs, using several colours. However, this takes some practice, and the best way to start is to make a sampler using two colours. The sampler illustrated was woven on the home-made loom described on page 41, and here on this page we give instructions for making a sampler which is like it. The warp threads are tough but fine cotton string, and the weft is rug wool. The only other equipment you need are two small bobbins for holding the weft, a knitting needle or similar pointed object for pushing the weft down into a compact shape, and a piece of cardboard about 5cm. (2in.) by the width of the loom. The bobbins can be made from pieces of card about 5cm. (2in.) square. Cut V-shapes into two of the sides. Make a slit at the top, so that you can push the bobbin into one of the warp threads to hold it. This will allow you to let the bobbin go if you are inter-

rupted when working without unravelling the thread.

The weaving
Put the warp threads on the loom (see page 41) to the desired width of the sampler. The one illustrated is 12cm. (4¾in.) wide. Use every nail on the loom, so that you have 8 warp threads for each 3cm. (1⅛in.). This procedure will give you a close warp.

Insert the pieces of cardboard into the warp threads at the bottom of the loom, going under one and over the next. This will raise the alternate threads slightly so that it is easier to pass the bobbin in and out. Wind white rug wool on to a bobbin and weave a few rows of plain white so that you get the feel of it and see how the wool covers the warp. Treat the two warp threads at each side as one so that you create a selvedge.

Now you can start experimenting with patterns and shapes. Variations of stripes can be made in the following ways. For instance, if you weave one row in colour A and one in colour B, the weft rows (picks) will cover the warp in such a way that thin vertical stripes are formed (Fig. 2). A thin wavy line is produced by weaving 2 rows in colour A and 2 in colour B (Fig. 3). Spots are made by weaving 3 rows of A and 1 row of B (Fig. 4).

When you introduce a new thread of colour, do not start at the very edge, but take the end into the weaving by a few warp threads. The next row will overlap and hold the end firmly. Always leave an end about 3cm. (1⅛in.) long.

Shape changes and joins
To make a diagonal of about 45°, increase the weft by one warp thread for every row (Fig 5). To produce a steeper incline, pass more than one weft around each warp (Fig. 6). For vertical lines, such as the sides of triangles and squares, the two blocks of colour must be joined. There are several ways of doing this. The simplest is as follows. Weave colour A to the edge of the block, go round the warp thread and return to the edge. Then weave colour B from the other side, pass it around the same warp thread and return (Fig. 7). The disadvantage of this method is that the threads build up and make a bulge in the weaving. The second method decreases this build up. If alternate groups of three weft rows are wound round one warp (Fig. 8) the loops will dovetail neatly into each other when the weaving is pressed down. In the third method colour A and colour B are joined over three warps (Fig. 9). This is the strongest join and can be continued to any depth without the weft rows building up.

To make gentle curves and lozenges, weave in colour A, taking weft over one warp, then back over two, and then back over three, building up until the shape is the width you want. Then decrease until the weft is covering only one warp. Do not make the shape too big or the design will pucker. Take colour B and weave across until it meets colour A, take over warp thread and return.

When you have completed the weaving, knot or braid the loose warp ends.

Tablet weaving

Tablet weaving is an ancient method of weaving, in which decorative braids are produced without using a loom. It is called tablet weaving because the warp (the set of threads running the length of the weaving) is formed by threading them through holes in a series of tablets (Fig. 1). The warp is then held under tension and the actual weaving begins, passing the weft (crosswise) threads over and under across the warp. As you can see from Fig. 1, because of the position of the holes in the tablets, two distinct groups of warp threads are formed, with a space betwen them. This space is called the shed, and the weft thread is passed through it for each row (pick) of weaving. The difference between ordinary flat-loom weaving (pages 38 and 41) and tablet weaving is that the tablets bearing the warp threads are twisted round as the weaving progresses (Fig. 2) so that a different shed, and hence a different arrangement of colours, is formed with each turn. The weft, which in ordinary weaving produces the pattern and colour, only shows at the edges in tablet weaving; its function is simply to hold the warp threads together.

Materials

Tablets These can be bought from crafts suppliers, or they can be made quite easily from stiff cardboard, following the measurements given in Fig. 3. The holes should be made with a punch, as they must not have rough edges.

Yarn The thread should be strong and smooth: mercerised cotton is most commonly used and it comes in a wide range of colours. Wool can be used, but beginners are advised to avoid it as it can easily break under tension.

Shuttle The weft thread must be wound on to a small shuttle, which passes easily in and out of the shed. You can make one from cardboard, by the method described on page 58.

Tensioning devices There are various methods of holding the warp under tension while weaving. The simplest is probably the one shown in the colour illustration. The end of the warp away from the weaver is knotted, and hooked over a door handle or hook on the wall, while the near end is knotted around the arm of the weaver's chair. An alternative is to make two tension posts by screwing G-clamps on opposite sides of a table. The clamps must be placed upside down, with the screw thread at the top so that they act as posts (Fig. 3). Wrap stiff paper or cardboard around the screw threads so that the warp does not become frayed and can be slid on and off easily.

The weaving

The arrangement of colours you use to thread the tablets helps to form the pattern, and as you grow expert you will soon know how to work out your own. The first step, however, is to understand the method, and the best way to do this is to practise. Try making a very simple warp, using 2 colours and 6 tablets. Thread holes 1 and 2 in all tablets with a light colour, and holes 3 and 4 in a dark colour. To do this, cut 4 pieces of yarn (2 light, 2 dark) about 2½m. (2½yd.) long. Take first tablet, and thread one end of each length of yarn through a hole, from front to back. Tie threads firmly at back. Cut another 4 threads, and repeat process for second tablet. Repeat for third. Do exactly the same for the remaining tablets, but thread them from front to back. This keeps the braid more even. When you have threaded all six, place them face upwards and draw the knotted ends together. Knot again firmly, or bind with cord (Fig. 4). Make sure all numbers correspond, and tie tablets together through the centre hole (Fig. 4). Place the knotted end on whatever post or hook you are using, and secure the near end. When you are sure the tension is correct, untie the centre tie. Hold all the tablets together

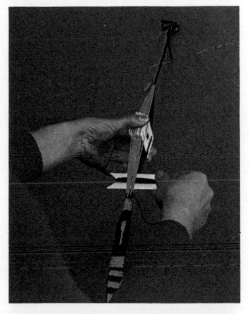

so that the numbers are all facing right or left. Wind weft yarn on to shuttle, and wind the end round the threads nearest you to give a firm start on the weaving. Put the weft through the shed, and turn all the tablets a quarter turn either away or towards you. (They can be turned in either direction, but if they are always turned one way large twists will build up at the other end, so it is a good idea to change direction frequently.) After each quarter turn, insert a line of weft (pick) and pull it tightly. If the weft picks seem loose, beat them down with the edge of a ruler.

You can try out various patterns as follows. Arrange tablets with 1 and 2 at the top. Turn tablet *away* from you twice and follow with two quarter turns *towards* you. Continue in this way and a light material will appear on the top with a dark material underneath. For another pattern make four quarter turns away from you followed by four quarter turns towards you. Alternate light and dark stripes will result. The width of stripes can be altered according to the number of quarter turns made before reversing. After practising these patterns try altering the positions of the numbers, e.g. turn the middle 2 tablets round so that numbers 3 and 4 are at the top. A great variety of patterns can be made without re-threading the tablets.

Finishing off

There will be a large number of threads in the fringe, these ends can be knotted, twisted, bound or plaited.

warp threads
Fig. 1

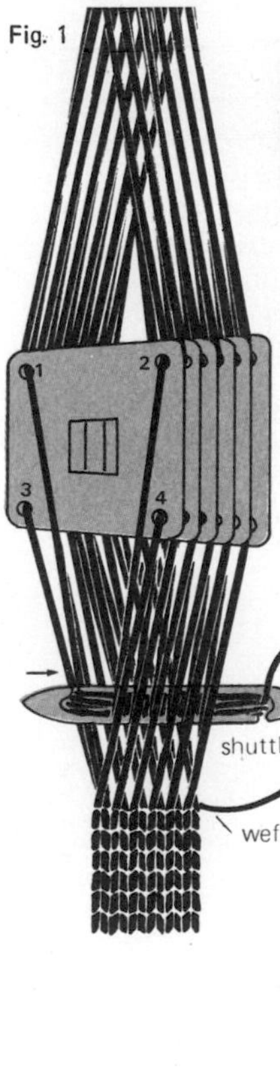

Tablets are pulled apart to show structure
Fig. 2

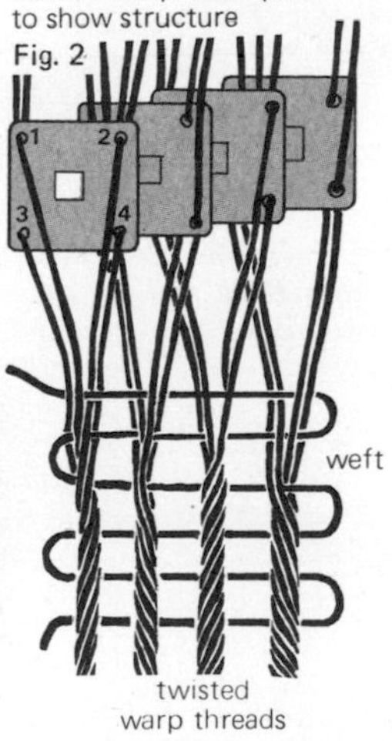

weft

twisted warp threads

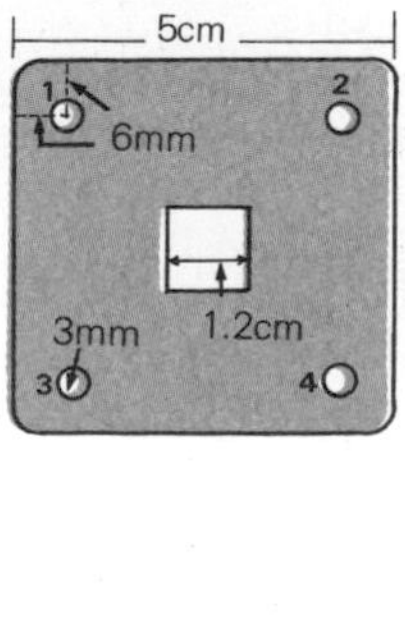

shuttle

weft

1
2
6mm
5cm
3mm 1.2cm
3
4
Fig. 3

Canvas work stitches

One of the most important elements in the creation of a really successful piece of canvas embroidery is the use of different stitches to provide textural effects. There is a wide variety of stitches which can be used, but this does not mean that you should use as many different stitches as possible in one piece of work. You should decide the type of stitch best suited to each part of a design – a large and bulky square stitch, or a small, neat flat stitch – and then the ultimate choice of stitch will depend upon both the shape and its relative position in the design.

A design can be carried out entirely in one colour, provided that a suitable selection of stitches is used for the working. There should be the maximum of contrast in the size and shape of the stitches, so that any tendency towards flatness in the finished surface is prevented. Differences in the slope or direction of a stitch can also make a great contribution to the general appearance of the work. By using a variety of stitches in this way, without a definite change of colour, it is possible to produce shadows, which in their turn introduce considerable tonal variation. This is particularly apparent when the work is hung so that a good strong light comes from one side.

An additional element in achieving a textured surface is the use of a variety of yarns. Nylon and cotton threads can be used in a piece and the reflectiveness of these yarns will contrast with the rather matt appearance of wool. Silk threads, used carefully, can introduce a beautiful sheen to a piece of work.

Satin stitch *The number of threads over which the stitch is worked can be varied according to the effect desired.*

Long-legged cross stitch *Can be worked over 2, 4 or 6 horizontal threads of canvas. Bring needle through at A, take yarn over 4 vertical and 4 horizontal threads into hole B. Bring out 4 threads down, at C. Take yarn diagonally over 4 horizontal and 8 vertical threads to D, and bring out 4 threads down for next stitch.*

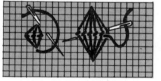

Smyrna stitch *(sometimes called double-cross stitch). Large diagonal cross stitch with straight cross worked over it. Can be worked over 2, 4 or more threads of canvas.*

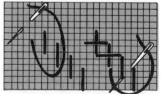

Upright cross stitch. *One horizontal and one vertical stitch, each over 4 threads. Bring out thread at arrow; insert at A and bring out at B (2 threads down and 2 to the left). Continue till end of row, then work horizontal stitches across.*

Diagonal Parisian stitch. *Worked diagonally over 3 and 1 intersections so that each long stitch fits into the short one of the previous row.*

Eyelet stitch. *Individual stitches worked from each hole around the perimeter into the centre hole. Can be worked over any number of canvas threads.*

Rococo stitch. *A group of vertical straight stitches worked by passing the yarn each time through the same hole. Each stitch is tied in the middle to a thread of canvas with a straight stitch if the threads are of even number (a), or a tent stitch if uneven (b).*

Mosaic stitch. *Each stitch is a group of 3 diagonal stitches worked over 2 horizontal and 2 vertical threads. The first stitch is over 1 intersection (tent stitch), the second over 2 and the 3rd over 1 again.*

Italian two-sided stitch. *Cross stitch bounded by straight stitches.*

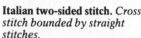

Cushion (or Scottish) stitch. *Set of 5 diagonal stitches worked over 1, 2, 3, 2 and 1 intersections, and surrounded by row of tent stitch.*

Rice stitch. *A large diagonal cross worked over an even number of threads with small diagonal stitches worked over each arm of the cross in finer yarn. The large cross is worked first.*

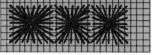

Rhodes stitch. *This is a square stitch worked over any uneven number of threads. Begins with an individual diagonal stitch running from one corner to the other of chosen square. Continues around square, moving in one direction, until a stitch has been worked into every hole around the edge, always passing across the centre.*

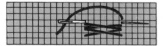

Oblong cross stitch. *Worked over 1 vertical and several horizontal threads.*

Fan stitch *(left). Square stitch usually worked over 3 vertical and 3 horizontal threads.*

Church kneelers

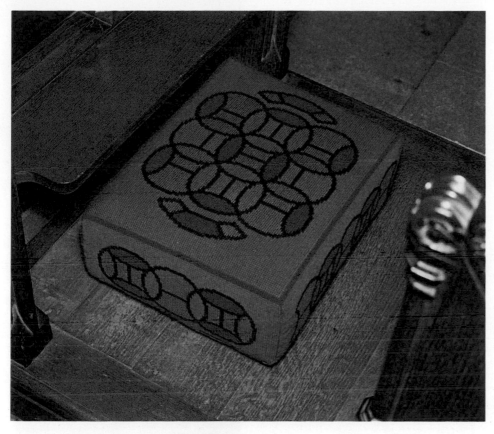

ink. If you are using cut out paper shapes, draw round them direct on to the canvas.

Finishing
Measure the finished work to make sure that the sides are the same size and are square. Stretch the canvas if it has pulled out of shape. Trim off the surplus canvas leaving 2cm. (¾in.) on the edges of the embroidery for seams. Join the seams with machine stitching or back stitches. Press seams flat.

Making up
Cut rubber or latex foam to size and twice the thickness of the kneeler because it must be compressed inside. (You can use several layers of carpet underfelt if you prefer.)

Make a case for the filling from washed unbleached calico (top and four sides seamed together). Push the filling into it. Cut a base piece from carpet underfelt and seam to the calico case. Slip a brass curtain ring on to a piece of tape. Sew the tape firmly to the casing (Fig. 2). Cut a piece of upholsterer's black linen to the base size plus turnings. Press the turnings. Press the turnings on the casework outer. Slip the outer on to the kneeler. Oversew the linen base to the canvaswork, so that the ring is outside.

Working church kneelers is often a group project, workers discussing and then selecting a single design, or each needleworker designing and working independently. There are points to be considered when deciding design.

Generally, large-scale motifs are more effective than designs with small detail. Traditional church motifs are popular but try and achieve a fresh, modern approach. Cut the motif in different sizes from paper and move them about on a sheet of paper for an interesting design idea.

Abstract and geometric designs look better than naturalistic or illustrative themes. A good way of judging the effectiveness of a design is to place it on the floor and look at it from above. This helps you to decide whether fine detail can be omitted without spoiling the effect.

Colour schemes
If kneelers are for a new church the architect may be helpful with colour schemes. For an old church, consideration should be given to other decorative features in the building such as stained glass windows, or altar frontals and banners. If a church has a dark interior, a bright colour for the background of the kneeler might be acceptable.

Size
A kneeler can be any reasonable size you like but generally they are about 23cm. by 35cm. (9in. by 14in.) and about 5.6cm. (2¼in.) thick. Fig. 1 shows the area of embroidery (top and sides in one piece). The sides can be worked as four separate pieces if you prefer.

Canvas and threads
Single-thread canvas 16 holes to 2.5cm. (1in.) is most suitable for this type of work. By working some areas of your design over 2 threads of canvas and others over 4 threads or more, exciting and interesting texture is achieved. If you prefer double mesh canvas, choose 11 threads to 2.5cm. (1in.). Wool yarn is usually used for working kneelers but silk threads can be included for contrast and sheen.

Preparing the work
Cut the canvas to the overall size of the kneeler plus surplus for mounting in a frame. Mark the centre of the canvas with tacking threads. Go over the lines of your drawing with thick black lines. Mark the centre (see Fig. 1). Lay the canvas on top of the design and you should be able to see the design through the holes. Mark the lines with a laundry marker or Indian

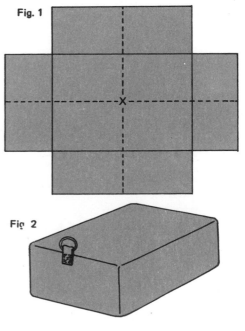

Fig. 1

Fig 2

Woven bookmarks

On page 51 we explained the basic techniques of tablet weaving, so if you want to make these attractive bookmarks, first read that page carefully.

You will need

12 tablets

Medium-weight mercerised crochet cotton in turquoise, black and purple

Small shuttle (optional)

Ruler for beating down weft

Tensioning device

Threading the tablets

You will need a warp 76cm. (30in.) long to make 2 bookmarks, each 25cm. (10in.) long, so cut 48 warp threads as follows: 18 black; 10 purple; 20 turquoise. Cut them about 80cm. (31½in.) so that you can knot the ends. In order to make a black selvedge, thread the top and bottom tablets with black. The others are threaded in the following way: Hole 1, black; Hole 2, purple; Holes 3 and 4 turquoise. When you have threaded each tablet arrange them so that the warp threads come from the back for the first six and the front in the second six. Place them in a pile on a table and tie them together through the hole in the middle. Even up the threads, knot them firmly at each end, and bind ends with strong cord.

Beginning the weaving

Secure the ends to whatever tensioning device you are using (see page 51). The simplest is to tie one end to a door handle or hook on the wall, and the other to the arm of the chair you will sit in to weave. Make sure the warp is kept taut throughout the weaving. Thread the shuttle with black thread, which is used throughout for the weft. Untie the tablets. They will now be lying in the same direction as the warp threads. Hold the tablets with Hole 1 nearest you, insert the shuttle bearing the weft into the shed (the space between two groups of warp threads) and leave about 10cm. (4in.) hanging down. This will be secured by the next rows of weaving.

The pattern

The tablets are turned between each row of weaving (pick) so that a pattern is formed. After each pick, press down the weft with the ruler.

The following instructions are for the bookmark on the right in the illustration.

The shorter striped band:

1 Make 8 quarter turns away from you, weaving a pick between each turn.

2 Make 8 quarter turns towards you, weaving a pick between each turn.

The central pattern:

1 Change the position of tablets 3, 5, 8 and 10 by giving them 2 quarter turns away from you. Weave 1 pick.

2 Make 8 quarter turns away, weaving a pick between each turn.

3 Make 8 quarter turns towards you, weaving a pick between each.

4 Repeat these 16 rows (2 and 3). This completes the central pattern.

The longer striped band:

1 Return tablets 3, 5, 8 and 10 to their original position. Weave 1 pick.

2 Make 8 quarter turns away, weaving 1 pick between each turn.

3 Make 8 quarter turns towards you, weaving 1 pick between each turn.

4 Make 8 quarter turns away, weaving 1 pick between each turn. Cut the weaving off, leaving sufficient warp ends for fringe. You will still have enough warp for a second bookmark, using a different pattern.

The second bookmark

Move the tablets up the warp so that you have a long enough warp for weaving in front of the tablets. The striped end bands are made in the same way as for the first bookmark; only the central pattern is different. When you have completed the stripes, turn tablets 3, 4, 9 and 10 2 quarter turns away from you. Weave 1 pick. Now weave for 16 rows in exactly the same way as for the first central pattern (steps 2 and 3) and return tablets 3, 4, 9 and 10 to their original position. Complete the longer striped band as before. Cut weaving and remove tablets.

Framework

This is a very old weaving technique which produces a knotted or tufted fabric. It can be used for anything square or oblong, so is ideal for cushions, mats and so on.

The yarn (any knitting yarn will do) is wound round nails on a wooden frame, then these threads are held into position by being tied together where they cross with a separate piece of yarn.

Various different patterns can be achieved by this method. For instance, an even number of nails on each side will produce a different effect from an odd number (however, remember that each side must always have the same number). Different effects can also be created by winding the yarn round the nails in different ways, and finally, some of the threads can be cut. See page 57, which provides a complete framework project for you to do.

Once the work is completed it is removed from the frame, and made up in whatever way desired, just like a piece of weaving.

To make a 46cm. (18in.) square frame, which is a good size for a cushion cover, you will need the following.

1. 190cm. (75in.) of 2cm. (¾in.) square planed wood
2. 4 4cm. (1⅝in.) panel pins
3. 76 3cm. (1⅛in.) panel pins
4. Wood glue
5. Hammer, steel rule, vice or corner cramps

Making the frame

Fig. 1 shows a top view of the completed frame with the nails in place. Cut the wood into four even lengths. Take care that the ends of the wood are square otherwise the frame will become warped when the joints are made. To make a joint, glue the end of one piece of wood, butt this glued end up to the side of the second piece, place both in a vice or corner cramp, check with a set-square that the corner is square, and finally nail into position. Leave the joint until the glue is set and repeat this process for the other three joints. Sand off any sharp edges.

Placing the working nails

These nails must be hammered in absolutely square and placed exactly 2.5cm. (1in.) apart down the centre of the top side of the wood. Measure and mark out their positions before hammering them in. Leave the last 2cm. (¾in.) of each nail sticking up.

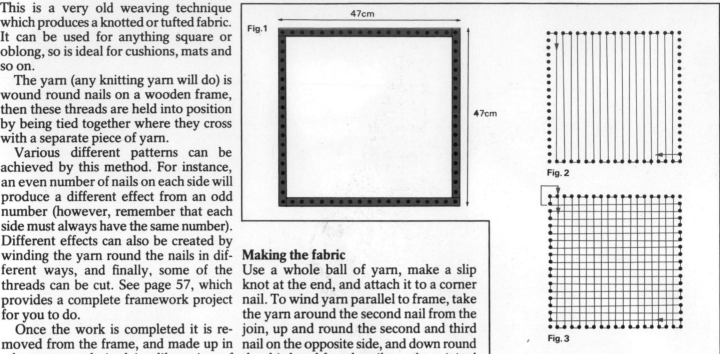

Fig.1

47cm

47cm

Fig.2

Fig.3

Making the fabric

Use a whole ball of yarn, make a slip knot at the end, and attach it to a corner nail. To wind yarn parallel to frame, take the yarn around the second nail from the join, up and round the second and third nail on the opposite side, and down round the third and fourth nails on the original side. Continue in this way, winding the yarn around two nails at a time, to the end (Fig. 2).

Now wind the yarn sideways across the frame, beginning at the 2nd nail on the next side (Fig. 3).

If a thick fabric is required, repeat the winding several more times, or just once more if you want a lace effect. Tie knots wherever the threads cross. The best way to do this is with yarn threaded in a tapestry needle so that you can make the knots in rows with no ends showing.

When you have made all the knots, take the work off the frame. If desired, the loops round the outside edge can be cut to form a fringe, as shown for the cushion cover on page 57.

By Carol Payton

Framework cushion cover

By Carol Payton

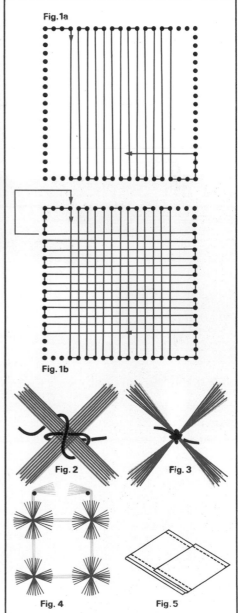

Fig. 1a

Fig. 1b

Fig. 2

Fig. 3

Fig. 4

Fig. 5

If you have read page 56, you will understand the principle of framework. This pretty cushion cover will give you a chance to try out the technique. You can use colours to match your furnishings.

You will need

A wooden frame 46cm. (18in.) square

14in. square cushion pad

38cm. (15in.) of 91cm. (36in.) wide fabric in a light shade

3 balls of double knitting in a medium shade and 3 balls in a dark shade

1 tapestry needle, matching sewing cotton

To make the framework

1. Using the 46cm. (18in.) frame described on page 56, wind dark wool around the nails parallel to the sides of the frame, omitting the last three nails at each end of each side (Figs. 1a and b). Continue winding until there are eight threads round each nail.

2. Now wind the medium colour round in exactly the same way until there are eight more threads round each nail. Fasten off both colours.

3. Take a piece of medium-colour yarn and thread it diagonally under the threads at every crossing, passing one end up and over, then down and up through the next space, then diagonally across, down the opposite space and up again through original space (Fig. 2).

4. Draw yarn tight and make a knot to secure (Fig. 3). Leave ends hanging.

5. Continue to tie all crossed threads in the same manner.

6. Cut through the medium colour only midway between every tie (Fig. 4).

7. Cut through all threads midway between the nails.

8. Trim off the knotted ends and trim the outside edge so that the dark threads are longer than the medium threads.

To make the cushion cover

With right sides together, fold fabric across 36cm. (about 14in.) from the selvedge. Fold remaining 25cm. (about 10in.) back and pin into position (Fig. 5). Stitch down either side. Turn cover right side out. Carefully stitch the front on to the cushion cover.

Indian weaving

These delightful, delicate wall hangings are woven on the simple home-made loom used for the place mats on page 41. If you have not made the loom, and would like to try it now, first study pages 38 and 41, which give full instructions and a list of materials needed for making the loom yourself.

The wallhangings are made from linen thread and cotton knitting thread, combined with dried leaves and grasses. You do not, of course, have to use the same leaves and grasses, but if you want to, they are quite easy to come by. Bay leaves (used in the small hanging) can be bought in any supermarket, and dried grasses in most florist's shops.

Hangings like these would look very dramatic mounted on coloured card, as this would show up the delicacy of the weaving, and they would make attractive and unusual presents for friends and relatives.

You will need
Linen thread or cotton knitting thread
Glue: PVA or wood glue
2 pieces cardboard: 25.5cm. by 7.5cm. (10in. by 3in.) and 25.5cm. by 5cm. (10in. by 2in.)
2 sticks or bamboo poles 5cm. (2in.) longer than the width of the weaving.

Setting up the loom
Thread the warp threads on the loom in the same way as explained on page 41 but this time put a thread round every nail. This gives a closer weave. Thread as many as you need for the width of weaving you want to do: the one on the loom in the illustration uses 63 warp threads and is about 22cm. (8½in.) wide.

Insert the wider piece of cardboard, threading it between the warp threads. This has two purposes: firstly it will help keep the weaving straight and secondly it will give the correct spacing for a fringe at the bottom.

As you will be using the same thread for the weft as for the warp you will need a shuttle. This is simply made by cutting a V-shaped piece from each end of the narrow piece of cardboard and winding the thread on to it (see colour picture).

Note
The leaves and dried grasses should not be too small as they will not be held firmly in place by the warp. It is a good idea to practise first with some grasses which extend more or less the width of the weaving, and can thus act as weft threads.

The weaving
Weave about 10 rows (picks), and then insert one of the sticks or bamboos as the 11th row. Weave another 10 rows. This will give a nice firm bottom edge which will hold the shape when the weaving is removed from the loom.

When putting in the decoration, always leave at least 3 weft picks of cotton between each to hold the shape. These can be shaped around the objects, as in the one illustrated, where the weaving is curved around the honesty leaves. The decorations will be easier to put in if you insert a ruler into the warp and turn it on its side so that every other thread is raised right across the warp.

When you have put in whatever decorations you wish finish in the same way as you started, with 10 rows of weaving either side of a stick.

Finishing
Before cutting the weaving off the loom, spread a small amount of glue at the back of it at top and bottom to hold the threads in place. This must be clear glue; do not use latex fabric adhesive as it tends to discolour. When the glue has dried cut the hanging off the loom. The piece of cardboard at the bottom will have insured that the warp threads at the bottom are the right length for a fringe. This can either be left plain or knotted in a decorative way, or you could even thread small wooden beads at the end of each warp thread.

Straight-stitch repeat patterns

These four patterns are all variations on Florentine embroidery (see page 46) in that the stitch used is always a straight upright one. However, not all the stitches are of the same length; the 'long and short stitch' pattern makes use of alternating stitches, worked over five and two meshes of canvas.

All these patterns rely for their success on the use of subtle colour shading going from dark to light in related colours, for instance, indigo shading to pale blue or dark red to pink. Never try to use a lot of bright colours in designs like these, or the result will be garish and the designs will be lost.

Diamond pattern

This design is worked mainly over four meshes of canvas, with the ends of each stitch going into the same hole as the one above or below it. However, as you obviously cannot make diamond shapes without the corner stitches being smaller than the others, those are worked over six, four and then two meshes. It sounds more complicated than it is. The best way to work this design is to outline each square first, after which the insides of the squares come quite easily. This pattern is well suited to furnishings –

Diamond

Cross and diamond

Long and short zigzag

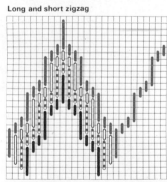
Scallop

cushions, chair seats and so on, and can also be used for accessories, such as handbags.

Cross and diamond pattern

This is rather slower, as the stitches are worked over two meshes of canvas. Each stitch is one mesh up or one mesh down from the previous stitch. Again, the way to work is by outlining the pattern, so work the white crosses and diamonds right across the canvas and then fill in with the colours. As you will see from the diagram, there are five stitches running diagonally between each diamond, and the diamonds have seven stitches on each side. This is a good stitch for smaller items, such as spectacle cases, and would look lovely worked in silks on fine mesh canvas.

Long and short zigzag

This uses stitches worked over five and two meshes of canvas. Work a complete row in one colour right across the canvas, then a row of the next colour and so on.

Scallop pattern

This is a delightful stitch for smaller accessories and, like the cross and diamond pattern, looks lovely worked in silks. If you use colours with rather low contrast, it can give a delicate brocade effect. It is worked mainly over four meshes in groups of one, three, five and seven stitches, each one mesh up or down from the last. Be warned, however: a few stitches are worked over only two meshes, and one in each repeat is worked over six. Unlike the other patterns, this is best worked motif by motif, as otherwise you tend to lose track.

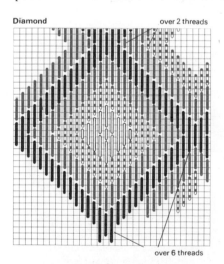
Diamond   over 2 threads
over 6 threads

Cross and diamond foundation rows

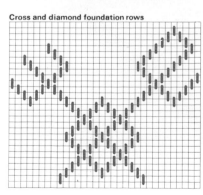

Long and short zigzag

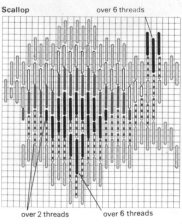
Scallop   over 6 threads
over 2 threads   over 6 threads

Purse and spectacle case

These pretty objects have been worked in Florentine stitch, using oddments of wool and silk left over from larger projects. Anyone who does a lot of canvas work soon collects a bag of leftovers. If you are a knitter, you can use knitting yarns just as successfully.

Items such as these are quick to work, and they make very nice gifts. You won't need a frame, as straight stitch does not distort the canvas, and the amount of canvas required is quite small.

The finished spectacle case will measure 10cm. by 18cm. (4in. by 7in.), the purse 9cm. by 15cm. (3½in. by 6in.).

You will need
For both items
51cm. by 23cm. (20in. by 9in.) single-thread canvas, 18 threads to 2.5cm. (1in.).
Spectacle case
Tapestry wool in 6 colours
Tapestry needle No. 18
Piece of felt 30cm. by 23cm. (12in. by 9in.) for lining
Purse
Stranded cotton in 5 colours
Piece of felt or taffeta, 23cm. by 20cm. (9in. by 8in.) for lining
15cm. (6in.) zip
No. 18 tapestry needle

Note
Florentine embroidery is not at all difficult, but if you have not done it before you may find it helpful to read the instructions on page 46.

To make the spectacle case
1. Cut two pieces of canvas, each 23cm. by 15cm.
2. Leave 2.5cm. (1in.) unworked all round, and commence pattern from centre thread at base (Fig. 1). Work the foundation row as shown in Fig. 1 in one colour. Work each stitch over four threads of canvas, placing each group of stitches two holes down or up from the last group.
3. Each succeeding row follows the foundation row, and each row is worked in a different colour.
4. Work other side in the same way.
5. Trim canvas to 1.3cm. (½in.) from embroidery.
6. Cut lining to same size.
7. Place right sides of case together and stitch close to embroidery, leaving open at top.
8. Make up lining in the same way.
9. Turn both bag and lining to right sides,

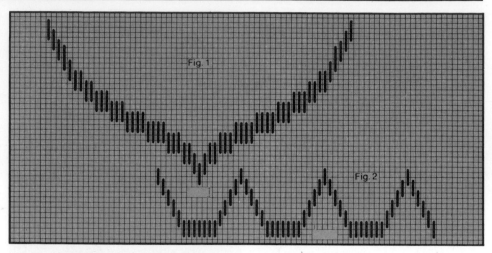

Fig. 1

Fig. 2

and slip lining into the completed case.
10. Turn in seam allowance at top and slip stitch to case.

To make the purse
Use five strands of thread throughout.
1. Leave 2.5cm. (1in.) unworked at base, and commence foundation row from central thread at base (Fig. 2). Work each stitch over three threads of canvas. Each stitch or group of stitches is one hole down or up from the previous one.
2. Work rows, following the foundation row, until work measures 18cm. (7in.).
3. Trim canvas to within 1.3cm. (½in.) of embroidery.
4. Cut lining to same size.
5. Fold purse in half and stitch close to embroidery, leaving one long side open.
6. Insert zip.
7. Fold lining in half, stitch sides and slip into purse.
8. Turn lining in at top and slip-stitch to zip.
9. Make two tassels from stranded cotton and sew on to each end.

Ribbon-woven evening bag

The evening bag illustrated is made from lurex ribbon.

Making up a purse

1. Cut strips of the lining 2.5cm. (1in.) on the cross for the piped edges. Fold along the length and pin to the right side of the main purse piece, raw edges of fabric together.
2. Machine stitch the piping in place.
3. Lay the smaller purse piece on top, right sides facing, and stitch on the same stitching line, so that both pieces of the purse are together, with the piping sandwiched in between.
4. Cut the lining from the same pattern pieces and sew both pieces together, right sides together.
5. Slip the lining into the purse and turn in the edges, slipstitching to the purse.
6. Sew on a press stud for a fastening.
7. If you want a shoulder strap, sew a length of lurex ribbon to both sides of the purse. Make a small pocket for the inside if you like.

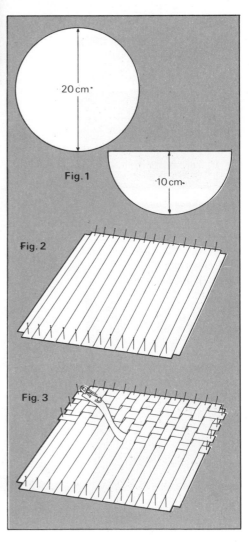

Ribbon weaving is a fascinating technique and can be used to make all kinds of pretty accessories. This glittery gold evening bag is made with lurex ribbon, edged in green. You can buy both silver and gold ribbon with different coloured edging, so that you can make an accessory to match your outfit. The weaving itself is simple, and no special equipment is needed other than the things in your sewing basket.

You will need
7m. (7yd.) gold lurex ribbon
Iron-on interfacing
Lining fabric, matching sewing thread
Large press stud
Pins

To prepare the weaving
1. Ribbon weaving can be done on a frame or on a flat padded surface. For this evening bag, work on your ironing board. Lay out a piece of iron-on interfacing, adhesive side up. This must be slightly larger than the main piece of the purse (see Fig. 1).
2. Cut lengths of ribbon to cover the area plus approximately 1.2cm. (½in.).

3. Arrange the pieces of the interfacing pinning each piece at both ends and stretching it slightly so that it lies smooth and straight. The edges should just touch (Fig. 2).
4. When you have completed the 'weft', cut more pieces of ribbon and weave each one under and over the weft, again pinning at both ends (Fig. 3). You will find it easier if you attach a safety pin to the end of the ribbon, as for threading elastic.
5. When the weave is neat and even, press the ribbon on to the interfacing following the manufacturer's instructions, without removing the pins.
6. Unpin and gently lift the weaving from the ironing board. Work tacking stitches round the edges to hold the ends of the strands securely.
7. Turn the weaving over and pencil in the circle for the main piece of the purse. Machine stitch just outside the seam allowance line.

Make up the second piece of the purse in the same way.

When you have two pieces of woven fabric you are ready to start making up your purse.

Straight-stitch cushion and hanging

Even if you have never tried canvas work before don't be daunted. This is a simple pattern and quite quick to work as it's satin stitch worked over three threads with double thread. You will find it easier to work on a frame, but it's not essential as satin stitch does not distort the canvas.

You will need
For the cushion
60cm. (⅝yd.) 58.5cm. (19in.) double-thread tapestry canvas, 10 holes to 2.5cm. (1in.)
Of tapestry wool: 17 skeins white, 3 skeins pale blue
3 skeins chocolate, 2 skeins magenta, 2 skeins peacock blue, 1 skein cyclamen
50cm. (½yd.) velvet or medium-weight fabric for backing
Thread to match velvet or fabric
Cushion pad
Tapestry frame (optional)
For the wall hanging
35cm. (¾yd) 48.5cm. (19in.) wide double-thread tapestry canvas, 10 holes to 2.5cm. (1in.)

Of tapestry wool: 19 skeins dark blue, 4 skeins cyclamen, 4 skeins light lilac, 2 skeins dark lilac, 3 skeins royal blue, 2 skeins magenta, 2 skeins pale blue, 2 skeins peacock blue, 2 skeins chocolate, 1 skein white
50cm. (½yd.) 90cm. (36in.) wide matching medium-weight fabric for backing
5 3cm. (1¼in.) diameter curtain rings
1 1.5cm. (⅝in.) diameter wooden rod or cane about 51cm. (20in.) long
80cm. (¾yd.) matching cord
Thread to match fabric
Tapestry frame (optional)

A pattern for cushion and wall hanging appears on the opposite page.

The embroidery
The procedure is the same for the cushion and the wall hanging.
1. Mark the centre of the canvas both ways with tacking stitches. To do this, run along a line of holes lengthways and between a pair of narrow double threads widthways.

2. If you are using a frame, mount canvas with raw edges to tapes.
3. We have given you half the pattern for the cushion. The top, which will be the centre of your pattern, should coincide with your tacking threads. The pattern for the wall hanging is complete.

4. The design is worked throughout in satin stitch, using the thread doubled. Each small block is made up of three double stitches worked over three double threads of the canvas (see diagram), thus each square of the pattern represents a block of three holes.
5. For both cushion and wall hanging, begin the design centrally and work following the patterns and the colour keys. The stitch may either be worked from left to right or from right to left. For the cushion, when the lower half is worked, turn round and work the upper half in reverse.

To make up the cushion
1. Trim canvas to within 2.5cm. (1in.) of embroidery all round.
2. Cut a piece of velvet or fabric the same size as the canvas, place both pieces with right sides together and sew close to the embroidery all round, leaving an opening on one side. Turn to right side.
3. Insert cushion pad. Turn in seam allowance and slipstitch opening neatly to close with matching thread.

To make up wall hanging
1. Trim canvas to within 2.5cm. (1in.) of embroidery on all sides.
2. Cut a piece of fabric the same size as the canvas. Place both pieces with right sides together and sew close to the embroidery all round, leaving an opening on one side. Turn to right side.
3. Turn in seam allowance and slipstitch.
4. Sew rings to top edge, spacing evenly.
5. Insert rod. Attach cord.

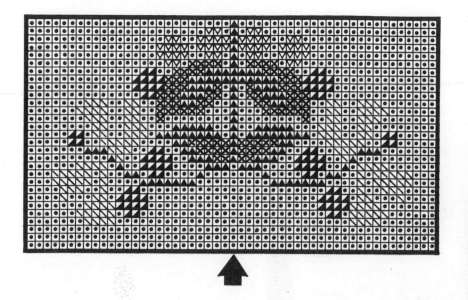

Straight-stitch cushion and hanging

- ◪ Magenta
- ▽ Light Lilac
- ✳ Dark Lilac
- ● Royal Blue
- ◥ Pale Blue
- ☐ Dark Blue
- ⊠ Peacock Blue
- · White
- ▲ Chocolate

Embroidered pocket

The embroidery

Mark the centre of the embroidery fabric both ways with a line of basting stitches. The diagram gives just over a quarter of the design, the centre being indicated by the blank arrows. Each square represents one thread of fabric. The embroidery is worked in satin stitch over a varying number of threads, using six strands of cotton throughout.

Start the embroidery six threads to the right of the crossed basting stitches and work upper left quarter from diagram. Work other three quarters to correspond.

To make up

Press the embroidery on the wrong side. Place lining fabric to embroidery right sides together, and stitch close to the embroidery, leaving an opening for turning to right side. Turn to right side, slip stitch opening closed, and sew to garment.

This colourful zigzag design worked in stranded cotton is used here as a pocket for a plain dress. It is a useful design, as it can so easily be adapted to fit different shapes, a belt or clutch bag for instance. You could also work it in wools or canvas to make a shoulder bag or cushion cover.

You will need

Stranded cotton:

3 skeins each dark violet, black; 2 skeins each pink, dark cyclamen, light violet, jade green, grass green, light moss green; 1 skein each light cyclamen, kingfisher blue, light blue, peacock blue, dark moss green, yellow, red

Piece white evenweave fabric 30cm. by 28cm. (11⅞in. by 11in.)

Piece lining fabric same size as above

Satin	1 – Pink	9 – Jade green
Stitch	2 – Light cyclamen	10 – Light moss green
	3 – Dark cyclamen	11 – Dark moss green
	4 – Dark violet	12 – Yellow
	5 – Light violet	13 – Red
	6 – Kingfisher blue	14 – Black
	7 – Light blue	15 – Peacock blue
	8 – Grass green	Stranded cotton

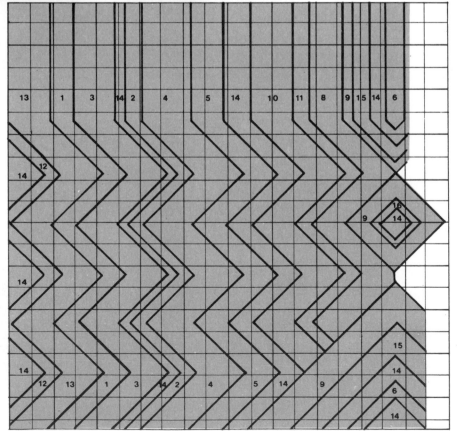

Florentine chair seat

This colourful embroidery is based on the famous Carnation pattern, one of the Florentine stitches which were very popular in sixteenth-century Europe. The beautiful pattern is worked entirely in straight stitch, developed from upright Gobelin. By using silks instead of yarns, it can be adapted and used for decorating evening bags and you can also use the pattern to make attractive cushions.

You will need
Fabric for pattern

Single weave canvas 10cm. (4in.) larger all round than your chair seat and 14 threads to 2.5cm. (1in.)

No. 18 tapestry needle

Tapestry wool in Wedgwood Blue (background), Moss Green (outlining green), yellow, orange, coral, cardinal red, raspberry, forest green, olive green, almond

Black upholstery linen for underside of chair

To make the pattern
Make a pattern (template) for your own chair with a piece of fabric. Pin it horizontally and then vertically, smoothing outwards as you pin. Mark the line where the fabric touches the edge of the seat with pins, then make a line with a soft pencil. Draw in a line marking the centre vertically, then horizontally so that you know the exact centre of your pattern.

Cut out the fabric pattern on your pencilled line. Mark a piece of canvas with vertical and horizontal lines to find the centre. Pin your pattern to the canvas matching the centre, horizontal and vertical lines. Draw round and allow 5cm. to 10cm. (2in. to 4in.) extra canvas all round the marked line. Oversew to minimise fraying.

Assessing yarn quantities
The only way to work out how much yarn you are going to need of each colour is to embroider one whole motif in the middle of your chair seat (red carnation) with the surrounding background and at least one quarter of the four surrounding green carnations. As you cut and use your yarn, cut the same length each time – about 30cm. (12in.) is about right. Note how many pieces you cut from each skein of colour. Once you have worked your test area you will have a very good idea of how much yarn you are going to need to complete your project.

Colours
The chair illustrated is a Regency chair and so the brilliant colours used suited its style.

If you prefer a softer colour scheme – perhaps you'd like all the carnations in tones of blue or in warm gold and yellow tones on a cream ground – simply choose your yarn colours and cut bits off. Glue them or pin them to a piece of card and mark code letters beside each cutting so that when you are following our colour guide you will know your own colour immediately.

To work the pattern
Usually Florentine patterns have a key line and this is worked right across the canvas. Florentine Carnation pattern does not have this key line but you will find it easier if you begin the first motif by outlining it in the dark green. Each stitch is worked over four threads of canvas and stepped down 2 threads. Once you have done the outline you will be able to fill in.

Completing
If the canvas work has stretched out of true when finished, prepare it by damping and pinning out as explained on page 39. To mount the work on the chair, spread it and temporarily tack on the underside of the chair, stretching for alignment as you tack. Fold and slip-stitch the corners. Permanently tack and then cover the underside of the chair with the black upholstery linen.

1. Red carnation
2. Green carnation

1. Moss green
2. Moss green
1. Yellow
2. Yellow
1. Orange
2. Almond
1. Coral
2. Olive green
1. Cardinal red
2. Forest green
1. Raspberry
2. Forest green
1. Almond
2. Almond
1. Olive green
2. Olive green
1. Forest green
2. Forest green
1. Wedgwood blue
2. Wedgwood blue

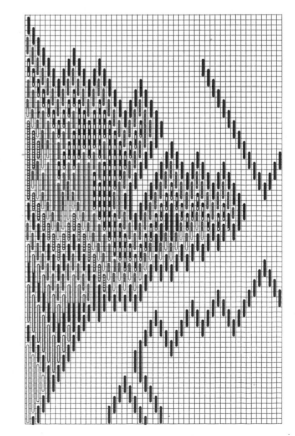

Cushion with canvas centre (1)

The picture on the right shows the canvas centrepiece for this attractively-shaped cushion and here we give instructions for only this element of the cushion. For the complete cushion and other instructions see page 68.

You will need

20cm. (8in.) square of fine gauge canvas, 20 threads per 2.5cm. (1in.)
1 skein each stranded cotton in the following colours: light red, medium red, dark red, light brown, medium brown, dark brown, light green, medium green, dark green, light turquoise, medium turquoise, dark turquoise, light orange, medium orange, dark orange, light blue, medium blue, dark blue, light salmon pink, medium salmon pink, dark salmon pink, light mauve, medium mauve, dark mauve, white.
No. 24 tapisserie needle

To make the centrepiece

Study the plan (Fig. 1) carefully before proceeding. All the single stitches are worked in tent stitch (see page 39). Work square blocks in satin stitch to complete areas of canvas work (Fig. 2) which will give you 'Scottish' stitch. Work from the centre of the design outwards building up each section to complete the area. Once the entire area has been worked the piece of canvas will probably be quite out of shape and must he 'damp-stretched' back into its correct shape once more. Follow the method which is described in detail in the instructions on page 39.

1st quarter	2nd quarter	3rd quarter	4th quarter
☑ Light brown	◻ Light turquoise	☑ Light orange	◻ Light pink
▲ Medium brown	◀ Medium turquoise	▼ Medium orange	▶ Medium pink
● Dark brown	● Dark turquoise	● Dark orange	● Dark pink
◕ Light mauve	● Light green	● Light blue	● Light red
■ Medium mauve	■ Medium green	■ Medium blue	■ Medium red
◨ Dark mauve	■ Dark green	■ Dark blue	■ Dark red
☑ Light turquoise	◻ Light orange	☑ Light salmon pink	◻ Light brown
▼ Medium turquoise	▶ Medium orange	▲ Medium salmon pink	▲ Medium brown
▲ Dark turquoise	◀ Dark orange	▼ Dark salmon pink	▶ Dark brown
White	White	◻ White	◻ White

This graph represents a quarter of the total canvas work area

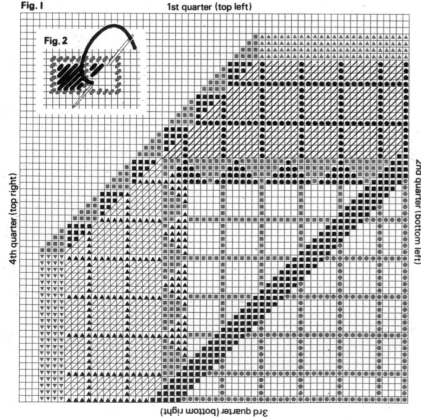

Fig. I — 1st quarter (top left) / Fig. 2 / 4th quarter (top right) / 2nd quarter (bottom left) / 3rd quarter (bottom right)

Cushion with canvas centre (2)

The illustration shows the entire cushion which measures approximately 32cm. (12½in.) square. The instructions for the canvas centrepiece are given on page 66. The cushion has an interesting shape but also serves to show how well colours and different types of material can blend together. For the floral-print cotton fabrics used, try to choose a small print in four different colour ways and similar colours for the larger print.

You will need

50cm. (19½in.) each narrow velvet ribbon in blue, green, turquoise, orange, salmon pink, pale pink, brown and mauve

30cm. (1ft.) of 8 different floral print cotton fabrics

34cm. (13½in.) of 1 of the above colours for underside of cushion

2-40cm. (16in.) squares of strong cotton backing fabric

2-40cm. (16in.) squares of light-weight iron-on interfacing

Cotton to match velvet ribbons

50cm. (19½in.) cambric or cushion lining fabric 91cm. (36in.) wide

Filling for cushion

Graph paper to the size indicated on diagram

Oddments of card

Sewing equipment

To make the cushion

Using one of the pieces of interfacing, place the canvas work in the centre and pin to hold it in place. Cut out four of the oblong shapes (Fig. 1) from the smaller floral prints and four of the angular shapes (Fig. 2) from the larger prints (one piece per fabric).

Now place these shapes on the iron-on interfacing carefully positioning them

around the canvas work following the colour plan (Fig. 3). Each piece should meet and slightly overlap the next one so that there is no bare interfacing. Carefully iron these and the canvas work on to the iron-on interfacing, thus holding it in position. Tack this layer of interfacing with the 'patches' on to one of the squares of backing fabric.

Following the colour sequence (Fig. 4) pin and tack the velvet ribbons in position along the edges of the patches, and using matching threads, machine stitch close to each side of the ribbons. This completes the upperside of the cushion.

Place the completed side of the cushion on to the material you have chosen for the underside. Pin together and cut out. With right sides together and seam lines coinciding with each other, machine back and front cushion together, remembering to leave an opening of sufficient size to insert the inner cushion. Turn to the right sides.

Make up the inner cushion from the cambric using the same cushion shape (Fig. 3) but slightly smaller and fill with

either foam chips, kapok or other filling.

To make the tassels

Use either stranded cottons or the machine cottons. Wind the threads around a piece of card approximately 5cm. (2in.) wide. Pass a length of thread under wound threads and tie it securely. Cut the opposite ends of threads releasing them from the card. Wind another piece of thread around the tassel and tie to secure it. Make two tassels per colour of velvet ribbon and sew each tassel in place at the corners of the cushion so that the colours all link up. Place the inner cushion inside and hand-sew the opening of the cushion or sew small press studs at regular intervals along the inner edge of the opening for easy access.

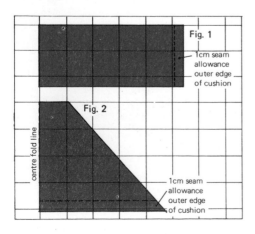

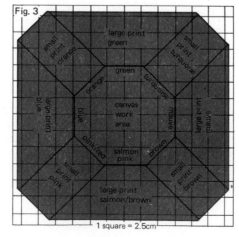

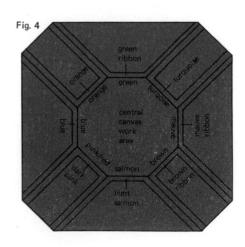

Cushion with canvas centre (3)

On pages 66-68, a specific canvas work design was given to be worked. Here we describe general techniques and tips regarding canvas work plus another idea for a cushion.

Canvas
This is available in a variety of types such as single thread or double thread, fine or heavy. Choice of canvas is determined by finished effect required. If in doubt, always work a small sample.

Threads and yarns
Traditionally canvas work is associated with crewel and tapestry wools which are available in a comprehensive range of colours. Other threads and yarns may also be used to great effect adding variety of texture and scale of work. Always test a small sample to experiment with the various yarns; some will be more effective than others.

Never have more than 45cm. (17½in.) of yarn in the needle as the sewing action will unavoidably cause friction as the thread is drawn through the canvas and it may become worn or even frayed. It is advisable to purchase all the yarn at one time, otherwise the dye shade may vary and spoil the overall effect.

Frames
Never work freely in the hand unless the area to be embroidered is very small or

Velvet stitch. Worked in loops then cut with sharp pointed scissors and neatly trimmed, this stitch produces a pile similar to an Oriental carpet. If preferred, loops may be left uncut or simply cut to give ragged effect.

Overcast (or trailing) stitch. Several strands of thread are closely worked over so that a raised effect is achieved.

just a sample. Likewise, never work in a circular hoop; always mount canvas on a square or rectangular frame ensuring the grain of the canvas is kept straight. There are several types of frame available. Your local needlework shop will advise you with regard to the most suitable frame for your purpose.

Needles
A needle with a rounded point and large eye is always used; called Tapestry Needles they are available in a variety of sizes. When choosing, remember the eye must be of sufficient size to allow the yarn to pass through easily but not too thick, otherwise the canvas threads will be forced apart causing distortion.

To work canvas embroidery
There is a wealth of canvas stitches ranging from the basic tent stitch to the more complicated stitches made up of several components. However, for the novice it is often advisable to choose one or two simple stitches and work these in a variety of yarns altering size and direction of stitch to explore the possibilities offered.

Starting and finishing off threads
Do not use knots as they stand out in relief when the work is finally stretched and mounted. To start, push the threaded needle through the canvas on the right side about 5cm. away from working area leaving a short end of thread. When the thread is nearly finished darn in about 2cm. (¾in.) of it on wrong side and trim surplus; also darn in original end on wrong side and trim to neaten.

Working method
Stitching should be accomplished in two or three movements (one hand kept on top of the frame, the other receiving the

needle on the underside of the canvas and returning it to the top).

THE CUSHION CENTRE
Canvas work is by nature often very time consuming, so it is often necessary to work only a small area. Remember you can always embellish this with a border of some complementary method of embroidery such as appliqué or patchwork. The cushion has a small central area of canvas work providing a detailed and rich focal point with a border of appliqué velvet ribbon and small print cotton fabrics.

Stitches used
This particular area has been freely built up with the use of three basic canvas work stitches:– satin stitch, cross stitch (see pages 39 and 52) and velvet stitch (Fig. 1) and is then embellished with freestyle embroidery and crochet. Overcast or trailing stitch is shown in Fig. 2.

The design is worked by finding the centre point of the area to be embroidered and working bands of colour along each 'leg' of the cross, then filling in the four triangles with flowers. The design is then contained within a border of cross stitch and straight stitch. The raised centre cross is built up by laying down several strands of thick wool which is closely overcast with the chosen colour of wool. Tapestry wools have been used. A length of single crochet chain is stitched down over this to give the appearance of it twined around the overcast cross. Cut out small green felt leaves and back stitch on to canvas at intervals along the crocheted chain. (Fig. 3).

Cut out and work buttonhole stitch in crewel wool around small felt circles and arrange along crocheted chain forming a cluster in the centre of the cross. Work two or three French knots in each flower to hold in position on canvas to complete.

To complete work
When work is complete remove it from the frame. It may be necessary to damp stretch it back into its correct shape. This is described on page 39. Remove from board and mount in desired way. It is often advisable to have the canvas work mounted professionally to achieve a high quality finish.

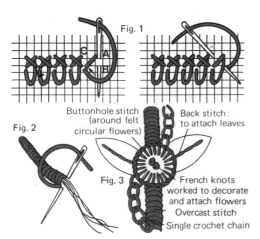

Fig. 1

Fig. 2

Buttonhole stitch (around felt circular flowers)

Back stitch: to attach leaves

Fig. 3

French knots worked to decorate and attach flowers
Overcast stitch
Single crochet chain

Sweetheart nightie case

This pretty case for sleepwear would be exactly right for a trousseau or you might make it as a gift for a friend or relative.

You will need
2 pieces taffeta for lining 44cm. (17in.) square
2 pieces thin polyester wadding 44cm. (17in.) square
Taffeta for weaving mound 44cm. (17in.) square
Ribbons as follows:
    Cream satin polyester 6mm. (¼in.) wide by 3.5m. (4yd.) long
    White satin polyester 6mm. (¼in.) wide by 3.5m. (4yd.) long
    Cream moiré taffeta polyester 2.2cm. (⅞in.) wide by 3.5m. (4yd.) long
    White moiré taffeta polyester 2.2cm. (⅞in.) wide by 4m. (4½yd.) long
    Cream jacquard ribbon 2.2cm. (⅞in.) wide by 3.5m. (4yd.) long
    White jacquard ribbon 2.2cm. (⅞in.) wide by 3.5m. (4yd.) long
    Pink satin ribbon 3mm. (⅛in.) wide by 3.5m. (4yd.) long
45cm. (½yd.) polyester satin for backing, to match pink ribbon
Piping cord
Sewing equipment

Preparing the pattern
From Fig. 1 draw up a paper pattern to scale. The direction lines on the pattern show the direction of the weaving and not the straight grain of fabric. The arrow shows the straight grain. Use the pattern to cut out two linings in taffeta and two pieces of wadding. Seam allowance is included in the pattern for these pieces. Use the pattern to cut out the backing satin but add 12mm. (½in.) all round. Do not cut out the last piece of taffeta – this is used as a weaving base. Baste the wadding to the lining pieces. Machine stitch all round taking 12mm. (½in.)

seams. Cut the wadding away almost up to the stitching line. Put aside for the moment.

Weaving
Prepare a padded table top on which to work. (You can use a folded blanket with a clean cloth pinned to it.) Have a quantity of pins ready. Spread the taffeta smoothly. Arrange the warp ribbons along one edge in the following order, (right to left) white moiré, white jacquard, cream narrow satin, cream moiré, cream jacquard, white narrow satin, then back to white moiré and continue ribbons in the same order. Cut each piece of ribbon 44cm. (17in.) long.

Pin a piece of the pink satin ribbon down the centre of each cream moiré strip. Tack all the ribbons to the taffeta with small tacking stitches so that they are secure. Pin the taffeta down on to the pad all round the edges. Smooth the ribbons down so that the edges are just touching and pin at the bottom edge of the taffeta.

The weft The pattern for the weft is exactly the same as for the warp. Begin with the same colour ribbon at the extreme right and use ribbons in the same order. Cut ribbons to the same length as before – 44cm. (17in.). Put a safety pin on the end of each weaving ribbon as you use it – it makes weaving easier. A kitchen fork will help to push the ribbons through. The weave is under 1, over 1, and you begin with white moiré and start with 'over 1'. Continue until pattern is complete. Without removing the pins, place the heart shaped pattern on top of the weaving (as the direction lines on Fig. 1 indicate). Pin round the shape and then tack so that the ribbons and taffeta are secured together. Unpin the weaving and machine stitch round the shape 9mm. (⅜in.) outside the tacking. Cut off the excess ribbons about 3mm. (⅛in.) away from the stitching.

Making up the case
From the remaining pink satin, cut bias strips 25mm. (1in.) wide and join them. Fold the strips wrong sides together over thin piping cord and tack along the cord. Tack the piping round the heart shape on the right side of the weaving, raw edges to raw edges and machine stitch using a piping foot on your machine. Stitch along the tacking line on the piping. Now lay the satin backing heart shape on the woven heart, right sides together. Pin and tack, taking a 12mm. (½in.) seam.

Machine stitch round from black dot to black dot on the pattern. Work on the wrong side of the weaving so that you can follow the stitching line you used when stitching on the piping. Turn the case to the right side. Stitch the two lining pieces together from black dot to black dot. Slip into case. Turn the edges of the lining in and slip stitch neatly to the inside of the outer case. Stitch a small press stud to the middle of the case opening if you like. Make a bow from the remaining pink ribbon and stitch it to the front of the case.

Using up oddments
You will have quite a lot of small pieces of ribbon left over from your weaving when you have cut out the heart shape. You can use these pieces to weave a matching handkerchief sachet.

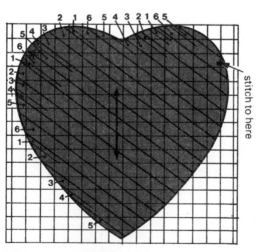

KEY
1 = Cream narrow satin   1 square = 2.5cm
2 = Cream moire
3 = Cream jacquard
4 = White narrow satin
5 = White moire
6 = White jacquard

70

Small tent stitch hanging

This effective little landscape is worked on canvas, using mainly tent stitch – an ideal stitch for a picture like this, in which small irregular shapes are required.

You will need

16cm. by 16cm. (6¼in. by 6¼in.) canvas, 18 threads to 2.5cm. (1in.)

Of pearl cotton No. 3 thread: 1 skein each in white, light blue, light turquoise, light green, medium green, dark green, light brown, dark brown, light mauve, dark mauve

1m. (1yd.) ribbon, 3mm. (⅛in.) wide in light orchid

40cm. by 20cm. (16in. by 8in.) heavyweight interfacing

40cm. by 20cm. (16in. by 8in.) small print fabric – cotton polyester etc.

Sewing thread to match fabric and ribbon

1 curtain ring

To make the picture

1. Work the canvas work landscape using the grid pattern as a guide (see Fig. 1). Most of it is worked in tent stitch (this is illustrated on page 39) or a variation of it (see Fig. 2). Use a relatively short length of thread so that it does not become worn when it is drawn through the holes of the canvas. Work one area of colour at a time, as much as is practical, and work methodically down the pattern so that you do not become 'lost' in the grid. When commencing work begin about 2cm. (¾in.) in from the edge of the canvas.

When working canvas embroidery it is usual to work it in a frame. However, this piece is very small and may be held in the hand without risk of becoming warped.

2. When the canvas work is complete, gently press it on the wrong side with a damp cloth, pulling it into shape if necessary.

3. Cut out two octagons 14.8cm. (5¾in.) wide in interfacing as Fig. 3. Cover one with fabric, turning a narrow allowance to the wrong side and tacking it in place. Cut out the centre section from the second octagon and cover the window piece with fabric, carefully snipping the fabric into the corners and folding to give a crisp shape.

4. Place the window piece over the canvas work to form a frame and tack it in position. Hand stitch around the inside edge of the window to attach it to the canvas work.

5. Hand stitch the ribbon around the window towards the inner edge, neatly folding it at the corners. Begin and end at the bottom right corner; tie a small bow and stitch it in place to neaten the join of the ribbon.

6. Stitch the canvas work octagon to the fabric covered piece, making sure corners match.

7. On the back of the picture stitch the curtain ring to form a hanger.

8. Carefully press the picture on the wrong side to complete.

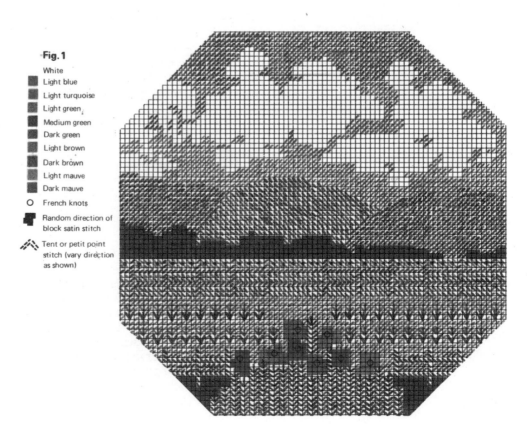

Fig. 3

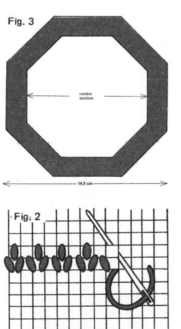

centre section

14,8 cm

Fig. 2

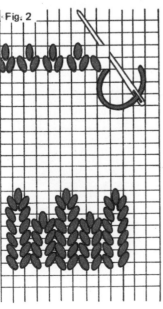

Fig. 1

White
Light blue
Light turquoise
Light green
Medium green
Dark green
Light brown
Dark brown
Light mauve
Dark mauve
O   French knots
Random direction of block satin stitch
Tent or petit point stitch (vary direction as shown)

Russian dolls

Russian dolls are traditionally toys but these canvaswork versions make lovely and unusual ornaments.

You will need
Of tapestry wool:
1 skein each Moss Green, Amber Gold, Tangerine, Orange, Flame, Chestnut, Coffee, White, Black, Gold, Spice Brown, Sage Green, Pink and Smoke
1 piece double thread tapestry canvas 30cm. by 68cm. (12in. by 26¾in.) 10 holes to 2.5cm. (1in.)
1 piece wine-coloured backing fabric 30cm. by 20cm. (12in. by 8in.) for large doll
1 piece brown-coloured backing fabric 20cm. by 16cm. (8in. by 6½in.) for small doll
Kapok
Thick cardboard 12cm. by 10cm. (4¾in. by 4in.) for bases
Tapestry frame with 46cm. (18½in.) tapes
Tapestry needle No. 18

To work the tapestry
Cut two pieces from the canvas 30cm. by 30cm. (12in. by 12in.). Mark the centre of each piece with a line of basting stitches run between a pair of narrow threads lengthwise and along a line of holes widthways. Mount one piece of canvas in frame.

Fig. 1 gives one half of each doll (A and B), and the centres are indicated by the blank arrows which should coincide with the basting stitches. Each background square on the diagram represents the double threads of the canvas. The design is worked throughout in Trammed Gros Point Stitch. (See Fig. 2). Commence the larger doll centrally and work half following diagram and key for em-

broidery. To complete, work other half in reverse. Work doll B in the same way.

To make up
Trim canvas to within 1.5cm. (⅝in.) of embroidery. Cut backing fabric to same size. Place canvas and backing fabric right sides together, then baste and stitch close to embroidery leaving lower edge open. Trim seams and press open. Turn to right side. Turn in seam allowance at

lower edge to wrong side. Stuff firmly. From cardboard cut one piece 9.5cm. by 3.5cm. (3¾in. by 1½in.) and one piece 7cm. by 2.5cm. (2¾in. by 1in.) for base of dolls. Round off the corners of each piece to fit. Cut fabric 1cm. (⅜in.) larger all round. Work a row of running stitches 5cm. (¼in.) from edge of fabric then place cardboard centrally and draw thread up tightly. Place base in position and oversew.

Work a Trammed Gros Point Stitch from left to right, then pull the needle through on the lower line; insert the needle diagonally into the upper line crossing the laid thread and one intersection of canvas threads (the point where a pair of narrow vertical threads cross a pair of narrow horizontal threads); bring the needle through on the lower line two canvas thread intersections to the left. Continue in this way to end of row.

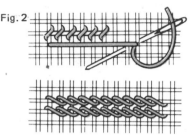

Fig. 2

This shows the reverse side of correctly worked Gros Point Stitch where the length of the stitches is greater than those on the correct side.

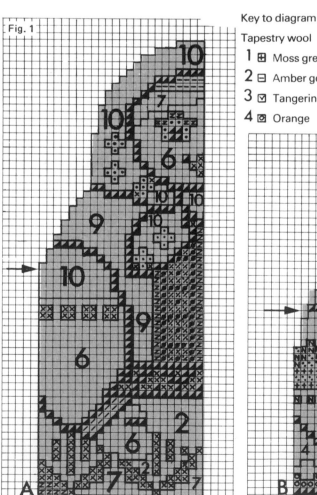

Fig. 1

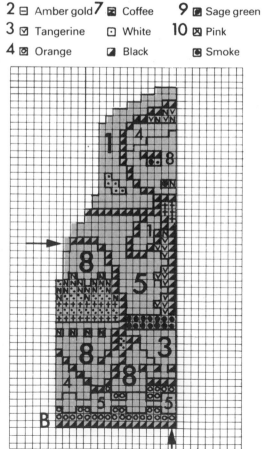

Key to diagram

Tapestry wool		
1 ⊞ Moss green	5 ⋈ Flame red	⊠ Gold
2 ⊟ Amber gold	6 ⊡ Chestnut	8 ⊡ Spice brown
3 ☑ Tangerine	7 ⊠ Coffee	9 ⊠ Sage green
4 ⊠ Orange	⊡ White	10 ⊠ Pink
	⊿ Black	ⓒ Smoke

Canvas work mirror frame

Lots of bathrooms and bedrooms have bare little nooks and crannies where this pretty mirror would look enchanting.

You will need

1 mirror tile 15cm. (6in.) square
25cm. (9¾in.) single thread canvas; 7 threads per 1cm. (⅜in.)
1 skein each of tapestry wool:
   Yellow green, grass green, bright blue, coral, pale pink, bright pink
15.5cm. (6.1/5in.) of heavy-weight pelmet interfacing
15.5cm. (6.1/5)in.) of firm card
Dark green sewing thread

15.5cm. (6.1/5in.) of iron-on adhesive tape
17cm. (6¾in.) floral print cotton fabric to complement wool colours
Clear household glue, 1 curtain ring
Square or rectangular embroidery frame or an old picture frame of suitable size

To make the mirror frame

1. Mount canvas on chosen embroidery frame. If using a rigid frame such as an old picture frame, mount with drawing pins or a staple gun.
2. Find centre of canvas and lightly mark (Fig. 1).
3. Following the colour and stitch chart (Fig. 2) work the canvas embroidery in tapestry wool, working from centre lines towards corners. Work the band of pale pink to establish the shape and make remainder of chart easier to follow. The entire frame is made up of straight stitch; the majority of it being stitched at right angles over the threads of the canvas and the plant leaves worked diagonally (Figs. 3a and 3b).
4. When the border is complete, remove canvas from frame and trim excess canvas away leaving a turning of 1.5cm. (⅝in.) on all sides and on inner edge. Carefully mitre outer corners and snip into inner corners as in Fig. 4.
5. Cut out centre window 10cm.sq. (4in. sq.) from card and cover frame with canvas work glueing in position. Turn edges and glue firmly to wrong side as in Fig. 5.

6. Using iron-on adhesive tape bond pelmet interfacing square centrally on wrong side of floral fabric.
7. Securely stitch the curtain ring to right side of floral backing. With wrong sides together glue mirror on to floral backing, turning edge of fabric over and glueing on to face of mirror as Fig. 6.
8. Glue canvas frame on to face of mirror and with double thread carefully slip stitch edge of floral backing to edge of canvas work frame to complete.

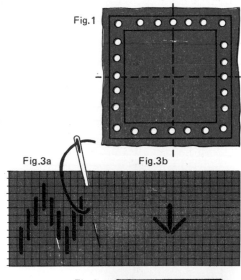

Fig.1

Fig.3a   Fig.3b

Fig.4

Fig.5

10cms

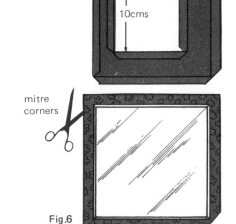

mitre corners

Fig.6

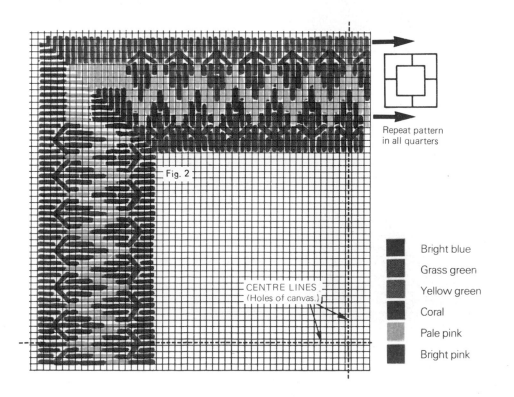

Fig. 2

CENTRE LINES
(Holes of canvas.)

Repeat pattern in all quarters

Bright blue
Grass green
Yellow green
Coral
Pale pink
Bright pink

Canvas work belt

This is a project for all those who enjoy canvas work but like to make something which can actually be used. The belt looks lovely on a dark dress or plain smock, and would make an ideal gift for anyone who likes unusual accessories.

The belt will fit a 61cm. to 66cm. (24in. to 26in.) waist, but can easily be adjusted to individual measurements by working extra squares. Each square is 5cm. (2in.).

You will need
Of tapestry wool:
   2 skeins plum, 1 skein each magenta, lilac, blue, beige, violet and cyclamen
80cm. by 20cm. (31½in. by 7⅞in.) piece of single-thread tapestry canvas, 14 threads to 2.5cm. (1in.)
10cm. (4in.) matching fabric, 91cm. (36in.) wide, for lining
Tapestry frame with 46cm. (18in.) tapes (optional)
2.70m. (98in.) matching cord
Tapestry needle No. 18

Working the embroidery
1. Mark the centre of the canvas lengthways and widthwise with basting stitches. Mount on frame, if you are using one, with short edges to tapes. Turn to side-on position to work.
2. The chart gives a section of the design (two complete squares), the centre indicated by blank arrows which should coincide with the basting stitches. It also shows the arrangement of the stitches on the threads of canvas, represented by the background lines.
3. Start the design in the centre and work from the chart and key. Cross stitch is illustrated on page 39. When working cross stitch, make sure that the upper halves of each cross lie in the same directions. The other stitches used, Gobelin stitch and Rhodes stitch, are illustrated here (Figs. 1 and 3).

4. Repeat central section twice more to the left to complete half the design. Work right half to correspond.

To make up
1. Trim canvas to within 2.5cm. (1in.) of embroidery on long sides and 1.3cm. (½in.) on ends.
2. Fold canvas to wrong side close to embroidery and herringbone stitch in position.
3. Divide cord into four equal pieces and sew two to each end of belt as shown in the photograph. Knot ends.
4. Cut a piece from lining to correspond with belt.
5. Turn 1.3cm. (½in.) of lining to wrong side and sew to back of belt.

Fig. 1 Gobelin stitch. This stitch may be worked from right to left or left to right. Bring the thread through at the left-hand side and insert the needle 2 canvas threads above. Pull the needle through 2 threads down and 1 thread to the right in readiness for the next stitch, continue in this way to the end of the row.
Figs. 2 and 3 Rhodes stitch. This is an attractive raised filling stitch which covers a square of canvas with an even number of threads. Fig. 2 shows the construction of a Rhodes stitch over a square of 6 horizontal and 6 vertical threads. Bring the thread through at A, insert the needle at B, bring through at C, insert at D, bring throuh at E, insert at F. Continue in this way following the direction of the arrows, each stitch overlapping the previous stitch until square is filled. Finish off with a small vertical straight stitch at centre taken through the layers of thread and canvas as shown in Fig. 3.

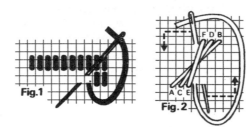

Fig.1 Fig.2 Fig.3

1	Magenta	
2	Violet	
3	Beige	cross stitch
4	Cyclamen	
5	Plum	
6	Lilac	
7	Blue	diagonal satin stitch
8	Plum	
9	Magenta	gobelin stitch
10	Beige	
11	Cyclamen	rhodes stitch

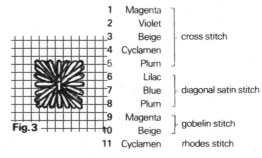

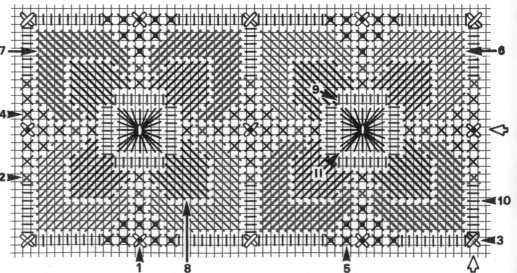

Learn to crochet (1)

Abbreviations used in crochet patterns

alt.	alternate	lct.	lacet
beg.	begin(ning)	patt.	pattern
blk.	block	pct.	picot
br.	bar	qd.tr.	quadruple
ch.	chain		treble
ch. sp.	chain	rem.	remaining
	space(s)	rep.	repeat
cl.	cluster(s)	sh.	shell
cont.	continue	sl.st.	slip stitch
d.c.	double	sp.	space(s)
	crochet	st.	stitch(es)
dec.	decrease	thr.	through
d.tr.	double	tog.	together
	treble	tr.	treble
foll.	follow(ing)	tr.tr.	triple
gr.	group(s)		treble
h.tr.	half treble	y.o.h.	yarn over
inc.	increase		hook

* in a pattern means that you must work instructions after first * until second * is reached, then go back to first * as many times as specified.

Beginning your work

The first step in crochet as in knitting is to make a slip loop. Make a circle of yarn, insert hook through it, pull a loop of yarn through the circle then tighten the slip loop that you have just made on the crochet hook.

Holding the hook in the right hand, the base of the slip loop between the thumb and first finger of the left hand, take yarn over 1st and 2nd fingers and under 3rd and 4th fingers.

Lift yarn with 2nd finger and lay the back of the hook against the strand; then, holding hook like a pencil, pick up the strand with the head of the hook and draw the yarn through the loop on the crochet hook.

Each time the yarn is taken through the loop on the hook, it makes 1 chain (Fig. 1). Continue until the required number of stitches in the chain have been worked. This is the foundation chain in which to work the crochet.

To work a slip-stitch

Slip-stitch forms a flat chain which is often used in the shaping of garments.

Insert hook into next chain, under both top loops, and pick up the strand of yarn with the head of the hook; draw it through the foundation chain, and through the loop already on the hook (Fig. 2).

Continue along foundation chain for length required, inserting hook into each chain.

To work double crochet

Insert hook into 2nd foundation chain, under both top loops. The 1st chain stands for the 1st double crochet and must be counted and worked into as such at end of each return row. Picking up yarn with the head of the hook, draw it through the work, making 2 loops on hook (Fig. 3).

Pick up the yarn as before and draw it through the 2 loops on hook (Fig. 4).

Work 1 double crochet into each chain until required number has been completed.

To work a treble

Pick up the strand held in the left hand with head of crochet hook, to bring the yarn over the hook, then insert the hook into 4th foundation chain, under both top loops. The first 3 chain stands for the 1st treble and must be counted and worked into as such at each end of each return row. Pick up the yarn with the head of the hook and draw it through the work, making 3 loops on the hook (Fig. 5). With the yarn over the hook again, draw it through the first 2 loops, then with the yarn over the hook once more, draw it through the last 2 loops (Fig. 6).

Work 1 treble into each chain until the required number has been completed.

Tension

The word 'tension' in crochet – as in knitting – refers to the number of stitches and rows worked to each square centimetre or inch of fabric. This measurement is a result of the combination of a particular weight and type of yarn with a suitable hook size, and can be varied by altering the yarn and/or hook used. It is possible, for instance, to work the same pattern in a variety of yarns and hook sizes and achieve entirely different results.

It is extremely important therefore before you embark on making up any pattern, to check that your work achieves the tension measurement quoted, otherwise you will never produce finished work to the correct size. Check your tension by working about 10cm. (4in.) of chain, using yarn and hook size recommended in pattern, and make up a sample of the stitch pattern (about 7.5cm. or 3in. should be sufficient). Press the sample, then using a ruler, measure across 2.5cm. (1in.) and mark this area with pins.

Now very carefully count the number of stitches between the pins. If this comes to a greater number than quoted in the pattern, you are working too tightly – make another sample, trying a larger size hook. Alternatively, if you have fewer stitches in your centimetre or inch than quoted in the pattern, you should try working with a smaller size hook. Keep on making sample pieces until you achieve the correct tension.

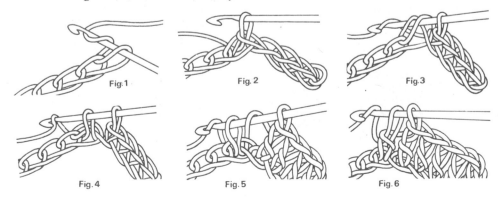

Fig. 1　Fig. 2　Fig. 3

Fig. 4　Fig. 5　Fig. 6

Crochet tablemats in string

6th Round *6ch., 1 d.c. into the next chain loop. Repeat from * all round.
7th Round As 6th.
8th Round *7ch., 1 d.c. into the next chain loop. Repeat from * all round. Fasten off.

To finish the string mats
The final end of the yarn will be too thick to darn in, so separate the strands and darn in each strand separately. Similarly, if there are any ends from joins during working, separate these into strands and darn in each of these separately.
The end of the yarn at the beginning of the work will only need clipping providing it was worked over with the 1st round of d.c. Steam press the mats to set the waxy surface of the string.

To finish the crochet cotton mats
Darn in ends and saturate the mats in water. While still damp, pin them out on an ironing board or similar surface, stretching the chain loops as much as possible with a pin in each loop around the edge. Leave to dry before removing pins.

These mats are strong and hardwearing and look well with a modern table setting. However, the hardwearing qualities of the string also mean that it is a harsh yarn to handle, and you may prefer to try out the pattern first in a softer yarn such as crochet cotton which will make up into small mats or coasters half the size.

You will need
String or cotton parcel twine (medium thickness). The quality will vary with the type used, but the mats shown used 2 large reels, with an ISR hook size 4.50mm. to make 4 mats of approximately 25cm. (9½in.) diameter.

1 ball of medium-weight mercerised crochet cotton with an ISR hook size 3.00mm., will make 4 small mats of approximately 12cm. (4½in.) diameter.

If you have never done crochet, first read page 75, which explains the basic method and the abbreviations used in crochet patterns.

To work the mats
Start with 6 ch., sl. st. into the first ch. to form a ring. Lay the tail end of the yarn around the chain and treat it as part of the ring.
1st Round Work 12 d.c. into the ring, sl.st. to first d.c. to join the round.
2nd Round * 5 ch., miss next d.c., 1 d.c. into the following d.c. Repeat from * 5 times more.
3rd Round Work 1 d.c., 7 tr., 1 d.c., all into the next chain loop (i.e., into the space. Push the stitches up together to make room for them all). Repeat * 5 times more.
4th Round Sl.st. into the next d.c. and also into each of the next 2tr. *(5 ch., miss 1 tr., 1 d.c. into the next tr.) twice, 5 ch., 1 d.c. into second tr. of next petal. Repeat from * 4 times more, (5 ch., miss 1 tr., 1 d.c. into the next tr.) twice, 5 ch., 1 d.c. into the first chain loop.
5th Round *5 ch., 1 d.c. into the next chain loop. Repeat from * all round.

Tatting

Tatting is a lace which is made directly on the fingers using a shuttle. Many people find the technique difficult to master as a certain amount of dexterity is required to form the basic knot. There is only one knot (or stitch) used in tatting – a double knot made up from a pair of half knots. These are built up into rings and chains from which the designs are produced.

All you need is thread, shuttle and a small hook. Some shuttles have a hook incorporated into their design, and some have a removable central spool which can be wound on a sewing machine. A smooth, firm thread is essential, one that gives or stretches is not suitable. Crochet cotton is ideal.

It is possible for a beginner to learn without a shuttle by practising with string. Simply wind the string into a figure-of-eight and secure it with an elastic band as a makeshift shuttle.

Working the double knot

To make the first half knot, hold the shuttle in the right hand with about 50cm. (20in.) of thread unwound. Holding the end of thread between the thumb and index finger of the left hand, pass it over the remaining outstretched fingers and back underneath to form a ring (Fig. 1). Lay the thread from the shuttle in a loop over the top of the left hand, and pass the shuttle upwards from underneath, through both ring and loop, from right to left (Fig. 2).

Now comes the difficult part and it is most important that this movement is correctly worked. The loop now on the shuttle thread is transferred to the thread around the left hand by lowering the middle finger of the left hand (to relax the thread) at the same moment as the shuttle thread is pulled horizontally to the right with a little jerk. When this transfer is correctly made, it is then possible to slide the loop along the shuttle thread by extending the middle finger again. Slide the loop up to reach the thumb, by which time it will have tightened, and hold it firmly in place with the thumb and index finger. This completes the first half knot (Fig. 3). For the second half knot, pass the shuttle from the top, downwards through the ring (Fig. 4). Transfer the loop from the shuttle thread to the left-hand thread as before, and slide this half knot up to reach the first half knot. This completes the double knot (Fig. 5).

Practise a series of double knots, holding each firmly with the thumb and index finger as it is made. When the thread becomes used up, unwind more from the shuttle and 'feed' the ring around the left hand as needed, by stretching the fingers. Note that all the knots should slide easily along the shuttle thread. If they do not the transfer has been incorrectly made. Tatting will not unravel, but any mistakes can be unpicked with a pin.

To make a picot

Leave a little space, say 6mm. (¼ in.) between one double knot and the next, and when the knots are pushed up together, this space will form a picot (Fig. 6).

To make a ring

When a number of double knots have been worked, release the ring from the left hand and gently pull the shuttle thread to close the ring tightly. If the ring proves impossible to close, the basic transfer of the loop is at fault.

To make a chain

Two threads are needed to make a chain. The second thread can be left on the original ball or wound on a second shuttle. Two different colours may be used. To make a chain, tie both threads together, hold the connecting knot with the thumb and index finger of the left hand, and wrap the ball thread (or second shuttle thread) over the hand and around the little finger (Fig. 7). Work double knots in the usual way to produce a chain.

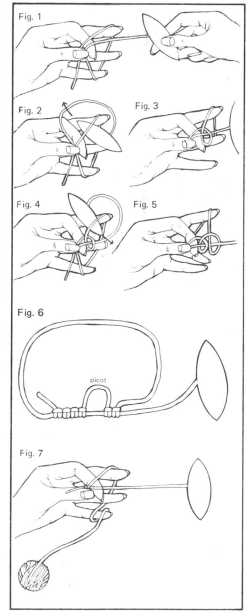

Fig. 1

Fig. 2

Fig. 3

Fig. 4

Fig. 5

Fig. 6

picot

Fig. 7

Tatted rings and chains

On page 77 we explained how to make the basic tatting knot and how to make chains and rings. Here we give further information on tatting as well as instructions for the decorations on the lampshades.

Reading tatting patterns

Tatting patterns can be worked entirely in rings or entirely in chains, but most designs are a combination of both. If after working a chain, the pattern directions then require a ring, drop the second thread from the left hand and use the shuttle thread on its own. Patterns often require the work to be reversed or turned upside down in the hands, when changing from rings to chains or vice versa.

Abbreviations

The usual abbreviations are: ds.–double knot or double stitch; p.–picot; rw. – reverse work.

Joining

The component parts of a design are joined together by the use of picots (see page 77). Rings can be joined to rings or to chains, and chains can be joined to chains or to rings by the method ex-plained in the following example.

To join two rings, work a ring of 4ds., p., 4ds., p., 4ds., p., 4ds., close ring. Start a second ring of 4ds., then join to the last picot of the first ring by inserting a hook through the picot, draw through a loop of thread from the left hand and pull it out sufficiently to insert the shuttle as shown in the diagram. Treat this loop as if it were the first half of a double knot and slide it along the shuttle thread and tighten as usual. Now work a second half knot, and complete the ring with 3ds., p., 4ds., p., 4ds., close ring. Note that the join plus a half knot is counted as a double knot.

PATTERN FOR TATTED DAISY RINGS

You will need

Plain lampshade
1 ball medium-weight mercerised crochet cotton
Tatting shuttle
Fabric adhesive

To work the daisies

Large daisy Ring of 1ds., (large p., 2ds) 6 times, large p., 1ds., close ring. Tie ends and cut close to knot.
Small daisy Ring of 1ds., (large p., 2ds.) 4 times, large p., 1ds., close ring. Tie and cut.
Large ring Ring of 20ds., close. Tie and cut.
Medium ring Ring of 14ds., close. Tie and cut.
Small ring Ring of 8ds., close. Tie and cut.

Arrange rings and daisies at random around the lampshade. Fix each with a dab of adhesive, making sure that the ends are tucked out of sight. This can be more easily managed if the head of a pin is used to manipulate the adhesive.

PATTERN FOR RINGS AND CHAINS TRIMMING

You will need

Plain lampshade
1 ball light-weight mercerised crochet cotton
Tatting shuttle

To work the trimming

Tie ball and shuttle threads before start-ing. * Ring (i.e., shuttle thread only) of 5ds., p., 5ds., close. Rw.
Chain (i.e., both threads) of 5ds., p., 5ds. Rw. Large ring of 3ds., join to picot of previous ring, (2ds., p.) 8 times, 3ds., close. Rw. Chain of 5ds., p., 5ds. Rw. Ring of 5ds., join to last picot of large ring, 5ds., close.
Repeat from * for the length required, allowing the tatting to stretch slightly for a good fit.

Sew the tatting into position, or attach with an adhesive.

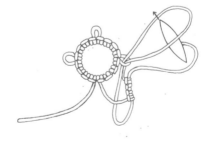

Learn to crochet (2)

On page 75 we listed the abbreviations used in patterns and explained how to work the basic stitches, chain, double crochet and treble. Here we tell you how to increase and decrease, and how to work some further crochet stitches.

Half treble
Pass the hook under the yarn held in the left hand, insert the hook into the stitch to the left of the hook. Catch the yarn and draw it through the stitch. This gives you 3 loops on the hook. Put yarn over hook and draw it through all loops on hook, leaving you with 1 loop (Fig. 1).

Double treble
Pass the hook under the yarn in left hand twice, put the hook into the next stitch, yarn over the hook and pull it through the stitch. This gives you 4 loops on the hook (Fig. 2). Put the yarn over the hook and pull it through 2 loops, leaving 3 loops, put yarn over the hook again and pull through the next 2 loops and finally put yarn over the hook and pull through the last 2 loops.

Triple treble
Pass the hook under yarn held in left hand 3 times, put the hook into the next stitch and draw the yarn through. This gives you 5 loops on the hook. (Fig. 3). Put yarn over the hook and draw through the first 2 loops (4 loops on hook), yarn over and draw through the next 2 loops (3 loops), yarn over and draw through next 2 loops (2 loops), yarn over and draw through last 2 loops.

Quadruple treble
Pass the hook under the yarn held in left hand 4 times, insert hook into next stitch and draw the yarn through. This gives you 6 loops on the hook (Fig. 4). Pass the yarn over the hook and draw through the first 2 loops (5 loops on hook), pass yarn over hook and draw through next 2 loops (4 loops on hook), pass yarn over the hook and draw through next 2 loops (3 loops on hook), pass yarn over and draw through next 2 loops (2 loops), pass yarn over and draw through last 2 loops.

Increasing and decreasing
Instructions for increasing are usually given in the pattern, but as a general rule, increasing can be done by working the required number of times in the same foundation stitch so that you make one or more extra stitches. To increase the overall width more chain stitches can be worked between pattern groups.

Instructions for decreasing are also given in patterns, and these will suit the particular design and the stitch being worked.

One method of decreasing is merely to omit a stitch, but this is only successful if the space created is not too obvious. Another method is to work stitches together. Do not complete either of the stitches but leave the last loop on the hook in addition to the loop already on hook. Draw yarn through all the remaining loops to leave a single loop on hook.

Joining and finishing
Never make knots in your work. When the yarn you are using is coming to an end, place the new yarn along the top of the work and crochet a few stitches over this. Before the old yarn has completely run out, change to the new yarn and work stitches over the old.

At the end of the last row, do not make any turning chain. Cut the yarn about 7.5cm. (3in.) from the work. Draw the end through the last loop on hook and pull tight. Finally, darn the loose end into the work so it is hidden.

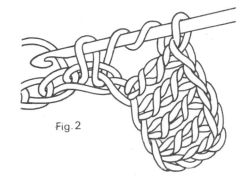
Fig. 2

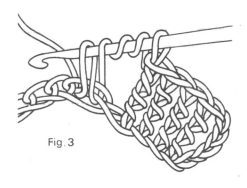
Fig. 3

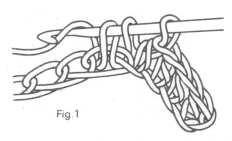
Fig. 1

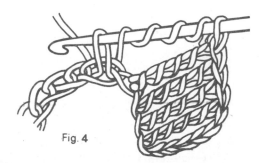
Fig. 4

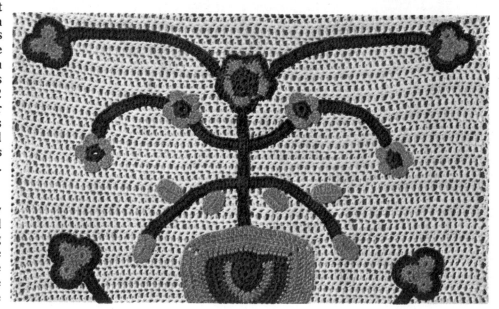

Crochet dressing-table mat

This charming mat in fine white crochet, will add the feminine touch to a bedroom, but it could equally well be used as a really lovely traycloth.

You will need
4 balls No. 20 fine mercerised crochet cotton
ISR Hook size 1.25

Measurements
Size of motif approximately 4.50cm. (1¾in.).
Overall size of mat approximately 46cm. (18in.) by 37cm. (14½in.).

To work the first motif
Start with 12 ch., join into a ring with sl.st.
1st Round 4 ch., 5 d.tr. into ring, (3 ch., 6 d.tr. into ring) 5 times, 3 ch., sl.st. to top of 4 ch. at beginning.
2nd Round 1 ch., 1 d.c. into each of next 2 d.tr., 5 ch., 1 d.c. into each of next 3 d.tr., (5 ch., 1 d.c. into each of first 3 d.tr. of next group, 5 ch., 1 d.c. into each of last 3 d.tr. of group) 5 times, 5 ch., sl.st. to 1 ch. at beginning.
3rd round 9 ch., (miss next 5 ch. loop, 6 tr. into 5 ch. loop between groups, 6 ch.) 5 times, miss the next 5 ch. loop, 5 tr. into last 5 ch. loop, sl.st. to 3rd of 9 ch. at beginning.
4th Round 8 ch., (1 d.c. into nearest ch. loop, 5 ch., 1 tr. into each of next 6 tr., 5 ch.) 5 times, 1 d.c. into last ch. loop, 5 ch., 1 tr. into each of next 5 tr., sl.st. into 3rd of 8 ch. at beginning. Finish off.

To work the second motif
Work as for the first motif for 3 rounds.
4th round 8 ch., 1 d.c. into nearest ch. loop, 5 ch., 1tr. into each of next 6 tr., 5 ch., 1 d.c. into nearest ch. loop, 5 ch., * 1 tr. into next tr., remove the hook from its stitch and insert the hook into the top of the opposite treble of any group on the 4th round of the first motif, pick up the dropped stitch and draw it through. Repeat from * 5 times more, and complete the second motif to match the first. All motifs are joined together at the groups of trebles by this method. Join 85 motifs as shown in diagram.

To work the edging
1st Round Join to 1st tr. of any group around outer edge by drawing a slip knot through. Work 1 d.c. into each of the 6 tr., * 2 d.c. into the following 5 ch. loop, 4 ch., 2 d.c. into the 5 ch. loop before the next group, 1 d.c. into each of the next 6

tr. Repeat from * all around the mat, ending with 2 d.c. into the following 5 ch. loop, 4 ch., 2 d.c. into the 5 ch. loop before group at beginning, sl.st. to 1st d.c.
2nd Round Work 1 d.c. into every d.c. and 4 d.c. into every 4 ch. loop, all around, joining finally with a sl.st. to 1st d.c. Finish off and press the work under a damp cloth.

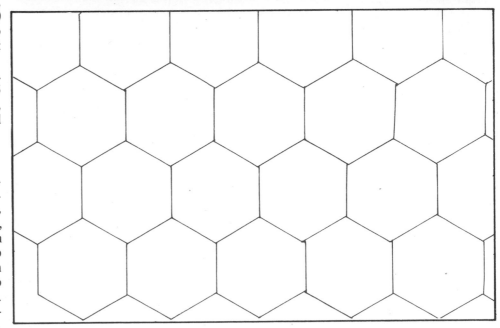

Mexican-style rug

Add a touch of luxury to your home with this Mexican-style crochet rug. It is not hard to make – you crochet a net first and then work the 'pile'. The finished size will be approximately 115cm. by 61cm. (45in. by 24in.).

You will need
Of a medium-weight mercerised cotton:
5 balls in Rust; 5 balls in Chocolate; 7
  balls in Pampas; 4 balls in Gold
Crochet hook No. 3.50

If you are not experienced at crochet, first read pages 75 and 79, which explain the technique and list the abbreviations used in crochet patterns.

To make the foundation chain
With Gold, make 173ch.
1st row 1 d.tr. into 9th ch. from hook, * 4 ch., miss 3 ch., 1 d.tr. into next ch., rep. from * to end, turn: 42 sp.
2nd row 8 ch., 1 d.tr. into next d.tr., * 4 ch., 1 d.tr. into next d.tr., rep. from * to end, finishing 1d.tr. into 4th of the 8 ch., turn.
Rep. 2nd row until there are 63 sp. Fasten off.
Mark the 11th square from foundation edge and side edge.

To work the 'pile'
1st round Join Rust to the d.tr. at right-hand side of marked square and following the diagram work thus: 4 ch., then work 2 d.tr. over same side (1), then work 3 d.tr. over lower side (2), right-hand side (3), top (4) and left-hand side (5) of square

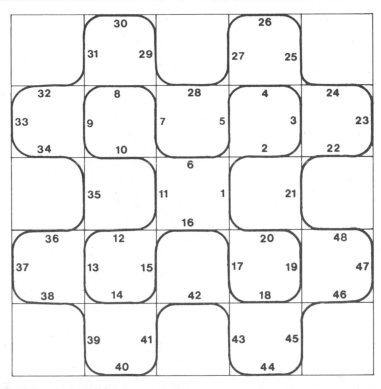

to right of first square but 1 row up. Now work 3 d.tr. over top side of original square (6). Continue to work 3 d.tr. over sides, following numbers in rotation, finishing with side 20, sl.st. into top of the 4 ch. Fasten off. 9 squares have now been worked over.
2nd round Join Rust to remaining side of square directly to right of original square, 4 ch., then work 2 d.tr. over same side (21), continue to follow numbers, working 3 d.tr. over sides as before, ending at side 48, sl.st. into top of the 4

ch. Fasten off. Join Chocolate to remaining unworked side of square. Continue to work over each side as before, work 2 rounds Rust, 2 rounds Chocolate, 2 rounds Pampas, 2 rounds Chocolate, 2 rounds Rust.
Now mark position of centre of 2nd pattern block, 11 squares from side edge and 11 squares from foundation edge. Work 'pile' for this block the same way as the first pattern block, following the illustration for the colour sequence.

Mark centres of 3rd and 4th pattern blocks, 11 squares from edge of 1st and 2nd blocks. Work 'pile' for each as before. Mark centre of 5th and 6th pattern blocks 11 squares from 3rd and 4th blocks. Work 'pile' as before.
Edging With right sides facing join on Pampas and finish each long edge, working 2 h.tr. into each large sp. and 1 h.tr., into each small sp.
Fringe Using 4 15cm. (6in.) lengths of Pampas together, knot fringe evenly along each short edge.

Tunisian crochet

This technique looks rather more like knitting than crochet, but is worked on a single long hook, and is begun in exactly the same way as crochet. There are a variety of different stitches, all of which produce a strong, hard-wearing fabric, particularly suitable for furnishings or blankets. On this page we explain how to work the two best-known of these, and also how to increase, decrease and shape.

Tunisian Simple Stitch

Two foundation rows form the basis of most Tunisian crochet patterns.

First make the basic chain (see page 75 for the basic crochet technique and abbreviations).

Now work foundation rows as follows:

1st row Insert hook into 2nd ch. from hook, y.o.h., and draw loop through, * insert hook into next ch., y.o.h., draw loop through; rep. from * to end, leaving all loops on hook. Do not turn work round.

2nd row 1 ch., then * y.o.h., draw through 2 loops on hook; rep. from * to end, leaving 1 loop on hook. Do not turn work round.

3rd row * Insert hook under next vertical thread from right to left, y.o.h., and draw loop through; rep. from * to end, leaving all loops on hook. Do not turn work.

4th row As 2nd.

The 3rd and 4th rows form the pattern; repeat them as required.

Tunisian Cross Stitch

Make chain

Work 2 foundation rows as Tunisian Simple Stitch.

3rd row * Missing 1 vertical thread, insert hook from right to left under following vertical thread, y.o.h., and draw loop through, insert hook from right to left under missed vertical thread, y.o.h., and draw loop through, rep. from * to end.

4th row As 2nd row of Simple Stitch.

The 3rd and 4th rows form the pattern; repeat as necessary, always ending with a 4th row.

Finishing

For a neat finish, work double crochet row as follows: * Insert hook into next stitch in chosen pattern, y.o.h., draw loop through, y.o.h., draw through 2 loops on hook; rep. from * to end.

Shaping

Tunisian crochet, just like knitting and other types of crochet, can be shaped to make garments in the following ways.

Increasing a stitch on the right-hand edge

To increase one stitch, make 1 ch., insert hook behind vertical thread of the first stitch (edge stitch), y.o.h. and draw loop through, continue in pattern to end of row.

Increasing a stitch at the left-hand edge

This must be worked on an even numbered row. Y.o.h. and draw through one loop, 1 ch., * y.o.h. and draw through 2 loops, rep. from * to end of row. On the next row patt. to the last stitch, insert hook into the 1 ch. and draw loop through, insert hook into last stitch and draw loop through.

Increasing 2 or more stitches at the right-hand edge

Make the required number of ch. then work basic stitch into each ch. and the first vertical thread (edge stitch) and continue in pattern to end.

Increasing 2 or more stitches at the left-hand edge

Using a separate length of yarn make the required number of ch. and leave for time being. Work in pattern to the end of the row then work in basic stitch into each of the separate ch.

Decreasing one stitch at the right-hand edge

Insert the hook behind 2 vertical threads, y.o.h. and draw through one loop only, continue in pattern to the end of the row.

Decreasing one stitch at the left-hand edge

Work as given for decreasing at the right-hand edge by inserting the hook behind the last 2 vertical threads together, y.o.h. and draw through one loop only.

Top left: Tunisian simple stitch; top right, Tunisian cross stitch; bottom, shaping Tunisian crochet.

Tunisian crochet cushion

Try making these bright cushion covers in Tunisian crochet. You can use up odd balls of wool, mixing colours as you please. The cushions illustrated were made up in double knitting wool. Tunisian Simple stitch is used for all three cushion covers (see page 82).

You will need
For all cushions
No. 5 Tunisian crochet hook
Large-eyed needle
Zip fasteners (optional)
Cushion pads to fit cushions

For the patchwork cushion
The cushion illustrated is made up with 64 10cm. (4in.) squares on each side and is 81cm. (32in.) square. It requires 56 25g. balls of double knitting. Smaller cushion covers can be made up with 9, 16, 25, 36 and 42 squares on each side. 14 25g. balls of wool would make a cover with 16 squares on each side measuring 41cm. (16in.) square.

Striped cushion
The cushion illustrated measures 51cm. (20in.) square, and has 8 stripes on each side, using 28 25g. balls of double knitting.

Rectangles cushion
The cushion illustrated measures 51cm. by 40cm. (20in. by 16in.) and is made up of 80 rectangles 5cm. by 10cm. (2in. by 4in.), 40 on each side, using 28 25g. balls of double knitting.

To work motifs
Patchwork square. Make 20 ch. and work 2 foundation rows. Work 32 rows in Tunisian Simple Stitch until work measures 10cm. (4in.) from beg. Work d.c. row and fasten off.
Strip. Make 12 ch. and work 2 foundation rows. Work Tunisian Simple Stitch until

work measures 51cm. (20in.) from beg. Work d.c. row and fasten off.
Rectangle. Make 12 ch. and work 2 foundation rows. Work 32 rows until work measures 10cm. (4in.) from beg. Work d.c. row and fasten off.

To make up motifs
Patchwork. Sew squares together to make large square. Make 2 large squares for cushion cover.
Strips. Sew 8 strips together on long sides

to make square. Make 2 squares for cushion cover.
Rectangles. Sew 5 rectangles together on short ends to make strip and then sew 8 strips on long sides. Make 2 cushion sides.

To finish cushions
Press work on the wrong side. Lay 2 covers together with right sides facing. Sew together on 3 sides and then insert zip fastener on 4th side. Alternatively, insert cushion pad after sewing 3 sides then turn in the edges of the 4th side and sew to close the opening.

Other patterns to try
You can make up all kinds of patterns with the three motifs. Try making 4 squares in the same colour for a centre motif, then sew strips 5cm. by 25cm. (2in. by 10in.) round the edges. Or you might try making up a pattern of rectangles and 5cm. (2in.) squares, as in diagram.

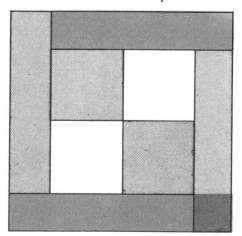

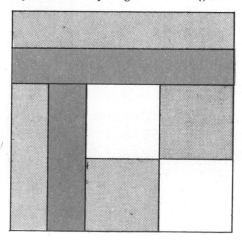

Shaped crochet basket

These delicate baskets are made by immersing a piece of crochet in a sugar solution and leaving it to dry over a mould. They are washable, but will need stiffening again after washing.

You will need
2 balls lightweight crochet yarn
No. 2 crochet hook

Tension 1st 5 rounds to 9cm. (3½in.).

To make fruit basket
1st round 5 ch., (1 tr. 2 ch.) into ring 7 times, sl.st. into 3rd of 5 ch.
2nd round Sl.st. into ch.sp. 3 ch., 4 tr. into same ch.sp. as sl.st. * 5 tr. into next ch.sp., rep. from * all round, finish sl.st. into top of 3 ch.
3rd round 3 ch., 1 tr. into each of the next 4 tr., * 3 ch., 1 tr. into each of the next 5 tr., rep. from * all round, finish 3 ch., sl.st. into top of 3 ch.
4th round (1 d.c. into each tr., 3 d.c. into each ch.sp.) all round, sl.st. into 1st d.c.
5th round 6 ch., * miss 1 d.c., 1 tr. into next d.c., 3 ch., miss 1 d.c., 1 tr. into next d.c., 3 ch., miss 3 d.c., 1 tr. into next d.c.,

3 ch., rep. from * all round, finish 3 ch., sl.st. into 3rd of 6 ch.
6th round 3 ch., * 3 tr. into sp., 1 tr. into next tr., rep. from * all round, finish sl.st. into top of 3 ch. omitting 1 tr. into tr.
7th round 4 ch., 4 d.tr. into same ch. as sl.st., * miss 3 tr., 5 d.tr. into next tr., rep. from * all round, finish sl.st. into top of 4 ch.
8th round Leaving last st. of each d.tr. on hook, 4 ch., 1 d.tr. into each of the next 4 d.tr., y.o.h. draw yarn through remaining st. to form a group * 6 ch., 1 group over the next 5 d.tr., rep. from * all round, finish 6 ch., sl.st. into top of 1st group.
9th round Sl.st. into sp. 3 ch., 6 tr. into sp., 7 tr. into each sp. all round, sl.st. into top of 3 ch.
10th round 6 ch., * miss 2 tr., 1 tr. into next tr., 3 ch., rep. from * all round, sl.st. into 3rd of 6 ch. (56 sp.) Turn.
11th round 3 ch., * 3 tr. into sp., 1 tr. into next tr., rep. from * all round, finish sl.st. into top of 3 ch. omitting 1 tr. into tr.
12th round 6 ch., 1 tr. into same ch. as sl.st., * 6 ch., miss 7 tr., 1 tr. into next tr., 6 ch. miss 7 tr., 1 tr. 3 ch. 1 tr. into next

tr., rep. from * all round, finish 6 ch., miss 7 tr., 1 tr. into next tr., 6 ch., sl.st. into 3rd of 6 ch.
13th round Sl.st. into sp., 4 ch. 3 d.tr., 2 ch. 1 d.tr., 2 ch. 4 d.tr., into same sp. as sl.st., * 3 ch. 1 d.tr. into next tr., 3 ch. 4 d.tr., 2 ch. 1 d.tr., 2 ch. 4 d.tr. into next 3 ch.sp., rep. from * all round, finish 3 ch., sl.st. into top of 4 ch.
14th round Sl.st. into 3 d.tr. and into sp., 4 ch. 3 d.tr. into same sp. as sl.st., 2 ch. 1 d.tr. into d.tr., 2 ch. 4 d.tr. into next sp., * 2 ch. 1 d.tr. into d.tr., 2 ch. 4 d.tr. into next 2 ch.sp., 2 ch. 1 d.tr. into d.tr., 2 ch. 4 d.tr. into next sp., rep. from * all round, finish 2 ch. 1 d.tr. into d.tr., 2 ch., sl.st. into top of 4 ch.
15th round Sl.st. into 3 d.tr. and into sp., 4 ch. 3 d.tr. into sp., 3 ch. 1 d.tr. into d.tr., 3 ch. 4 d.tr. into next sp., * 1 ch. 1 d.tr. into next d.tr., 1 ch. 4 d.tr. into next 2 ch.sp., 3 ch. 1 d.tr. into d.tr., 3 ch. 4 d.tr. into next sp., rep. from * all round, finish 1 ch. sl.st. into top of 4 ch.
16th round Sl.st. into 3 d.tr. and into sp., 4 ch. 1 d.tr. into same sp. as sl.st. 4 ch., sl.st. into 4th ch. from hook (to form a picot), 2 d.tr. into same space as last d.tr., 1 picot, 2 d.tr. into d.tr., (1 picot 2 d.tr.), twice into next sp., * 2 ch. 1 d.tr. into d.tr., 2 ch. (2 d.tr. 1 picot) twice into next 3 ch.sp., 2 d.tr. into d.tr. (1 picot 2 d.tr.) twice into next sp., rep. from * all round, finish 2 ch. 1 d.tr. into d.tr., 2 ch., sl.st. into top of 4 ch. Fasten off.

To stiffen and shape
Take 2 tablespoons granulated sugar and 1 of boiling water. (Do not use brown sugar.) Pour water over sugar in small pan, place over low heat and stir until dissolved. Place crochet in sugar solution, making sure every part is damp. Squeeze out gently if necessary. Place the damp crochet over a tin or bowl with a diameter of about 20cm. (8in.) and mould around it. Leave to dry. This can take anywhere up to two days.

Crochet chairbacks

This elegant set of settee cover, chairback and armrests is quite a simple crochet pattern, and you don't have to make them all if you don't want to. The measurements are approximately as follows: settee cover 87cm. by 56cm. (34½in. by 22in.); chairback 76cm. by 56cm. (16½in. by 22in.); armrests 26.5cm. by 53cm. (10½in. by 21in.).

You will need
Settee cover
15 balls medium-weight mercerised crochet cotton
Chairback
7 balls medium-weight mercerised crochet cotton
Armrests
5 balls medium-weight mercerised crochet cotton
For all
Crochet hook No. 3.00 (10)

Notes
When purchasing materials be sure that you buy enough to finish the articles also allowing extra yarn if article is made larger as dye-lots vary. The quantitites of yarn stated are based on average requirements and are therefore approximate.

For all abbreviations see page 75.

Tension
2 patts. to 7.5cm. (3in.) over main part.

Tension check
Before you crochet this design check the tension by working a 15cm. (6in.) square in the stitch pattern. If the tension is tight use a size larger hook, if loose use a finer hook.

To work the crochet
Make 4 ch. Work 2 tr. 1 ch. 3 tr. into 4th ch. from hook, turn.
2nd row 3 ch. 3 tr. 1 ch. 3 tr. into 1 ch.sp., turn.
Rep. 2nd row until 30 rows have been worked for armrest, 50 rows for chair backs and 102 rows for settee back. Fasten off.
Foundation row Rejoin yarn into 1st 3 ch.sp. (i.e. at end of row). 3 ch. 2 tr. 1 ch. 3 tr. into sp., 3 ch. * 3 tr. 1 ch. 3 tr. into next sp., miss 1 sp., 6 ch. Rep. from * ending 3 ch. 3 tr. 1 ch. 3 tr. into last sp. (9 groups for armrest, 14 groups for chair back and 27 groups for settee back.)
1st patt. row 3 ch. 3 tr. 1 ch. 3 tr. into 1st 1 ch.sp., 3 ch. * 3 tr. 1 ch. 3 tr. into next 1 ch.sp., 6 ch. Rep. from * ending 3 ch. 3 tr. 1 ch. 3 tr. into last ch.sp.

2nd patt. row Rep. 1st row.
3rd patt. row 3 ch. 3 tr. 1 ch. 3 tr. into 1st ch. sp., 3 ch. * 3 tr. 1 ch. 3 tr. into next 1 ch.sp., 5 ch. 1 d.c. working into next sp. 3 rows below, (joining ch. loops together) 5 ch. rep. from * ending 3 ch. 3 tr. 1 ch. 3 tr. into last 1 ch.sp.
4th patt. row Rep. 1st patt. row.
Rep. these 4 rows until work measures 53cm. (21in.) for armrest, 56cm. (22in.) for chairback and settee back, ending on a 2nd patt. row.
Last row 3 ch. 3 tr. 1 ch. 3 tr. into 1st ch.sp., * 3 ch. 3 tr. 1 ch. 3 tr. into next 1 ch.sp., 3 ch. 3 tr. 1 ch. 3 tr. working into sp. 3 rows below, rep. from * ending 3 ch. 3 tr. 1 ch. 3 tr. into last 1 ch.sp. Fasten off.

Springtime lamb

A charming little lamb to make for a gift. Worked in nylon courtelle yarn, it is washable and thus suitable for a young child.

You will need
7 20g. balls of double knitting nylon courtelle in white (W)
1 20g. ball in black (B)
3mm. (No. 10) crochet hook
Washable stuffing
Scraps pink and black fabric for eyes and nose
Sewing threads
Ribbon for neck

Measurement
Length from top of head to feet: 28cm. (11in.)

Note
If you have not done crochet before, first read pages 75 and 79.

Tension
4½ st. to 2.5cm. (1in.)

Special stitch for this pattern
Loop stitch. Work with wrong side facing. Wrap yarn once completely around first finger on left hand. Keeping finger as close to work as possible, insert hook in next stitch, then insert it from left to right under the 2 strands of yarn on the finger. Draw all through first loop on hook, yarn over hook and draw through all 3 loops on hook.

Body
Starting at centre front and using W, ch. 4, join with a sl.st. to form a circle. Work 6 d.c. in circle. Now work in loop st.
2nd round. Increase in each st. (12 loop st.) now increase 6 st. on each of next 4 rounds (36 st.). Continue on these st. until work measures 20cm. (8in.) from last row. Now stuff. Decrease 6 st. on each of next 5 rounds, stuffing as you go. (6 st.). Decrease 3 st. Break off, pull yarn tight and finish off.

Legs (four required)
Starting at foot and using B, ch. 4, join with a sl.st. to form circle and work 6 d.c. in circle.
2nd round. Increase in each st. (12 st.) Then 6 st. on next round on each alternate st. (18 st.) Now work 6 rounds on these 18 st. Fasten off. Change to W and work in loop st. for 14 rounds.
Shaping top of leg. Work 12 loop st. 1 ch., turn.

2nd row. Work 12 d.c. into loop sts., turn. Repeat last 2 rows once more, then first row once more. Fasten off. Put circles of cardboard the size of a 10p piece in foot, stuff leg and sew on to body, stuffing shoulder as you go on.

Head
Starting at crown and using W, ch. 4, join with a sl.st. to form circle, work 6 d.c. into circle. Now work in loop st.
2nd round. Increase in each st. (12 loops), now increase 6 st. on each of next 5 rounds. (42 st.). Continue on these st. until work measures 10cm. (4in.). Now decrease 3 st. on every round until 7 st. remain. Fasten off. Stuff and attach to body.

Tail
Using W, ch. 4, join with a sl.st. to form circle, work 6 d.c. into circle, now work in loop st.
2nd round. Increase in each st. (12 loops). Continue on these st. until work measures 5cm. (2in.). Fasten off. Attach tail to body.

Ears (two required)
Using W, ch. 12 and work one row in d.c. Then one row in loop st. Repeat last 2 rows until work measures 5cm. (2in.) Now decrease one st. at each end of next and every following alternate row until 3 st. remain. Fasten off. Attach ears to head as illustrated.

Nose
Using B, ch. 3 and join with a sl.st., 5 d.c. into circle.
2nd round. 2 d.c. into each d.c. of previous round (10 d.c.).
3rd round. 1 d.c. into each d.c. of previous round.
4th round. 2 d.c. into each d.c. of previous round (20 d.c.).
5th round. 1 d.c. into each d.c. of previous round.
6th round. 2 d.c. into each alternate d.c. of previous round (30 d.c.).
7th round. 1 d.c. into each d.c. of previous round.
8th round. 1 d.c. into each d.c. of previous round.
9th round. 1 d.c. into each of next 20 d.c., turn.
10th round. 1 d.c. into each of last 20 d.c. Now decrease one st. at each end of every row until 4 d.c. remain. Fasten off. Stuff and attach to head.

To make up
Cut 2 circles of black fabric using coin as template, turn under edges and sew to head. Cut a pink fabric circle for the nose, turn under the edges and sew on, stuffing as you stitch.

Leaves and trellis bedspread

For crochet fanatics, or even for those who have always wanted to try their hands at it, here's a marvellous occupation for the winter evenings. You'll love this pretty leaf-pattern bedspread and, if you put it over a coloured blanket, it will really give a glow to your bedroom.

You will need
For a double bedspread
Of medium-weight cotton yarn:
    40 100g. hanks or 80 50g. balls
Single bedspread
Of medium-weight cotton yarn:
    31 100g. hanks or 62 50g balls
King-size bedspread
Of medium-weight cotton yarn:
    48 100g. hanks or 96 50g. balls
For all sizes
5.00 crochet hook

Tension
1 motif to 14cm. (5½in.) across

Abbreviations
The standard crochet abbreviations are given on page 75.

To make each motif
Commence with 10 ch. sl.st. into 1st ch. to form a ring.
1st Round 3 ch. (standing as 1st tr.) 3 tr. into ring, 2 ch. (4 tr. into ring 2 ch.) 3 times, sl.st. into top of 3 ch.
2nd Round 3 ch. 1 tr. into sl.st. 1 tr. into each of the next 2 tr. 2 tr. in next tr. 4 ch. (2 tr. in next tr. 2 tr. 2 tr. in next tr. 4 ch.) 3 times, sl.st. into top of 3 ch.
3rd Round 3 ch. 1 tr. into sl.st. 4 tr. 2 tr. in next tr. 6 ch. (2tr. in next tr. 4 tr. 2 tr. in next tr. 6 ch.) 3 times, sl.st. into top of 3 ch.
4th Round 3 ch. 1 tr. into sl.st. 6 tr. 2 tr. in next tr. 8 ch. (2 tr. in next tr. 6 tr. 2 tr. in next tr. 8 ch.) 3 times, sl.st. into top of 3 ch.
5th Round 3 ch. 1 tr. into sl.st. 8 tr. 2 tr. in next tr. 10 ch. (2 tr. in next tr. 8 tr. 2 tr. in next tr. 10 ch.) 3 times, sl.st. into top of 3 ch.
Fasten off.
For the single size make 285 motifs.
For the double size make 361 motifs and for the king-size make 441 motifs.

To join motifs
Sewing tr. parts together, join motifs in 19 (19: 21) lines of 15 (19: 21) motifs.

Border
1st Round Join yarn to first tr. of one 12 tr. gr. at centre of one edge, 1 ch. 1 d.c. into each of 12 tr. make 18 ch. (1 d.c. in each of 12 tr. of next gr. 18 ch.) all round, ending sl.st. into 1st ch.
2nd Round St.st. into first d.c. 5 ch. miss 2 d.c. (1 tr. in next d.c. 2 ch. miss 2 d.c.) 3 times, * (1 tr. in next ch. 2 ch. miss 2 ch.) 6 times, (1 tr. in next d.c. 2 ch. miss 2 d.c.) 4 times, rep. from * all round, ending (1 tr. into next ch. 2 ch. miss 2 ch.) 6 times, ending sl.st. into 3rd of 5 ch.
3rd Round 5 ch. (1 tr. in next tr. 2 ch.) all round, ending sl.st. into 3rd of 5 ch.
Fasten off.

Fringe
Cut remaining yarn into 13cm. (5in.) lengths. Taking 2 strands at a time knot through every 2 ch.sp. Trim fringes.

Fabric and crochet mats

The beauty of these pretty mats is that you can use remnants or leftover pieces of fabric for the centres and chose a matching or contrasting colour for the crochet edgings. You can make a set of place mats or a dressing-table set, as illustrated. The large mat is 25cm. (9⅞in.) in diameter; the small ones 17cm. (6¾in.)

You will need
(For one large and two small mats)
1 ball No. 20 fine mercerised crochet
    cotton in chosen colour
Steel crochet hook 1.25 (No. 3)
30cm. (12in.) fabric 91cm. (36in.) wide
Sewing thread

Tension
Depth of edging – 3.5cm. (1⅜in.)
If your crochet is loose, use a size finer hook than specified; if tight use a size larger.

Note
If you are not familiar with the abbreviations used in crochet patterns, first read page 75.

To make the large mat
1st Round Commence with * 7 ch., 1 d.tr. into 7th ch. from hook; rep. from * 47 times more or for length required having an even number of loops, taking care not to twist, join with 1 sl.st. into first commencing ch.
2nd Round * Into next loop work 1 d.c. 1 h.tr. 5 tr. 1 h.tr. and 1 d.c., into next loop work 1 d.c. 1 h.tr. and 3 tr., 7 ch., 1 sl.st. into last tr., into same loop on previous row work 2 tr. 1 h.tr. and 1 d.c.; rep. from * ending with 1 sl.st. into first d.c.
3rd Round 1 sl.st. into each of next 4 sts., 1 d.c. into same place as last sl.st., * 5 ch., into next 7 ch. loop, work (1 d.c., 7 ch.) 3 times and 1 d.c., 5 ch., 1 d.c. into centre tr. on next loop; rep. from * omitting 1 d.c. at end of last rep., 1 sl.st. into first d.c.
4th Round 1 d.c. into same place as sl.st., * (3 ch., 3 d.c. into next 7 ch. loop) 3 times, 3 ch., miss next 5 ch. loop, 1 d.c. into next d.c.; rep. from * omitting 1 d.c. at end of last rep., 1 sl.st. into first d.c.
5th Round * 1 d.c. into each of next 4 sts., 1 h.tr. into next st., 1 tr. into each of next

5 sts., 3 tr. into next st. 1 tr. into each of next 5 sts., 1 h.tr. into next st., 1 d.c. into each of next 4 sts., miss next st.; rep. from *, ending with 1 sl.st. into first d.c. Fasten off.

To make the small mat
Work as large mat but with 28 loops, or number required, on first row.

To make up
Damp crochet work and pin out to measurements.
    There are two ways of making the mats. The first is as follows. Place the crochet edging on the fabric. Baste and machine zig-zag stitch the inner edge of the crochet to fabric, and cut away excess fabric. This is probably the easiest method. The other way is to mark the outline of each circle on fabric, cut out leaving 6mm. (¼in.) seam allowance, face edges with bias binding and sew crochet in position.

Hairpin crochet

A lovely type of openwork crochet lace can be worked by using a special implement called a 'hairpin' prong. These prongs were originally the actual 'U'-shaped hairpins used by Victorian ladies for their hair, but today they are made especially for the purpose. Prongs can be purchased from any good wool shop and come in a variety of widths from 1.3cm. (½in.) to 7.5cm. (3in.), these measurements representing the gap between the points. Any yarn can be used for hairpin crochet, from the thickest wool to the finest cotton, though of course the size of the prong must be in keeping.

Trimmings, edgings, collar and cuff sets, table mats and even complete garments can be made by this simple technique, but the work always has to be square or rectangular as hairpin crochet cannot be shaped.

To make a length of hairpin crochet make a slip knot and place it on a crochet hook held in the right hand. Holding the hairpin prong in the left hand with the prong pointing downwards, place the crochet hook between the prong, wrap the yarn from the front round the right-hand side to the back. Hold this yarn also in the left hand, pick up a loop and pull through the loop on the hook (Fig. 1). Remove the loop from the hook and turn the prong half a turn in a clockwise direction. There will now be a loop round the other prong. Insert the hook into the drooped loop (Fig. 2) pick up a loop and pull it through (Fig. 3).

You have now made a complete loop. Secure it by working a double crochet (see page 75) into the front thread of the loop on the left-hand prong (Fig. 4). Repeat the process until you have made the number of loops required. As the work proceeds, allow the loops at the base to fall from the prong, thus allowing room for the new loops to be made.

To finish, remove the prong, break the thread and draw this through the loop on the hook, draw tight.

All hairpin is made in this way; it is how the loops are joined or twisted together which gives the infinite variations. However, all patterns will describe the basic loop in the instructions, for instance here is a pattern for a simple edging:

1st side Twist first loop half a turn in an anti-clockwise direction, attach yarn to top of this loop, 1 d.c. into same place as join, * 1 ch., twist next loop half a turn in the same direction, 1 d.c. into this loop; rep. from * to end. Fasten off.
2nd side Work as 1st side.

It is a good idea to practise before starting a project, as your work may be uneven at first. Also the wider the prong you use the more difficult it is to keep the stitches central. However, after a little practice the loops on either side will soon become neat and even, with each double crochet lying neatly in the centre.

Carol Payton

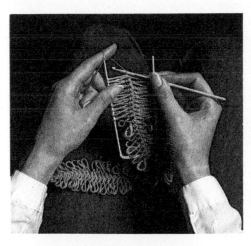

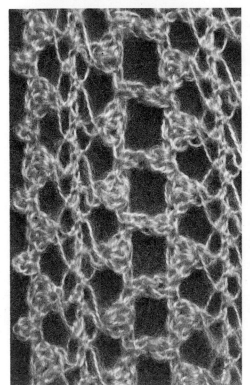

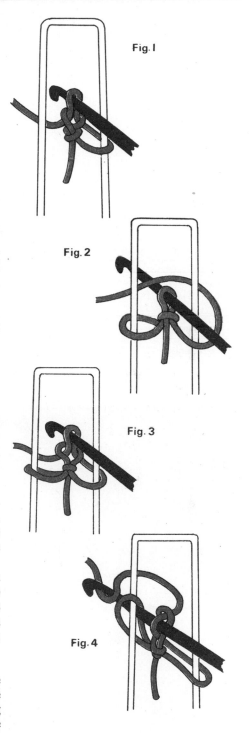

Fig. 1

Fig. 2

Fig. 3

Fig. 4

Hairpin crochet scarf

If you have read page 89 you will now be ready to try out a hairpin crochet project. This scarf is a good one to start with. Although the stitch pattern resembles a delicate open-weave lace it is surprising how warm and snug it is.

If you want to make the scarf longer, simply work more loops on each length of hairpin. To make it wider, work and join a few extra raws of hairpin. But don't forget to allow for extra yarn if you increase the size.

You will need
3 balls of lightweight mohair yarn
5cm. (2¼in.) wide hairpin prong
ISR crochet hooks 4mm. and 6mm.

Measurements
135 by 30cm. (52 by 11½in.) excluding the fringe

Note
If you have not done crochet or hairpin crochet, first read pages 75 and 89.

To make the scarf
Make 3 lengths of hairpin with 100 loops on every side, using a 4mm. hook.

Edging
With the 6mm. hook and right side facing, take the first 2 loops on one side of any length of hairpin, twist them half a turn to the left, insert the hook into the top of the 2 loops and make a d.c., 2 ch., 2 tr. into same place as d.c., (3 ch., 1 sl.st. into top of last tr. made, take the next 2 loops on same side, twist them half a turn to the left and work 3 tr. into these 2 loops.) 49 times. Fasten off. Work this edging along the first side of every hairpin length.

Lay out the strips of hairpin side by side.

Joining
Take the last 2 loops made on the first hairpin length, twist them half a turn to the left, insert hook into the top of the 2 loops, and make a d.c., 2 ch., 2 tr. into same place as d.c., (1 ch., 1 d.c. into 3 ch. loop in first side of 2nd hairpin length, 1 ch., 1 sl.st. into top of last tr., take the next 2 loops on first hairpin length, twist them half a turn to the left and work 3 tr. into these 2 loops) 49 times. Fasten off. Work and join 2nd side of 2nd hairpin length to first side of 3rd hairpin length in the same way. Work edging along 2nd side of 3rd hairpin length to complete the side.

Designed by Carol Payton

Tenerife lace

This is a simple, attractive, but little-known method of making square and round lace motifs. Yarn is wound around a circle or square of pins stuck into cardboard (or a cork or polystyrene tile) and then woven in and out of these threads.

Large motifs, made in thick string, can be used singly as doilies or teapot stands, while small ones, in fine yarns, can be sewn together into groups to form edgings, collars, shawls and so on. The list of items you can make is really endless.

Instructions for a pretty collar made in a light-weight metallic yarn are given on page 92.

Preparing the weaving 'frame'

Draw a circle or square the size of the motif you want on a cork or polystyrene tile or piece of cork board. Now you must place on this at least 32 pins at an equal distance apart from each other and push them down firmly into the board. If you are making a square, place a pin in each corner and then divide each line into equal parts of not more than 1cm. (⅜in.). If you are making a circle, imagine it as a clock face, and place a pin at each of the following points: 12 o'clock, 6 o'clock, 3 o'clock and 9 o'clock. Now place a pin at an equal distance between each of the first 4 pins (8 pins altogether).

Place a pin at an equal distance between each of the 8 pins (16 pins), and then another at an equal distance between each of the 16, making 32 altogether (Fig. 1).

This is the most useful number of pins to work with, but if the motif is quite large and fine thread is used, then repeat the process so that there are 64 pins.

Making the lace

Hold the end of the yarn at the centre of the circle, and then wind it round the pin at 12 o'clock, and down round the pin at 6 o'clock (Fig. 2). Take it up round pin to the left of 12 o'clock, and then down round the pin the right of 6 o'clock (Fig. 3). Continue in this way until the thread has been wrapped round every pin, and end back at the centre (Fig. 4).

For a square motif the procedure is exactly the same: start with central pin at the top, taking the yarn to the central pin at the bottom, and then back to the one at the left of the central top pin, and so on.

Now you have the foundation threads. The next stop is to decorate them. Break the yarn, leaving a good length to work with. Thread the end into a tapestry needle and, beginning at the centre, weave round by working alternately under and over the foundation threads. Draw the yarn tight so that the centre is closely worked to hold the foundation threads firmly in position (Fig. 5). Work at least three rounds. A round or two of decorative knotted stitches may then be worked if desired 2cm. (¾in.) out from woven centre. To finish, weave end into back of work.

To join motifs, place together with right sides facing inwards, then oversew the loops and secure. Join all the motifs in a similar manner.

By Carol Payton

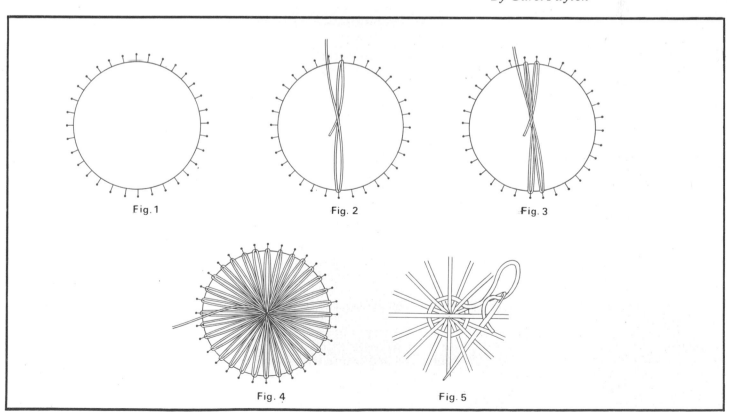

Fig. 1

Fig. 2

Fig. 3

Fig. 4

Fig. 5

Tenerife lace collar

Neck edging

Thread the needle with a length of yarn, and with right side of work facing, attach the yarn to the fourth loop from the motif joining on the first motif. Tie a knot with the end of the yarn, then knot the yarn into the second loop 6mm. (¼in.) from the previous knot. *Knot together the two remaining loops on the motif and the first two loops on the next motif 6mm. (¼in.) from the previous knot, (make a knot into next loop 6mm. (¼in.) from the previous knot) four times; rep. from * to end, omitting two knots at the end of last repeat. Fasten off.

Pin collar into shape and lightly press with a hot iron over a damp cloth.

By Carol Payton

If you have read page 91, you may like to try a project in Tenerife lace. This pretty collar in metallic yarn can be made very quickly and easily, and really does look rather special.

You will need
1 ball of lightweight metallic yarn
1 tapestry needle
A piece of cork, thick cardboard or polystyrene
Dressmaker's pins

To make the foundation threads
Draw a circle 5cm. (2in.) in diameter on the cork, card or tile. Place 32 pins round it and wind the yarn round them as explained on page 91. Cut yarn 90cm. (36in.) from work.

Thread the end of the yarn into the tapestry needle and weave over and under the foundation threads for two rounds around the centre of the motif. Push the weaving well into the centre to keep the work firm.

Last round
Insert needle under the next two threads with the yarn under the tip of the needle and draw it tight (Fig. 1 and 2). Continue in the same way all round. To complete the round, insert needle through the first stitch made on this round (Fig. 3), draw tight and secure. Carefully remove the motif from the pins.

Make nine more motifs to match in the same way. This will fit the average neck fairly closely; if you want a lower collar it will have to be longer, so you will need to make extra motifs.

To join up the motifs
Lay the motifs side by side, all with their right sides facing. Thread the needle with a length of yarn. Take the first and second motifs and place right sides and loops together. Then, working through double thickness throughout, thread the yarn through the first loop and secure by tying a knot. Thread the needle through next loop (Fig. 4), pass it back over and through the loop just made (Fig. 5) and draw the yarn up to within 6mm. (¼in.) of the previous knot. Repeat this twice more, and fasten off.

Place the second and third motifs with right sides and loops together, miss the next eight loops on the second motif for the neck edge, and tie the yarn to next loop (Fig. 6). Join the second and third motifs as before. Continue in this way until all motifs have been joined together.

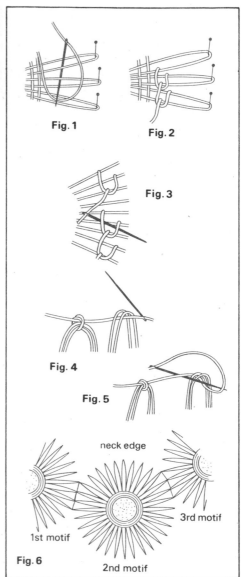

Fig. 1

Fig. 2

Fig. 3

Fig. 4

Fig. 5

neck edge

1st motif

3rd motif

2nd motif

Fig. 6

Beaded crochet flowers

These pretty little flowers have hundreds of uses. They make lovely hair decorations for a bride and bridesmaids, or for a young child's party outfit. They can be used as motifs sewn on to an existing dress, thus giving it a new look. Or you could use them as part of an artificial flower display, with tissue paper flowers.

You will need
1 ball of light-weight mercerised crochet cotton (several flowers can be made from one ball)
12 small beads, small piece fuse wire
1 U-shaped hair pin for each flower (if using as hair decoration)
ISR crochet hook, 2.5mm.

If you have not done crochet before, first read page 75.

To make a flower
Thread twelve beads on to yarn. To do this take a piece of fine fuse wire about 10cm. (4in.) long, loop this round the yarn, fold it in half and twist the two ends of fuse wire together. Now thread the beads on to the fuse wire and push down on to the yarn (see diagram). This is an ideal method for threading beads on to a thick thread.

Put the yarn round your finger once to form a ring.

1st Round
1 d.c. into ring, (drop a bead down behind work, 1 d.c. into commencing ring) 11 times, drop last bead down behind work, end with 1 sl.st. into back loop only of next d.c. Draw commencing ring right, and then turn.

2nd Round
Working into front loops only, make *(1 h.tr., 3tr., 1 h.tr.) into next d.c., 1 sl.st. into next d.c., rep. from * 4 times more, ending with (1 h.tr., 3 tr., 1 h.tr.) into last d.c., 1 d.c. into back loop of next d.c.

3rd Round
Working into back loops only of 1st round make * (1 tr., 4 d.tr., 1 tr.) into next d.c., 1 d.c. into next d.c., rep. from * 4 times more, ending with (1 tr., 4d.tr., 1 tr.) into last d.c., 1 sl.st. into first d.c. Fasten off.

To complete
Darn in all ends. Thread the U-shaped hairpin through the back of the flower at the centre. The hair pin is now decorated and ready for use.

Carol Payton

Crochet shawl

This lovely warm shawl is in an easy crochet stitch and won't take you too long to finish. It is made in a light-weight mohair, a soft, slightly fluffy yarn which comes in a range of lovely pastel shades.

You will need
8 balls light-weight mohair yarn
Crochet hook No. 5.50mm.

Measurements
Depth excluding fringe 91cm. (36in.)

Tension
2 patt. to 6.35cm. (2½in.)
It is essential to test your tension by working the first few rows before starting the pattern. If your tension is tight use a size larger hook, if loose use a size finer hook. Provided the tension quoted is obtained then your measurements will be the same as those given.

Note
The abbreviations and the basic crochet technique are given on pages 75 and 79.

To make the shawl
Commencing from lower corner, make 4 ch.
Foundation row 3 tr. into 4th ch. from hook, turn.
1st row 6 ch., 1 tr. into first tr., 1 ch., (1 tr., 2 ch., 1 d. tr.) into 3rd of 3 ch., turn.
2nd row 4 ch., 3 tr. into first d. tr., 1 ch., 4 tr. into next 1 ch. sp., 1 ch., (3 tr., 1 d. tr.) into 4th of 6 ch., turn.
3rd row 6 ch., 1 tr. into first tr., * (1 ch., 1 tr., 2 ch., 1 tr.) into next 1 ch. sp., rep. from * ending with 1 ch., (1 tr., 2 ch., 1 d. tr.) into 4th of 4 ch., turn.
4th row 4 ch., 3 tr. into first d. tr., * 1 ch., 4 tr. into next 1 ch. sp., rep. from * ending with 1 ch.,(3 tr., 1 d. tr.) into 4th of 6 ch., turn.
Rep. last 2 rows until work measures 76cm. (30in.) from beginning, ending with a 3rd row.
Last row 4 ch., 3 tr. into first d. tr., * 3 ch., 1 sl.st. into last tr. made, 4 tr. into next 1 ch. sp., rep. from * ending with 3 ch. 1 sl.st. into last tr. made, (3 tr., 1 d. tr.) into 4th of 6 ch. Fasten off.
Edging With right side facing, attach yarn to top corner, (1 d.c., 2 ch., 1 tr.) into same place as join, (1 tr., 3 ch., 1 tr.) into each row-end down side and up other side. Fasten off.
Fringe Cut remaining yarn into 46cm. (18in.) lengths, then with 6 thicknesses, make a tassel into every 2 ch. sp. made.

Hairpin table centre

This pretty, festive-looking table centre is made in the hairpin crochet technique shown on page 89 combined with ordinary crochet.

You will need
2 balls lightweight metallic yarn
1 hairpin prong 6cm. (2½in.)
1 2mm. crochet hook

Abbreviations
The standard crochet abbreviations will be found on page 75.

To make the mat
With crochet hook make 8 ch. Sl.st. to form ring.
1st round 3 ch., 23 tr. into ring, sl.st. to top of 3 ch.
2nd round 4 ch., 1 tr., 1 ch. in each tr., sl.st. to top of 4 ch.
3rd round Sl.st. in next sp., 6 ch., 1 d.c. in next space. Rep. all round. Sl.st. into 1st sl.st. to close.
4th round 1 d.c. in next space, 6 ch., 1 d.c. in next space, rep. all round. Sl.st. into 1st d.c. (24 sp.)
Make hairpin strip of 96 loops.

5th round Join strip to mat thus: sl.st. over 3 ch. on next sp., 3 ch., 1 d.c. over 4 loops of strip, 3 ch., 1 d.c. in next sp. Continue in this way all round. Sl.st. into 1st d.c. Join strip.
6th round Anchor thread to 3 loops with d.c., 6 ch., rep. all round. Sl.st. to 1st d.c.
7th round Sl.st. over 2 ch. of a 6 ch. loop. 5 ch., 1 d.c. in same sp., 5 ch., 1 d.c. in same sp., cont. making 2 loops in each 6 ch. sp. (65 sp.)
8th and 9th rounds Repeat 7th round (make a strip of 260 loops).
10th round Sl.st. over 2 ch. of next 5 ch. sp., 1 d.c. over 4 loops of strip. 1 d.c. in next sp., rep. all round, sl.st. to 1st d.c. Join strip neatly, leave other side of strip free. Pin out to shape, cover with a damp cloth for two to three hours. Lift off damp cloth and leave to dry.

Geese table centre

If you enjoy crochet and want a change from flat shapes, you will love this original table centre with its four geese, which are made by stiffening and stuffing the crocheted shapes.

You will need
2 balls light-weight mercerised crochet cotton
Small amount contrast for beak
8 sequins for eyes

Abbreviations
The standard crochet abbreviations are given on page 75.

Centre mat
8 ch., sl.st. to form a ring.
1st round 3ch., 23 tr. into ring. Sl.st. to top of 3 ch.
2nd round 5 ch., miss 1 tr., 1 tr. into next tr. (2ch., miss 1 tr., 1 tr. into next tr.) 10 times, 2 ch., sl.st. into 3rd of 4 ch., 12 sp.
3rd round Sl.st. into sp., 3 ch., 2 tr., 3 ch., 3 tr. into same sp. as sl.st. (3ch., miss one sp., 3 tr., 3 ch., 3 tr.) into next sp. 5 times, 3 ch., sl.st. to top of 3 ch. to close.
4th round 6 ch., 3 tr. into centre sp. of gr., 3 ch., 4 tr. between gr., rep. all round, finishing with 3 tr. and sl.st. into 3rd of 6 ch.
5th round 7 ch. (1 tr. in each of the next 3 tr., 4 ch., 1 tr. in each of the next 3 tr. and 2 tr. in the next tr. 4 ch.) all round, ending with 4 tr. and sl.st. into 3rd of 7 ch.

6th round 8 ch. (1 tr. in each of the next 3 tr., 5 ch., 1 tr. in each of the next 4 tr., 2 tr. in the next tr., 5 ch.) all round, ending with 5 tr. and sl.st. into 3rd of 8 ch.
7th round 9 ch. (1 tr. in each of the next 5 tr., 2 tr. in next tr., 6 ch.) all round, ending with 6 tr. and sl.st. into 3rd of 9 ch.
8th round 10 ch. (1 tr. in each of next 3 tr., 7 ch., 1 tr. in ech of next 6 tr., 2 tr. in next tr., 7 ch.) all round, ending with 7 tr. and sl.st. into 3rd. of 10 ch.
9th round 11 ch. (1 tr. in each of next 3 tr., 8 ch., 1 tr. in each of next 7 tr., 2 tr. in next tr., 8 ch.) all round, ending with 8 tr. and sl.st. into 3rd of 11 ch.
10th round 12 ch. (1 tr. in each of next 3 tr., 9 ch., 1 tr. in each of next 8 tr., 2 tr. in next tr., 9 ch.) all round, ending with 9 tr. and sl.st. into 3rd of 12 ch.
11th round Sl.st. into next 2 ch., 6 ch., miss 2 ch., 1 tr. in next ch. (3 ch. miss 2 ch., 1 tr. in next ch.) all round, sl.st. into 3rd. of 6 ch.
12th round Sl. st. into next st. and into sp., 7 ch. (1 tr. into next sp. 4 ch.) all round, sl.st. into 3rd of 7 ch. Fasten off and press.

Body
Commence with 60 ch. 1 d.c. into 3rd ch. from hook. 1 d.c. in each d.c. to end 2 ch., turn.
2nd row 1 d.c. in each d.c. to end, 2 ch., turn.

3rd and 4th rows As 2nd row.
6th row Sl.st. over 5 d.c., 1 d.c. in each d.c., leaving last 4 d.c. unworked, 2 ch., turn.
6th, 7th and 8th rows As 2nd row
9th row As 5th row
10th, 11th and 12th rows As 2nd row
13th row As 5th row
14th, 15th and 16th rows As 2nd row. Fasten off.

Fold in half, sew together to within 2.5cm. (1in.). Attach thread to join at tail end, (7ch., 1 d.c. in next point) 3 times more, (4ch., miss 3 d.c., 1 d.c. in next d.c.) 8 times more, 7 ch. and 1 d.c. in each point to complete round.
Next round Sl.st. into next 3 ch. and into loop. 7 ch. 1 d.c. in each loop to end. Fasten off.

Head
Commence with 15 ch., 1 d.c. into 3rd ch. from hook. 1 d.c. to end, 2 ch., turn. 13 d.c.
2nd row 1 d.c. into next 11 d.c., 2 d.c. in next d.c., 1 d.c. in top of turning ch., 2 ch., turn. 14 d.c.
3rd row 1 d.c. into each d.c. to end, 2 ch., turn.
4th row 1 d.c. into next 12 d.c., 3 d.c. in next d.c., 1 d.c. in top of turning ch., 2 ch., turn. 16 d.c.
5th row As 3rd row.
6th row 1 d.c. into next 14 d.c., 3 d.c. in next d.c., 1 d.c. in top of turning ch., 2 d.c., turn. 18 d.c.
7th row As 3rd row.
8th row 1 d.c. into next 14 d.c. Dec. 2 in next d.c., 1 d.c. in top of turning ch., 2 ch., turn, 16 d.c.
9th row As 3rd row.
10th row 1 d.c. into next 12 d.c. Dec. 2 in next d.c., 1 d.c. in top of turning ch.
11th row As 3rd row. Fasten off.

Back
Attach contrast thread to edge of shaped end and work 10 d.c., 2 ch., turn. Dec. 1 st. each end of every row, reducing to 2 d.c. Fasten off. Join neck and beak, gathering slightly under the head part. Sew head to body. Sew on sequins for eyes. Make 3 more geese. Starch, pull and pin into shape. Place a little terylene stuffing into neck, head, beak and body to firm. Remove when thoroughly dry. Attach geese to mat at equal distances.

Shawl in hairpin lace

This attractive shawl is marvellous to wear over an evening dress but should you wish to make one as a gift for a relative or friend and you're uncertain whether it will be used for evening wear, the silver lurex can be omitted. The shawl can be worked in three sizes, 7 bands short, 8 bands average and 9 bands tall. The abbreviations used can be found on page 75.

You will need
225g. (8oz.) 4-ply white yarn
1 hairpin frame 6.5cm. (2½in.)
3.50 crochet hook
1 reel silver lurex thread
1 piece card 15cm. (6in.) wide, for fringe

To work the shawl
1st band (60 loops). Slip loops off the frame carefully and work 7 ch. pick up 15 loops tog. with 1 d.c., 5 ch., 30 loops tog., 5 ch., 15 loops tog., 7 ch., 1 d.c., in centre of band at end, 7 ch., continue working down second side by picking up 3 loops tog., with 1 d.c., and 5 ch., between 7 ch., join with sl.st. to the base of first 7 ch. Fasten off and work ends in. Roll the band carefully to use later.
Important. All bands are worked by this method. The first side varies according to the number of loops in the band. The second side of every band is worked with 3 loops tog., with 1 d.c., and 5 ch., between. The ends of every band are closed with two lengths of 7 ch., joined in the centre.
2nd band (114 loops). On first side join 15 loops tog., 3 loops tog., 9 times, 30 loops tog., 3 loops tog., 9 times, 15 loops tog.
3rd band (162 loops). On first side join 15 loops tog., 3 loops tog., 17 times, 30 loops tog., 3 loops tog., 17 times, 15 loops tog.
4th band (216 loops). On first side join 15 loops tog., 3 loops tog., 26 times, 30 loops tog., 3 loops tog., 26 times, 15 loops tog.
5th band (264 loops). On first side join 15 loops tog., 3 loops tog., 34 times, 30 loops tog., 3 loops tog., 34 times, 15 loops tog.
6th band (318 loops). On first side join 15 loops tog., 3 loops tog., 43 times, 30 loops tog., 3 loops tog., 43 times, 15 loops tog.
7th band (366 loops). On first side join 15 loops tog., 3 loops tog., 51 times, 30 loops tog., 3 loops tog., 51 times, 15 loops tog.
8th band (420 loops). On first side join 15

loops tog., 3 loops tog., 60 times, 30 loops tog., 3 loops tog., 60 times, 15 loops tog.
9th band (468 loops). On first side join 15 loops tog., 3 loops tog., 68 times, 30 loops tog., 3 loops tog., 68 times, 15 loops tog.

To join bands
Work with wool and lurex thread together. The shaped side of band 2 is joined to the edge of band 1. That is, worked in groups of 3. Join yarn to centre of 30 loops on band 2, 5 ch., 1 d.c., in centre loop of the 30 loops on band. 5 ch., 1 d.c., in next loop on band 2, 1 d.c., in next loop on band 1, continue in this way to end.

Turn work over and again join yarn to centre of 30 loops on band 2, 5 ch., 1 d.c., in centre loop of 30 loops on band 1 (there are now two lengths of 5 ch., joining bands 1 and 2 in the centre). 5 ch., 1 d.c., in next loop on band 2, 5 ch., 1 d.c., in next loop on band 1, continue to end, fasten off. Work all ends in.

Each band is joined in the same way. By joining each half separately, you will

be certain to keep the 30 loops in the centre of the shawl, which is the beauty of this design.

To work the bottom, attach yarn to right hand corners, work 11 ch., and 1 d.c., in each 5 ch., loop. When you have reached the left hand corners, continue along top working a row of d.c. to firm the edge. Work a 2nd row along bottom with 5 ch., and 1 d.c., in each 11 ch., loop. It is in these 5 ch., loops you put the fringe. Fasten off and work all ends in.

Fringe
Take yarn 6 times round the card loosely and cut. Slip off the card and keeping the loops tog. draw one end a little way through the 5 ch., loop, thereby forming a small loop. Pass the other end of fringe through this loop and pull tight. Repeat in each 5 ch., loop. Cut ends of fringe.

Crochet jewellery

It is quite amazing the number of uses crochet can be put to and this lovely necklace and pendant are a good example of the versatility of the craft. The jewellery is quick and inexpensive to make and would be ideal for bazaars or gifts. If you have never done crochet before, be sure to read the basic instructions which are given on page 75.

You will need
1 ball light-weight metallic yarn (gold)
2.5mm. crochet hook
13-2.5cm. (1in.) curtain rings
1-3.8cm. (1½in.) curtain rings
1 decorative button
small piece white card
strong white paper same size as card
1 safety pin
clear household glue

Abbreviations: ch. chain, d.c. double crochet.

To make the pendant
Cover the 13 smaller curtain rings by working directly into the ring as many d.c. that are required to completely cover each ring. Lay the finished covered rings on a flat surface to form the design. When you are satisfied with the design, stitch together where necessary very neatly on the wrong side. Make a ch. of required length and sew neatly to each of the end rings.

To make the brooch
Cover the remaining curtain ring with d.c. Using the glue, stick button (which should fit on the inside edge of worked curtain ring) on to the ring. Cut a circle of

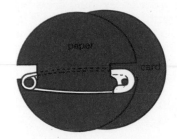

card, slightly smaller than the back of the brooch. Cut a circle of strong white paper the same size as the card. Make a small cut in the paper on each side of the circle and place the safety pin behind it as in the diagram. Stick paper to card which will then secure the pin in position. Stick card to back of curtain ring.

Apron with crochet motifs

This pretty gingham apron has that special fresh and clean look which will make it a pleasure to wear.

You will need
1m. (1yd.) polyester gingham (blue)
2 balls No. 20 fine mercerised crochet cotton (white)
Crochet hook 1.25mm.
Sewing cotton and needle

Abbreviations
The standard crochet abbreviations are given on page 75.

To work each motif
10ch., join with sl.st. to form a ring.
1st row 4 ch., 14 d.tr. into ring, sl.st. to top of 4 ch., turn. (15 d.tr.)
2nd row Rep. 1st row, turn.
3rd row Rep. 1st row, but increase 1 d.tr. at each end of row, turn. (17 d.tr.)
4th row 4 ch., 1 d.tr. into 1st sp. * miss 1 sp., 2 ch., 1 d.tr. into next 2 sp. * rep. from * to * to end, turn.
5th row 4 ch. 1 d.tr. into 1st sp., * 6 d.tr. into next sp., 1 d.c. into next sp., * rep. from * to * to end, turn.
6th row 5 ch., 1 d.c. into d.c. between 1st and 2nd scallop, 5 ch., 1 d.c. into next d.c., turn.
7th row 4 ch., 9 d.tr. into each sp., 1 d.tr. into 1st ch., turn.
8th row 4 ch., 20 d.tr., turn (21 d.tr.)
9th row As 8th row.
10th row (Waist) sl.st. 7., 3 ch., 8 tr., turn. (Make sure waist is in centre of row).
11th row 4 ch., 9 d.tr., turn (10 d.tr.)
12th row 4 ch., then as row 11, but increase 1 d.tr. at each end, turn (12 d.tr.)
13th row 4 ch., 11 d.tr. with 1 ch. between, turn.
14th row As 13th row, but increase 1 d.tr. at each end and 2 ch. between, turn.
15th row 4 ch., 2 d.tr. into 1st sp. 3 d.tr. into each sp. to end, ending with 1 d.tr. into last sp. and 1 in top of turning ch., turn.
16th row (Skirt) 3 ch., 1 tr. 1 ch. 2 tr. into sp. 1 ch., miss 3 sp. (2 tr. 1 ch. 2 tr.) into next sp., 1 ch., rep. to end, turn. (10 patterns)
17th row As 16th row, but 3 ch. between gr.
18th row As 16th row, but with 4 ch. between each gr.
19 - 22nd row As 18th row.
23rd row 3 ch., 1 tr., 1 ch., 2 tr. into 1 ch. sp., * 4 ch., 1 d.c. over the 2 previous rows, 4 ch., (2 tr. 1 ch. 2 tr.) into next 1

ch. sp., * rep. from * to * to end. Fasten off.
Make 5 motifs and put to one side.

To make the edging
Attach cotton to 1st blanket stitch, * 3 ch., miss 2 st., into next st. work 5 d.tr., with picot between, 3 ch., miss 2 st., 1 d.c., into next st. * Rep. from * to * for length required.

To make up the apron
From the gingham, cut pieces as follows:
1 piece 46cm. by 92cm. (18in. by 36in.) for the apron
2 pieces 15cm. by 15cm. (6in. by 6in.) for the pockets
1 piece 15cm. by 51cm. (6in. by 20in.) when folded and turned makes a 6.3cm. (2½in.) band.
2 pieces 5cm. by 61cm. (2in. by 24in.) for the ties.
Make up the apron in the usual way but before putting on the pockets, turn and sew a hem 2.5cm. (1in.) wide, across the top of both pockets. Round off the bottom corners, turn and tack a narrow hem round the remaining raw edges. Work this edge with blanket stitch as a base for the lace edging. Work the edging and sew pockets to apron.

Work both sides of apron with blanket stitch, then work edging as for pockets. Sew motifs along bottom edge of apron joining each edge of skirt. Allow the skirts to form a scalloped edge along the bottom of apron. Sew remaining edges of motifs to apron.

Looped hat

The wool used for this hat is very thick and warm. As a close fabric is required, it is necessary to work a loop in every stitch of a loop line. Should a finer fabric be required, work in alternate stitches with a double crochet between.

You will need
115g. (4oz.) 4 ply random-dyed wool
Small quantity of contrast wool for peak
4.50mm. crochet hook

Note
The abbreviations and basic crochet techniques are given on pages 75 and 79.

Special abbreviations
y.r.h. yarn round hook.

Loop. Insert hook in next d.c. Hold yarn across first and second fingers of the left hand. Extend yarn to required length by lifting the second finger, keeping hook to the right of the yarn over the fingers, place the hook round the yarn lying between second and third fingers. Draw loop through d.c. now take the hook to the left of the yarn over the fingers, y.r.h. from main ball, and draw through both loops on hook. Remove second finger from hook and repeat.

To work the hat
Make 72ch. join with sl.st. to the first chain to form a circle.
1st round 2 ch. to stand for first d.c., 1 d.c. in each chain to end, join with sl.st. to top of 2 ch.
Repeat round one twice.
4th round This and every alternate round is worked in loops (see abbreviations).
5th round This and every alternate round is worked in d.c.
Repeat 4th and 5th round four times more.
14th round Loops
15th round Dec. every 12 d.c.
16th round Loops
17th round Dec. every 11 d.c.
18th round Loops
19th round Dec. every 10 d.c.
20th round Loops
21st round Dec. every 9 d.c.
22nd round Loops

23rd round Dec. every 8 d.c.
24th round Loops
25th round Dec. every 4 d.c.
26th round Loops
27th round Dec. every 3 d.c.
Then dec. every 2 d.c. until ring is closed. Fasten off.

To make the peak
1st round With right side towards you attach wool to any d.c. on first round. Work 1 d.c. in every stitch half way round the brim. Turn.
2nd round Sl.st. 3 st. 1 d.c. in each d.c. leaving 3 st. unworked at end. Turn.
3rd round Repeat 2nd round.
Fasten off.
4th round Attach wool to first stitch of brim. Work 1 d.c. right round edge of hat. Sl. st. into first d.c.
Fasten off.

Tatted compact cover

If you have never tried tatting before first read pages 77 and 78. It is worth persevering with this craft as some very pretty designs can be worked.

You will need
1 ball No. 20 fine mercerised crochet cotton in main colour
1 ball No. 20 fine mercerised crochet cotton in contrasting colour
Tatting shuttle
Piece of fabric 20cm. by 11cm. (7¾in. by 4¼in.)
Piece of lining 20cm. by 11cm. (7¾in. by 4¼in.)
Pearls or beads to decorate
Polyester thread

Measurements
Finished size of tatting is 7.5cm. (3in.) square.
Finished size of cover is 9cm. (3½in.) square.

Abbreviations
ds. – double stitch; r. – ring(s); ch. – chain; p. – picot(s); sep. – separated; cl. – close; rw. reverse work; rep. – repeat; M. – main colour; C. – contrasting colour.

To work the tatting
1st Row: Tie ball of M. and shuttle of C. together. R. of 8 ds., p., 8 ds., cl., rw. Ch. of 6 ds., p., 6 ds., rw. * R. of 8 ds., join to p. on previous r., 8 ds., cl. (R. of 8 ds., p., 8 ds., cl.) 3 times, rw. Ch. of 6 ds., join to p. on previous ch., 6 ds., rw. (Corner). (R. of 8 ds., join to p. on previous r., 8 ds., cl. R. of 8 ds., p., 8 ds., cl., rw. Ch. of 6 ds., p., 6 ds., rw.) twice; rep. from * three times more omitting a r. and a ch. at end of last rep., join by shuttle thread to base of first r. Tie ends, cut and oversew neatly on wrong side.
2nd Row: Tie ball and shuttle of M. together. Attach by shuttle thread to first joining of r. on previous row. * Ch. of 10ds., join to next corner p., 8 ds., join to next corner p. (Ch. of 10ds., join to joining of next 2 r.) 3 times; rep. from * 3 times more working last join into same place as first.
3rd Row: * Ch. of 4 ds., 5 p. sep. by 2 ds., 4 ds., join to same place as next joining on previous row; rep. from * 19 times more. Tie ends, cut and oversew neatly on wrong side.
Damp and pin out to measurements.

To make up
1cm. (⅜in.) has been allowed for seams on fabric and lining.

Fold fabric section in half, right sides together, short ends meeting. Stitch short sides. Turn to the right side. Sew on tatting and pearls or beads. Make up lining in the same way but do not turn to the right side. Place lining inside main section, turn in top edges and sew in position.

Lunch mats

These delightful lunch mats look superb on laminated and other shiny surfaces. The quantity of yarn given is sufficient for two mats.

You will need
4 balls No. 10 mercerised crochet cotton (20g.) in main colour (M)
4 balls No. 10 mercerised crochet cotton (20g.) in contrasting colour (C)
Steel crochet hook 1.50 (No. 2½) (if your crochet is loose use a size finer hook, if tight, use a size larger hook)

Tension
Width of strip, 5.5cm. (2in.)

Measurements
Finished size, 30cm. by 38.5cm. (11¾in. by 15in.)

Abbreviations
These can be found on page 75.

First Strip
Using C commence with 9 ch.
1st Row * 1 tr. into 7th ch. from hook – 1 pct. made at end of strip, 11 ch. 1 h.tr. into 5th ch. from hook, 1 h.tr. into each of next 4 ch. * (16 ch. 1 h.tr. into 5th ch. from hook, 1 h.tr. into each of next four ch.) 15 times, 9 ch. rep. from * to * once more, work along opposite side of strip, ** 3 ch. 1 tr. into centre ch. on next 7 ch. sp. on first side, 12 ch., 1 h.tr. into 5th ch. from hook, 1 h.tr. into each of next 4 ch; rep. from ** 14 times more, 1 sl.st. into first ch. Fasten off.
2nd Row Attach M. to 1 p.c.t. at first end of strip, 6 ch. 1 d.c. into 4th ch. from hook – a pct. made ** 1 tr. into same 1 pct., 1 d.c. into last tr. – another pct. made, into same 1 pct. work (1 tr., a pct.) 6 times and 1 tr. 2 ch. miss 1 tr. 1 d.c. into each of next 7 st. * 2 ch. remove 1 pct. from hook. Insert hook into last tr. made and draw dropped 1 pct. through – a joining st. made, into next 1 pct. on previous row work (1 tr. a pct.) 4 times and 1 tr. 2 ch. 1 d.c. into each of next 8 st., miss next st. 1 d.c. into each of next 8 st.; rep. from * along side omitting 9 d.c. at end of last rep., 2 ch. a joining st. into last tr. made, 1 tr. into next 1 pct. a pct.rep. from ** along opposite side omitting 1 tr. and a pct. at end of rep. 1 s.s. into 3rd of 6th ch. Fasten off.

Second Strip
Work as first strip until 10 pct. have been made on 2nd row, * (1 tr. into same 1 pct. 1 ch. 1 s.s. into corresponding pct. on first strip, 1 ch. 1 d.c. into last tr. made on second strip (a joining pct. made) twice. * 1 tr. into same 1 pct. cont. as first strip until next pct. has been made; rep. from * to * once more, ** cont. as first strip until next 2 pct. have been made; rep. from * to * once more; rep. from ** 12 times more, cont. as first strip until next joining st. has been made. Into next 1 pct. work (1 tr. a joining pct.) twice. Complete as first strip.
Make 5 more strips joining each as second strip was joined to first.

Embroidery stitches

We shall be giving you patterns and suggestions for embroidery on other pages, but first you must know how to do the basic stitches, illustrated on the right. Practise these on a piece of fabric in a hoop until you can do them easily.

Outline stitches

Stem stitch. This can be used as an outline, and is ideal for the stems of flowers. Work from left to right, taking regular, slightly slanting stitches. The thread is kept below the needle and always emerges on the left side of the previous stitch.

Back stitch. Working from right to left, bring thread through on stitch line, insert it a short step back and bring it out again at an equal distance from starting point.

Running stitch. Working from right to left, pass needle over and under fabric, making upper stitches of equal length. The under stitches should be half the length of the upper, but also of equal length.

Laced running stitch. As above, but laced with a contrasting colour. Use a round pointed needle for lacing and do not pick up fabric.

Flat stitches

Straight stitch. Bring needle out at beginning of stitch, insert at end and bring out again ready for next stitch. The stitches can be of varying size, but must not be either too long or too loose.

Satin stitch. This is straight stitch worked closely together across the shape. Keep stitches parallel. Do not make them too long as they will pull. Satin stitch can be padded by working running or chain stitch underneath first.

Long and short stitch. This is the same as satin stitch, but the stitches are of varying lengths. In the first row stitches alternately long and short are used and in the following rows the stitches are of even length. This is generally used for shading effects.

Fishbone stitch. Make a small stitch at top of centre line. Bring thread through at side of shape and make diagonal stitch to just across central line. Bring thread up at other side and make a similar diagonal stitch to overlap first one at centre. Used for filling small shapes.

Chevron stitch. Bring thread through on lower line, insert a little to right and take a small stitch to the left emerging halfway between stitch being made. Now insert needle on top line a little to right and bring out just to left on top line. Insert again to right and bring out at centre of

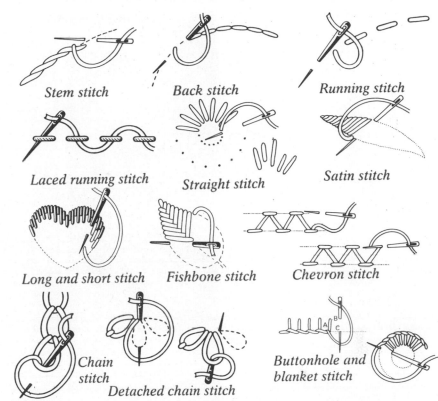

Stem stitch   *Back stitch*   *Running stitch*

Laced running stitch   *Straight stitch*   *Satin stitch*

Long and short stitch   *Fishbone stitch*   *Chevron stitch*

Chain stitch   *Detached chain stitch*   *Buttonhole and blanket stitch*

stitch. Continue to work alternately. Used as line or filling.

Looped stitches

Chain stitch. Bring thread out at top of line and hold down with left thumb. Insert needle and bring it half way out a short space down the line. Before pulling it through, pass thread under point of needle. Now pull through, forming a loop. Start next stitch inside loop.

Detached chain stitch (daisy chain stitch)

Work in the same way as chain stitch but fasten each loop down with a small stitch. This can be worked in groups to form flower petals.

Buttonhole and blanket stitches. Bring thread out on lower line (A), insert needle at top (B) and bring out again directly underneath (C), holding thread under needle. The only difference between blanket and buttonhole stitch is that for buttonhole stitch the stitches are worked close together.

Bird of paradise

of the large pink flower on the bird's tail are worked in long straight stitches. Work the design, following the colour key. If stranded embroidery threads are being used, use three strands throughout.

Dry press the finished embroidery on the wrong side, setting the iron to the correct heat for the background fabric.

Mounting the picture

Lay the embroidered material on a flat surface, wrong side up. Place the card mount on top, centring it. Cut off the corners of the material diagonally, 3mm (⅛in.) away from the mount corners. Spread a band of glue around the edges of the mount and turn the edges of the embroidery on to it. Press the fabric down firmly. Check the right side of the embroidery to make sure that the design is still centred and straight. Smooth any excess fabric to the back so that the picture fits the mount neatly. Leave to dry under a weight, such as a large book, until the glue has dried.

Other ways of using the design

The Bird of Paradise design would make a pair of matching cushions. Reverse the tracing for one cushion so that the birds are looking towards each other. The design could also be worked on a magazine cover or, using crewel wools on even-weave linen for a firescreen. You might also try a toned colour scheme for a different effect.

This delightful embroidered picture is worked on a yellow felt background, but a woven fabric would be equally suitable – cotton or cotton mixture, linen or even silk for a rich effect. Only three basic embroidery stitches are used, chain stitch, satin stitch and straight stitches.

A pattern for the embroidery appears on the opposite page.

You will need

Piece of stiff cardboard for the mount, 40cm. by 27cm. (16½in. by 10½in.)
Yellow felt or fabric for the background, 47cm. by 32cm. (18½in. by 12½in.)
Soft embroidery threads or stranded embroidery threads in the following colours (1 skein of each): parrot green, laurel green, moss green, light cyclamen, violet, dark cyclamen, old rose, chestnut, amber gold, black
Clear all-purpose adhesive

Tracing paper and blue dressmaker's carbon paper
Embroidery needle
Pencil

To work the picture

Trace the outline and pattern lines from the separate pattern sheet. You will see that the lines of the embroidery are keyed to the numbers of the embroidery threads.

Transfer the design on to the fabric by the following method. Tape the material flat to a table, place the carbon paper face down on top, and the tracing on top of that. Make sure the three layers are firmly held together and the design is placed in the centre of the fabric. Now trace the design with a sharp pencil, using an even pressure.

The design is worked mostly in chain stitch, satin stitch being used for the flower centres and the bird's beak (see page 103 for stitches). The petal details

Turning the fabric on to the card, trimming the corners diagonally.

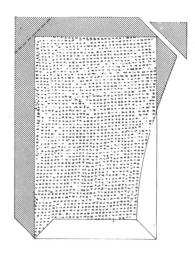

Bird of paradise

Colour key

1 Parrot Green
2 Laurel Green
3 Moss Green
4 Light Cyclamen
5 Violet
6 Dark Cyclamen
7 Old Rose
8 Chestnut
9 Amber Gold
10 Black

Smocking

Smocking is a form of decorative needle-work in which material is gathered and held with small stitches. It is the easiest of all embroidery stitches, and possibly the most useful, as the gathering gives an elasticity to the fabric so that it can be shaped to make all kinds of clothes and accessories.

The smock was one of the earliest and most widely used articles of dress, and it is from this garment that the word smock-ing comes. The labourer's smock was quite plain until, during the 18th century, it evidently occurred to someone that the loose folds of material, which tended to impede the wearer, could be gathered and the fabric made thicker and more weatherproof by stitching.

Method

The purpose of smocking is to contain gathers, and the most important rule is accurate and even gathering. The dis-tance between each row of gathers must also be even. Smocking spots are a useful aid; these are sold in sheets, and are ironed on to the wrong side of the material, pro-ducing accurate lines which can be picked up by the needle and thread. However, they are not always easy to obtain, so it is advisable to practise smocking methods on a cotton fabric with a small check pattern. The gathering is then worked along the lines of the check.

The gathering is done as follows. Take a fine sewing needle with strong cotton in a contrasting colour to the fabric. Cut the thread a few inches longer than the width of the fabric—the thread must never be joined in the middle of a row of gather-ing. Knot one end. Work from right to left, first making a backstitch to secure the thread. Pass the needle under one check and through the next, and continue in this way across the fabric. Leave the end of the thread hanging loose, and start a new one for the next row. Each row is worked in the same way, with the thread passing under the same check and through the next. Make sure that the spaces between rows are absolutely even. When all the rows are completed, gather the loose threads together and gently push the gathers back towards the knots. When they are back as far as they can go, pull on each individual thread until the gathers are side by side. These small folds are known as reeds. If the gathers are far apart there is more material between the reeds and consequently less stretch; if close together there is maximum stretch.

When buying material for smocking, calculate that the finished work gathers into only about one third of the original width, so cut the material three times the width required. Widths of fabric can, of course, be joined.

The stretch is also affected by the stitch used. The most frequently used stitches are stem stitch, which is tight hold; cable stitch (medium hold), and surface honey-comb, the loosest hold. Stem stitch is worked in the same way as for surface embroidery (see page 103) but each stitch takes up one reed. Start at the left side of the work, keeping the thread below the needle at each stitch. Cable stitch (Fig. 1) is worked in the same way, but the thread is laid first on one side of the needle and then on the other alter-nately. Surface honeycomb (chevron in surface embroidery) is worked in the fol-lowing way. Take a stitch through the left-hand reed, then through the next reed. Pull them together, so that a straight stitch lies over both reeds. Take the thread over and up the right-hand reed to the level of the next row of gathering thread, take a stitch through this reed, then through the next reed, and pull these together. You will now have another straight stitch across two reeds and two threads which come out between them (Fig. 2).

In Fig. 3, surface honeycomb is worked over 3 rows of gathering and become Vandykes.

Uses

Smocking can be used in a variety of dif-ferent ways and for many different things. It is, of course, ideal for children's clothes, as it stretches to fit the growing child, provided the tight stem stitch has not been used lower down in the band of smocking. A smocked top for an apron looks very attractive, and is more prac-tical than gathers, while smocking is in-valuable on a maternity dress below a short yoke. The same dress can later be worn with a belt.

But smocking need not only be used for clothes: on page 107 we have shown you a smocked dressing-table set.

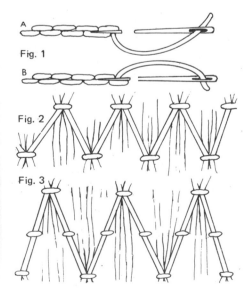

Fig. 1

Fig. 2

Fig. 3

Smocked dressing-table set

These pretty dressing table accessories are fairly simple to make and might be your first project in smocking. Choose a fabric which has a geometric pattern or lines of pattern as a guide for your gathering threads and then you will not need a dot transfer.

You will need

Patterned cotton fabric, 122cm. (48in.), 90cm. (36in.) wide
Toning lining fabric for bag and pin tin, 45cm. (18in.)
Stranded embroidery threads, 2 colours to tone with fabric
Small amount of interfacing
Latex fabric adhesive
4 brass paper fasteners

First read page 106, which explains the method of smocking and the stitches that are used.

To make the curler bag

Cut 2 pieces of the patterned fabric across the width, 40cm. deep (16in. approximately). Cut a piece of lining fabric to the same depth, across the width of the fabric. The bag is made in two pieces in the same way. Turn and press a 5cm. (2in.) hem on the top edge of the patterned fabric. Start gathering 2.5cm. (1in.) down from the hem edge. Work gathering through both thicknesses of the hem. (Make sure that you cut your gathering threads long enough to work right across the fabric.) The rows of gathering should be about 1cm. (3/8in.) apart. Work gathering for 4cm. (1 5/8in.). Pull up the rows of gathering evenly. Wind the first three rows round pins in figures-of-eight. As you smock, move the pins down the rows, adjusting the reeds of each row before you continue smocking.

The bag illustrated has 3 rows of stem stitch first to hold the reeds tightly and then 2 rows of cable stitch (see page 106). Finally, surface honeycomb stitch is worked as Vandyke honeycomb (see page 106). Gather up and work the bottom hem of the pieces in the same way. When smocking on both pieces is completed, pull out the gathering threads. Join the side seams to make the bag. Run a gathering thread round the bottom and pull up tightly. Hem a small circle of fabric into the bottom to close the hole. Make the lining in the same way, gathering the top to fit. Put it into the bag. Make a strap, lining it with Vilene. Sew the strap to the inside of the bag. Finish hemming the lining to the top edge of the bag.

To make the tissue box cover

Cut and join strips of the patterned fabric, 14cm. (5 1/2in.) deep, to make a strip 132cm. (52in.) long. Cut a square of the same fabric to the size of the tissue box top plus 1.2cm. (1/2in.) all round. Cut a piece of interfacing to the same size. Turn and press a hem on both long edges of the strip. Gather the fabric from top to bottom hem. Work 3 rows of cable stitch at the top, then surface honeycomb and finish with 2 rows of cable stitch on the bottom hem. When smocking is completed, pull out the gathering threads. Join the side seam to fit the box cover.

For the box top use the detachable piece from the top of the tissue box as a pattern for cutting the hole. Lay it on the interfacing and draw round the shape. Baste the interfacing to the square of fabric. Cut out the hole, cutting 1.2cm. (1/2in.) away from the pencilled line. Snip into the edge and glue the tabs to the wrong side. Work embroidery round the hole edges to strengthen it because this part of the box gets a lot of wear. Remove tacking threads. Sew the box top to the smocked cover smocking.

To make the pin tin

The pin tin illustrated is made on a 1/2lb coffee tin. Cut a piece of the patterned material across the width and 13cm. deep (5 1/8in. approximately). Cut a piece of the lining material to the circumference of the box plus 2.5cm. (1in.) and to the depth plus 3.7cm. (1 1/2in.). Stand the tin on a piece of cardboard and draw round twice. Cut out 2 circles of card. Cut out 2 circles of the lining fabric to the same size plus 1.2cm. (1/2in.) all round. Turn and press a 1.2cm. (1/2in.) hem on both long edges of long strip.

Gather and smock the fabric as you did for the tissue box. The pin tin illustrated has 2 rows of cable stitch, then surface honeycomb and finally 2 more rows of cable stitch at the bottom.

When all smocking is completed, pull out the gathering threads. Join the side seam so that the smocking fits the tin. Take the smocking off the tin. Join the seam of the lining piece. Put inside the tin. Snip into the bottom edge. Turn the top edge to the outside of the tin and glue down. Glue the bottom edge to the bottom of the tin. Cover one piece of card with lining fabric, padding it a little with a scrap of cotton wool. Glue the padded circle to the inside of the tin.

Put the smocked cover on.

Cover the second piece of card with lining fabric. Push the paper fasteners through for feet. Open the prongs on the card side. Glue the covered circle to the underside of the tin.

Free embroidery

Free embroidery is usually worked over a design that has been transferred on to the cloth, unlike counted thread embroidery, which is done by working each stitch over a precise number of threads. It is very important to use good materials in the right combination, so always use the needles recommended for each project, and do not be tempted to buy poor quality fabrics, as the embroidery would be wasted on them.

Hints

Whatever the work you are doing keep the thread fairly short (about 40cm. or 15½in.). This prevents it becoming frayed by continuously passing through the material, and also decreases the likelihood of knots forming. If you are working on tough fabric it may be necessary to wax the thread with beeswax to strengthen it.

A thimble should be used if possible, and must fit the finger well. Some people, however, find it difficult to work with a thimble; an alternative is to tape the index and middle fingers with masking tape. This is very effective and easy to work with.

You will need a pair of small sharp scissors with points. Always use these for cutting the thread, never break or bite it as this weakens it (and can hurt your teeth). Never start with a knot, but with a small back stitch or by working the 'tail' under succeeding stitches.

Keep all your needles in a box with a small piece of fine emery paper, as this will help them to stay sharp and not rust. If a needle becomes bent or damaged, throw it away.

Method of working

Most free embroidery is worked in an embroidery hoop. There are various kinds, both wooden and metal, and they come in different sizes. Metal frames are better as fine materials can be stretched much tauter than in a wooden one. If you prefer to have both hands free to work with you can buy clamps to attach the frame to a table.

Always work in a good light; try to have it coming over your shoulder on to your work. Hold the work in front of you, not in your lap, and sit in a comfortable position, preferably in a straight-backed chair.

Embroidery is hard on the eyes, so when you are sewing, keep glancing up and focusing on something on the other side of the room. This will help to cut down on eye strain.

Enlarging and transferring designs

Embroidery designs are often printed on a grid background which has to be enlarged before it can be transferred to the fabric. Using squared paper, scale up the work to whatever size you require. Remember that if one of the squares on your paper is 2cm. (¾in.) and one of the original squares is 1cm. (⅜in.) the new diagram will be twice the size of the original. Work systematically from the top to the bottom and from left to right, carefully copying the patterns from each square. If you work one square at a time you will not find it difficult.

There are several ways of transferring designs. One of the simplest methods is to use dressmakers' carbon paper. This is made in various colours, light for dark fabrics, and dark for pale fabrics. It is used in the same way as ordinary carbon paper. Tape the material to be worked flat to a table or board. Place the carbon paper face down on the fabric and secure it at the corners, and place the design sheet on top of that. All three layers must be held firmly in place. Trace the design out with a hard, sharp pencil, using an even, steady pressure. Be careful not to lean on the work and cause smudges.

Another method is to tack the design sheet directly on to the fabric and then stitch out the design with running stitches through both paper and fabric. When you have finished, tear the paper away. This method is useful for transferring an original design of your own on to the fabric. The running stitches are removed when the embroidery is complete.

Damp stretching

When the work is finished you will probably need to damp stretch it, to remove any ring marks left by the hoop, and to straighten any distortion of the fabric. For this you need rustless drawing pins and a board or similar surface larger than the embroidery. You also need either an absorbent white towel, or white blotting paper to hold the moisture. These must be absolutely clean, and must be white so that there is no risk of dye getting on to the work.

Lay the blotting paper or towel on the board, with the work on top of that. Now pin the work in the following manner. Put one pin in the middle of one of the long sides, then, pulling the fabric sideways, put in another 5cm. (2in.) to the left, and a third 5cm. (2in.) to the right. Put in three more on the opposite long side in the corresponding places, pulling the fabric down before pressing them in. Do the same to the short sides, always pulling away from the centre of the fabric. Now fill in the long sides, straightening the fabric all the time so that it is absolutely flat. Fill in the short sides. Damp the work evenly and completely (a gardening spray is useful for this). Fine fabrics such as silk may stretch quite a lot and will need repinning to take up the slack. Leave the work to dry thoroughly before you unpin it. The time this takes will vary from fabric to fabric, for example, silk will dry in about 18 hours whereas canvas will take up to 3 weeks to dry and for the glue in it to reset. Unpinning work too soon results in distortion. If it has dried completely and it is not straight, the whole process must unfortunately be repeated.

Embroidered notebook cover

this flap into the spine and glue it in place. Check that the design is straight on the book and turn the spare fabric (about 3cm. or 1¼in. at top and 5cm. or 2in. at bottom) under the cover to the inside of the book. Glue in place. Cover the raw edges either by sticking the first and last pages of the book to the inside of the cover, or by cutting a piece of paper 1cm. (⅜in.) smaller all round than the book, and glueing this in place.

This design is worked in free embroidery on silk, using only three kinds of stitches, chain stitch, satin stitch and stem stitch. The measurements are for a book 14cm. by 22cm. (5½in. by about 8½in.), but the design can be adapted to fit any size of book.

You will need
Piece of silk fabric 28cm. by 38cm. (11in. by 15in.)
1 skein each of stranded cottons in the following colours: parrot green, forest green, coral, white, grey
Crewel needle No. 8 sharp
Small embroidery hoop
Fabric adhesive

If you are new to embroidery, first read the information which appears on page 108, explaining the technique of free embroidery, and page 103, on which a selection of the stitches is illustrated.

Note
Satin stitch looks easy, but does require some practice, so if you have not done it before, try it out on a spare piece of fabric in a hoop. Make sure you place the stitches next to each other without leaving any gaps. Keep your stitches firm but do not pull them too tight or they will cause the fabric to pucker and distort. Practise filling in a curved shape where the stitches have to be closer on the inside of the curve than the outside.

Working the embroidery
Trace off the motifs from this page, arrange them following the illustration, and transfer them on to your silk, using dressmaker's carbon paper (see page 108).

Put the work into the embroidery hoop, making sure it is nicely taut and not distorted in any way. Only 2 strands of the cotton are used throughout the design. Always use a short length (about 40cm. or 15½in.) and divide the threads carefully. Using coral thread, work the chain stitch along the straight lines of the design. Start the line with a tiny back stitch to secure the thread; this will be covered by the first chain stitch.

Keep the stitches of an even length and take care not to twist the thread.

Now work the stem stitch between the flowers and the leaves in forest green. Work the satin stitch on the leaves, using the forest green first on the inside and then the outside of the leaves. Leave a gap for the parrot green, and then fill it in. Work satin stitch on the flowers, doing the bottom ones in white and the others in grey.

When you have finished take the embroidery out of the hoop, damp stretch it and leave it to dry (see page 108).

Making up
If the book has a wide spine, you will have to make slits in the silk, one each side of the spine, from the edge of the fabric to just below the spine edge. Tuck

Machine embroidery

There are two categories of embroidery which are within the scope of most modern domestic sewing machines–that which is done with a foot, and 'free' embroidery, which is done without a foot.

Embroidery with a foot
Most machines have a variety of feet designed for specific purposes such as shell hemming or seam neatening. Some machines even have double needles for special stitches. These different feet and needles are worth experimenting with for the decorative effects they can produce.

The most versatile machine embroidery stitch is the satin stitch produced by the swing-needle action of the machine. This can be used for all kinds of appliqué work or for stitching down wool and other decorative threads. Every machine has an instruction booklet which will give you precise information about what your particular machine will do.

Embroidery without a foot
Any machine that has a swing needle, and on which you can lower the feed dog (sometimes called the feed teeth), can be used for machine embroidery. Some instruction booklets describe this as 'darning'. It is done with the fabric tautly stretched in an embroidery hoop. Set the machine up by removing the foot, lowering the feed dog, putting the needle in the central position, and setting the stitch width at 4 on the zig-zag selection, and the length at 0. You must lower the foot lever even though you have no foot, as otherwise the top tension of the machine will not operate properly.

Turning the machine by hand, bring the bottom thread up through the material before you begin sewing. The way you hold the hoop is very important. The hands move the hoop so that the fabric is moved about under the needle to work the design. The hoop must be held firmly so that the needle does not pull the work up with it as it moves. The hoop must be right side down so that the fabric is actually in contact with the needle plate. Hold the hoop with both hands, thumbs towards you, little fingers on the fabric just inside the frame for guiding. When you begin sewing, hold the two threads firmly in place so that they are not drawn down in to the race. You may need to slack off either the top tension or the bottom tension; much depends on your individual machine. For this work to be effective the machine must run quickly.

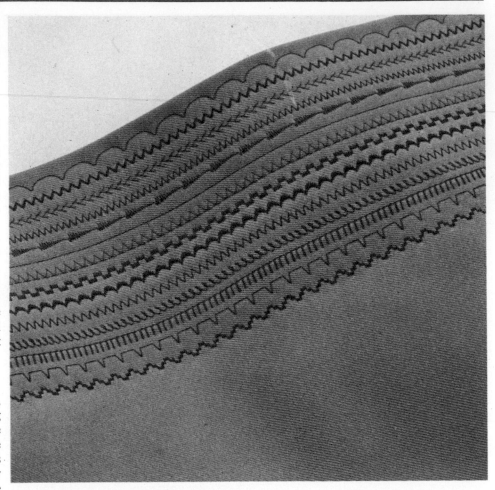

The hoop can be guided with your hands to the left and right, or in circles, or indeed in any way that enables you to fill in shapes or obtain the effects you want, but you must always keep the hoop flat. It is best at first to press it down slightly.

This type of machine embroidery is very effective, but it does require practice. You may find that the thread keeps breaking, or that the needle snaps. If the thread breaks, check the top tension–if it is correct it probably means that you are using a poor quality cotton. The best choice is machine embroidery thread No.50. If the needle breaks, it probably means that you are machining too slowly so that the movements of the frame are pulling the needle and bending it.

Be very careful of your fingers–until you are really expert it is all too easy to sew them up. Keep them well away from the needle. Rest the tips of the fingers just inside the embroidery hoop.

Unless you are sewing on heavy material, such as calico or linen, you will need another layer of fabric in the frame as lining. The work is sewn through both layers. This serves two purposes, holding the fabric tighter in the frame, and giving a neater, less puckered finish.

Once you have sufficient control of the technique, experiment with all the stitches and widths your machine can do. You can also try out different tensions, for example, loosening the bottom tension and tightening the top one will give a whipped effect on top of the fabric. Interesting effects can be created by using a different coloured thread in the bobbin for contrast. Thicker threads are threaded on to the bobbin by hand. You can also experiment with different ways of filling in shapes, moving the hoop in curves and circles as well as from left to right. Pile stitches on top of one another for a solid effect.

Machine embroidery will nearly always need damp stretching (see page 108), especially if it is closely worked.

Child's embroidered skirt

The skirt is made from a straight piece of fabric gathered into a waistband and fastened at the back with a button. It can be adapted to fit any age of child, and the simple machine embroidery around the hem can be done in any colours you choose.

You will need
1 piece of medium weight cotton fabric
  (for quantity see below)
Mercerised machine embroidery cottons
  in 5 colours
Sewing machine with swing needle
Buttons, hooks and eyes, or zip
  fastener

The fabric
Calculate the amount of material you need as follows. For the waistband you need a strip 8cm. (3in.) wide. The length must be the child's waist size plus 10cm. (4in.) for seam and overlap fastening. For the skirt itself you need an oblong piece of fabric, the width being at least the waist size doubled. The length from waist to knee is a matter of choice, but allow 5cm. (2in.) hem allowance.

The embroidery
Most modern machines have a swing needle, which produces a zig-zag stitch and some also have some decorative stitches. These are usually on top of the machine and are selected by a lever.

Before starting work, try all the stitches your machine can do on a spare piece of fabric, and select the one you like most. Two further factors will affect its appearance. The first is the stitch width, or the swing needle width, which is usually controlled by a knob on the top right-hand side of the machine. The range is usually from 1 to 4, 1 being the narrowest and 4 the widest. The second factor is the stitch length, that is, the number of stitches the machine sews per inch. Some machines have settings from 0 to 4; in this case 4 represents the fewest number of stitches to the inch (about 6), and 0 the most, so close together that they are almost in the same place. Other machines have settings from 20 to 6, directly stating the number of stitches per inch. Thus, if you select a decorative stitch setting that gives you a wavy line, set the stitch length to 0 (the closest) and the swing needle width to 4 (the widest) you will get a close wide wavy line. If you then lengthen the stitch to 2, and leave the width setting on 4, you will get a very different stitch, just as wide, but less closely spaced.

The pattern on the skirt uses only three stitches at different settings, those found on most domestic machines. It consists of a simple shape that is repeated all the way round the hem (see diagram).

Mark the position of the hem and the main lines on the material before sewing, using a pencil and ruler. This is not strictly necessary but will enable you to keep the machined lines straight and parallel. Then work the embroidery with your chosen stitches round the hem of the skirt.

To make up the skirt
When the embroidery is complete, press the fabric. It may even be necessary to damp stretch it if it has puckered under the machine (see page 108). Run a gathering thread through the top of the skirt and draw it up to the required length. Fit it into the waist band, leaving enough overlap (about 4cm. or 1½in.) on the left side to allow for the buttonhole. With right sides together, machine the band to the skirt, turn it over the top of the skirt and slip stitch the back down by hand. Turn the end in to the level of the skirt on the right-hand side and neaten the overlap on the left-hand side. There is only one seam in the skirt, and this goes at the back. Sew this seam, leaving an opening below the waistband, which is fastened with hooks and eyes. You may prefer to insert a zip, if so, sew it in before neatening the waistband so that the zip ends are correctly placed in the band. Turn up the hem and slip stitch. Finish by working a buttonhole on the left-hand overlap, the button on the right side.

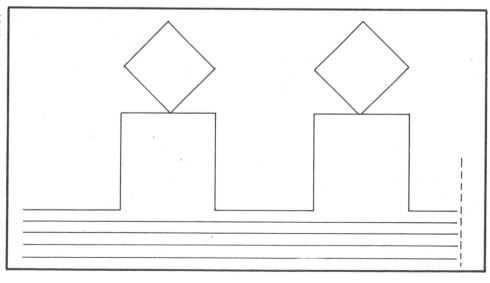

Smocked aprons

braid along the hems but do not cut off the braid yet as it may stretch a little as you stitch it. Feather stitch the braid to the hem, and trim the ends. Tack and then feather stitch the ricrac to the top of the pockets, and stitch them to the apron skirts.

Cut one of the strips for the larger apron in half and sew the halves to the ends of the other piece. This avoids a join in the centre front of the waistband. Measure the width of the smocked area at the top of the apron and mark the same width with pins along the centre of the waistband strip. With right sides together sew up the strip, leaving the centre width open. Turn the two tubes you have made right sides out. Sew the centre unjoined piece to the smocking and feather stitch along the band above the smocking. Turn the apron to the back and hem the band down covering the stitches. This makes it neat and tidy.

The child's apron is made in exactly the same way, but there is only one strip instead of two to make the waistband and ties.

The doll's apron is also made in the same way.

Matching aprons for mother and daughter and one for the favourite toy.

You will need
1.5m. (1½yds. approximately) brown and white check gingham
Stranded cotton: 2 skeins brown, 1 skein white
2.5m. (2½yds. approximately) ricrac braid

Note
First read page 106, which explains the technique of smocking and illustrates the basic stitches.

To make the apron
Cut from the full width of gingham a piece 60cm. (23½in.) deep. Cut another piece 40cm. (15¾in.) deep and from the side of this piece cut off enough to make the doll's apron. The one illustrated is 24cm. (9½in.) wide, but if you need a larger one just cut a little more from the child's apron; a few centimetres won't make very much difference to its size.

From one end of the remaining piece of gingham cut the 2 pockets. The strip left over makes the waistband and ties for the two aprons. Cut it into 3 separate strips, 2 wide ones about 12cm. (4¾in.) in width and a narrower one about 6cm. (2¼in.) wide. These measurements need not be exact, so it does not matter very much if they do not fit exactly with the material strip you have left; just cut the 3 strips as wide as you can. Sometimes in straightening up a badly cut piece of gingham you may loose a few centimetres.

Gather and smock the waist edge of the mother's apron as follows: 3 rows stem stitch, 1 row cable stitch, 4 rows surface honeycomb, honeycomb worked over 4 rows to make vandykes. For the daughter's apron, smock 1 row stem stitch, 1 row cable stitch, 2 rows surface honeycomb and 4 rows of honeycomb to make vandykes. The doll's apron is smocked with 1 row stem stitch, 1 row cable stitch and 3 rows of honeycomb to make vandykes. Hem round the sides and turn up bottom hems. Tack ricrac

Valentine keep-sake card

This Valentine card is bound to stay in someone's keep-sake drawer for ever as it is so beautiful. Not only will it give its recipient a lot of pleasure but the giver, too, can have hours of fun making it.

You will need
20cm. by 20cm. (8in. by 8in.) pale blue cotton fabric
20cm. by 20cm. (8in. by 8in.) white nylon tulle net
27cm. by 27cm. (10½in. by 10½in.) pale blue floral print cotton fabric
Scraps of white organdie
1m. (3ft.) of 2.5cm. (1in.) wide white nylon lace edging
2m. (6ft) of 3mm. (⅛in.) wide mauve satin ribbon
Polyester/terylene wadding
Small sachet of rose-scented pot pourri
Sewing threads – pale mauve, white, light brown
Shaded sewing threads – mauve, pale blue, pink
25cm. (9¾in.) square of thick white card 24.5cm. by 49cm. (9⁷/₁₆ by 19¼in.)
Clear glue
Iron-on adhesive tape
Sewing equipment

To make the Valentine card
1. Using pattern cut out two pale blue cotton hearts and two white tulle hearts (Fig. 1).
With the layers of tulle sandwiched between the blue cotton fabric, pin, tack and stitch around edges on seam line. Leave a small opening. Trim and clip edges. Turn to right side and stuff with wadding.
2. Insert pot pourri sachet in centre of stuffing. Pin open edges of heart together and slip stitch neatly to close.
3. Gather up lace to fit around heart and with small stitches attach to heart along seam line. Join ends of lace neatly.
4. Divide mauve ribbon into four equal lengths and tie all four together as one to make a 'quadruple' bow. Stitch it firmly at top of heart. Clip ends of ribbons to neaten.
5. Trace three butterfly motifs with a pencil on to a double layer of organdie. Hand-embroider each butterfly using a combination of colours and stitches or alternatively, set sewing machine to satin stitch width 2, minimum length and with the shaded sewing threads carefully work along all design lines of wings to give one butterfly of each colour. Work antennae in light brown (Fig. 2). With sharp-

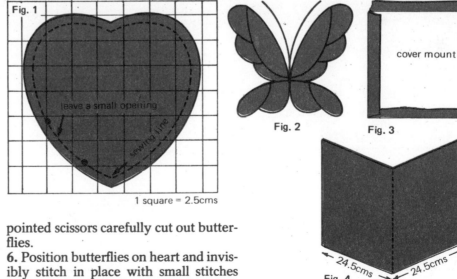

Fig. 1

leave a small opening

sewing line

1 square = 2.5cms

Fig. 2

cover mount

Fig. 3

24.5cms   24.5cms

Fig. 4

pointed scissors carefully cut out butter-flies.
6. Position butterflies on heart and invisibly stitch in place with small stitches along centres of bodies so that the wings and antennae are free standing.
7. Following instructions supplied, apply adhesive tape to wrong side of square of floral fabric and then afix it to square of thick card, clipping fabric at corners to achieve neat points (Fig. 3).
8. Glue wrong side of heart and stick centrally on to fabric-covered card. Place a heavy weight (large book) on top of heart and leave until thoroughly dried and set.

9. Fold thinner card in half (Fig. 4) and stick front side to wrong side of thick card to complete Valentine card.

113

Butterfly belt

The butterfly design on the belt is worked entirely in cross stitch using different coloured threads in alternating combinations. This technique is called counted thread embroidery. It is similar to canvas work in that you do not use a transfer, but work from a chart, each square of which represents threads of the material.

You will need
Strip of linen (12 threads to 1cm. or ⅜in.) 8cm. by 84cm. (3in. by 33in.)
Strip of cotton or calico the same size for lining
Heavy-weight interfacing 76cm. by 4cm. (32in. by 1⅝in.)
Wooden buckle without tongue and with 4cm. (1⅝in.) bar
Pearl cotton in 4 colours: scarlet, rose pink, cardinal, violet

The belt in the illustration has 9 butterflies and will fit a 61 to 66cm. (24 to 26in.) waist. Each butterfly, with the square motif, takes up about 7.5cm. (3in.), so if you want a longer belt, add extra motifs.

Following the chart
Every square on the chart (Fig. 1) represents 2 threads of the linen. Thus the large crosses on the chart, which cover an area of 2 squares by 2 squares will actually cover an area of 4 threads by 4 threads. Study the chart before you start to sew and you will see that some of the crosses start half-way over another cross.

Working the embroidery
All the crosses must be worked in the same direction, with the first thread running from the bottom right-hand corner to the top left-hand corner, and the second thread running in the opposite direction. Following the chart, work the embroidery from left to right, alternating the colours of the body and wings. Follow a colour order of red body and pink wings, then pink body and violet wings, violet body and pink wings, pink wings and red body, and finally violet body and red wings. The small square motifs in between the butterflies are worked in the dark red. The butterflies' antennae are made by working one long stitch and 2 short ones.

Making the belt
Lay the embroidery wrong side up. Lay the interfacing on top. Tack the layers together. Press the embroidery on to the interfacing, cutting the corners off di-

agonally. Tack the turnings down. Turn and press the edges of the lining so that it is 3mm. (⅛in.) smaller than the stiffened belt. Slip stitch the lining to the embroid-

ery (Fig. 3). Pass the left end through the buckle. Sew the buckle in place. Sew on a press fastener to hold the belt if it needs it.

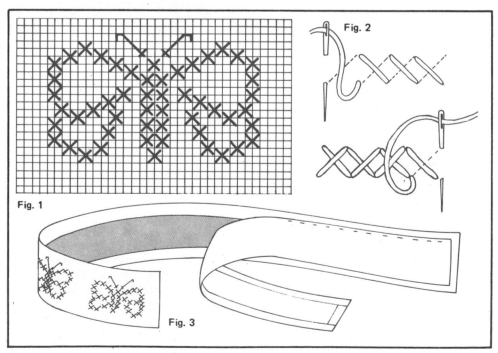

Fig. 1

Fig. 2

Fig. 3

'Happy apple' tablecloth

The motif on this tablecloth is worked mainly in chain stitch, which can be used for following the line of a design, for bordering and for filling. There are at least 10 variations on the stitch, one of which is the popular lazy daisy.

Chain stitch is one of the stitches which cannot be worked in an embroidery hoop. It is far easier worked in the hand and you'll find that the fabric puckers less if you curve it over your finger and take only a thread or two of fabric on the needle, keeping the stitch fairly loose.

The bright apple design on the tablecloth illustrated is worked with chain stitch used as a filling stitch, French knots for texture and long and short stitch and stem stitch for the leaves. As a tablecloth is likely to be laundered frequently, soft embroidery cotton has been used for the apple because this both washes and irons well.

You will need
Even-weave linen to the size of the desired tablecloth
Matching sewing thread
Squared dressmaker's paper, chalk or dressmaker's transfer paper
Soft embroidery cotton in the following colours: 1 skein yellow, olive green, gold
Stranded cotton: light green, dark green
Crewel embroidery needle

The pattern
Fig. 1 is the pattern for the apple motif. On the tablecloth illustrated, the apple is 18.2cm. (7½in.) across and if you want to work the motif to this size, you should enlarge the pattern so that each square is 2.5cm. (1in.). To achieve a smaller motif, perhaps for a matching set of napkins or for a border of apples, draw up your pattern so that each square represents 1.2cm. (½in.) for a 9cm. (3¾in.) apple or, for a really small apple simply trace the outline from the card.

Transfer the pattern to the fabric. Either use dressmaker's transfer paper as described on page 108 or rub the back of your tracing with chalk.

Preparing the fabric
The tablecloth must be absolutely square. Pull warp and weft threads from the borders and cut the tablecloth out along the lines marked by the pulled threads.

Transfer the motif and work the design. Start working the chain stitch on the outside edge of the design and follow the solid lines indicated on the pattern to fill

the area. Work French knots as shown in Fig. 2. Work the leaves in long and short stitch and the stem in stem stitch (see page 103) using 6 strands of thread together. Follow the key beside Fig. 1 for colours.

Fig. 1

To finish the cloth
Press the finished embroidery on the wrong side over a padded ironing board so that the embroidery is not flattened by pressing. Iron a narrow hem on all four sides of the cloth and then turn a 2.5cm. (1in.) hem. You can either machine stitch the hem or finish it with a line of chain stitch worked right on the fold of the hem. A closely matching cotton will give the best effect, but a colour from the apple embroidery would look bright and attractive if you prefer.

Other uses for the motif
Used large, the apple would make a good cushion embroidery. For a set of cushions, work it in reds, oranges and greens, as well as yellow. Used small, it could be worked on play clothes–using stranded embroidery threads instead of soft cotton.

Traced off and cut out of cotton fabrics, the apple motif would look delightful for a simple appliqué.

If you enjoy canvas work, you might like to try the apple as a kind of sampler, using only a small range of yarns but trying out all kinds of texture stitches to get the roundness of the apple. Your finished sample could either be mounted and framed for a wall panel or you might use it for a stool top or a cushion.

A Chain stitch	yellow	**b** French knots	yellow
B Chain stitch	olive green	**D** Stem stitch	dark green
C Chain stitch	gold	**E** Long and	
a French knots	olive green	short stitch	light green

Fig. 2

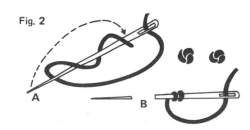

Stitching on patterned fabric

Embroidery on patterned fabrics is a fascinating craft and the results can be used for decorating a variety of home furnishings and clothes. You do not need transfers because you work your stitches to highlight the fabric's pattern, following lines, filling in certain areas, outlining others, using yarns and threads to give your work texture. Furnishing fabrics are usually heavy enough to take the weight of embroidery but dress fabrics are sometimes too light. If you were planning to embroider the hem ot a cotton skirt, for instance, you should back the area with lightweight cotton or thin, iron-on interfacing first. To mount fabrics, tack the two layers together, keeping the surface absolutely smooth, working stitches from corner to corner and then side to side. Then work the two layers together.

Patterns to choose
Although almost any design can be embroidered, floral patterns are usually too detailed for the embroidery to show up. Spots can be embroidered to look like flowers with lazy daisy petals round them. Indian cotton prints decorate well with chain stitch, applied braids and even beads. With all-over patterns the first thing to decide is which part needs the added interest or weight. Take a few beads, sequins, braids or bunches of threads and just lay them on your material. Move them around and you'll get some idea of which parts of the pattern need highlighting. It also helps you to decide which colours to use. Some patterns need toning down and others need brightening up. You can sometimes buy a furnishing remnant with a pattern of curves or a large flower, not enough for a curtain but ideal for making a cushion, and emphasise the shapes with stitching.

Choose striped fabrics for your first practice piece. The red piece illustrated is made from striped furnishing linen and embroidered with stranded embroidery threads and thick soft embroidery cotton. The two threads provide interesting texture against the fabric's weave.

Mattress ticking is ideal for working on but is rather expensive unless you're working a piece or several cushions. Striped dress fabric is suitable if it is mounted.

Threads
If a big project is being undertaken embroidery threads can be very costly. Try to find balls of knitting or crochet cottons

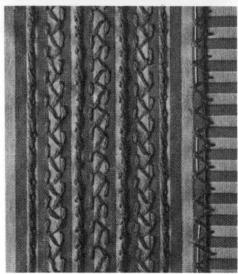

in the colours you need. Although they are more expensive than a skein of thread they have much more yardage. If using stranded cotton try varying the number of strands used, working one part of your design in one or two strands and another part in four or six strands. It is surprising how it varies the texture of your work. If the finished article is going to have hard wear and you have used ric-rac braid, stitch down each curve–fly stitch or detached chain stitch is useful for this–then the braid edge can't pop up and look untidy. Bias binding can have tape down the centre or ric-rac tucked under each side which is then overstitched with thread.

Stitches
Any kind of embroidery stitch can be used, but the craft lies in combining stitches for effect. The red sample, for instance, uses herringboning in two different threads, soft cotton and one strand of embroidery thread; chain stitch threaded with another colour; stem stitch, cable stitch, detached chain stitch and feather stitch. Check page 103 for stitches, and have fun practising them in combinations of colour and thread. Add beads, braids and ric-rac if you like for added effect. There are no rules in this fascinating embroidery.

Crewel embroidery

The term 'crewel embroidery' comes from the spun, two-ply wool yarn which is used for the stitchery. It is also known as Jacobean wool work because in the 17th century it was much used for decorating bed curtains and wall hangings. There were two distinct styles of design: one had flowers, leaves, trees and scrolls. The other looked rather oriental with birds and beasts, the colours shaded and subtle. The design on page 118 is a combination of both styles.

Crewel embroidery is distinctive. in that some of the background fabric is left unworked and is an integral part of the design.

Fabrics and yarns

Cream-coloured linen twill is traditionally used for crewel embroidery. You can also use plain-weave linen, slub-weave linen or cotton and a variety of medium-weight closely woven dress fabrics and home furnishing materials. Both crewel yarns and tapestry wools are available in an enormous range of shades. You can also use 2-ply knitting wool but the effect will not, of course, be quite the same.

Other equipment

Most of the stitches in crewel work can be worked without a frame. However, laid work and couching **are** easier to work in a frame.

You'll need two types of needles: crewel

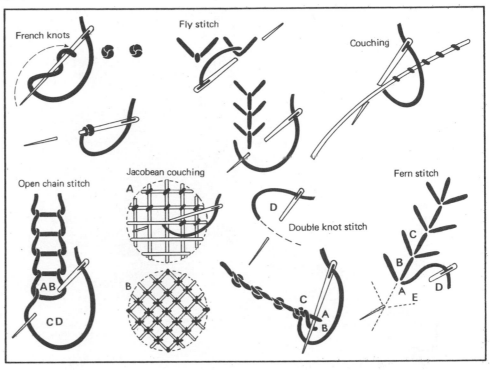

needles have a long narrow eye and the size will depend on the number of strands of yarn being used. Tapestry needles are useful for threading under stitches and for laid work.

Approach to design

Crewel is a free technique. In the past embroidresses would work out the design on the fabric in charcoal or chalk and then apply stitches and colours as they felt the design required. This should be your aim in crewel embroidery.

Stitch Library

Most of the popular embroidery stitches you'll need are on page 103. Here are some other stitches which you'll meet in crewel work.

French knots Bring the thread out at the required position, hold it down with the left thumb. Wind the thread twice round the needle. Hold the thread firmly, twist the back to the starting point and re-insert it just behind, gently pulling the thread through.

Fly stitch Bring needle through at top of stitch, hold thread down, insert needle at top right of stitch and bring out at centre a little below, thread below needle. Insert needle again below the stitch at centre, bringing it through in position for the next stitch.

Couching Lay a double thickness of thread along the line of the design. Tie, or couch

it down to the fabric with another thread, worked at intervals. The couching thread can be in a contrasting colour.

Open chain stitch This is worked in a similar way to chain stitch but you can vary the depth. Bring the needle through at A and, holding the thread down with the left thumb insert the needle at B. Bring the needle through at C for the required depth of stitch. Leave the loop loose and re-insert the needle at D and, with the thread under the needle point, bring it through in readiness for the next stitch. Secure the last loop with a small stitch (at each side if necessary).

Jacobean couching This stitch consists of long, evenly spaced stitches (laid threads), taken across the space horizontally and vertically (A) or diagonally (B). The crossed threads are then tied (or couched) down at all intersecting points, with a small slanting stitch or a cross stitch.

Double Knot Stitch Bring the thread through at A. Take a small stitch across the line at B. Pass the needle downwards under the surface stitch just made, without piercing the fabric, as at C. With the thread under the needle, pass the needle again under the first stitch at D. Pull thread through to form a knot.

Fern stitch This stitch consists of three straight stitches, radiating from the same point, A. From the third stitch D, bring the needle through at E to start the next three stitches.

Crewel work picture

Direction of stitches
Study the colour illustration first. Then look at the pattern. You will see that certain areas of the design have lines showing stitches worked in one direction. The tree trunk (squares D6, 7) for instance, have stitches worked down the trunk. The little fawn (squares E,F,6,7,8) has stitches worked down the body but across his hind leg. The squirrel, squares (B7,8) has some stitches worked across the body, but the tail stitches follow the shape of the tail.

Helpful hints
When you are working a design with a number of colours in it, start by cutting a snippet of yarn from each skein. Glue the snips to a piece of paper and write the number shade clearly beside it. Lay your yarns out in the same order. This will help you to pick up the correct yarn quickly when you need it.

Mounting the embroidery for a picture
Press the finished embroidery on the wrong side. Place over backing board and pull the surplus fabric to the back. Lace from side to side both ways with strong thread to hold the fabric taut. Frame or use the mounted embroidery as desired.

Crewel embroidered pictures are a popular furnishing accessory, fitting into every style of home. This Jacobean-style design of a fabulous tree with birds and animals can be worked as a picture, as a fire screen or as a cushion. The overall dimensions of the embroidery are 40cm. by 35cm. (16in. by 14in.) The pattern appears on the opposite page.

You will need
60cm. (24in.) cream-coloured medium-weight fabric 91cm. (36in.) wide
Dressmaker's carbon paper.
Chenille needle No. 18
Tapestry wool: 2 skeins each orange, chestnut, chocolate, olive green, sea foam green, light sage green, dark sage green; 1 skein each tangerine, flame red, snuff brown, gold, sea green, light turquoise, dark turquoise, biscuit
Backing board, frame etc. for picture

Trim fabric to 60cm. by 70cm. (23⅝in. by 27½in.). Iron or press the fabric smooth. Spread it on a firm, padded surface and pin down. Lay dressmaker's carbon paper on top, chalked side down and the pattern sheet on top. Pin in position. Draw over the lines of the pattern firmly to transfer them to the fabric. Unpin and lift two corners only to check that all lines have been traced down.

Using the pattern
You will see that the pattern has various numbers on it from 1-98. These numbers are the key to the yarn colours and stitches you use for different parts of the design. For instance, the flower motif top left (squares A1, 2, B1, 2) has the numbers 24, 25, 26, 62, 69 and 90. Check these numbers on the key on the pattern and you will see that you use yarn light turquoise and sea green for the leaves in stem stitch and back stitch, and sea foam green and dark turquoise in stem stitch, daisy stitch in chocolate and double knot stitch in flame red in order to complete the flower.

Most of the stitches used are familiar embroidery stitches and these are explained and are also illustrated on pages 103 and 117.

Crewel work
picture

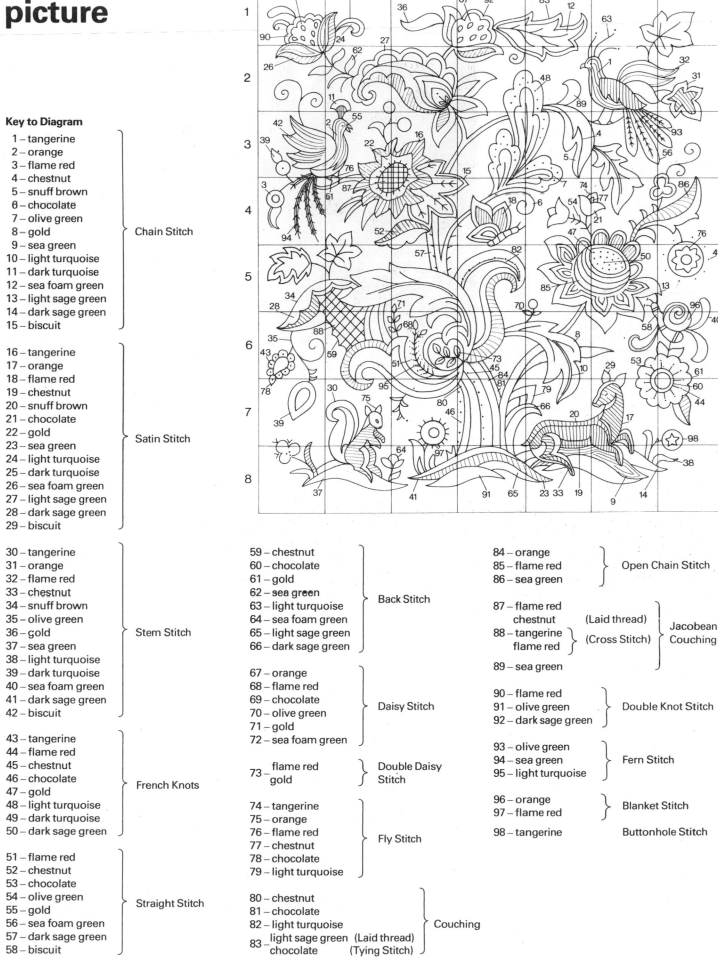

Key to Diagram

1 – tangerine
2 – orange
3 – flame red
4 – chestnut
5 – snuff brown
6 – chocolate
7 – olive green
8 – gold
9 – sea green
10 – light turquoise
11 – dark turquoise
12 – sea foam green
13 – light sage green
14 – dark sage green
15 – biscuit
} Chain Stitch

16 – tangerine
17 – orange
18 – flame red
19 – chestnut
20 – snuff brown
21 – chocolate
22 – gold
23 – sea green
24 – light turquoise
25 – dark turquoise
26 – sea foam green
27 – light sage green
28 – dark sage green
29 – biscuit
} Satin Stitch

30 – tangerine
31 – orange
32 – flame red
33 – chestnut
34 – snuff brown
35 – olive green
36 – gold
37 – sea green
38 – light turquoise
39 – dark turquoise
40 – sea foam green
41 – dark sage green
42 – biscuit
} Stem Stitch

43 – tangerine
44 – flame red
45 – chestnut
46 – chocolate
47 – gold
48 – light turquoise
49 – dark turquoise
50 – dark sage green
} French Knots

51 – flame red
52 – chestnut
53 – chocolate
54 – olive green
55 – gold
56 – sea foam green
57 – dark sage green
58 – biscuit
} Straight Stitch

59 – chestnut
60 – chocolate
61 – gold
62 – sea green
63 – light turquoise
64 – sea foam green
65 – light sage green
66 – dark sage green
} Back Stitch

67 – orange
68 – flame red
69 – chocolate
70 – olive green
71 – gold
72 – sea foam green
} Daisy Stitch

73 – flame red / gold } Double Daisy Stitch

74 – tangerine
75 – orange
76 – flame red
77 – chestnut
78 – chocolate
79 – light turquoise
} Fly Stitch

80 – chestnut
81 – chocolate
82 – light turquoise
83 – light sage green (Laid thread)
83 – chocolate (Tying Stitch)
} Couching

84 – orange
85 – flame red
86 – sea green
} Open Chain Stitch

87 – flame red / chestnut (Laid thread)
88 – tangerine / flame red (Cross Stitch)
89 – sea green
} Jacobean Couching

90 – flame red
91 – olive green
92 – dark sage green
} Double Knot Stitch

93 – olive green
94 – sea green
95 – light turquoise
} Fern Stitch

96 – orange
97 – flame red
} Blanket Stitch

98 – tangerine Buttonhole Stitch

Fabric boxes (1)

Making fabric boxes is an old needle craft that is becoming popular again with needlewomen. They make exquisite gifts and home accessories and they are also an opportunity for trying new embroidery techniques such as beading or goldwork. Essentially, fabric boxes are structures made of cardboard which is padded and then covered with fabric. Any embroidery or other decoration must be worked on the box sections before they are assembled.

Note
This page is intended to be used in conjunction with page 121, which explains the final steps in making fabric boxes and gives instructions for working the embroidery.

Tools and materials
Most of the tools used are in your sewing box. You will also need a steel rule, a sharp crafts knife, a geometric square and a surface for cutting on, such as a piece of hardboard. Fabric adhesive and a spreader are also required and some cellophane tape.

Fabrics
Thin fabrics such as silk, satin, fine cotton and lawn, silk or cotton velvet, and metallic fabrics are all suitable. Linings should be thin and smooth. Additional decoration can take the form of patchwork appliqué, surface embroidery of all kinds, machine embroidery, beadwork and goldwork.

Padding fabric
Soft brushed cotton, such as wincyette, used to be used for padding but a light to medium weight interfacing is just as good.

Cardboard
If you can obtain it, a weight of card known as 'four-sheet' is best for the base and top of the box. The sides are made of a lighter weight called 'ticket card'. Bristol board is obtainable from art shops and some stationers and they will usually be able to supply a heavier weight of card for the box lid and base.

Making a start
A round box is the easiest for beginners, but the basic technique is the same for joining pieces of a square or rectangular box. Decide first the dimensions of the box you are going to make. Then do an exploded drawing (see diagram) so that

the various parts of the box can be seen. A round box has a circular top and bottom of the same size, a lining for the top, a rim for the lid, a piece for the sides of the box bottom and a lining piece for the box bottom so that the lid stays on. On the diagram these are marked A top, A/1 top lining, B base, B/1 base lining, C top rim, D bottom side, E lining. The lining is 1.2cm. (½in.) deeper than the box side to accommodate the lid rim.

Cutting the card
Cut the side piece (D) first. Then cut the lining (E) 1.2cm. (½in.) deeper. Join the ends into a ring with cellophane tape. Do not overlap ends because this would make a bump and show through the fabric. Mark the inside of the box side and the outside of the lining clearly so that you know what the piece is and where it goes. Later, when one side of each piece is covered with fabric, it is very easy to get them mixed up. From the heavier card, cut the lid (A). This circle should be exactly the diameter of the box side (D). Cut a lining for the lid (A/1), about 3mm. (⅛in.) smaller than the lid itself, from light-weight card. Mark the inside of the lid and the outside of the lining piece.

Cut the rim of the lid next (C). This should be exactly the diameter of the lid and 1.5cm. (⅝in.) deep. Finally cut the bottom of the box (B) in heavy card to the same diameter as the top and then cut the lining (B/1) from the lighter card slightly smaller. Mark all pieces.

Cutting fabric
Fabric is cut to the sizes of the various

box pieces plus 1.2cm. (½in.) turnings all round. Two pieces have an extra allowance of 1.8cm. (¾in.). Piece E, the box lining, has an extra allowance on the top edge so that it can be turned over the lip. Piece C, the lid rim, has the extra allowance on the bottom edge so that it turns under the lip.

Padding the pieces
For the bottom, cut three pieces of interfacing, two to the same size as the bottom circle and the other one 1.2cm. (½in.) larger all round. Glue the smaller piece to the outside of the box bottom and then glue the larger pieces on top, taking the allowance over to the wrong side so that the card edges are padded. Snip into the allowance for a smooth turn. Now cover the lining piece in the same way, covering the top side of the lining. Pad the lining of the box lid with three layers in the same way. Pad the top of the box with an extra layer so that it is soft. Cut strips of interfacing to cover the box lining and the lid rim. Butt joins, do not overlap them.

The instructions are continued on the next page.

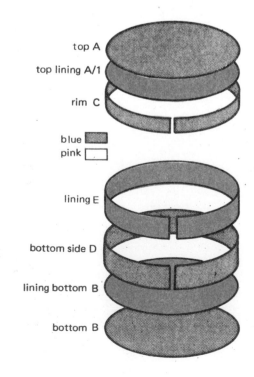

top A
top lining A/1
rim C

blue
pink

lining E

bottom side D

lining bottom B

bottom B

Fabric boxes (2)

Page 120 explained how to make the cardboard base of the box. Now you are ready to embroider the design and make the fabric outer.

Embroidery motif

The stylised flower design is worked in simple machine embroidery techniques and can be done on any zig zag sewing machine. The motif is 17.6cm. (7in.) in diameter and can be used on any box larger than this. The box illustrated is about 20cm. (8in.) across.

You will need

Closely woven fabric in blue and pink, 25cm. (10in.) square
Pink sewing thread
Small sharp scissors
Spool of silver machine thread
Sequin waste (scraps from a sheet)
Embroidery hoop
Dressmaker's carbon paper (light and dark colours)

Draw up the design from the diagram. Each square = 1.2cm. (½in.). Pin the pink fabric to a board and trace down the design using dark-coloured dressmaker's carbon paper. Tack the pink fabric to the blue fabric, wrong side of pink to right side of blue. Tack first across from corner to corner, then vertically down the middle and horizontally across, and finally round the edges. Keep the fabric absolutely smooth. Lay the larger hoop on the table, lay the fabric on top, pink side up, and then press the small ring into the larger. Thread up the machine with pink sewing thread. (Read page 110 for the technique of machine embroidery, and practise on a piece of waste material if you have never done it before.) Work the lines of the design in pink, using a small stitch.

Remove the fabric from the hoop and unpick the tacking. With tiny sharp scissors, cut away the surplus pink fabric, leaving pink motifs on the blue ground. Put the fabric back in the hoop and work a narrow, close zigzag stitch over the edges of the pink motifs.

Wind silver thread on to the bobbin by hand, keeping it evenly wound. Leave the pink thread on top of the machine. Trace the silver parts of the design on the blue side of the fabric. Mount the fabric in the hoop pink side down. Work the silver areas of the design in silver satin stitch, setting the machine to a close zigzag. Clip pieces of sequin waste and stitch to the embroidery, following the illustration for position.

Making the fabric outer

Cut the pieces of fabric for the rest of the box, following diagrams on page 120.

Next stitch the short ends of the box side (D) so that it forms a circle. Press the seam open. Join the piece for the box lining (E) in the same way. Join the fabric for the rim (C) into a circle and press the seam open. Cover box side D with fabric, turning the allowance to the inside and glueing down. Cover piece E with lining fabric in the same way. Leave to dry and then slip E into D. Slip the rim fabric over the padded rim circle C so that the raw edges are level. You do not glue this piece but oversew the raw edges together, smoothing the fabric for a neat fit. Cover the box bottom (B) with fabric, taking the turnings to the wrong side. Cover the lining of the box bottom (B/1) in the same way. If you are adding a bead or a button for a knob, cover the lid with fabric and then sew on the knob, taking stitches right through the padding and card.

Joining the sections

The box is assembled with open Cretan stitch (Fig. 2) using stranded embroidery

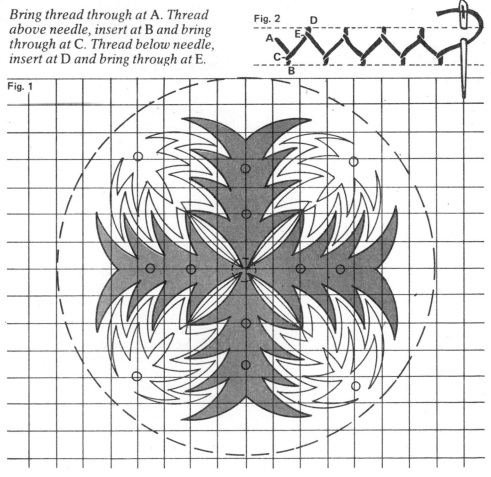

floss. Use 6 strands together. Stitch the lid rim to the box top. Stitches should go through fabric and padding only. Join the box bottom to the sides. Spread glue on the bottom lining and carefully push down into the box. Glue in the lid lining in the same way.

Bring thread through at A. *Thread above needle, insert at* B *and bring through at* C. *Thread below needle, insert at* D *and bring through at* E.

Darning on net

Embroidering on net, using the darning technique, is an easy, quick and inexpensive way to make really individual-looking curtains for the home. Net can be bought by the yard almost anywhere and the threads for darning at most wool shops. Choose strong terylene net with double strands each way, forming the hole. This washes well, drip dries, and shrinks very little. It is available in a range of widths, some wide enough for quite large windows. If terylene net is not obtainable, cotton net is just as good and is soft to work on. Both types of net should be washed before starting the embroidery. Cotton net is inclined to shrink quite a lot and unless it is pre-shrunk, the embroidery will be spoiled. Terylene net shrinks less but it is still advisable to wash it.

The darning pattern borders can be straight lines working in and out of the net holes, or in short zigzags up and down. You will soon discover how easy it is to work out geometric line patterns of your own. Besides the simple running in and out of the net holes, stitches such as herringbone can be used. It is surprising how different a stitch can look worked on net, as you can see some of the back of the stitch as well as the front.

Threads

Many different types of threads can be used in this technique. Dishcloth cotton and vest cotton are both soft, dull-surfaced and cream coloured. Medium weight mercerised crochet cotton is a harder yarn and is slightly shiny. Pearl cotton yarn looks very good worked in fine lines and if a slight glitter is needed, silver or pale metallic yarn can be used. Use this only in small quantitites, or the overall effect will be too glittery and detract from the embroidery itself. Two or three different thicknesses of thread can be used for textural contrast.

It is important for the needle to pass easily through the net and not strain the holes. Try needle and thread out on a spare piece of net before you begin, to be sure you can darn without jerking the thread through. A large and blunt-ended needle such as a rug needle or tapestry needle can be used if the holes are large enough.

Making curtains

Turn down the top allowance once and run several in and out running lines through the two thicknesses of net, leaving enough space for the wire or rod. If you wish to have a top frill allow for this

and run lines along to hold it. If the sides of the net are puckered turn them in and run a line of stitches to hold the edge. Measure the window carefully and if you are worried about future shrinking turn up a hem 5 to 7cm. (2 to 3in.) deep and run a single row of darning along this. This would be easy to slip out to adjust the hem later if necessary. Thread a long length of thread in the needle and work from the edge of the curtain. If a thread needs to be joined in the middle of a pattern, take the old thread through to the back, lay the new thread over it, if possible darning it in for a few stitches. Using a matching sewing cotton, stitch the two threads together firmly, taking in a piece of the net, if you can do it without it showing on the front.

Monograms and ciphers

Embroidered monograms are intended as ornament – of clothing, accessories or household items – and it is important that they should be of good design and perfectly worked. A monogram is a combination of two or more letters, where one letter forms part of another. When two or more letters are placed together or interlaced, each being a separate entity, it is called a cipher.

Two techniques are illustrated here, satin stitched letters worked on a zigzag sewing machine and an appliqué technique, suitable for towels, where the fabric letters are outlined in satin stitch.

Note

If you have not done machine embroidery, you will find it helpful to read the information on page 110.

Machine-stitched letters

Mark out the letters on smooth fabric using dressmaker's chalk or using the dressmaker's carbon paper method of transferring (see page 108). Spread the fabric across the larger section of an embroidery frame and push the smaller section down on to it. Tighten the screws, pulling the fabric so that it is smooth and taut. Thread up the machine and bobbin with machine embroidery thread 50. Fit a needle sized 70-80. Remove the foot from the machine. Set the stitch width between 2 and 4, depending on the width of satin stitch you want. Set the stitch length at 0. Set the machine for zigzag with the needle position at centre. The drop feed control should be lowered.

Set the hoop under the needle and lower the foot even though you have no foot on the machine. Bring the needle down into the fabric and stitch a few straight stitches to bring the bottom thread up through the fabric. Cut the thread ends and you are ready to begin. The line of the letter you are working should be in the middle of the zigzag (see diagram). Allow the machine to run quickly if you want the best effect. Keep your finger tips away from the needle, resting just inside the frame. Move the frame slowly and steadily and do not stop until the monogram is complete.

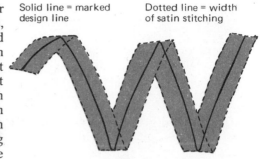

Solid line = marked design line   Dotted line = width of satin stitching

Hand embroidery

To work satin stitch (or other embroidery stitches by hand) on rough fabrics like towelling, mark out the design on a piece of even weave fabric such as organdie. Tack it to the fabric and work the stitches through both fabrics. Afterwards, withdraw the threads of the organdie one by one. The embroidery is left on the fabric surface. This is the only way to work a counted stitch such as cross stitch on rough fabrics. Cross stitch is a particularly suitable stitch for working initials on towels.

Appliqué initials

Mark out the monogram on a piece of closely woven fabric, such as cotton or a washable satin. Tack it to the right side of the item to be decorated. If you are working on a thick fabric such as towelling, you may need to clip down the surface of the pile where the letters are to be placed. Work the outline of the marked letters in a small running stitch, using an embroidery frame and removing the foot from the machine as before. With a small sharp pair of scissors, cut the excess fabric away outside the stitched line. Replace the fabric in the ring and work a narrow satin stitch over the cut edges.

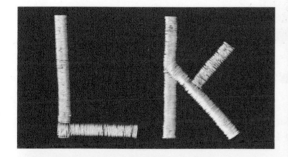

Candlewicking

Tufted candlewicking

Thread the needle with a long length of yarn and pull the two ends level. Start on the right side of the fabric at the end of a design line. Leave the ends of the yarn on the right side of the fabric. Work even running stitches in and out of the fabric. The stitches should be about 6mm. (¼ in.) apart. Pull the yarn through so that small loops are left standing on each stitch. Lay a pencil on the work as you pull the thread through to make sure that the loops are all the same size.

When all the work has been completed, cut the loops evenly and cleanly with sharp scissors. In massed areas of stitches, the rows of running stitch should be worked as closely as you can without straining the fabric weave.

Candlewicking is an easy technique, though not quick to do. It originated in America more than 200 years ago and was used to decorate cotton and linen quilts with the cotton wick used for making candles.

Originally, the traditional candlewicked quilts were worked white on white but now that cotton yarn is available in a wide range of colours, candlewicking can be done in colours to match room schemes. You can use candlewicking for throw-over bed-covers, cushions or for making bath mats.

Fabrics and yarns

There are two methods of doing candlewicking; one has a tufted finish and the other, called 'smooth candlewicking', leaves beads of thread on the surface of the work.

For both techniques, bleached calico or linen is used. Fabric must not be pre-shrunk, as the process involves the fabric shrinking on first washing to hold the stitches in position. Thin fabrics such as cotton are not suitable.

Soft cotton thread, sold in skeins, is used for candlewicking. Dishcloth cotton is available in a range of colours.

A special candlewicking needle is used for the work. It is large, has a flattened, curved point and a large eye. You will also need sharp embroidery scissors, and tracing paper and dressmaker's carbon paper for transferring designs on to the ground fabric (see page 106 for the method).

Designs for candlewick

Designs for candlewick are usually large and flowing because they are best appreciated from a distance. You can work out designs on a block basis, repeating a block pattern over the work. Look at commercial patterns for cutwork as these sometimes have the simplicity of design required and it is possible to abstract patterns from them.

Stitches

The stitch used for both techniques is running stitch. You will find it easier if the fabric is set in a frame but alternatively, spread the work on a table top and work sitting in front of it.

Cutwork embroidery

This method of embroidery has its origin in 16th century Italy, its inspiration being the Venetian lace which was then in demand all over Europe. The French Cardinal Richelieu, objecting to the high taxes on Venetian lace, set up schools and workshops in France, and the more elaborate type of cutwork became extremely popular – it is sometimes called Richelieu work after the Cardinal. A full project for using cutwork appears on page 126.

Cutwork is normally used nowadays to decorate table linen, napkins, pillow-slips etc. It consists, quite simply, of a design outlined in buttonhole stitch with the background cut away.

Materials
The best material to use is a firm linen which does not fray too easily, with an embroidery cotton such as soft embroidery cotton or stranded cotton. Fine material can be used, of course; broderie anglaise, which is a type of cutwork, is usually done on fine cotton lawn. However, if fine fabric is used, the design should be backed with organdie before working. This is cut away when the stitching is complete. Cutwork looks very effective worked on white or natural coloured fabric and a thread which is close in colour, but the simpler work, such as the example illustrated above, can make particularly good use of a contrasting colour.

The design
The best type of design for this work is a very simple stylised one, in which all parts are linked to the main fabric so that the material does not fall apart when the background is cut away. For your first project, try copying the design illustrated on the left or the one shown on the right, in which buttonhole stitch is combined with satin and stem.

Starting the embroidery
Trace the design on to the fabric, using dressmaker's carbon paper (see page 108). Mount the work on an embroidery hoop if you normally use one.

Before starting the buttonhole stitch, work two rows of running stitch just inside each of the edges to be cut. This will strengthen them. Sometimes a padded buttonhole outline can look attractive. If you want to create this raised effect, work two further rows of running stitch, but remember, if you are using soft embroidery thread, the buttonhole outline will be fairly well raised anyway.

Now work buttonhole stitch (see page 103) round the outlines, with the heading of the stitch against the edge to be cut. You can vary the length of your stitches to follow the line of the design, for instance, the scalloped edge on the example illustrated has stitches of carefully graded lengths. Otherwise, keep the stitches even and close together to prevent the fabric fraying. Work all the embroidery before cutting.

Finishing
To cut the fabric you must use very sharp-pointed scissors. You may find it helpful to make a small hole in the middle of each area to be cut with a knitting needle or with the point of the scissors before cutting. Work on the right side and cut as close to the stitching as possible, as otherwise the fabric will fray out. Press embroidery carefully on the wrong side.

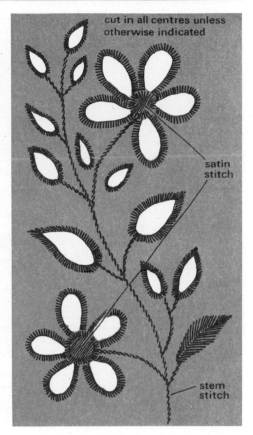

cut in all centres unless otherwise indicated

satin stitch

stem stitch

Cutwork tablemats

corner of one long side of one mat. Turn fabric round and transfer on to the opposite corner. Join up parallel lines, keeping them in line with tacking stitches.
5. Repeat procedure for remaining two mats.

The embroidery
1. Follow Fig. 2 for colour and stitch. Work the buttonhole stitch first, making sure that the looped edge of the stitch is on the edge that will be cut away (these parts are shown as solid red in Fig. 2.
2. When the embroidery is complete, press it on the wrong side.
3. Using small, sharp-pointed scissors, cut away the marked parts and the surplus fabric around the edges. Cut very carefully, taking care not to snip the stitches themselves.

Now we have introduced you to this lovely embroidery technique (see page 125) you may like to try out a project. These mats are cleverly designed, making good use of contrasting colours, and combining the cutwork and buttonhole stitching with stem and straight stitch. Each mat measures 41cm. by 24cm. (16⅛in. by 9¼in.).

You will need
For three mats
Of stranded cotton: 6 skeins cobalt blue; 2 skeins white
(or of No. 8 pearl cotton 2 balls cobalt blue; 1 ball white)
50cm. (½yd.) fine blue embroidery linen, 90cm. (35⅜in.) wide
1 crewel needle No. 6
Dressmaker's graph paper, dressmaker's carbon paper

You will find it helpful to read page 125, which explains the technique of cutwork embroidery.

To prepare the mats
1. Draw up the pattern (Fig. 1) to scale.
2. Cut 3 pieces of linen, each 46cm. by 30cm. (18in. by 11⅞in.).
3. Work a line of basting stitches along the thread of the fabric on each side

2.5cm. (1in.) in from the edge to make a rectangle 41cm. by 25cm. (16⅛in. by 9½in.).
4. Using dressmaker's carbon paper, transfer the design on to the right-hand

'1 square = 2.5 cm
Fig. 1

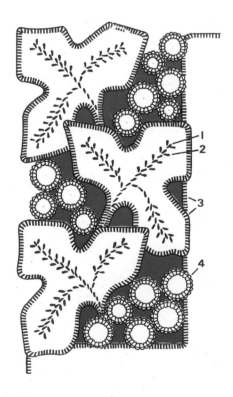

Fig. 2
1 blue   stem stitch
2 blue   straight stitch
3 blue } buttonhole
4 white } stitch

Cross-stitch tablecloth

Fig. 1

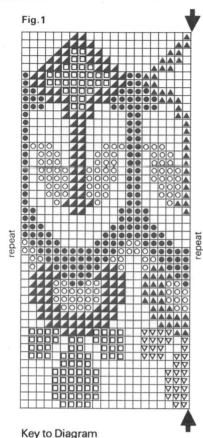

Fig. 2

repeat

The embroidery

1. Fold fabric vertically and horizontally, and mark the centre both ways with a line of tacking stitches.

2. Fig. 1 gives a section of the design. The centre is indicated by a blank arrow which should coincide with the tacking stitches. Fig. 2 shows half the corner. Each background square represents two threads of fabric.

3. Working from Fig. 1, start the design 96 threads down from the crossed tacking stitches and work section shown. Using 4 strands of thread, work cross stitch throughout over two threads of fabric, making sure that the upper half of every cross lies in the same direction.

4. Work the central half-motif and three complete motifs, then work section B.

5. Work right side to correspond, then work other sides in the same way.

To make up

Press embroidery on wrong side. Turn 2.5cm (1in.) hems, mitre the corners and then slipstitch.

Key to Diagram

Stranded Cotton

☑ = jade		◪ = laurel green	
⊙ = blue		◉ = light brown	
▽ = magenta		▲ = violet	

Pearl Cotton

☑ = jade		◪ = grass green	
⊙ = cobalt blue		◉ = light brown	
▽ = rose madder		▲ = violet	

This lovely design is worked entirely in cross stitch in a range of glowing but subtle colours. A 'special occasion' tablecloth anyone would be proud of.

You will need

Of Stranded Cotton: 5 skeins each blue and light brown; 4 skeins each violet and laurel green; 3 skeins each magenta and jade
1.50m. (1½yd.) 150cm. (59in.) wide pale blue even-weave embroidery fabric, 21 threads to 2.5cm. (1in.)
Tapestry needle No. 24

Alternative threads
Of No. 8 pearl cotton (10g. balls): 1 each rose madder, violet, cobalt blue, jade, grass green, light brown

Drawn thread work

Drawn thread embroidery is a type of counted thread work in which a certain number of threads, either from the warp or the weft, are cut and drawn out. This gives an appearance rather like a laddered stocking, in which threads are left running in one direction only. The remaining threads are then pulled together in one of several different ways, creating a decorative effect.

Drawn thread work is found all over the world, and is the basis of many national embroidery styles. It can be as simple as the hemstitch illustrated (top left) or extremely complex. Any even-weave fabric can be used, though cotton and linen are the most usual. Obviously a

coarser material is easier to work as it is easier to see the individual threads. If you use a fine fabric, you may have to use a magnifying glass.

The actual embroidery should be done with thread of a similar weight to the background fabric. You can use the withdrawn threads themselves, but if you want a contrast colour, use stranded cotton for cottons, and soft embroidery thread for linen. Use fine embroidery needles, and a very sharp, pointed pair of embroidery scissors. The following instructions relate to the three examples illustrated.

Hemstitching
Work out the required depth of the hem and mark where the top of it is to be. The next step is to withdraw the threads, but do not withdraw them right across the fabric – they must form a square or rectangle at the top of the hemline. Insert a pin under one thread at the centre, cut it and withdraw the thread gradually outwards on each side to within the hem measurement, leaving enough thread at the corners to darn in. Follow this procedure until sufficient threads have been drawn. (Two or three will usually be sufficient for coarse fabric, while a fine cotton will need more.) Turn back the hem to the space of the drawn threads, mitre the corners and tack.

Now you are ready to start the stitching. Work on the wrong side from left to right, with the hem at the top. Fasten the thread at the left, then pass it from right

to left under 3 or 4 of the border threads and both turnings of hem, bring needle out and pass it from below upwards under 1 or 2 threads of turning at right of group of threads (Fig. 1). When a corner is reached, work buttonhole stitches close together over both edges of hem.

Ladder hem stitch
This is worked in exactly the same way as simple hem stitch, but both edges of the drawn-thread border are worked (Fig. 2).

Zigzag hem stitch
Begin by working simple hem stitch along one edge, but be sure to pick up an even number of border threads each line. Then work the other edge, taking half the threads from one group and half from the next group together, as shown in Fig. 3. The row will start and finish with half a group.

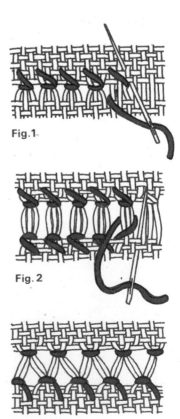

Fig. 1

Fig. 2

Fig. 3

Shadow work

Shadow work embroidery is not as well known as many other forms of embroidery, which is a pity as it's very attractive. It is called shadow work because it is worked on the wrong side of very fine fabric, using fine herringbone stitch between double lines. On the right side you will see a 'shadow' of the herringbone stitch between two continuous lines of backstitch. Obviously, it is best to use strong colours, as otherwise the stitch will not show through.

The example illustrated is a shower cloth, a cover used to protect laid-out food from flies, wasps and pre-dinner pickers. These are popular in America,

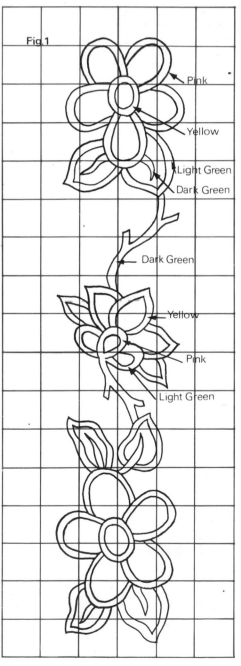

but the technique would be equally effective used for net curtains, or even a bridal veil. The instructions below are for the shower cloth, but you could adapt the design for other items.

You will need
Stranded cotton: 2 skeins pink; 1 skein each yellow, dark green, light green
122cm. (48in.) square white terylene, nylon or voile
1 crewel needle No 7
Squared paper for pattern

To work the embroidery
1. Draw up the design (Fig. 1) to size on squared paper.
2. Fold fabric in half both ways and mark creases with matching thread. This will act as a guide for placing the design.
3. Place fabric face downwards on a firm table over the design, which must be centred under the tacking thread 20cm. (7⅞in.) from edge.
4. Trace the outlines lightly with a soft pencil. Repeat design on the other three sides of cloth.
5. Working on the wrong side and using two strands of cotton in the correct shade (see colour key), work a small even herringbone stitch (Fig. 2) between the traced lines. It will be necessary to lengthen one 'arm' of the stitch from time to time to follow the line of the design. On the right side of the cloth, the backstitch should show as a continuous line.
6. Take great care to fasten off all surplus ends of cotton or they will show through the fabric.

To make up
1. Turn 1.3cm. (½in.) hem all round and slip stitch in place.
2. Work a row of chain stitch on the right side of the hem, using one of the colours used in the design.
3. Press the embroidery lightly on the wrong side with a cool iron.

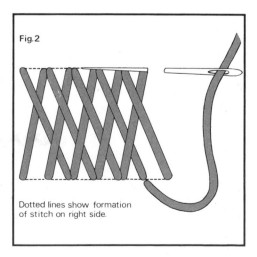

Fig.2

Dotted lines show formation of stitch on right side.

Chain stitch cat

A picture of a favourite pet, done in wools or silks, makes an attractive decoration for the home, and is a better tribute to the animal itself than a photograph, as it's something you've designed and worked on yourself. You don't need an embroidery frame for this kind of picture, so you can carry it about and work on it at odd moments. Once the main design is drawn in, an embroidery like this can be worked quite freely, so you can give full rein to your imagination.

Our embroidery measures 45cm. by 30cm. (18in. by 12in.) and is done with wool in chain stitch. This is the simplest of all stitches to do, and covers a lot of ground quite quickly. You can make convincing flower petals by using lazy daisy stitch, as each of the large single chain stitches can represent a petal. If you're not sure how to do these stitches, first read page 103.

Chain stitch uses a great deal of yarn, so make sure you have plenty of the colours you want before starting.

You will need
Wools (embroidery or knitting) in blue, mauve, white, browns, black, red, green, orange, etc.
Sharp, large-eyed crewel needle
Piece of soft, open-mesh material, at least 5cm. (2in.) bigger all round than the finished work is to be
Waterproof pencil or crayon to draw on the material.
Squared paper

To prepare the embroidery
1. Hem the edges of the fabric to prevent them fraying during work.
2. If you are good at drawing you will be able to sketch the outline of your own cat, but if not, copy our chart, enlarging it to the required size by enlarging the squares. Once you have the main outline, you can add details as you wish.
3. Sketch the outlines on to the fabric with waterproof pencil or crayon.

The embroidery
Start by stitching the cat in chain stitch, looking at a picture of a cat or at your own pet to get the markings convincingly. Use several different shades of brown as well as black, as this will make the picture richer in colour.

When it comes to the flowers and leaves, you can make them as simple or as complicated as you like, but do put plenty of colours into the flowers.

Do not ignore the background, as it is an important part of any picture. It will give a richer and more interesting effect if you stitch it in more than one colour. The background of our picture, for example, is not just plain dark blue; it has bits of indigo, black and pale mauve in it.

When the picture is finished, wash or damp it and stretch it on to a drawing board with pins to dry. Then you can frame it, but make sure the glass is well fitting and the picture is thoroughly sealed from behind, as otherwise the moths will be able to get in.

One square = 2.5cm

Picture pram cover

Here is a really unusual idea – a padded pram cover embroidered with children's pictures. The lady who designed and made this was a teacher, and she simply chose the children's pictures she liked best and used them as embroidery designs.

If you have older children and are expecting a new one, use their pictures for the pram cover; this will please them and prevent them feeling left out.

You will need

5 23cm. (9in.) squares light pink felt
About 75cm. (¾yd.) dark pink for border and contrasts
Felt-tipped pen
Pencil
Crewel needle
Crewel embroidery wools
About 113g. (¼lb.) kapok
50cm. (½yd.) cotton fabric for lining

The embroidery

1. Draw the designs you want to use on paper with the felt-tipped pen. Keep them simple, and try to contrast outlines with solid areas.
2. Copy the designs on to the squares of pink felt, or make tracings if you find this difficult.
3. The embroideries themselves are done in simple stitches, backstitch, blanket stitch, running stitch, chain stitch and Y stitch, and we give diagrams for all these stitches here. Embroider the pictures using these stitches, or use others, such as satin stitch, if you prefer. Our cover uses five embroideries, but you can use fewer if you want to.

To make cover

1. Cut cotton squares about 6mm. (¼in.) larger all round than the measurements of embroidered squares.

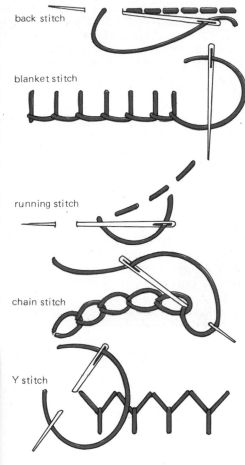

back stitch

blanket stitch

running stitch

chain stitch

Y stitch

2. Turn a hem all round on each one, pin to the embroidered squares and blanket stitch them together, lightly stuffing them with kapok before finishing the stitching.
3. Decide how far apart you want the embroidered squares to be and cut dark pink rectangles to fill the spaces. The cover illustrated uses two rectangles measuring 15cm. by 23cm. (6in. by 9in.) and two measuring 11cm. by 23cm. (4½in. by 9in.).
4. Line, stuff and stitch the dark pink rectangles in the same way as the embroidered squares.
5. Stitch squares and rectangles together by using the eye end of the needle and catching the loops of the blanket stitch together. This is very quick.
6. Add a border made of double felt. In the pram cover illustrated, the top and bottom borders are made from a 23cm. (9in.) strip of felt folded in half. Side borders are made from a 19cm. (7½in.) strip folded in half. Stuff and stitch the borders as before, and join to the central squares by catching the loops of the blanket stitch together.

Introduction to bead embroidery

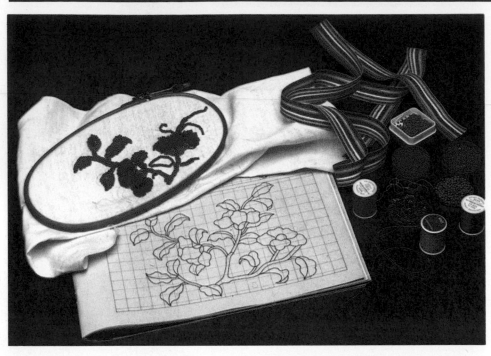

Embroidery with beads was very popular in Europe in the 19th century, particularly in England. Victorian ladies decorated all kinds of things with beads – not just their clothes and fashion accessories – but also every kind of home furnishing – cushions, lampshades, antimacassars, bell-pulls, book covers, box lids and picture frames. Beadwork is a charming craft and, updated to modern materials and designs, is still used to decorate clothing and home furnishings, as well as for making lovely evening bags, belts, hair ornaments, dress ornaments and so on.

Materials and equipment
Traditionally, silk thread was used for beadwork, but, modern polyester threads are quite suitable and come in a wide range of colours. For very small beads, special beading needles are used, but you can use any ordinary small sewing needles for most beads. Choose the size that passes through the beads easily.

Fabrics should be firm and strong enough to carry the weight of the beads. Cotton and cotton blends, firm silks and satins, wool and wool blend fabrics, velvets and materials of similar weights are all suitable. Avoid sheer fabrics if possible – or use them doubled or mounted on a firmer fabric.

Small pieces of beadwork can be worked in the hand, but for larger areas an embroidery frame is essential.

For easier working, line a cardboard box lid with felt or velvet, arrange your beads in colour groups and work from the box lid. You'll find the fabric helps to prevent the beads from leaping about as you pick them up.

Designs
Embroidery or canvas work designs can be used for beadwork, but choose those with bold, uncluttered motifs. Beads look best when they are clustered together richly rather than worked in thin lines. You might like to start by embroidering a piece of printed dress fabric with beads, massing beads in certain areas of the design. The finished fabric can be used to make a matching evening bag or a belt.

Methods of applying beads
Method 1 (Fig. 1) is used for putting down single beads. Fasten the thread firmly on the wrong side of the fabric and bring the needle through to the right side. Pick up one bead on the needle tip and slide it along onto the thread. Take the needle through a single thread of fabric the exact length of the bead along from the point where you brought the needle out, and draw it through. The bead is now anchored to the fabric. If the next bead is to be placed immediately alongside, simply pick up another one and continue. If the next bead is to be placed a distance away, pass the needle back into the fabric and bring it up where the next bead is to be positioned.
Method 2 (Fig. 2) This method is used where beads are being put down to cover large areas. It is a couching technique in which two needles and thread are used simultaneously. Fasten thread 1 to the wrong side. Bring the needle through and slide several beads onto the thread. Position a bead on the fabric, then bring needle 2 through from the wrong side and make a small slanting stitch after the bead with thread 2 holding thread 1 down onto the fabric (Fig. 2). Continue positioning and fastening down each bead in turn.

An alternative method, which is a little faster, is to bring thread 2 up between every 3rd or 4th bead and couch down thread 1, then take thread 2 back to the wrong side of the fabric (Fig. 2b).
Method 3 (Fig. 3) This technique is used for filling smaller areas, such as leaves or petals. Bring the thread through from the wrong side. Pick up three or four beads, pass them along the thread and insert the needle back into the fabric, picking up a single thread.

Finishing beadwork
Beadwork should not be pressed, but if the finished work looks puckered it can be stretched as for canvas work. Dampen the work and pin it out on a padded board with rust-proof pins, pulling gently to remove the puckers. Leave to dry before removing pins.

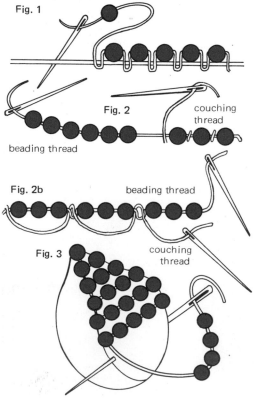

Fig. 1

Fig. 2

couching thread

beading thread

Fig. 2b

beading thread

Fig. 3

couching thread

Bead embroidered book cover

Beading on printed or woven patterned fabric produces a rich jewelled effect. You can follow the lines of the design and follow the colour scheme also, massing beads in some areas or applying beads singly in others. Read page 132 before making a start.

You will need
Fabric, twice the width of the book plus ⅓ and by the depth plus ¼
Glass and ceramic beads
Matching threads
Beading needle
Embroidery frame
Medium-weight iron-on interfacing
Clear household glue
Embroidery threads (optional)
Pencil, ruler

Preparing fabric
Prepare the fabric by ironing on interfacing following manufacturer's instructions. Spread fabric, interfacing side up, on a flat surface. Lay the book on its back about 12.5cm. (5in.) from the right hand edge. Pencil round the book ABCD (Fig. 1). Move the book and hold it on its spine along line ABCD. Draw the spine E to E. Take away the book and draw another line outside all lines 3mm. (⅛in.) away. Put the book back against the new spine line EE face down, and draw round FGHI. Add a new line 3mm. (⅛in.) away (Fig. 2). This extra allowance is so that when the cover is finished it does not fit the book too tightly.

To add the end flaps, draw a line from B to C then a line from B to b and C to c

for 10cm. (4in.). Draw corresponding lines from G to H, G to g and H to h (Fig. 3). Now add the 3mm. (⅛in.) top and bottom allowance along the two flaps. Draw a further line 2.5cm. (1in.) from b to g and c to h for hem (Fig. 4). Cut out cover on these lines.

To work the beading
Work the decoration on the book cover, on both front and back if liked, but avoid the book edges areas and the spine edges. Avoid the inside flap areas. Add surface embroidery if you like.

To finish book cover
Cut into spine flaps for 1.8cm. (¾in.) as marked with black dots in Fig. 4. Fold to inside and glue down. Fold in 6mm. (¼in.) on both end flap edges. Glue down. Fold top and bottom edges 9mm. (⅜in.) and glue together. Fold another 9mm. (⅜in.) and glue down. Leave to dry under weights. Try the book in the cover, tucking in the end flaps. Close the book and then with a pencil lightly mark where the flaps lie on the inside. Remove the book and spread glue neatly along the inside of the end flaps only, top and bottom and both back and front. Press down with the fingertips and then leave to dry overnight. The book's covers are slipped under the flaps.

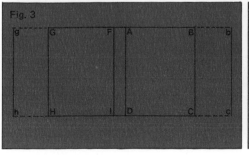

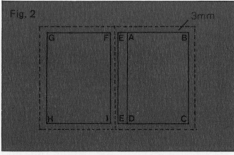

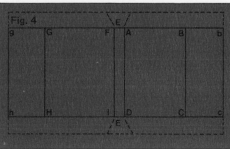

133

Using small motifs

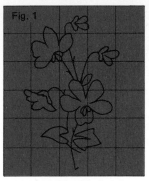

Handkerchiefs

The drawing (Fig. 1) gives the whole motif. Scale this up to size on squared paper, make a tracing and transfer on to one corner of each handkerchief, using the carbon paper. Follow Fig. 2 and colour key for the embroidery, using one strand only for stem stitch and two strands for both satin stitch and long and short stitch. When embroidery is complete, press on the wrong side.

Bedlinen

The drawing (Fig. 3) gives half the motif. Draw up to size on squared paper, make a tracing, and transfer on to the fabric, using the carbon paper. Reverse tracing and transfer other half, making sure centres meet. (You may find it helpful to crease the fabric slightly in the place where you intend the centre of the embroidery to be.)

Work the embroidery following Fig. 4 and colour key, using three strands throughout. When complete, press on the wrong side.

Even if embroidery is your passion, you don't always want to embark on a huge project that will take you years to complete. Sometimes it is pleasant to work on something fairly small, like handkerchiefs or a pillowslip, and hand-embroidered linens are something to treasure for always. Here we give you two simple but pretty floral motifs for linens, using satin stitch with other stitches for outlines.

You will need

For two handkerchief motifs
Of stranded cotton: 1 skein each moss green, yellow, shaded mauve or shaded pink
Tracing paper; dressmaker's carbon paper; squared paper
Crewel needle No. 8
For two bed linen motifs
Of stranded cotton: 1 skein each light violet, dark violet, lilac
Crewel needle No. 7
Tracing paper; dressmaker's carbon paper
Squared paper

Note

The colours for the bedlinen embroidery have been chosen for the pale blue sheets illustrated. If you are embroidering white sheets, or some other colour, choose your own embroidery cotton colours to give the best effect.

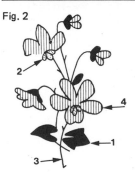

Fig. 1

Fig. 3

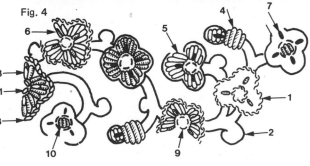

Fig. 2

Fig. 4

KEY

1	■	Satin Stitch moss green
2		Satin Stitch yellow
3	—	Stem Stitch moss green
4		Long and short stitch shaded mauve (pink)

Stranded Cotton or Pearl Cotton

1 –	light violet	
2 –	dark violet	} Stem Stitch
3 –	lilac	
4 –	light violet	
5 –	lilac	} Satin Stitch
6 –	light violet	
7 –	dark violet	} Straight Stitch
8 –	lilac	
9 –	light violet	
10 –	dark violet	} Back Stitch
11 –	lilac	

134

Assisi embroidery

This form of embroidery takes its name from the small town in Italy, home of St Francis, where it was traditionally used for ecclesiastical linens. It has remained popular, as it is relatively quick and easy, and looks very effective on household items such as tablecloths, place mats, napkins and so on. It also looks effective and unusual worked on garments, for instance on a belt or round the hem of a skirt.

Basically it is a cross stitch technique, the only other stitch used being double running, or Holbein stitch (Fig. 1). The difference between this and other cross stitch embroideries is that in Assisi work the motif is the part of the fabric left plain; the cross stitch forms the background. For this reason the designs are usually worked in two colours only on a cream or white ground, and the darker of the two colours chosen is restricted to the running stitch outlines. Motifs should be kept simple and stylised like those shown here, as the best effect is gained by contrasting blocks of stitching against blocks of plain fabric.

Materials
As this is a counted-thread technique it must be worked on evenweave fabric. This can be either linen or cotton and, although cream or white is traditional, colours can be used if desired. Indeed, a red or yellow linen with the stitches worked in black or another dark colour can look very effective indeed.

Yarns can be varied also. Suitable yarns are soft embroidery cotton, stranded cotton or pearl cotton, but silks and metallic threads can be used for effect, particularly for the running-stitch outlining.

Designing and working
Many of the simpler cross stitch designs can be used for Assisi work, or you can adapt your own from patterns you see about you. Wallpaper, carpets and vinyl flooring are all excellent sources for the kind of stylised designs required; if you are really keen, get a book on Oriental carpets out of the library and you will find a wealth of ideas. Chart your chosen motif on graph paper like the examples shown here, and bear in mind that the plain areas must be large enough to stand out from the stitched background.

The embroidery itself is simple; there are only two points to remember. Firstly, make sure that all the tops of the cross stitches go the same way and secondly, make sure that each stitch of the double running stitch goes over the same number of threads as the cross stitch. Always work the outline stitches first and, when they are completed, work the cross stitches in neat horizontal lines so that there are no long threads carried from one part of the work to another.

Fig. 1. Holbein stitch. Working from right to left, work a row of running stitches by passing needle over and under 2 (or more) threads of fabric. Work a second row from left to right, filling in the spaces left in the first row.
Fig. 2. A repeating motif, useful for borders.
Fig. 3. A central motif. The size will depend on the number of threads used for each cross stitch.

Red = cross stitch
Black = Holbein stitch
Fig. 2

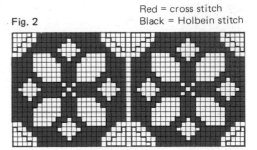

Fig. 3

Fig. 1

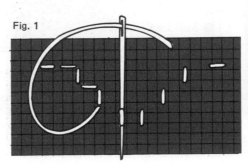

Red = cross stitch
Black = Holbein stitch

Birds in a tree

If you enjoy crewel embroidery you'll like this project – it's a fairly simple design, but there are a lot of different stitches, and beads and sequins are used to create a sparkling effect. You could use the same motif for a small embroidery too; it would look lovely on household linens, for example.

You will need

Of stranded cotton: 2 skeins snuff brown; 1 skein each rose madder, raspberry, cyclamen, moss green, gorse yellow, nasturtium

Piece fine white embroidery fabric 76cm. by 61cm. (30in. by 24in.)

50 gold cup sequins; 236 crystal beads; 89 seed pearls

Crewel needles nos. 5 and 7

Squared paper for pattern, tracing paper

Dressmaker's carbon paper

Note

The techniques of crewel embroidery are explained on page 117. All the stitches you will need are illustrated on that page or on page 103, except fishbone stitch, which is illustrated here (Fig. 1).

The Embroidery

1. Fig. 2 gives half the design. Draw it up to size on squared paper and make a tracing.
2. Using the carbon paper, transfer the design centrally on to the fabric, then turn the tracing over and transfer the other half, making sure the two halves match.
3. Work the embroidery following the diagram and number key, referring to the colour illustration if necessary. Use six strands and the No. 5 needle for double knot stitch and 3 strands with the No. 7 needle for all other stitches.

4. When you have completed the embroidery, press on the wrong side before sewing on beads and sequins with one strand of thread.
5. To make up, place embroidery over mounting board and fold surplus over the back. Secure by lacing from side to side, vertically and horizontally.

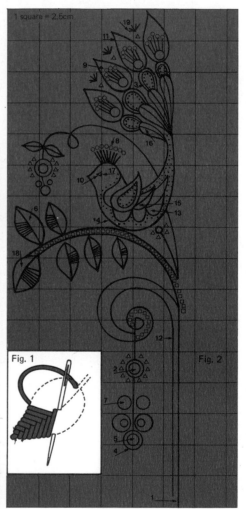

Pearl Cotton or Stranded Cotton

Chain Stitch	**Double Knot Stitch**
1 – Raspberry	11 – Cyclamen
2 – Moss green	12 – Snuff brown
3 – Gorse yellow	
4 – Nasturtium	**Stem Stitch**
	13 – Gorse yellow
Satin Stitch	14 – Nasturtium
5 – Rose madder	
6 – Moss green	**Fishbone Stitch**
7 – Nasturtium	15 – Gorse yellow
	16 – Nasturtium
French Knots	
8 – Rose madder	**Back Stitch**
9 – Gorse yellow	17 – Gorse yellow
10 – Snuff brown	18 – Snuff brown

Straight Stitch
19 – Nasturtium

Embroidered brooches

Make these dainty brooches from just a few scraps of felt and lace. They make inexpensive and unusual gifts – ideal for a little girl's Christmas stocking.

You will need
(per brooch)
2-5cm. (2in.) diameter circles of felt in main colour
20cm. (8in.) lace edging, 2.5cm. (1in.) wide
Scraps of three shades of felt to complement main colour
Scrap of green felt

Fig. 1

Fig. 2

size of flower circles

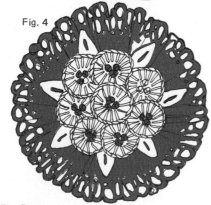

Fig. 3

Fig. 4

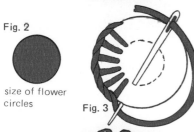

Fig. 5

size of leaf

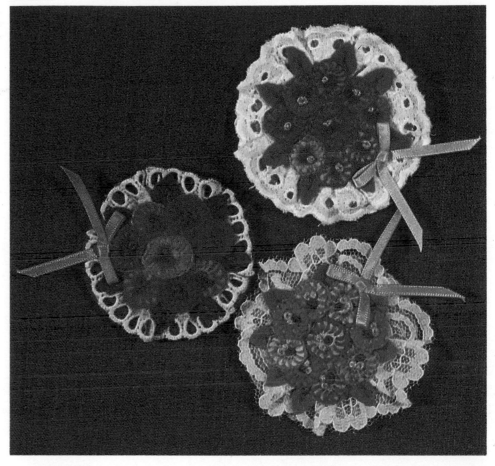

1 safety pin
10cm. (4in.) satin ribbon, 3mm. (⅛in.) wide, in the following colours: lilac, yellow, pink
Stranded embroidery cotton to match main colour felt
Sewing cotton

To make the brooches
1. With sewing cotton, neatly join the ends of the lace with a narrow seam. Run a line of small gathering stitches along the raw edge of the lace and draw thread up to form a 'rosette' (see Fig. 1).
2. Stitch the rosette centrally on to one of the large felt circles.
3. Cut out eight or nine small circles from scraps of felt which complement the main colour felt (see Fig. 2).
4. With crewel wool work buttonhole stitch around the edge of each small felt circle (see Fig. 3), varying the colours used.
5. Arrange these flower circles on top of the lace rosette and attach by working French knots in the centre of each flower, using two different colours plus green wool (see Fig. 4).
6. Cut out 8 small leaves (see Fig. 5) from the green felt and arrange them around the flowers. Stitch in position with green wool, working two or three neat back stitches along the centre of each leaf to form the leaf vein.
7. Tie a small bow with the very narrow satin ribbon and trim the ends at a slanting angle; securely stitch the bow on the edge of the posy.
8. With three strands of embroidery cotton to match the main colour felt, stitch the safety pin very securely in a central position on the other large felt circle, then place the two circles together back to back and neatly buttonhole stitch around the edge with the stranded embroidery cotton to complete the brooch.

Note
You can vary your brooches by omitting the lace or ribbon or use a greater variety of coloured felts and wools. Also, to give a richer effect, beads may be stitched on to the centres of the flowers instead of working French knots.

Crewel-work Christmas scene

The embroidery

1. The diagram gives the complete design, reduced in size. Scale it up on to squared paper, using the red outlines. The stitch detail can be found on the pattern opposite.
2. Trace design on to the fabric, placing it centrally.
3. Work the embroidery from the diagram, following the key for colour and stitch. Use three strands throughout. The stitches themselves are all illustrated on page 117. Note that all parts similar to the numbered parts are worked in the same colour and stitch, and that the back stitch is worked on completion of the satin stitch.

To make up

1. Press embroidery on the wrong side.
2. Place the embroidery centrally over the backing board, and fix temporarily by pinning the fabric to the edges of the board.
3. Secure at the back by lacing horizontally and vertically with strong thread. Remove pins.
4. Cut a mount with a 'window' measuring 19.5cm. by 29.5cm. (7¾in. by 12in.).

A very attractive project for those who enjoy crewel embroidery. The bold, simple design could be adapted for other purposes too, for instance it would make a lovely Christmas card.

You will need

Of stranded cotton: 2 skeins each spring green, white; 1 skein each cardinal red, apple green, grass green, yellow, light tangerine, dark tangerine, flame red, terracotta and black

40cm. (16in.) light-weave embroidery fabric, 92cm. (36in.) wide

Picture frame with backing board or cardboard 33.5cm. by 45cm. (13in. by 17¾in.)

Blue mounting card 33.5cm. by 45cm. (13in. by 17¾in.)

2 picture rings

Crewel needle No. 7

Squared paper

Tracing paper, dressmaker's carbon paper

Craft knife

1 square = 2.5cms

Crewel-work Christmas scene

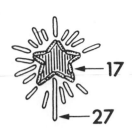

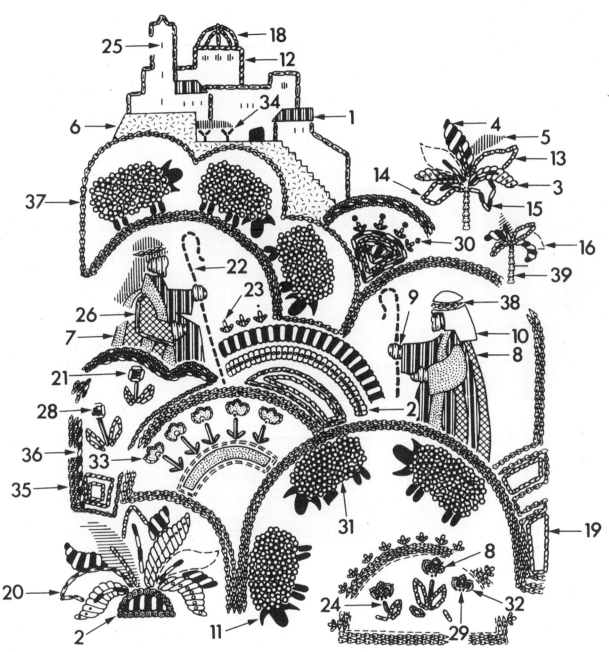

Free-style embroidered picture

This pretty embroidered picture is just right for that empty space on the wall. You can make more than one picture and arrange an attractive group. You can give the pictures more meaning by using scenes from either your own garden or favourite places you have visited.

You will need
36cm. by 18cm. (14in. by 7in.) floral print cotton fabric
48cm. by 16cm. (18¾in. by 6in.) pelmet weight interfacing
Iron-on adhesive tape
16cm. by 16cm. (6in. by 6in.) white linen-type fabric
Pearl cotton embroidery cottons in light green, medium green, orange, light brown, medium brown
1 curtain ring
Sewing thread to match floral print
Squared paper

To make the picture
1. Draw the design to size on grid paper. Using this as a pattern cut out one 'window' frame and two solid pieces in pelmet-weight interfacing (see Fig. 1).
2. Using iron-on adhesive tape, fix linen-type fabric to one of the solid frame pieces and trim away excess fabric around edges.
3. Using iron-on adhesive tape, cover the other solid frame piece and the window frame with the floral print fabric clipping and snipping the narrow turning around the curves. Tack turned edge to wrong side of frame (Fig. 2).
4. Place window frame over linen-covered piece, pin and slip stitch layers together around inner edge of frame. Trim away excess of linen layer under frame edge (Fig. 2).
5. Using design layout (Fig. 1) as a guide, work free-style embroidery. In the embroidery illustrated straight stitch was used for the stone wall and clusters of grass in front of and behind wall. Back stitch was used for the gate. Stem stitch in single lines was used for the branches and in several lines side by side for the trunks. Chain stitch was used to represent leaves. All these stitches can be found on page 103. Fly stitch, which is illustrated on page 117, was used for the abstract flowers above the grass behind the wall and on the single clump in the foreground.
6. When embroidery is complete, press gently with a steam iron or damp cloth on the wrong side to flatten fabric but emboss the stitchery.
7. Stitch the curtain ring centrally on the right side of the fabric frame back.
8. Pin the back and front frame pieces together and with matching thread slip stitch around edges to complete. Press on wrong side to flatten if necessary.

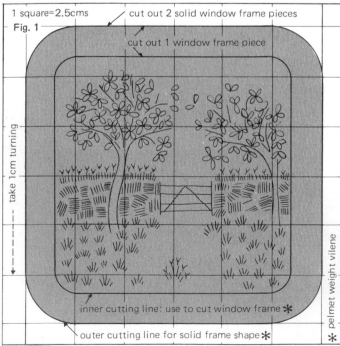

1 square=2.5cms
Fig. 1
take 1cm turning
cut out 2 solid window frame pieces
cut out 1 window frame piece
inner cutting line: use to cut window frame *
outer cutting line for solid frame shape *
* pelmet weight vilene

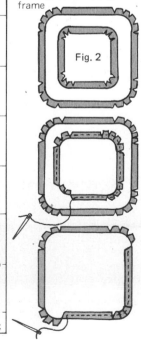

making and covering frame
Fig. 2

Spanish blackwork traycloth

This delicate and beautiful traycloth uses whipped back stitch as a feature in its design. This stitch is always associated with Spanish blackwork. The amount of material given is enough for you to make two traycloths.

You will need
Stranded cotton, 3 skeins black
50cm. (19½in.) of 150cm. (59in.) wide evenweave embroidery fabric, 21 threads to 2.5cm. (1in.)
Tapestry needle No. 24
Sewing equipment

To work the embroidery
From the fabric cut out two pieces each 39.5cm. by 54.5cm. (15½in. by 21½in.). Mark the centre lengthwise with a line of basting stitches. Fig. 1 gives one complete motif and part of second motif. The centre is marked by the blank arrow which should coincide with the basting stitches. The diagram also shows the arrangement of the stitches on the threads of the fabric represented by the background lines.

When working the embroidery, use two strands of cotton for whipping and

Fig.1

KEY **1** Back stitch (squares and circles pattern) **2** Whipped back stitch
3 Cross stitch **4** Back stitch (octagon pattern)

three for the remainder of the embroidery.

With one short side of fabric facing, commence the design twelve threads to the right of the basting stitches and 7cm. (¾in.) from lower edge. Work given motif following the diagram and number key for the embroidery. The stitches can be found on pages 103 and 114, with the exception of whipped back stitch which is shown in Fig. 2. All parts similar to numbered parts are worked in the same stitch. Repeat motif once more to the left in the position when on the diagram.

To complete, turn the fabric and work other short side in same way. Press the embroidery on the wrong side. Turn back 1.3cm. (½in.) hems, mitre corners and slip stitch.

Work normal back stitch first.
Whip over each back stitch without entering the fabric.

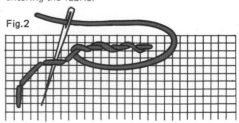

Fig.2

Dorset feather stitch tablecloth

This form of embroidery can be approached with confidence by the average needlewoman. It is a combination of buttonhole stitching with the addition of chain and stem stitch, all of which can be found on page 103.

You will need
A plain linen tablecloth
Stranded cotton in 3 shades of beige
Graph paper
Dressmaker's carbon paper
Tracing paper the size of the cloth
Pencil

To work the embroidery
1. Prepare the tablecloth by checking that the hem is finished properly and then iron it.
2. Enlarge the design on to squared paper to the size as instructed.
3. Measure the tablecloth inside the hem and work out how much to extend the side pieces.
4. Slip the pattern under the tracing paper and trace the entire pattern on to it extending the length as necessary.
5. Pin the tracing paper with the complete pattern to the cloth on the inside of the pattern lines (Fig. 1). Keep as flat as possible.
6. Slip the dressmaker's carbon paper under the design with the waxed side facing the cloth and carefully trace the pattern through slipping the carbon paper along as you go. Make sure you do not rest your arm on the pattern or you will smudge the work.
7. Following the chart on the pattern and the colour code, work the embroidery. Fig. 2 shows twisted chain stitch.
8. When the border has been completed, trace six or eight motifs (depending on the size of the cloth) on to the centre and work in the same way.
9. To complete, press on the wrong side of the work over a damp cloth with a moderately hot iron.

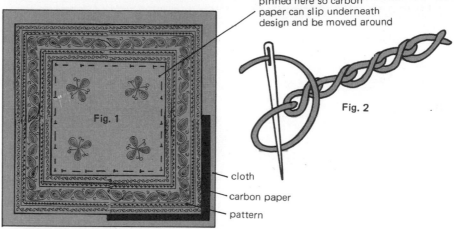

pinned here so carbon paper can slip underneath design and be moved around

Fig. 2

Fig. 1

cloth
carbon paper
pattern

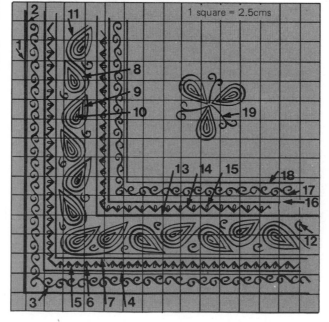

1 square = 2.5cms

Shades of beige		
dark	1	stem
med.	2	twisted chain
light	3	chain
med.	4	twisted chain
light	5	straight stitch
med.	6	detached chain
	7	twisted chain
light	8	
med.	9	blanket stitch
dark	10	
	11	
med.	12	twisted chain
	13	
light	14	straight stitch
med.	15	detached chain
	16	twisted chain
light	17	chain
med.	18	twisted chain
	19	

Dorset crosswheel buttons

These delightful buttons are an attractive finish to smocking, patchwork or any handmade item.

You will need
for each button
A plastic curtain ring – practise on one about 2.5cm. (1in.) diameter
Thread – such as pearl cotton, crochet cotton, crewel embroidery wool or a variation
A tapestry needle

To make
You will need about 2 metres of thread. Hold the ring in your left hand and tie the thread end round it with a single overhand knot. Buttonhole all round clockwise (Fig. 1). The last few stitches will catch in the thread end. Stitches should not be packed too tightly although the ring should be completely covered.

When buttonholing is complete take the needle through the loop of the first stitch. Now turn the outer edge of the stitches inwards with your finger and thumb. The next step is to lay the spokes. For this size ring 8 spokes are sufficient to make a button similar to A in (Fig. 2). Think of the ring as a clock face and hold it with the loose end of the thread at 6 o'clock in front of the ring. Take it up to 12 o'clock and over the ring behind to half-past four, round in front to half-past

ten, over and behind to 3 o'clock and so on until 8 spokes in all are laid. Make sure the crossover point of each pair of threads at the front is in the middle and do not wind the thread too tightly or it will be impossible to complete the next stage satisfactorily.

Still using the same thread come up from the back to one side of the centre crossing and make a firm cross stitch in the middle so that you catch in at the same time all the spokes at the back. (Fig. 3) Now work the centre. With the thread at the front back stitch in clockwise direction backstitch over one spoke and forward under two, so as to make a spider's web. Leave a small gap between the edge of the 'web' and the edge of the buttonholing. Finish off the thread at the back. (Fig. 4).

Button B has 12 spokes laid as in a clock face at the hours. With a different colour darn under and over each pair of spokes separately.

Button C has the spokes and spider's web worked in a different colour.

For Button D whip round 4 spokes of the 12 laid with the basic colour, then darn under and over the remaining 4 groups of 2 with a different colour.

In Button E there are 12 spokes which are divided into 4 groups of 3; pairs of 3 spokes are darned with 2 colours.

Button F has 10 spokes and is worked the same as Button A except that a few rounds of a different colour are worked into the spider's web.

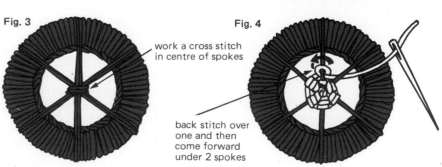

Fig. 1

buttonhole round clockwise

Fig. 2

arrangement of buttons on photograph

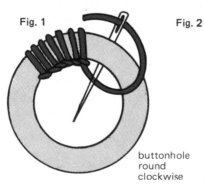

Fig. 3

work a cross stitch in centre of spokes

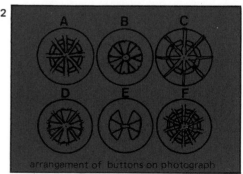

Fig. 4

back stitch over one and then come forward under 2 spokes

Stumpwork embroidery

Stumpwork is an English embroidery technique which was popular during the 17th century. It has a kind of three-dimensional effect because some areas of the design are raised or padded. Originally, stumpwork was called 'stamp work' and was a kind of do-it-yourself kit for children. Professional embroiderers supplied fabric already stamped out with a design together with scraps of appliqué fabrics, embroidery threads, beads, bits of glass, ribbons and lace, and children were encouraged to use as many stitches and techniques as possible. Stumpwork examples in museum collections mostly consist of boxes, frames, jewel caskets, trays and mirror frames.

Fabrics and materials
It has been said of stumpwork that 'anything goes'. Any fabrics at all can be used for the backgrounds and appliqué, as long as the worker feels that she can handle them. 'Slips' (separate pieces of embroidery worked on fabric or mesh canvas) are applied to background fabrics. Beads, pearls, gold threads, lace ribbons, sequins, artificial flowers – all can be used for decoration. Silks, yarns and metallic threads are used for embroidery.

Stitches
Couching and appliqué techniques are used extensively in stumpwork but a wide variety of surface embroidery stitches are used – especially filling stitches. Many of the following stitches have been identified in collected items; satin stitch, braid stitch, bullion knots, buttonhole stitch variations, chain stitch, cloud stitch, wave stitch, Roumanian stitch, cross stitch, feather stitch, French knots, needleweaving, stem stitch, fishbone and split stitch.

Designs for stumpwork
It is a good idea to study museum examples of stumpwork before attempting to adapt the technique to modern designs. Look at the effects achieved and try to work out the various stages of assembly. There are stumpwork examples in many of the larger museums and, if they are not on show, ask the curator in charge of historical textiles if there are stumpwork examples which you can see.

Working procedure
Stumpwork has no exact technique because a worker having decided on the 'picture' or design was able to assemble his or her work in any way that suited

Victoria and Albert Museum, Crown Copyright

them. In general, the design is first outlined on the ground fabric. You could use embroidery chalk or tacking stitches. The areas which are to be simply padded are then applied with polyester filling or cotton batting. This is 'tied' down with a series of crossed stitches. The padded sections can be padded to different thicknesses, depending on the design concept. The raised or padded area is then either covered with appliquéd fabric or, if it is a fairly small area, with embroidery stitches, such as one of the needleweaving trellis stitches. Sometimes, padded areas are covered with a 'slip'.

Slips
Slips are areas of the design worked separately and then applied to the background, usually over a padded area. They can be pieces of embroidery on fabric or worked on a fine mesh canvas. They can also be a separate stuffed piece. This latter kind of slip is often used for faces.

Originally, slips would have been glued on to a paper backing to prevent the edges fraying when they were cut out. Nowadays, clear nail polish is used. When the embroidery has been worked, paint the polish around the stitches, close up to the edge and for about 6mm. (¼in.) all round. Cut out close to the stitches but taking care not to snip them. If edges show, it is permissible to touch them up with a waterproof felt-tipped pen. The slip is then stitched down to the background with blind stitches.

Padded faces
Scraps of nylon tights or stockings are good for working faces in stumpwork

designs. Cut out the shape in thin cardboard. Pad the surface with wadding and then stretch the nylon fabric over the top. Draw the edges to the back and fasten off with a few stitches. Make sure that the stitches do not show through on the front. Now embroider the features carefully using one strand of embroidery thread and a fine needle. Work carefully because you will not be able to unpick mistakes without laddering the nylon.

Padding on contrast fabrics
You may occasionally want to have a padded figure in a patterned or textured fabric which is different from the main background. Trace off the design shape on the patterned fabric twice, reversing one shape. Work any embroidery or embellishment you desire. Cut out the shape leaving about 6mm. (¼in.) extra all round. Cut out the second shape from the same fabric. Put the two pieces together right sides together and sew all round leaving a gap for turning. If it is a very small or intricately shaped piece, simply turn in the edges of both pieces as you sew using oversewing stitches. Stuff the piece and close the open seam. Now sew it to the background work.

Freestanding areas
In some of the collected pieces of stumpwork you may see certain areas of the design which are freestanding. These can be anything from bird's wings or an insect's leg, to a flower petal or a butterfly's wing. To raise an area of stumpwork, such as a petal, first work the whole flower in the 'flat'. The raised petal is worked in two pieces, the front and a back. Trace the shape on the same kind of fabric as the background twice. Work both shapes, the front and the back of the petal, as close to the flat embroidery in colour and technique as possible. Cut a piece of thin wire – fuse wire will do – and bend it roughly to the shape of the petal. Paint all round the two worked shapes with nail polish and leave to dry. Cut out closely. Lay the two pieces of embroidery together, wrong sides together with the bent wire in between following the shape of the petal. The two wire ends should protrude from the bottom of the petals. Keep the ends of the wire together. Oversew all round the two petals joining them together. Thread the wires through to the back of the work and couch them down securely.

Fabric painting

If you have ever wanted to design dress fabrics, have table linen to match your china or bedlinen carrying your personal monogram, now is your chance.

If you are artistic, you can probably produce your own designs, but even if you are not, you are surrounded by designs which can be copied. You can trace motifs off the wallpaper, from a dinner plate, from an existing fabric, or from something in a book. Embroidery transfers are a good source of motifs, you can paint a design with the aid of stencils, and fabrics can be printed by using simple printing blocks such as half potatoes, the cut surface carved into interesting designs.

Fabric paints come in many intermixable colours which are ideal for painting or printing natural and synthetic fabrics. They are colourfast, so anything you paint is washable and dry-cleanable. Although fast on fabric, these paints wash easily from fingers and equipment with cold water. They are also non-toxic and are therefore quite safe for children to use.

For the best results, new washable fabrics should be washed and ironed before patterning to remove any dressing which would prevent the paint from being properly absorbed.

To paint your fabric

Iron on a transfer or draw your design on to the fabric with a soft pencil or a dressmaker's chalk pencil. Lay the fabric on paper, or if painting a garment, pillowslip, or anything with two sides, slip some paper inside to prevent the paint penetrating right through. Kitchen paper is ideal for this purpose, but you can use newspaper as long as it is at least a week old – fresh newsprint can mark your material. Secure silky fabrics with adhesive tape to stop them slipping as this could smudge the paint. Stretch T-shirts and stretchy fabrics over a piece of card.

The choice of brushes will be dictated by the kind of design you are painting. Soft artist's brushes are best for small, intricate designs, but for covering large areas you can use a 1.3cm. (½in.) household brush. Stencilling requires a fairly hard bristle brush such as those used for oil painting.

Except when you are putting one colour on top of another you need not wait for one colour to dry before painting on the next. Brushes, however, should be washed and dried between each colour change. For vivid colours on deep-coloured fabrics, paint on a white base coat and allow this to dry before painting on the colour.

When the finished painting is dry, remove the paper or card, cover the painted areas with a cotton cloth and iron with a hot iron for 2 minutes to fix the paint.

Block printing

This is the easiest way of patterning fabric with a repeat design; even one motif printed in several different colours can produce an exciting effect. Virtually anything that has a raised pattern and will hold the paint until pressed into position on the fabric can be used as a printing block. An effective block can be made by cutting away the background from a halved potato to leave a raised motif, but remember to blot the potato regularly during printing to dry up excess moisture. Half an apple or pear will print the fruit's shape. More complicated designs can be made from string twisted into a pattern and glued on to off-cuts of wood. If you are really ambitious you could make lino blocks, but for this you would need special tools for cutting the lino.

Besides the printing block and fabric paints you will need printing pads (squares of synthetic sponge – one for each paint colour), two plates, paper and, if mixing colours, a small dish.

Work out your design and make the printing block. Mark the fabric very lightly in chalk with guide lines for positioning the block. Lay the fabric on paper and secure with pins or adhesive tape to prevent it from slipping; put paper or card inside garments. If you are printing lengths of fabric, move the fabric and paper together as you progress, taking care not to fold the still wet printed areas, and making sure that each section of fabric to be printed is secured to a clean sheet of paper.

Pour a small quantity of fabric paint on to a plate, press the sponge into it and lay it paint-side up on another plate. Press the block on to the sponge so that it takes up the paint evenly, then press the block firmly on to the fabric. Repeat until the design is complete. If using several paint colours, finish everything in one colour, allowing it to dry before printing the next. Wash blocks, sponges etc. in cold water between each colour change and do not use again until thoroughly dry.

When printing is complete and the fabric is dry, fix the paint as described, using a hot iron.

Designing with batik

The ancient craft of batik, which was developed in Indonesia centuries ago, has now become a popular hobby. The word itself means 'wax writing' and the principle is quite simple: areas of fabric are painted with hot liquid wax, and the cloth is then dyed. The wax acts as a barrier so that only the unwaxed areas take the dye. This process can be repeated several times, using different dye colours, to build up a more complex design or picture. The wax is then removed, leaving the fabric soft, supple and translucent.

A unique characteristic of batik is the attractive marbling or crackling effect produced by dye seeping in to tiny random cracks in the wax. Some of the best effects are, in fact, produced by chance, as it is necessary to work rather fast with hot wax. This, and the control of colour gained by repeated dyeings, make batik a particularly exciting way of decorating fabric. It is not necessary to be an artist, as fine batiks can be created just by using bold geometric shapes, while more elaborate patterns can be made with the aid of embroidery transfers, stencils or simple batik blocks.

Materials

The best batik fabrics are white or cream coloured cotton, linen or silk. Avoid synthetic fibres, as they will not take the dye properly. The wax used for batik is usually a mixture of paraffin wax and beeswax, but ordinary white candles can be used. The dyes must be cold-water dyes, as hot water would melt the wax; they give a good choice of colours, all of them intermixable, and have the advantage of being colourfast. For applying the wax you will need bristle paintbrushes, domestic ones for covering large areas and artist's brushes for straightforward work. Very detailed work is done with the traditional batik tool the *tjanting* (wax pen). This consists of a small copper bowl with a narrow spout attached to a wooden handle. It is dipped into the wax and used just like a pen.

You will also need a double saucepan, or a can which can be placed in a saucepan, for melting the wax, and some kind of frame on which to stretch the fabric so that the wax penetrates right through it. Special frames can be purchased in craft shops, but you can easily make one with 4 strips of wood joined at the corners with rightangle braces, or you can use an old drawer or box.

Working method

Wash and iron new fabrics to remove any dressing. Lightly pencil the design on to the fabric, or iron on a transfer, and stretch the fabric on the frame with thumb tacks.

Heat the wax, either in a double saucepan or in a can placed inside a saucepan with about 5cm. (2in.) of water in it. Do not allow the wax to get so hot that it smokes; turn it down when it begins to bubble. If it is at the right temperature, it should look transparent when applied to the fabric. Paint the hot wax over your design where you wish to retain the existing colour. If it looks milky the wax is not hot enough and is not penetrating the fabric – for a good dye-resist the wax must penetrate right through.

Repeat patterns can be produced with blocks or stencils, while such everyday objects as forks, fish slices and pastry cutters dipped in hot wax can create intriguing patterns. Other motifs can be made by pushing nails into corks or blocks of wood.

When your design is complete remove the fabric from the frame, wet it in cold water, crumple it a little if you want the crackled effect, and dye it, following the instructions on the dye tin. If using more than one dye colour always start with the lightest, and remember that where two colours overlap a third will be created, for instance yellow overdyed red gives orange. Rinse thoroughly in cold water and drip-dry. This sequence may be repeated several times until the design or picture is complete.

To remove the wax, sandwich the batik between sheets of absorbent paper or old newspapers (never use new ones as the ink could run), and iron over the top. Remove any remaining wax and dye residue by washing the batik in very hot detergent in a bowl. Never pour water containing wax down the sink.

Painted waistcoat

Clothes you once loved but have grown tired of can be given a new lease of life with an exciting decorative treatment. Denim, in particular, is so durable that you tend to lose interest in it long before it wears out, and since becoming so popular much of it has lost its individuality. This plain denim waistcoat looked like any other until it was revamped and updated with fabric paints. Any fabric, not just denim, can be painted, and this colourful chevron design can be adapted to pattern other things, too. Try it around the hem of a skirt, down the legs of jeans or on a plain shirt front.

A pattern for the chevron design appears on the opposite page.

You will need
Of fabric paints:
1 pot red
1 pot gold
1 pot blue
1 pot white
Small soft paintbrush
Small dish for mixing colours
Tracing paper and pencil
Dressmaker's carbon paper
Ruler
Piece of string, 60cm. (24in.) long
6 beads

Note
Before painting new denim, or any new washable fabric, wash it in very hot water to remove any dressing which will prevent the paint being properly absorbed.

To paint the design
From the paper pattern, measure the overall area covered by the chevron design and mark the corresponding areas on the waistcoat. Open out the waistcoat, lay it flat on a wad of paper and paint a white base coat over the areas to be pat-terned. You cannot paint bright colours directly on to a dark background. If necessary put on a second coat of white, and leave to dry. (Omit this white under-coat if painting a light-coloured fabric.)

To transfer the pattern on to the white-painted areas of the waistcoat, make a tracing and pin it right side up on the waistcoat with a sheet of carbon under-neath. Go over the pattern with the pencil so that the outline appears on the white paint. Turn the tracing over so that the pattern is reversed, pin into position on the opposite side of the waistcoat and trace off the design as before.

Paint in the design, using the colour-key as a guide. There is no need to wait for one colour to dry before painting on the next, but complete one colour at a time and wash and dry the brush between every colour change. Additional shades can be mixed from the basic colours as follows:

yellow + blue = green
blue + white = turquoise
yellow + red = orange
red + blue = purple
white + red = pink

When the painting is finished and com-pletely dry, cover the waistcoat with a cotton cloth and iron each of the pat-terned sections with a hot iron for 2 min-utes to 'fix' the paint.

Complete the new look by adding some beaded strings. Paint a 60cm. (24in.) length of ordinary parcel string green and when dry iron it as above. Cut into 6 pieces, 10cm. (4in.) long, dividing them into 2 sets of 3 and knot together at one end. Thread a bead on to each string and secure with a knot. Sew into position and trim ends.

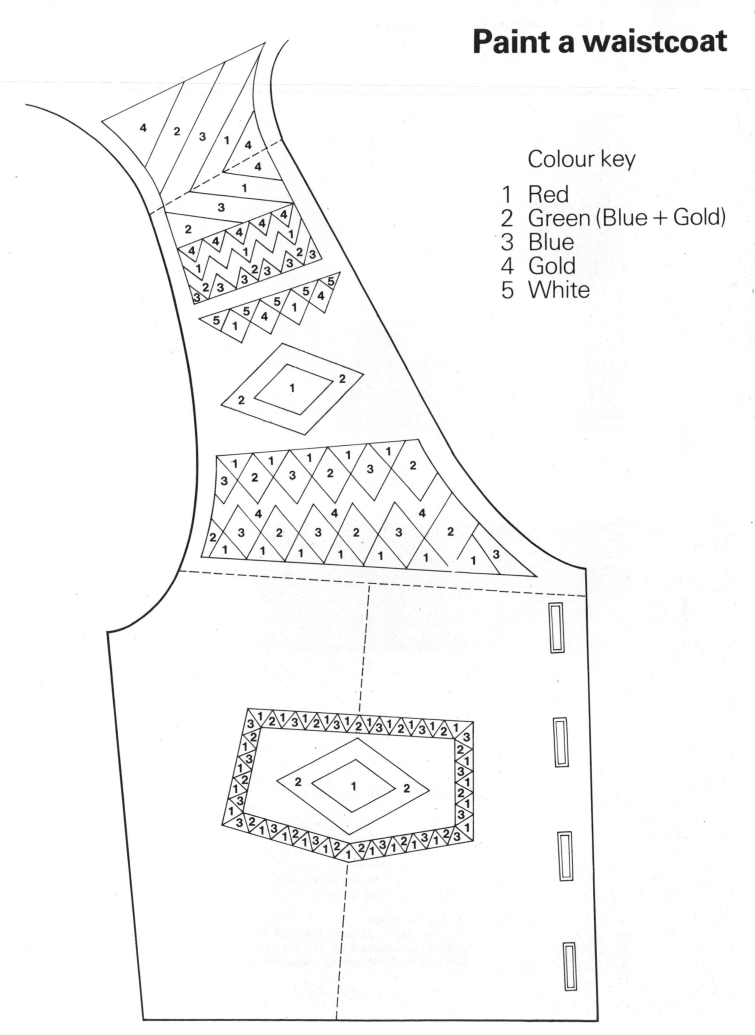

Paint a waistcoat

Colour key

1 Red
2 Green (Blue + Gold)
3 Blue
4 Gold
5 White

Batik blind

The beauty of a batik blind is that it comes alive like a stained glass window when the light shines through it. This design is suitable for any room and can be scaled up to fit any size window. The same design could be used to make a matching tablecloth, placemats, cushion covers or a wall hanging.

You will need
White cotton fabric to fit window plus
   hem allowance
DIY roller blind kit
Of cold water dyes:
2 tins each yellow and green
4 sachets cold dye fix
Salt
Wooden frame or drawer
Batik wax or white candles
Old saucepan
Medium size artist's bristle brush and
   1.3cm. (½in.) domestic paintbrush
Dressmaker's graph paper
Soft pencil, ruler and drawing pins
Rubber gloves, old newspapers or
   kitchen paper

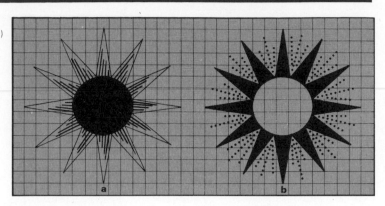

Scale:
1 square = 7.62cm (3in)

a Black =
areas for 1st waxing

b Black =
areas for 2nd waxing

First read page 147, which explains the principles of batik.

To make the design
Wash the fabric, if new, to remove any dressing which will prevent the dye being properly absorbed. Scale up the design (Figs. a and b) on to dressmaker's graph paper, using a ruler, and mark in both the first and second waxings. As the graph paper is sold in fairly small sheets you will need to tape several together. Pin the fabric over the enlarged drawing and trace the design. Remove the graph paper and stretch the fabric on to a wooden frame or over a drawer, keeping it taut with the drawing pins. As this is too large a design to fit on most frames you will have to paint section by section.

Heat the wax and, using a medium size artist's brush, outline the sunrays and paint in the stripes on each ray with hot wax. Wax in the centre circle with a 1.3cm. (½in.) domestic paintbrush. When the first waxing is complete, mix the first dye colour, yellow. Remove the fabric from the frame, wet thoroughly in cold water, crumpling it to crack the wax for the 'marbling' or crackled effect, and dye for an hour.

Rinse the batik in cold water until it runs clear, and drip-dry. Check that the pencilled outlines for the second waxing are still visible and re-trace if necessary. Stretch the fabric back on to the frame. Wax in the sunrays with the domestic paintbrush and paint dots of wax with the artist's brush between the rays where you wish to retain the yellow. Wet the batik and dye it green, following the same procedure as before. Rinse well and then drip-dry.

To remove the wax, lay the batik on a wad of old newspapers topped with clean kitchen paper, cover with more kitchen paper and iron over with a hot iron, changing the paper as necessary until most of the wax is absorbed. Remove the residue of wax and any excess dye by washing the batik in very hot detergent in a bowl, as water containing wax should not be poured down the sink.

Make up the blind following the instructions accompanying the kit.

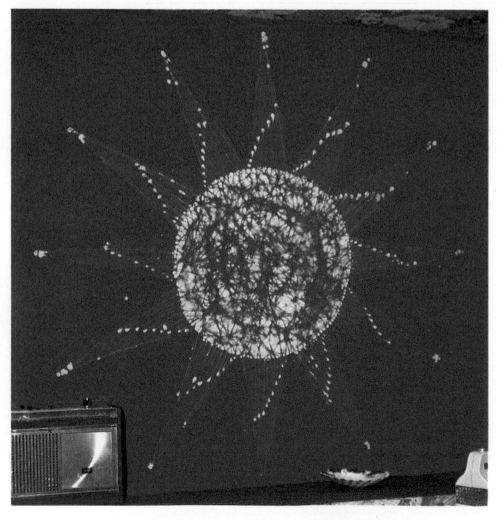

Tie-and-dye

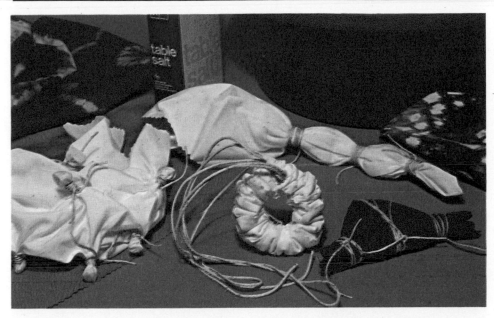

Tie-and-dye is probably the oldest dye-craft of all. Tie-dyed silks and fine cottons were popular in India, China and Japan around the 6th century A.D. As the craft developed different methods evolved, and fabrics were folded, pleated and knotted, tied tightly with thread or string and then dyed. As the dye cannot penetrate the tied up areas, a pattern is produced, and the way the fabric is tied determines what the pattern will be. Other designs can be made by tying stones into the fabric or by sewing and ruching it.

For a sharp pattern contrast the fabric must be wet before it is dyed. Attractive patterns can be produced with just one dyeing, but by using several dye colours in different stages you can achieve very intricate designs. Rinse well after dyeing and remember that where two colours combine a third will be produced, e.g. yellow + blue makes green. Always start with the lightest colour and either reposition the bindings or completely refold and re-tie the fabric between each dyeing so that some of the first colour is retained and only the newly exposed areas of fabric take the next dye.

Tie-and-dye can be used to pattern clothes – everything from dresses, skirts and tops to underwear and scarves – or to liven up plain household linens.

Natural fabrics (cotton, linen, silk) viscose rayon and fabrics with a high natural fibre content (polyester/cotton) are best dyed with colourfast cold water dyes.

Synthetics and acetates should be dyed with hot water dyes but these are not as colourfast as the cold water dyes.

Rinse well after the final dyeing, remove the bindings and wash in hot, mild detergent to remove any dye residue.

TIE-AND-DYE PATTERNS
Stripes
Several variations are possible depending on how the fabric is pleated and tied. Pleat lengthways for vertical stripes, horizontally for horizontal stripes and diagonally for diagonal stripes. To make candy stripes fold narrow pleats, and make wide pleats for broader stripes. Iron to make the folds crisp, and tie string bindings at regular intervals. If you are using more than one dye colour you might like to reposition some of the bindings before re-dyeing for a good effect. Add the new bindings before removing the old to avoid disturbing the pleating. The new bindings will then resist the next dye.

Circles
Tie stones, marbles or dried beans into the fabric to create a pattern of small circles. Either mark out a specific design or tie them in at random. If you want another dye colour, repeat the process, tying the stones, marbles or beans in different places.

Sunbursts
These larger circles can be varied in size and complexity according to the number and position of the string bindings. Pick up the fabric to form a peak and arrange it in even folds as it falls away. For a 5cm. (2in.) circle bind the fabric and string 2.5cm. (1in.) from the top of the point; for a 10cm. (4in.) circle position the binding 5cm. (2in.) down from the point, and so on. Several sets of bindings will produce concentric circles.

Triangles
Pleat the fabric lengthways into four then fold it back on itself, concertina-style, into a series of triangles. Bind the ends and across the centre with string.

Ruching
Lay a length of doubled string across one corner of the fabric and roll the fabric diagonally around it. Form a circle with the rolled fabric, ruche it tightly along the string and tie ends.

Tritik (sewing)
This is used for motifs, names and initials. Working freehand or with stencils, lightly pencil the design on to the fabric and with strong thread, knotted at the end, sew over the outlines with small tacking stitches. Sew a double row 6mm. (¼in.) apart on thick fabrics. Ruche the fabric tightly along stitches; secure with a knot.

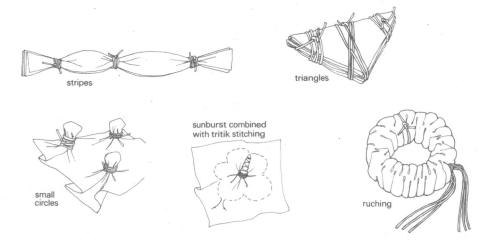

stripes

triangles

small circles

sunburst combined with tritik stitching

ruching

Tie-and-dye placemats

These pretty tie-dyed placemats will brighten up your mealtimes, and making them will give you a lot of fun. If you have some linens that are past their best, or if you have become tired of plain pastels, give them a new lease of life and enjoy using them again. Tie-and-dye can be used to pattern table-cloths and napkins, too, but you may prefer to cut something up and make several placemat sets in different co-ordinating colours so that you can ring the changes.

The placemats illustrated were made from a well-washed cotton damask tablecloth that was beginning to fray; you can make several sets from a medium-size cloth. The good parts of worn sheets or remnants can also be used. Fringe the edges of the mats or trim them with lace to complete the transformation.

The most suitable dyes are the cold water dyes, which come in a wide range of fast colours. These are ideal for tie-and-dye and are particularly suitable for household linens which are always in the wash. They will give the best results on cotton and linen. They can also be used on polyester/cottons, but as only the cotton content absorbs the dye the colours will be paler. If you are using an already coloured fabric, or are doing several dyeings, remember that the colours will blend together, e.g. a red dyed blue will give purple.

You will need

For the four placemats illustrated
1m. (1 yard) 90cm. (36in.) white cotton
6.50m. (7 yards) 2cm. (¾in.) wide white cotton lace
1 tin each of cold dyes in yellow and coffee colours
2 sachets cold dye fix
Salt
String

To make the mats
Make sure the fabric is clean and stain-free. It's a good idea to use a colour and stain remover to shift any stubborn stains, as these may still show through even after the fabric is dyed. Cut out four placemats, 45cm. by 35cm. (18in. by 14in.). This includes a 1.3cm. (½in.) hem allowance all round.

Mix the orange dye in 500ml. (1 pint) warm water and pour it with the salt into a large bowl (or the sink) containing enough cold water to cover the place-mats and lace. Dissolve the cold dye fix in 500ml. (1 pint) boiling water and add to the dye. Wet the fabric and lace in cold water and put them into the dye solution. Dye for one hour, stirring continuously for the first 10 minutes and intermittently thereafter, keeping the materials submerged and spread out. Afterwards, rinse until the water runs clear. Iron the placemats when almost dry.

Taking each placemat in turn, lay wrong-side up, fold in half horizontally, crease and open out. Fold in top and bottom edges up to the half-way line, then fold in half again to form a narrow strip a quarter of the original width with the outer edges folded in and the centre of each mat on the outside. Now fold the strip of fabric back on itself to form a series of right-angled triangles. Bind each corner and the centre of the resulting triangular shape with string.

Mix the brown dye as above, wet the tied-up placemats and lace and dye for one hour. Rinse thoroughly, untie the placemats and wash them, together with the lace, in hot, mild detergent, to remove any excess dye. Iron the lace and placemats while still damp. When dry, turn in the hems and trim edges with lace.

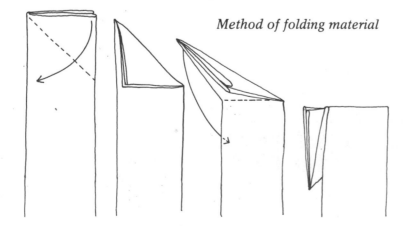

Method of folding material

Paint a quilt

cloth and iron with a hot iron for 2 minutes to fix the paint. Dye fabric for backing according to the instructions which appear on the tin.

To make up the quilt
Sandwich the wadding between the backing fabric and the painted fabric with the painted design towards you. Pin and tack round the edges, vertically, horizontally and diagonally to hold the three thicknesses together. Using a machine zig-zag stitch, set at width 1, length 2, quilt round the design shapes, working from the middle to edges. You will have to roll the quilt up under the machine arm to get to every part of it.

To finish the quilt
Fold, pin and stitch bias binding round the raw edges, tacking one side at a time. For neat mitred corners stitch up to 2.5cm. (1in.) from corner. Hold binding along stitched edge flat right up to the new unbound edge as you fold the binding at right angles at the corner, and then fold this new side for binding flat.

Attractive bedspreads can be quite expensive, but you can make your own individual designs by painting on cotton sheeting. Here we have given you three different designs to choose from, and you can use any colours you like.

You will need
Pure cotton sheeting. We used 4.50m. (5yd.) 160cm. (63in.) wide, or use an old cotton bedsheet
2m. (2yd.) washable terylene wadding, 90cm. wide
8m. (8yd.) 5cm. (2in.) wide bias binding
Fabric paints: for the quilt illustrated 1 bottle each green, sun, coral and blue
1 can cold water dye in blue for the backing
1.2cm. (½in.) household paintbrush

Preparing the fabric
Boil sheeting to remove dressing, damp dry, iron smooth. Cut sheeting in half to make two pieces each 91m. by 2m. (36in. by 78in.). Or cut double bed sheet in half lengthways. On one piece of fabric faintly pencil 15cm. (6in.) squares. Draw up your chosen design from one of the diagrams – each square represents a 15cm. (6in.) square. Spread marked out

sheeting on newspaper to prevent any paint seeping through.

To paint the design
Paint one colour at a time, and allow each to dry before starting the next. When complete and dry, cover with a

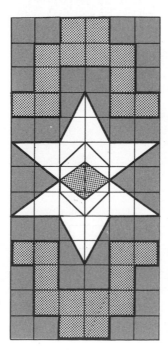
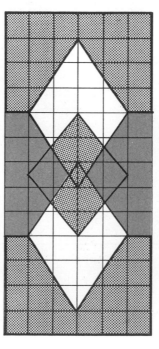
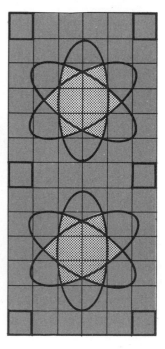

Scrap printing on fabric

This technique needs only a minimum of materials, all of which are easily obtainable, to produce individual, exciting results. You can print a range of items from useful articles like tea-towels, to decorative ones such as curtains and wallhangings. It is not necessary to be an artist; care and planning only are needed to produce attractive results.

Materials and equipment

The best colouring material to use is fabric paint, which can be used on any type of fabric as it is a paint, not a dye.

The next requirement is printing pads. These can be any absorbent pieces of material, such as felt, thin plastic foam or flannel. They should be about 15cm. (6in.) square, but always larger than the motif to be printed, and you should have one for each different colour.

You also need clean newspaper, paint brush, cellophane tape, rag, an apron and rubber gloves, and a cutting knife.

The printing units can be almost anything that takes your fancy. Collect bottle tops, small jars, corks, cotton reels and spools, sponges, polystyrene tiles and anything else that will print. Patterns can be cut into cut ends of carrots, turnips and potatoes. Brussels sprouts and cabbages cut in half print very well (see illustration), as do dried leaves and ferns with strongly marked veins.

Techniques

The dyes Fabric paint is ready to use straight from the bottle. To prepare the printing pad, simply brush the dye evenly over the pad, adding more dye as required.

Printing First cover a table with several layers of clean newspaper, smoothing it flat. Then tape an old handkerchief or piece of fabric to the newspaper. Lay the printing pad on your working side of the table on a plastic bag, tin lid, tile or a piece of kitchen foil. Press one of your printing units on to the prepared pad so that it takes up the dye evenly and then apply firmly to one corner of the piece of fabric. Repeat the process, working across the width, and always pressing the unit on the pad between each print. Try to make a complete design by printing several colours on top of or by the side of other prints using differently coloured pads. When you have experimented enough, and are sure of the technique, try printing a cushion cover, table mats, or a length of material for a bedspread.

If you are printing with a leaf or other flat unit, you do not use a printing pad. Instead, place it on newspaper with the printing surface uppermost and paint it evenly with dye. If it is a leaf, lift it by its stem and place it, dye side down, on the fabric. Cover it with a piece of clean newspaper and gently smooth the hands over the paper. Remove paper and leaf carefully from the fabric. Use fresh newspaper for each print.

Fixing the dyes. After printing with fabric paints, allow prints to dry, cover printed areas with clean cotton cloth and iron for 1 to 2 minutes, using as hot a setting as the type of fabric will allow. (Be careful not to leave the iron stationary on the fabric.) Wash in luke-warm water after ironing.

Notes

Always hang printed fabrics to dry away from direct heat, allowing air to circulate around the fabric. Never allow wet printed fabrics to lie in piles.

Lino block printing

This method of printing enables you to turn quite complicated designs into a permanent form ready to print. Lino blocks can be used for fabric or paper, and you can achieve exciting effects with simple patterns as well as with more complex ones.

Materials and equipment

The best surface for printing is a firm, flat-topped table covered with a smooth piece of blanket with a sheet of PVC or plastic sheeting on top. You will need a lino roller, and lino tools, which can be bought either singly or in a box containing several assorted cutters and a handle.

The lino should be plain and smooth, at least 3mm. (⅛in.) thick. It is a good idea to start with a 10cm. (4in.) square which is glued on to the same sized piece of hardboard, blockboard or plywood before the design is cut.

You will also need inking slabs to roll out the ink (pieces of hardboard, tiles or large tin lids will all serve), clear household glue, paraffin, greaseproof paper, rags and clean newspaper, an apron and rubber gloves. Fabric printing oil-based inks, sold in tubes, will print on most non-pile fabrics, and are colourfast.

Designing and cutting the block

Draw a simple design such as a star or sun shape on paper, and trace. Place the tracing face down on carbon paper on the lino and draw over the design so that your design appears in reverse on the lino. When printed, it will, of course, appear the right way round on the fabric.

To cut the lino, hold the tool with the handle in the palm of one hand, and hold the lino block with the other hand. Always keep both hands *behind* the tool nib when cutting and cut *away* from your body. Use a V-shaped nib to cut lines, dots and the edges of large spaces, and a U-shaped nib to clear out large spaces. Be careful not to cut into the lino backing. You can cut out either the design or the background; only the uncut areas will print.

Printing

Try a few prints on newspaper or scrap fabric before trying a real print. Tape the fabric corners down to the plastic sheeting on the table top. Squeeze out about 5cm. (2in.) of fabric ink on to the smoothest side of your inking slab. Use the rubber-covered lino roller to spread the ink evenly over the slab. Roll the inked roller over the cut surface of your lino block to give an even coating of ink sufficient to make a clear print without clogging up the cut-out areas. Apply the inked block to one corner of your fabric. 'Bump' the back of your block with the handle end of a mallet or hammer. Remove block, re-ink and reprint until the pattern is complete. (Always re-ink the block between each print.) Replenish the ink on the slab as required. Prints can either touch each other to give an all-over pattern or be left as separate units. Non-symmetrical shapes can be printed alternately upside down or in brick patterns. If you want to use more than one colour, you can either make two or more blocks or use small units such as cotton reels or spools, on top of the first print when it is dry.

When you have experimented enough, and are sure of the technique, remove the trial prints and tape down your proper fabric. Try to work it out so that the block size fits into the fabric size a certain number of times, for instance a 50cm. (20in.) square cushion cover will take 25 10cm. (4in.) square units, or 20 12.5cm. (5in.) units. Allow margins for making up.

After printing hang up the fabric to dry away from direct heat. When thoroughly dry place between two sheets of greaseproof paper and iron on the reverse for 2 to 3 minutes, using the hottest setting the type of fabric will take. (Never leave the iron stationary on the fabric.) After ironing, wash in luke-warm water and finally iron again while still damp.

Notes

Clean up roller, block and slab with paraffin and rag. Work on several sheets of newspaper because it is a messy job.

Screen printing on fabric

Screen printing, which developed from the ancient craft of stencilling, provides a very simple method of printing designs on small and large articles. It works on the principle of stretching material over a frame, blocking out certain areas and squeezing ink or dye through the un-blocked areas. There are different methods of blocking out, but here we deal only with the simplest one, a stencil made from greaseproof paper.

Materials and equipment
For the actual printing you will need the following.
1. A frame. This can be bought or home made.
2. Fabric to cover the frame. The most suitable fabrics are cotton organdie or terylene voile.
3. A squeegee to fit inside frame. The squeegee can be bought or it can be made from hardboard.
4. Waterproof cloth masking tape, 5cm. to 7.5cm. (2in. to 3in.) wide.
5. Roll of greaseproof paper.
6. Fabric paints.
7. Water, rags, clean newspaper containers for dye, spoons, scissors, iron, an apron and rubber gloves.
8. Fabric for printing: 100% cotton fabrics give the best results. (Before any fabric is printed it should be well-washed to remove any dressing, rinsed and ironed flat.)

You will also need a firm, flat surface covered with a smooth blanket and a piece of plastic sheet on top on which to print your fabric.

Making a frame
This can be made from ordinary planed softwood 5cm. by 2.5cm. (2in. by 1in.). The corners must be absolutely square, and can be butt-jointed (Fig. 1), glued with waterproof glue and pinned with 5cm. (2in.) oval nails. The completed frame must lie quite flat and must be smoothed down with sandpaper and then varnished all over with exterior quality varnish.

A convenient size of frame to begin with, for printing small articles and all-over patterns, would be 43cm. by 38cm. (17in. by 15in.), and would require four strips of wood each 38cm. (15in.) long.

The fabric to cover the frame should be 5cm. (2in.) wider all round than the outside screen measurement. Fold or iron the fabric 2.5cm. (1in.) in on all sides, wet it and spread over the frame. Put a drawing pin through the double edge at the centre of one side, and then continue pinning in the order shown, pulling the fabric evenly outwards and keeping edges level with the frame edge.

Turn the frame round and pin the opposite side in the same manner, pulling the fabric as taut as possible across the frame as well as outwards, to give a flat, drum-like surface. Pin the other two sides in the same way, tucking in the corners neatly.

Now you must mask the frame to provide dye 'reservoirs' inside it. Turn the frame the other way up and using self-adhesive waterproof cloth tape, mask a minimum 5cm. (2in.) margin on each edge of the screen.

The squeegee
The function of the squeegee is to press the colour through the screen. You can use a rubber-edged window cleaning squeegee, but file down any sharp metal corners to avoid damaging the screen covering, or you can cut one from a piece of hardboard with the lower edge bevelled by rubbing with sandpaper.

How to start printing
Before starting on fabric, practise on sheets of newspaper. When you have got the hang of it, you can move on to the real thing.
1. Place a sheet of clean, flat newspaper on your working surface.
2. Cut some greaseproof paper to the outside dimension of the screen and fold it into quarters.
3. Cut out a pattern in the folded paper, making sure that, when opened out, the pattern (cut-away parts) will fit within the printing area.
4. Open out the pattern and iron it flat between clean newspapers.
5. Place the greaseproof pattern on the printing newspaper and position the screen centrally on top of it.
6. Spread fabric paints along the bottom inside edge of screen. Hold screen with hand and, keeping squeegee almost up-right, push the paint across the screen in one firm stroke. Now place the squeegee behind the paint and pull it back to its original position, leaving the pattern area clear of paint.
7. Lift the screen carefully from the print, starting at one side, and prop it on a piece of wood, leaving the squeegee in position.

If you find the greaseproof pattern slips, you can tape the edges to the edges of the screen. When the paint is dry other colours and designs can be printed on top.

Wash all equipment in cold water when you have finished printing, and fix paint to the manufacturer's instructions.

Designs for screen printing

If you have read page 156, you will now understand the principle of screen printing. Here we give some ideas for a basic design that could be used by itself, as a border or as an allover pattern on a wide range of household furnishings.

Note
The materials and equipment you will need are listed on page 156.

Planning your design
Cut a piece of greaseproof paper to the outside dimension of your screen. Fold it in half, either on the diagonal or from one edge to another, and cut out a design on the folded edge similar to those shown on the front of the card. Keep the cut design to within the printing area of your screen. Open out the paper and iron it flat between the sheets of clean newspaper.

Preparing the fabric
You will obtain best results from 100% cotton or linen fabrics, but mixtures, such as polyester/cotton, rayon/cotton etc., or synthetics will give reasonable results. Make sure that the fabric is well washed to remove any dressing, rinsed and ironed flat when damp, then dried thoroughly.

For each placemat cut a piece of fabric 38cm. by 43cm. (15in. by 17in.). The cushion covers illustrated have zipped openings, and measure 38cm. (15in.) square. For this size of cushion, cut two 43cm. (17in.) squares. For a similar, but sewn up cushion, cut one piece of fabric 43cm. by 81.5cm. (17in. by 32in.).

Printing
Make a trial print first. Place the greaseproof pattern on top of a piece of clean flat newspaper placed on your printing table or surface. Position the screen centrally on top of the greaseproof pattern. The whole cut-out design should show through the screen printing area.

Place the dye in a line along the top inside of the screen. Hold the screen with one hand and use the other hand to hold the squeegee. Holding it almost upright, press the dye right across the screen with one firm stroke. Then place the squeegee behind the dye and pull it back to the original position, leaving the screen printing area clear of dye.

Lift the screen carefully, starting at one side. When it is clear of the fabric, prop it up on a strip of wood to prevent dye running back onto the printing area. The greaseproof pattern should adhere

to the underside of the screen ready for the next print.

If the print is satisfactory start printing on your fabric, adding more dye as necessary. (Most poor printing arises because the dye is too thin or too thick in consistency.)

When the dye is thoroughly dry, other colours or shapes may be printed on top, or the screen can be turned round to vary the design.

When completed fix the colour according to the manufacturer's instructions. Clean up with cold water as soon as the printing is completed. Never leave dye to dry on the screen or squeegee. Do not try to save the greaseproof paper.

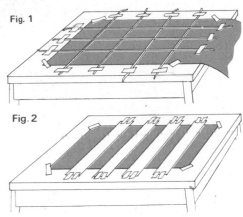

Fig. 1

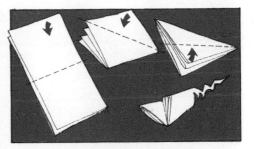

Fig. 2

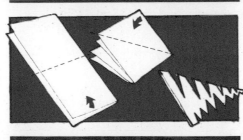

Printing a border or allover pattern
Obviously these are slightly more complex than individual motifs, as they must fit together with no gaps or overlaps. The fabrics must therefore be marked out, but never mark out a fabric with ballpoint or felt-tipped pens, pencils or even ordinary chalks as these may not wash out. Instead use fine white threads stretched across the fabric and fastened down with cellophane tape (Fig. 1). For band and stripe patterns, lay down strips of newspaper, fasten with cellophane tape and print between them (Fig. 2).

For allover patterns print alternative shapes to avoid wet dye coming off onto the underside of the screen and thus marking the fabric.

157

Transfer-printed apron

8. Attach apron strings by hand sewing or machine stitching.

Further decoration
Using the same method, you can apply any other details you like to the apron, for instance a name.

The pens and brushes illustrated have been applied to the apron using iron-on adhesive tape. Alternatively, they could be stitched into place. If you want to use these, draw them free-hand, using Fig. 3 as a guide, cut them out and stick or stitch them on. As interfacing does not fray it is perfectly suited to these small decorative details.

Transfer printing is fun and easy to do, but you must use synthetic fabric if you want the printing to last. Heavy sew-in interfacing is ideal for this project as it doesn't fray and can be cut in any direction. It is also washable. This work apron allows scope for the imagination and requires only basic skills. It's an ideal project for a child to make – you could help with the cutting and sewing if necessary.

You will need
Plain fabric for apron – the one illustrated took about 60cm. (23⅝in.) square
Heavy sew-in interfacing for pockets
1 pkt. transfer fabric crayons
Paper, pencil
Sewing thread
Ribbon/tape for apron strings
Iron-on adhesive tape (optional)

To make apron
1. Cut out basic apron shape (Fig. 1) to suitable size.

2. Cut out pocket shapes (Fig. 2) once in paper and once in heavy interfacing or other synthetic fabric.
3. Draw designs onto the paper pocket in pencil. Either make up your own designs or use Fig. 2 as a guide.
4. Fill the design in with the transfer print crayons.
5. When the design is complete, iron it, face down, onto the right side of the pocket. Iron with a steady pressure over entire design until an image becomes slightly visible through the back of the paper. Make sure the iron does not scorch fabric. Do not iron excessively or the design may blur. The longer you press, the deeper the colours become.
6. Remove the paper carefully, The image, transferred in brilliant colours, will remain on the fabric. Patterns can be reused as often as desired if colour is reapplied.
7. Machine or hand stitch pocket into place on the apron.

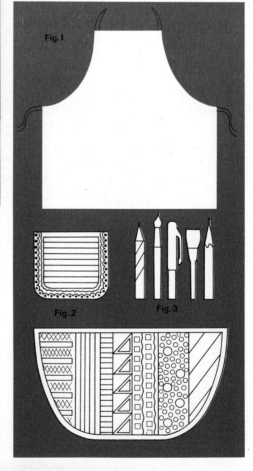

Fig. 1. The basic apron shape.

Fig. 2. The basic pocket shapes, showing the designs used on the apron illustrated

Fig. 3. The pencils and brushes. Draw up to a suitable size

Felt wall hanging with secret pockets

This is an ingenious idea for hiding your valuables – so long as they are flat valuables! Either copy this pattern or invent your own design. Here the front wall of the castle and the bush on the left are four separate pockets kept shut with touch-and-close tape, but you could easily add an extra big cloud or another hiding place in the castle itself.

You will need

Blue felt, 46cm. by 61cm. (18in. by 24in.)

Beige felt, 33cm. by 35cm. (13in. by 14in.)

Strip of darker beige felt, 46cm. by 20cm. (18in. by 8in.)

Yellowy green felt, 46cm. by 18cm. (18in. by 7in.)

Small pieces of cotton fabric for lining the wall and the bush

Other scraps of white, orange, greens, browns and red felt

Fabric adhesive

Felt nib pen

Strip of touch-and-close tape about 20cm. (8in.) long

Interfacing to back the hanging

Strip of wood slightly wider than the hanging

Ribbon

To make the picture

1. Draw a castle similar to the one illustrated and cut out a pattern.
2. Cut out the beige castle base and stick it to the blue background. Add two side turrets if you like, as in the picture.
3. The wall in front of the castle is the pocket, so cut out and at the same time cut out a matching lining piece to help stiffen the pocket.
4. Stitch the pocket lining to the felt pocket with horizontal lines of stitching, either with a sewing machine if you have one, or by hand. To save time, mark in the vertical lines of the bricks with felt nib pen.
5. As you sew the lines, sew in small strips of touch-and-close tape at four points along the castle wall, making sure they will not show from the front. Mark where the matching touch-and-close tape strips are to go on the castle base and then sew them on.
6. Sew the bottom of the wall to the bottom of the castle and the sides of the wall to the sides of the hanging. (They will be hidden later when the sides are turned in.)
7. Divide the pocket by sewing it on to the castle base with two vertical lines on either side of the gate.
8. Stick on the yellowy green foreground.
9. Sew on the left-hand pocket bush to the hanging along the base and along one side and sew touch-and-close tape to the bush and to the green base to shut the pocket.
10. Finish by sticking on trees, bushes, flowers and anything else you like.
11. Mount the hanging on interfacing and stick it to a strip of wood.
12. Stitch ribbon to the sides of the hanging to make a neat edge.

Paint a tablecloth

A pretty border design gives a new look to a plain tablecloth that's right for any occasion. Based on a traditional embroidered cross-stitch design, the pattern is painted on with fabric paints – an idea which can be adapted for place mats, table napkins, cushion covers and curtains, as well as for clothes. It's quicker than embroidering and permanent, too.

You will need

1 pot each fabric paints in red, green, gold

Fine soft paint brush (an eye-liner is ideal)

Squared maths graph paper

Tracing paper/greaseproof paper

Soft pencil; old newspapers

To work the tablecloth

If using a new cloth, wash and iron it to remove any dressing which may prevent the paint being properly absorbed.

Copy the motifs to the size required on to the squared paper and trace off on to the tracing paper with a soft pencil. If you prefer, you can use the motifs to the size shown in the diagrams. Turn the tracing over and pencil over the outline again. Place the tracing right-side up on the fabric and trace off the design, equally spacing the smaller motifs along the bottom of the cloth and using the larger outline in the corners.

It will be necessary to pencil over the back of the tracing paper after it has been used twice to renew the 'transfer'.

Lay the cloth on a base of old newspapers and paint in the pattern with a fine brush. There's no need to wait for one colour to dry before applying the next.

When completely dry, cover each motif with a cotton cloth and iron with a hot iron for two minutes to 'fix' the paint for a permanent, washable finish.

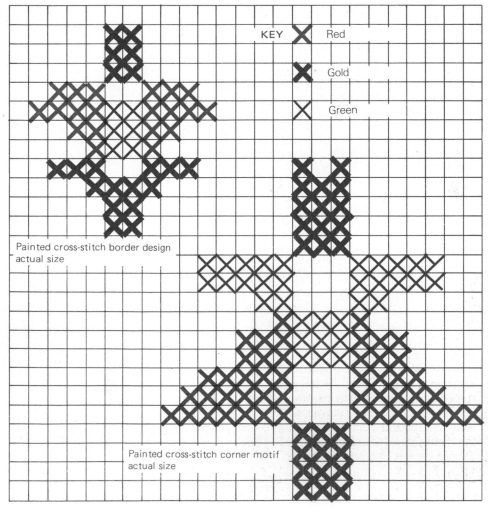

KEY

X Red

X Gold

X Green

Painted cross-stitch border design actual size

Painted cross-stitch corner motif actual size

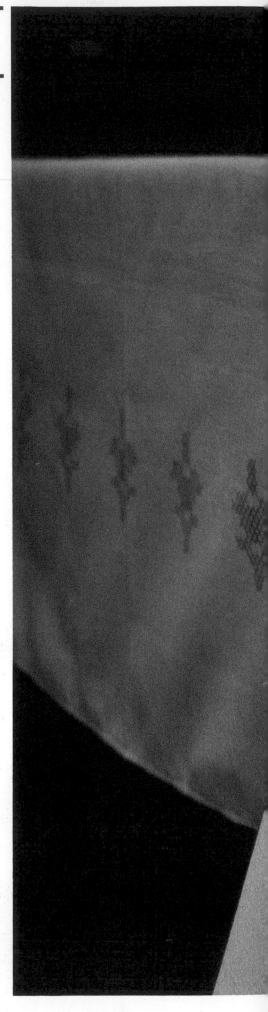

Stripping wooden furniture

If you have acquired or own an old piece of furniture and want to improve its appearance by polishing or painting it, the first step is to get rid of the paint or varnish already on it. This is called stripping. But before you decide to strip furniture, be wary. You must be sure that the wood underneath is in fairly good condition, as otherwise you may discover a knotted, stained, or heavily damaged surface underneath the paint which really was better covered up. So be prepared for re-painting or re-varnishing.

The types of finishes which you would want to remove are opaque paints – enamel, plastic, or water based – which do not allow you to see the wood beneath them, and clear finishes which include varnishes, shellacs, and French polish. Natural clear finishes such as beeswax and linseed oil should not be removed. This kind of finish, a soft sheen, is known as 'patina' and is much prized by antique collectors. Patina is satiny to the touch, does not obscure the grain of the wood underneath and, because it is a natural finish, allows the wood to 'breathe'. When one of these finishes needs reviving, simply apply any non-silicon-based wax, let it dry, and buff with a soft cloth.

To remove paint

Before starting work, assemble the following materials: paint remover; old newspapers to place beneath the object; a paint scraper 2.5cm. to 7.5cm. (1in. to 3in.) wide; an old toothbrush for getting into crevices; an old paintbrush for applying the stripper; rubber gloves to protect your hands. Wear old clothes as the strong chemicals in the stripper can stain and burn materials.

Place the object on a thick layer of newspaper and open the windows to provide ventilation.

Apply the stripper with the paintbrush over an area not exceeding 30cm. by 30cm. (2ft. square). Wait about 5 minutes until the bubbling action of the stripper stops, and then start to scrape off the paint with your paint scraper. Work with the grain if possible, and use the toothbrush to get into awkward places. Pro-

ceed in the same way, re-applying the stripper and scraping off each layer of paint, until the wooden surface has been completely exposed. If the paint is thick, the process may take several days to complete.

When dealing with stubborn paint or large objects which can be stripped outside, replace the stripper with one cup of potash, caustic soda, or drain-clearing crystals mixed with 2 pints of cold water and apply the solution with a sponge or large mop, turning the piece as necessary. Use in the same way as the paint stripper, re-applying as necessary.

When the stripping is done, rinse the object with warm water to remove any residue of the stripper and leave it to dry. If you are working out of doors use the garden hose. The effect of the water on the wood will give you a good idea of how most clear finishes will slightly darken the wood and highlight the grain. If it appears too dark or if you have uncovered defects in the surface then you may decide to repaint rather than sand and polish. However, if you are happy with the colour and quality of the wood, you are ready to start sanding (which is covered on page 164).

To remove varnishes

You will need fine wire wool, methylated spirits, and paper towels. Spread a thick layer of newspaper under the piece and wear old clothes and rubber gloves.

Working on a small piece of the surface at a time, about 9cm. (3½in.), apply a drop of the spirits and rub it into the wood with a finger-sized piece of fine wire wool. A gravy-like liquid will appear; continue rubbing until you reach the base wood and then wipe up the 'gravy' with a paper towel. Continue working, bit by bit, until all traces of the shellac, or varnish, or French polish have been removed. It may be necessary to go over stubborn patches more than once. If methylated spirits fails to shift the existing finish, try the following in this order: turpentine, paint strippers, caustic soda, ammonia.

When the piece has been stripped, wash down with cold water.

Sanding wooden furniture

On page 162, we told you how to remove the paint or varnish from an old piece of furniture in order to prepare it for re-surfacing. The next step is to smooth the wood by sanding it, a process often neglected by amateurs, but essential in order to ensure a professional finish. This applies not only to furniture, but also to woodwork which you intend to paint or varnish. Stripped wood must be sanded to smooth the raised grain, and so must painted surfaces, because sanding gives the new coat of paint something to adhere to.

You will need three grades of abrasive paper: M2 medium coarse, F2 medium fine, and extra fine (sometimes called flour paper). You also need fine steel wool, preferably grade 000, to give the surface a final rub, and a sanding block, which is a flat piece of cork, rubber, or wood around which the abrasive paper is wrapped. This keeps the paper flat so that you do not sand the wood unevenly.

Abrasive papers

Sandpaper, properly called glasspaper, is a tan-coloured paper with particles of crushed glass stuck to it. At one time sand was used, hence the name.

Garnet paper is a reddish paper with the grit made from crushed garnet stone stuck to it. It costs a little more than glass paper, but it lasts much longer, and is therefore recommended.

Sanding stripped and raw wood

If you are preparing a stripped piece for refinishing, or smoothing wood for shelving, begin with the coarsest paper (M2), using the sanding block for smoothing all the flat surfaces. Use torn strips of paper 2.5cm. to 5cm. (1in. to 2in.) wide for getting at awkward places. Obviously these areas are the most frustrating and you may have to resort to wrapping a piece of paper around one finger. Never sand in circles or across the grain.

Once the initial rough sanding has been completed, proceed to a medium grade paper (F2) and go over all surfaces again. Finally, finish off with extra fine paper followed by the finest grade of wire wool to achieve the maximum smoothness. By this time, if you have sanded thoroughly, the wooden surface should feel as smooth as a bedsheet. Never try short cuts such as using only two grades of paper – the surface will not be perfect.

Preparing painted furniture

To smooth already painted furniture so that it is ready for another coat of paint, simply sand the whole piece with a medium fine abrasive paper followed by flour paper. In both cases, remove the fine sawdust after each sanding with a soft cloth and, after the final dusting, wipe all surfaces with a rag saturated with white spirit (turpentine substitute) to remove the final traces of sawdust. You are now ready to choose your finish. Pages 165-167 tell you about the various kinds of paint, varnishes and stains you can use.

Sanding hints

Always store abrasive papers in a warm, dry place and never use them on damp surfaces.

While sanding, occasionally snap the paper on an edge to 'unclog' it.

Never use an electrical orbital sander to smooth wooden surfaces – the circular motion tends to produce 'dishes' in the very surface you are trying to smooth. If you have a lot of sanding to do, invest in, or rent, a belt sander, which has a back-and-forth motion, perfect for working with the grain.

Use a light pressure when working with abrasive papers, and a heavier one for wire wool.

When smoothing very large flat areas, wrap a brick in towelling and then abrasive paper to achieve an even surface with little effort.

When sanding, it is a good idea to tie a handkerchief over your nose and mouth to protect your throat and lungs from the fine particles.

Staining wooden furniture

New wood or newly stripped wood sometimes looks too 'raw' or too light a colour. If you do not want to paint it, but to keep the grain showing, the solution is to stain it – either a natural wood shade or a colour. Woods such as cherry, maple, mahogany and walnut are often stained to bring out their grain, but pine and other lightwoods can be treated in the same way, either to make them look like some other wood, or simply because coloured wood can look very attractive.

You can buy powdered stains or dyes to mix into a water or oil base or you can get them already mixed in a varnish or polyurethane base; the latter are less trouble. All stains are translucent – they should let the grain underneath show through.

Water stains and dyes
These are sold in powdered form in a range of colours and are the least expensive kind. They dye very thoroughly, sinking deep into the wood, but should not be used on veneered furniture or on very large areas as it can be difficult to achieve even spreading. Water stains are easily mixed, but sometimes need straining after mixing – an old mesh tea strainer is ideal.

Mix the stain as directed, until you have the colour you want, and thin with water to lighten if necessary. Before applying, test the stain on an inconspicuous place, and let it dry. If you are not satisfied with the colour adjust it by lightening or darkening.

Apply the stain with a clean 5cm. to 7.5cm. (2in. to 3in.) brush, stroking with the grain and tilting the object slightly (if it is light enough) to encourage the stain to spread. Do not overload the brush as this will cause dark patches. Apply another coat if necessary.

When the desired shade has been reached and the piece is completely dry, protect the stain by applying a clear sealer such as thinned shellac.

Clean the brush with soap and warm water.

Oil and alcohol stains
These are easier to use than water stains, but more expensive. Mix as directed on the label, blending two or more colours if required. The advantage of these stains is that they do not raise the grain of the wood and are therefore suitable for veneers and softwoods. The disadvantage is that they do not penetrate so deeply as water stain. This makes re-staining difficult as the wood is already saturated. It also means that they will wear off if not immediately protected with a clear sealer coat of thinned shellac followed by a coat of varnish.

Other stains
The most convenient method of staining is to buy ready-mixed sealer stains in a varnish base, as these stain and varnish in one operation. These are a little tricky to apply, but usually one coat will suffice (although table tops need a second). These stains can also be intermixed.

Stains are also available in polyurethane bases. These are extremely hard-wearing, and are recommended for furniture which will get a great deal of use, such as children's toy boxes and cupboards. They are rather less refined looking, with a hard, glassy look.

There are also many chemicals which will produce interesting effects on wood. Sulphate of iron imparts a blue-grey tone to oak and takes some of the redness out of mahogany. If applied to sycamore, it turns it grey, producing what is known as 'harewood'. The crystals are dissolved in water, and the liquid applied with an old paintbrush. This must be used with great caution, as it is poisonous.

Strong ammonia (880) mixed with water will darken oak and mahogany, the degree of darkness depending on the strength of the mixture. This must be used in a very well-ventilated room or outside, and applied with an old brush.

Hints
If you are staining a table top you will notice that the stain sinks more readily into the end grain and therefore darkens it more. To prevent this, paint the end first with a solution of 50% shellac and 50% methylated spirits.

Water-based stains tend to raise the grain of the wood. To lessen this effect, first wet the wood with plain water, let it dry, and smooth it with fine abrasive paper. Repeat the process and then apply the stain.

If the stain looks too dark when dry, it can be lightened by applying a commercial wood bleach. These are very much stronger than ordinary domestic bleaches, so wear rubber gloves and use an old paintbrush.

Sometimes the 'pores' of the wood may open slightly after staining, particularly if a water stain was used. To remedy this, seal with a coat of 50% shellac and 50% methylated spirits and then apply one of the following fillers. 1. Plaster of Paris, darkened with powdered pigment (raw umber). This is applied with a soft rag, working in circles. 2. 'Brummer stopping' thinned with turpentine and applied with a brush.

After filling the pores, let the filling dry completely and then apply the shellac mixture again; let this dry and apply a final coat of varnish (see page 166).

Polishing and varnishing

When a piece of furniture has been stripped or stained, it must be protected with some kind of clear finish or varnish. If it is not, dust and grime will settle into the pores of the wood and be difficult to remove, while many wood stains will begin to wear off in patches. There are two main groups of protective clear finishes – the natural oils and waxes and the shellacs and varnishes. French polish is in the latter category.

Before waxing or varnishing (unless you are using polyurethane or plastic-based varnishes) the wood must be sealed. Wipe the entire piece with lacquer thinner or white spirits to remove dust and grease. Apply shellac thinned with methylated spirits in equal measures, using a clean 5cm. to 7.5cm. (2in. to 3in.) paintbrush. Work in a dry room if possible – if the air is damp, the shellac tends to absorb the water and turn white. If you have to work in a damp atmosphere thin the shellac with lacquer thinner instead of meths.

Let the sealer dry for 24 hours, lightly rub it down with the fine 000 steel wool, and repeat the complete procedure once again. You are now ready to decide whether to apply wax, a natural oil or one of the varnishes.

Waxing

A waxed surface has a beautiful soft gloss and is warm to the touch. It takes some time to build up as several coats must be applied, but it is well worth it. Use any non-silicon furniture polish, applying one coat daily for 15 to 30 days, buffing each time with a clean soft cloth. Alternatively make your own beeswax polish as follows and apply in the same way.

Use 100g. (4oz.) beeswax to 25g. (½ pint) pure spirits of turpentine, adding a small amount (25g. or 1oz.) of carnauba wax or powdered resin to make the polish less tacky.

Grate the wax into flakes into a clean tin can and cover them with the turpentine. Place the can in a larger container and pour boiling water into the outer vessel, being careful not to get any of the water into the polish mixture. The turpentine must be kept from the heat source as it is inflammable. The heat from the water should cause the flakes to dissolve. If you wish, stir gently with a wooden spoon or wire whisk.

Pour the liquid into a clean jar or can but do not seal if for 24 hours.

Varnishing

There are two main groups of varnishes, the shellac-based, and the modern polyurethane or plastic-based varnishes. The method of application is much the same for both.

If possible, wear synthetic fabrics to keep down dust and work in a warm but well-ventilated room. Stretch a wire across the top of the varnish can so that you can wipe the excess off the brush. If using shellac varnish, never shake or stir it as varnish does not need mixing, and movement causes bubbles which are difficult to brush out.

Use the best-quality brush you have. Unless advised otherwise by the manufacturers, apply the varnish brushing hard in one direction and then stroke more gently the other way. Leave to dry for 2 to 3 days (a week in damp weather). If the finish is too shiny rub down with fine 000 steel wool, going in the direction of the grain and using even strokes to prevent scratching. Wax if desired, with a non-silicon polish.

Polyurethane and plastic-based polishes do not require previous sealing with the shellac mixture, and dry much more quickly than shellac varnish. They are usually available in high gloss, satincoat (a medium shiny gloss) or mattcoat (a low gloss). The latter does not have to be rubbed with steel wool, but as with shellac-based varnishes, always sand lightly between coats with fine abrasive paper and never apply the next coat if the previous one is even slightly wet.

These modern varnishes are highly resistant to heat and water stains, and are thus ideal for anything which will get a lot of wear, such as kitchen tables.

Linseed oil

This gives the deepest, finest finish of all but it is also the most time-consuming. It is particularly suitable for old oak furniture, but should not be used on Cuban mahogany, rosewood, ebony or any other close-grained wood.

Use boiled, not raw, linseed oil diluted with ⅓ pure turpentine and ⅓ vinegar. This will lessen the darkening qualities of the oil, though it can be used neat if you wish to darken the wood. Put the mixture in a cup and warm it by placing it in a bowl or pan of hot water. Make sure that turpentine is kept away from direct heat. Apply the warmed mixture with a rag or brush until the wood begins to reject it – little pools will collect on the surface when the wood is saturated. Wipe the surface hard with a soft cloth and leave it to dry undisturbed for three weeks. Build up the finish by rubbing more oil into the wood either with the palm of your hand or with a soft flannel cloth, once a week, for six months.

Either apply linseed oil twice a year from then on, or wax the surface after the final rubbing.

Painting wooden furniture

On pages 162-164 you were told how to strip and sand furniture to produce a perfect surface for painting, staining or polishing. Here we explain the technique of painting furniture and the paints to use.

Before painting, check the surfaces carefully for any dents and chips. These must be filled before painting. Use a proprietary wood filler such as plastic wood, and apply it with a filling knife (sometimes called a putty knife). Always overfill slightly because most fillers tend to shrink while drying. Allow the filler to dry thoroughly. Smooth with sandpaper.

Types of paint

There are three main types which are suitable for furniture: enamels, lacquers and plastic-based paints, all of which impart a tough, high-gloss finish to the surface of the wood. These are usually soluble in white spirits although some manufacturers may recommend their own solvents. Water-soluble high-gloss paints cannot be recommended for furniture.

All bare wood – that is, stripped wood or whitewood furniture, must be primed with an undercoat the same shade or lighter than the final coat. Most manufacturers make one which is compatible with their paint, but you can use thinned emulsion (water-based) paint as a substitute. A primer is not necessary if you are re-painting.

Working method

Spread a thick layer of newspapers and wear old clothes.

You will need, as well as the paint, clean cotton rags, a glass jar, white spirit (turpentine substitute), and a paintbrush 5cm. to 7.5cm. (2in. to 3in.) wide. Swish out the brush in white spirit.

Remove cushions and/or fabric from upholstered pieces or cover the upholstery with plastic bags taped into place. Remove any fittings such as drawer pulls, door knobs, etc.

Using blocks of wood, raise the piece off the newspapers.

Apply undercoat, allow to dry thoroughly, and sand lightly with a very fine abrasive paper. Repeat process.

Apply two coats of enamel, lacquer or plastic-based paint, sanding lightly between coats.

Hints

1. When painting chests-of-drawers, remove all the drawers and stand them face up. Paint them separately.
2. When painting chairs, do the underside first, then the tops of the chair legs, then the bottoms of the legs, then the back of the chair (both sides). Paint the seat last.
3. Work in a clean, dust-free room. Wear synthetic fabrics to reduce dust.
4. When sanding between coats of paint, dampen the newspapers to keep down dust or sand in another room.
5. Always apply paint in one direction and then stroke across it to blend it in, unless advised otherwise by the paint manufacturer.
6. Shake or stir the paint before applying unless directed otherwise.

Spray painting

The enamel or lacquer-based paints sold in aerosol cans are ideal for giving an even finish on anything with intricate areas which are difficult to reach with a brush, such as wicker or wrought iron. They are available in a wide variety of colours. It is usually necessary to apply spray primer first and at least 2 coats of the final colour, letting each dry thoroughly.

Spread newspapers everywhere; wear old clothes and tie a handkerchief over your nose and mouth – the fumes can be very irritating.

Shake the can for 60 seconds and hold it 15 to 20cm. (6 to 8in.) from the object, pressing the nozzle to apply an even film. If the paint runs this means you are spraying for too long in one place.

Some problems and their remedies

1. Blistering – caused by exposure to heat from the radiator or sun. This occurs most often with young, raw wood. To remedy, remove the paint with the recommended solvent and apply a coat of shellac first.
2. Checking or crazing – looks like irregular lines on the surface of the paintwork. Sand well and rinse with turpentine substitute; leave to dry and apply next coat.
3. Chipping – occurs when the top coat cannot adhere to a too-smooth undercoat. Rough up the surface with medium-fine abrasive paper, dust, and apply another coat.
4. Crawling – when paint seems to avoid a certain area because that area is dirty or greasy. Rinse with turps, leave to dry, and repaint.

French polishing

On previous pages in this section we have explained various ways of finishing wooden furniture, including polishing and varnishing. Here we are dealing entirely with French polish, which is the finest finish of all; it produces a high gloss but does not have the rather hard and over-bright appearance that characterises the glossy polyurethane varnishes. However, it does not wear very well, being easily marked by both water or alcohol, and should not be used on furniture which has to take a lot of wear and tear.

French polish is best suited to close-grained woods such as cedar, mahogany and walnut.

The most important thing to remember is that French polish must be applied in several thin layers – one or two will not give a satisfactory result. The application itself is a little tricky for beginners; we suggest trying it out on off-cuts of wood until you have mastered the technique.

The ingredients of French polish were for some time a closely guarded trade secret, but it can now be bought ready mixed from DIY shops and ironmongers.

How it is done

You will need French polish, boiled linseed oil, white spirit, soft cotton rag, cotton wool, flour paper.

First make sure that the surface to be polished is thoroughly stripped and sanded smooth (see pages 162-164). Remove all traces of dust with a soft cloth dampened with white spirit.

The polish is applied in several thin layers with a polishing pad, made by wrapping some cotton rag around a piece of cotton wool. Sprinkle polish on to the cotton wool and wrap the rag round it; the polish will seep through the rag. Always sprinkle the polish on to the cotton wool, not the rag, as this avoids a sticky build up of polish forming. Make sure that the surface of the pad is smooth, as wrinkles could make ridges in the finish. Apply polish in a long figure-of-eight motion, rubbing hard but evenly, and keep the pad moving all the time to avoid sticking. When the pad feels dry, sprinkle more polish on to the cotton wool and remake the pad. When the first application is finished leave it to harden for an hour or so and then repeat the procedure. When the second coat has completely hardened, rub it lightly with a worn-out piece of flour paper. (If you have just bought the flour paper, cut it in half and rub the two pieces together so that it is almost smooth.)

For the third coat, apply more polish to the cotton wool and then dip the pad itself in linseed oil. This will prevent the polish sticking. Go over the surface in the same way as before until you reach the edge, and then slide the pad off. Do not lift it. Repeat this process two or three times, applying more polish as necessary. If the pad sticks, use a little more oil.

For the final coats, work with polish only: if any oil is left it will leave smears. Continue polishing until a good shine is achieved, indicating that all the oil has been removed. Leave for 3 or 4 days to harden completely. No further treatment is necessary.

Restoring French polished furniture

A French polished surface which has become dull and needs reviving can be treated in the following way. Wash the surface thoroughly with a weak solution of soda crystals in water, or pure turpentine. Leave to dry and then apply French polish using the technique described. You will not need as many coats as you would if you were polishing bare wood.

If you are not sure whether a piece of furniture has been French polished or not test it, as follows, on a part which is out of sight, such as on the inside of a leg. Remove any wax polish with white spirit, and rub the area lightly with a rag dipped in methylated spirits. French polish will immediately soften and stain the rag, while other finishes will not.

A surface which is badly scratched or marked will have to be completely stripped. Follow the procedure which is given on page 162.

Removing blemishes

Most old furniture purchased in a junk shop needs something doing to it, either mending, stripping or a bit of restoration. Don't be put off by superficial appearances. Damage is often more fearsome-looking than it really is. And though it's best to start on something small, remember that it is sometimes possible to split a large piece of furniture into its component parts – for example, to turn a dressing table into a mirror and a chest.

Try to find out as soon as you can what sort of wood you are dealing with. A beautiful piece of pine may be lurking under layers of varnish and paint – though conversely, it could only be a piece of rough deal!

Cleaning

A good clean enables you to see what the wood needs in the way of further treatment. Clean gently because wood warps if it is soaked too generously in water and old water-based glues may come unstuck. Wipe over with a soft cloth dipped in warm water and detergent and wipe dry at once. Paint can be cleaned with a proprietory paint cleaner. Grease marks and heavy wax build up should be cleaned with domestic abrasive on a cloth which is slightly damp.

What type of polish?

Underneath the dirt there may be a centuries-old patina of wax, which is very difficult to reproduce quickly, or it could be French Polish, or it could be cellulose lacquer. Test on a part that won't show. Rub well with real turps to remove wax polish, then if there is any polish still left, rub with methylated spirits, which will soften French polish. Another test is to shave off a little varnish from an unseen place. Oil varnishes produce thicker shavings; French polish produces thin shavings and curls, while cellulose varnish forms a powder.

Woodworm

Woodworm is caused by larvae eating their way out of the wood. They do this slowly, and as they are on the inside, their presence is often undetected unless you happen to spot a tiny pile of sawdust. When the larvae have eaten their way to the surface, they change into chrysalis and hatch into small beetles. It is now that you can see the familiar woodworm holes, although by now it is sometimes too late to do much about them. However, you can buy some woodworm fluid and if the damage is not too bad, this can

be brushed on, or each hole soaked by use of the can-top applicator. When the holes have all been treated, fill them with a filler, so that the woodworm beetles will not return to their homes.

Surface blemishes

Burns Rub these down with fine flour paper to remove the charred edges, then fill with several applicaions of coloured wax tinted with oil paint to match the existing wood, gradually building up until it is level with the rest of the surface.

Dents and scratches Dents can sometimes be raised by laying a damp rag over the dent and placing a warm iron on top – but take care not to scorch the wood. Scratches can be dealt with by using a proprietary remover or by gently rubbing with flour paper dipped in linseed oil, then adding a dab of French polish. Or fill in the same way as for burns.

Heat rings can be removed by rubbing with equal parts of linseed oil and pure turps. Clean off with vinegar and repeat until the marks have gone.

Inkstains Treat with a 5% solution of nitric acid or with vinegar and sterilising fluid. Dab vinegar on the stain with a soft brush, then brush a 10% solution of sterilising fluid on this. Repeat until the stain has gone. Rinse off and polish.

Water marks Slight white water marks can be removed by rubbing with metal polish. Bad ones should be rubbed with finest steel wool and oil.

The corner cupboard

This piece of late Victorian furniture had been painted black to imitate lacquer and was gloomy and battered-looking. The key fitting was removed and treated with rust remover. As the piece was so intricate, paint remover was used to remove all the old paint and varnish.

Paint remover removes old paint without scraping. It doesn't drip, the only smell you notice is a clean, fresh odour after use and it is not inflammable. It consists of a paste applied with a knife and should be worked well into crevices and mouldings. Leave it on for anything from fifteen minutes to fifteen hours, then lift the paste, with the dissolved paint, with a knife. Scrub the surface well with a scrubbing brush and water and wipe down.

The cupboard was sanded as described on page 164 and the interior paper removed. It soon became clear that the cupboard was composed of two different types of wood, pale pine for the shelves and heavy dark wood for the doors and top. Wood dye was applied with a rag and rubbed in, and it was used to match up the two different woods. Hints on staining wood can be found on page 165. After a day, another coat of dye was applied, then another coat of dye with a small addition of a darker shade applied to the pine portions only, so that the whole thing finally matched up.

The inside of the cupboard was relined, the lock restored and three coats of matt polyurethane brought out the colour and imparted a beautiful sheen to the cupboard.

Upholstering a drop-in seat (1)

Upholstery is a fascinating craft combining the skills of soft furnishing and carpentry. Although it takes many years to master the art completely, it is a satisfying and worthwhile hobby to tackle at home. Bargain secondhand chairs are still widely available, and most need only a little help to be restored to their former glory. Doing a really good re-upholstery job is the best way to bring about a complete restoration.

A good piece with which to begin is the drop-in seat. This type of upholstery is used on a variety of chairs and stools, and it does not have the complication of chair springs.

Tools

There are several special tools used by upholsterers, but you can quite easily substitute more common tools found around the house.

1. Hammers used in upholstery have small heads, designed to hit only the head of the tack and not the surrounding wood. A small carpenter's hammer is a good substitute.

2. A ripping chisel and a wooden mallet are used to remove old tacks. As an alternative, use an old blunt wood chisel or a blunt screwdriver with a large head. A pair of pliers also helps.

3. Sharp scissors are a must for upholstery, and they must be heavy enough to cope with coarse, heavy fabrics.

4. A tape measure is necessary for measuring fabric, webbing, etc.

5. A webbing stretcher stretches the webbing taut across the seat frame to provide a good base on which the new upholstery will rest. You can use a small block of wood instead.

Materials

1. Tacks are always used for attaching fabrics to the seat frame. For attaching the final cover, use improved 1.2cm. (½in.) long tacks. Use 1cm. (⅜in.) fine tacks for attaching the remaining layers. Cut tacks have long tapering points which make them easier to fix into position.

2. Webbing forms the base of all the upholstery that is worked on an open frame, criss-crossing the frame in interwoven strands. If it is broken, the upholstery sags. When working with the traditional hair filling, a woven jute webbing is used. It comes in different widths, but 5cm. (2in.) is the most common width. To estimate the amount of webbing you will need, measure across the frame between its outside edges, and allow an extra 5cm. (2in.) for each strip. Allow for enough strands to make the spaces between the strands slightly less than the width of the webbing.

3. Hessian is also a woven jute and is the fabric that covers the webbing to prevent the filling from falling through. Use a proper upholstery hessian, and allow for enough to cover the seat frame plus a 2.5cm. (1in.) margin all round.

4. Horsehair is really a misnomer, as nowadays it is usually a mixture of hair from several different animals. This traditional filling is the most hard-wearing of all paddings and, if the chair is old or of value, it would be unwise to use any but the traditional materials. Horsehair is expensive and is often hard to find in the shops, but it can easily be recycled from the seat of the chair you are working on, so when stripping the chair do not throw it away. You will need about 450g. (1lb.).

5. Twine and needles are needed to fix the hair filling in place. Use a strong waxed upholsterer's twine and a curved needle.

6. If for some reason you cannot re-use the hair filling in your chair seat, and you prefer not to buy it, sheet foam may be used instead. This is a good substitute for hair filling, but bear in mind that it won't last as long. Buy latex or polyester foam, 5cm. (2in.) deep, allowing for the size of the seat plus 1.2cm. (½in.) all round.

7. Strong cloth-backed tape and latex adhesive are used to attach foam pads. The tape should be 4cm. (1½in.) wide and as long as all four sides plus 10cm. (4in.)

8. Calico, an unbleached woven cotton fabric, covers the padding to make a smooth foundation for the final cover. If not properly applied, it will ruin the look of the seat. Allow enough to cover the seat, plus 8 to 10cm. (3 to 4in.) all round.

9. Wadding, which is a material rather like cotton wool, is used to give additional padding to the seat. Allow enough to cover it.

10. The top cover should be a fabric that is recommended for upholstery. These fabrics are firmly woven and are therefore hard-wearing enough to make the cover last. Some suitable fabrics are linen, velvet, brocade, heavy cotton, twill, and some closely woven wools. Allow enough to cover the seat, with a margin of 8 to 10cm. (3 to 4in.) all round.

11. Bottoming is a black linen fabric that is applied to the underside of the seat. It finishes the seat off neatly and prevents the inside of the chair from becoming dusty. Allow enough for the size of the seat plus an allowance of 2.5cm. (1in.) all round.

Instructions for stripping the drop-in seat and beginning to upholster it are given on page 171.

Right. A dining chair with a drop-in seat, sadly in need of re-upholstering.

Upholstering a drop-in seat (2)

If you have followed page 170 you should now have the tools and materials needed to strip off the old seat and begin re-upholstering it.

Stripping the seat

1. Cover the floor with newspaper and have a waste bin handy for the old tacks and fabrics as they are removed.

2. Remove all the old tacks holding fabrics in position as follows. Place the chisel (or screwdriver) parallel to the side of the frame, with the top against the tack head. Tap the handle smartly with the mallet until the tack is worked loose and then prise it up. If the tack proves obstinate pull it out with a pair of pliers. Always drive with the wood grain and not across it, to avoid splitting the wood. Do not leave any tacks in the wood, even if they are hard to remove, as they might get in the way of the new tacks.

3. After removing the coverings, cut and remove the twine holding the filling in place. Release the filling and keep it for re-use if possible.

4. Finally take off the hessian and the old webbing, removing the tacks as before.

5. If the frame needs repairing, do this before you begin to upholster. Also treat the wood with woodworm fluid if needed and fill in any holes with wood filler.

Replacing the webbing

The foundation of the seat must be tight, and this depends on the firmness of the webbing.

1. On the top of the frame mark the centre points of each side with a pencil. Repeat to mark the centre points on the underside of the frame.

2. Always keep the webbing in a continuous length as you work, to save waste. Turn under 2.5cm. (1in.) on one short edge of the webbing. Place it centrally over the centre back mark on the frame top, just over halfway from the inner edge of the frame. Fix it in position with five tacks in a staggered formation, placing a tack through the fold of webbing at each corner and one centrally between them, then placing two more tacks in the gaps behind the first three.

3. Pull the webbing over to the centre mark on the front edge of the frame. To achieve a taut finish, wind the webbing round a web strainer or small block of wood and pull against the frame edge (see colour illustration). Hammer in three tacks in a row, as before, through the single thickness of webbing, keeping the webbing as taut as possible. Cut off the excess webbing, leaving 2.5cm. (1in.). Fold back this excess on to the webbing and tack it in place with two tacks placed as before on the back, to complete the formation.

4. Repeat this procedure on either side of the first central strand of webbing, always working from the back of the seat frame to the front. The space left between each length should be slightly less than the width of the webbing.

5. If the seat is wider at the front, graduate the strands of webbing so the gaps between the webbing at the front are slightly wider, but the webbing is still equally spaced.

6. To complete the webbing, repeat the process from side to side across the seat frame, treating one side as the back of the frame and one side as the front of the frame, but weaving the strands of webbing alternately under and over the previous rows.

Covering the webbing

1. Cut out the pieces of hessian on the straight of the grain. They should be the size of the seat frame plus an allowance of 2.5cm. (1in.) all round.

2. Centre the hessian over the webbing on the top of the seat frame. Turn back the allowance on itself at the back edge of the seat frame, so the fold is about 6mm. (¼in.) from the outer edge. Fasten it in place through the double thickness at the centre. Fasten in place again through the double thickness at both back corners. Insert more tacks between the centre and the corners at 2.5cm. (1in.) intervals.

3. Stretch the hessian to the front edge, keeping the fabric grain straight, and tack at the centre point through the single thickness of fabric. Pull the hessian taut at the front corners and tack. Add more tacks between the centre and the corners at 4cm. (1½in.) intervals. Fold back the hessian on itself, trimming if necessary. Fasten in place through the double thickness of hessian with tacks at 2.5cm. (1in.) intervals between the previous ones.

4. Repeat this process at the side edges, treating one side as the back edge and one side as the front edge, still keeping the fabric grain straight.

Instructions for finishing the upholstery of the drop-in seat are on page 172.

Upholstering a drop-in seat (3)

If you have followed pages 170-171, you should now be ready to pad the drop-in seat and put on the covers.

Attaching the padding

If you are using the hair filling from the seat, sew a row of bridle ties round the hessian to hold the filling in place (Fig. 1). To do this, measure a length of twine the circumference of the seat plus half again. Fasten the twine at one corner of the hessian with a slip knot. Pull up the knot and work round the seat with 2.5cm. (1in.) long back stitches at about 15cm. (6in.) intervals, leaving a loop between each stitch large enough to accommodate two fingers. Finish off by tying the twine to the first knot.

Tease out handfuls of filling and put on top of the seat under the twine loops, extending the filling to the edge of the seat frame. Use your judgment to achieve an equal quantity of filling all over – a good 2.5cm. (1in.) deep. Insert more filling in the centre in order to give a domed effect.

If you are using sheet foam instead of the hair filling, attach the padding with cloth tape. Cut four pieces of tape, each the length of one side of the foam plus 2.5cm. (1in.). Fold each piece in half lengthwise and, using latex adhesive, stick half the width along each edge of the foam. Leave the other half of the width unglued, and overlap the tape at the corners. When the tape is dry, place the foam on the hessian, tape side up. At the back, tack the free edge of the tape to the frame; then, pulling the tape taut, tack the front edge of the tape to the frame. Do the same for the sides. Because the foam is a little larger than the seat, it will have an attractive, slightly domed effect.

Fixing the calico cover

On the straight grain cut out a piece of calico the size of the seat frame plus 8 to 10cm. (3 to 4in.) all round. Mark the centres of the calico both ways.

Place the calico flat on the working surface. Position the seat centrally over the calico, matching centre marks. Hold the calico in place at the centres of each side with a half-fixed tack in the side edges of the frame.

To fix the calico firmly in place, begin at the back edge. Place the tacks in the underside of the seat frame through the single thickness of calico and about 1cm. (3/8in.) in from the outer edge. Work from the centre outwards, half fixing the tacks

and placing them about 2.5cm. (1in.) apart and within 5cm. (2in.) of the corners (Fig. 2).

Lift the seat frame up so that it rests on the back edge. Release the temporary tack holding the calico at the front. Smooth the calico over the seat round the front edge and tack to the underside front edge about 1cm. (3/8in.) from the outer edge of the seat frame. Place the tacks in position in the same way as for the back edge, continually smoothing the calico over the seat with your hand for a good finish.

Repeat this process at the side edges, keeping the fabric grain straight and treating one side as the back edge and the opposite side as the front edge.

At each corner, pull the fabric hard diagonally over the corner and fasten underneath with a temporary tack. Fold the fabric on either side of the corner tack into a small single pleat. Cut away any extra fabric from within the pleat and temporarily tack in place at both sides of the corner.

Check that the seat looks even and that there are no wrinkles in the calico. If necessary, remove and reposition tacks to gain a smoother fit. When you are satisfied, hammer all the tacks firmly in position.

Attaching the top cover

Cut out a piece of wadding the same size as the calico seat. Following the straight of grain, cut out a piece of fabric the size of the seat, making sure that any design is central and allowing an extra 8 to 10cm. (3 to 4in.) all round. Mark the centres of the fabric both ways.

Lay the fabric on the working surface with the wrong side uppermost. Place the wadding centrally on top of the

fabric, and place the seat centrally over the wadding.

Matching the centres, fold the fabric round the seat frame to the underside. Temporarily fix each centre of the fabric to the frame just over the calico edges with a half-fixed tack.

At the back of the seat, working from the centre, tack the fabric in place just over the edge of the calico to within 5cm. (2in.) of the corners. Half-fix the tacks in position through the single thickness of fabric.

Lift up the seat, so that it rests on the back edge. Release the temporary tack holding the front. Smooth the fabric over the seat to the front, round the front edge, and tack in place as for the calico cover.

Repeat the process at the sides, keeping the fabric grain straight and treating one side the same as the back edge and the opposite side the same as the front edge.

Complete the corners in the same way as the corners on the calico cover.

Check that a good shape has been achieved, and remove and replace any tacks if necessary. When you are satisfied, hammer all the tacks firmly in position.

Bottoming

Cut out a piece of fabric the size of the seat frame plus 1cm. (3/8in.) all round. Mark the centres of the fabric both ways.

Fold under the edges all round the fabric for 2cm. (3/4in.), neatly folding the corners. Turn the seat over. Position fabric centrally over the underside of the frame, matching centres and with the folded edges 6mm. (1/4in.) from the outer edge. Tack in place down the folded edge, starting at the back and working from the centre points outwards. Place the tacks at 2.5cm. (1in.) intervals. Replace the seat in the chair.

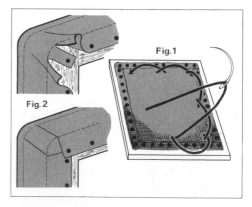

Work around edge, making backstitches and leaving loops between them.

Simple upholstery repairs

Many upholstery repairs are not as difficult as they seem. Here are some repairs you can do yourself to save the cost of re-upholstering or even replacing chairs, stools and sofas.

Re-covering a stool or simple chair seat
If the seat is the drop-in type, first lift the seat away from the surround before beginning to work.

Using pliers or the claw end of a hammer, prise out the old tacks and remove the covering. Also remove any wadding, but leave calico and horsehair, coconut fibre or other stuffing in place.

Cut out a piece of furnishing fabric the size of the old cover plus 5cm. (2in.) all round, and a piece of upholstery wadding the size of the visible area of the covering. Place the wadding over the seat, and position the new covering on top.

Pulling the fabric tight, secure with 10mm. (³/₈in.) small-headed tacks in the same vicinity as the old tacks. (On some seats, this will be on the underside, while on others it will be on the sides, next to the show wood.) Begin with one tack in the middle of each side, then add more tacks at 2cm. (³/₄in.) intervals, working out towards the corners. Do not hammer any of the tacks right in until you have pulled the fabric really tight and adjusted the tacks as necessary. At each corner fold the fabric so that there is a pleat on each side of the corner.

If the raw edges of the fabric are exposed at the sides of the seat, you can cover them with braid trim. Glue it in place with latex fabric adhesive being careful not to cover up too much of the wood, and tack the turned-under ends in place.

If the fabric extends right round to the underside of the seat, tack a piece of hessian over the underside, folding the edges under.

Replacing webbing
If the upholstery itself is not in too bad condition, a sagging chair, sofa or stool can sometimes be given a new lease of life by replacing the webbing. The amount of new webbing needed is the same as the old webbing, plus 8cm. (3⅛in.) per strip, plus 50cm. (19⅝in.).

Turn the item upside down and remove any hessian covering the webbing by prising out tacks with pliers or the claw end of a hammer.

Note the position of the old webbing, then remove it by taking out the tacks. Place the end of the new webbing where

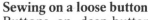

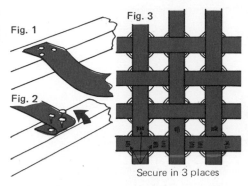

Fig. 1

Fig. 2

Fig. 3

Secure in 3 places

one of the old strips was fixed, with the raw edge near the inner edge of the frame. Using 1.3cm. (½in.) tacks for a stool, or 1.6cm. (⅝in.) tacks for a large chair or sofa, secure the webbing with three tacks (Fig. 1), then fold it back and secure with three more tacks (Fig. 2).

Wrap the webbing round a block of wood about 15 by 15 by 3cm. (6 by 6 by 1in.), then stretch it across the frame. Place the block of wood against the outside edge of the opposite side of the frame to help you pull the webbing as tight as possible.

Secure with three tacks and cut off, leaving an extra 5cm. (1⅝in.). Fold this end over and secure with three more tacks positioned as on the other side.

Repeat the procedure for each strip along the frame, then do the same for the strips going across, interweaving each before tacking in place.

Now stitch each spring to the webbing in three places (Fig. 3) using strong button thread or upholstery twine. A special curved needle will make this easier. Tack a piece of hessian on the underside, turning under the edges.

Sewing on a loose button
Buttons on deep-buttoned chairs and sofas can often work loose, so it's useful to know how to sew these buttons on again.

First you must lift the cover on the back side of the chair or sofa back. Using pliers or the claw end of a hammer, carefully prise out the tacks holding the cover in place along the bottom edge. There may also be some stitching along the sides of the back, which should be snipped with a pair of sharp scissors. Some sofas and chairs will have a layer of calico underneath the fabric, which should be lifted in the same way.

Cut off the loose button, and pin the loosened cover out of the way. Cut a 30cm. (12in.) length of strong button thread or upholstery twine, and thread it through a long needle. From the back, push the threaded needle through to the spot on the front where the button was fastened. Now push it through the canvas at the back of the button, then back through to the rear of the chair or sofa.

Fold a 10cm. by 4cm. (4in. by 1⅝in.) scrap of fabric in half crosswise, and place it between the two ends of thread at the back. Pulling the thread fairly tight, so that the button is as tight as the other buttons, tie a secure knot in the thread. Be careful to catch the fabric 'butterfly' in as well, to prevent the knot from working into the upholstery.

Unpin and reposition the cover. Working from the centre out towards the corners, tack it in place on the underside of the chair or sofa, with 1cm. (³/₈in.) tacks placed at 2cm. (³/₄in.) intervals. Then stitch by hand with matching sewing cotton wherever there was stitching previously.

Replacing foam padding
A chair or stool may look flat and unattractive simply because the foam padding in the seat has worn out.

To replace the padding, first remove the cover by prising out the tacks, then take off the old foam. With latex fabric adhesive glue a new piece of foam, of the same thickness as the old and as dense as you can find, to the top.

Cut four 12cm. (4¾in.)-wide strips of calico and glue half their width along each edge of the top of the foam. When the glue is dry, pull the calico down and tack it underneath the seat, so that the edges are nicely rounded. Replace the cover as described for re-covering a stool or simple chair seat.

Repairing cane seats (1)

Canework is a useful repairing craft to learn, as there are not many professionals nowadays who specialise in it. Also you can often pick up cane furniture quite cheaply because the canework itself is damaged, though the woodwork is perfectly sound.

Note

Although this is not a difficult process, it does have several stages, and clear diagrams are needed to explain each one properly. Thus, this page explains stages 1-3, while page 175 gives the final stages (4-7). This is the classic seven-step pattern to be found in most cane furniture.

Materials

You will need the following. Cane (one bundle will usually do a chair bottom and back). Nos. 2, 3 and 4 are normally used, but to be absolutely sure take samples of the old cane to your supplier for matching. Pegs, 5cm. (2in.) in length, to hold the canes in place while weaving. Sawn-off dowelling, golf tees or long rawlplugs will do. Strong scissors and a knife to cut the cane. Clearer; a metal knitting needle or small screwdriver with

a diameter of not more than 3mm. (⅛in.). Small hammer for flattening the knots and for tapping the pegs in. Bodkin (or large hatpin or sacking needle) to help the cane through tight places. Basin of hand-hot water and a cloth for dampening the cane.

Preparing for work

First remove all the canework from the chair, and knock out any old pegs. Soak the new cane in warm water for a few minutes to make it more pliable, and keep it damp while working. If it dries, pass it through the water again, stroking the underside with wet fingers to help absorption. Be careful not to overwet

the cane and always discard any cracked lengths. Do not dampen more cane than you need for one work session.

Working the caning

The classic cane pattern is worked in 7 steps as follows.

Step 1

Starting at the left side of the chair seat back, insert one end of the No. 2 cane into the hole nearest that corner. Place it glossy side up and peg it into the hole so that the cane is held firmly in place (Fig. 1). Leave a 10cm. (4in.) length hanging below. Bring the length of cane to the front of the seat and pass it down through the hole nearest the left front, taking care not to let it twist around as it passes through the hole. Pull the cane tight, peg it in place, bring it up through the next hole, to the right, and peg it (Fig. 2). Now take the cane back across the seat of the chair into the hole next to the starting one, pull tight, and peg. Leave the first back peg in place until later, but the second pegs, front and back, can be removed when the cane is held firmly in place by the next row of weaving. Continue in this way until the seat is covered. When the cane runs out, leave an end hanging on the underside of a hole and peg it to hold. Begin a new cane in the adjacent hole, leaving at least 10cm. (4in.) of cane hanging under the seat. Peg the new cane firmly and leave this peg in position.

Step 2

This is started and worked exactly as Step 1, with the cane crossing over and lying on top of the first (Fig. 3). As before, peg to hold loose ends.

Step 3

A repeat of the first step using the same holes but crossing over the second step and lying slightly to the right of the first step (Fig. 4).

The instructions are continued on the next page.

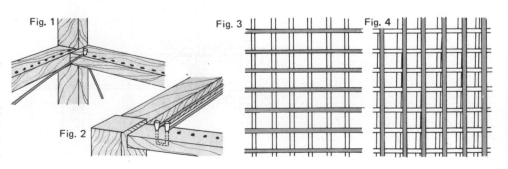

Fig. 1

Fig. 2

Fig. 3

Fig. 4

Repairing cane seats (2)

If you have followed steps 1-3 on page 174, you are now ready to start on Step 4, described below.

By the end of Step 3 there will be several loose ends hanging from the underside of the chair seat. Dampen the ends with a wet finger to make them pliable, cut them to a point with the scissors, and pass the ends twice over and under the canes between the holes on the underside to secure them (Fig. 5). Use the bodkin or similar tool to ease these ends through untwisted and with the glossy side out. Tap the strands with a hammer to flatten them and cut off any excess. Remove the pegs.

Step 4

Similar to Step 2, and begun in the same way, but this time the cane is woven under then over the vertical canes (Fig. 6). This process will probably take much longer than any previous steps. This time, do not pull the cane tight until you have gone under and over six pairs of vertical canes. The weaving will not look perfect, but the next two steps will produce the desired regularity.

Step 5

The first diagonal step. A wider cane, No.3 or 4, is used for this step. Peg the end of the cane in the back left-hand corner. Start weaving over the first pair of horizontals, then under the first pair of verticals, then over the following horizontals and so on (Fig. 7). When you reach the opposite corner, bring the cane through the next hole in front, to the left of the first, and weave backwards in the same way. Continue until ending in a

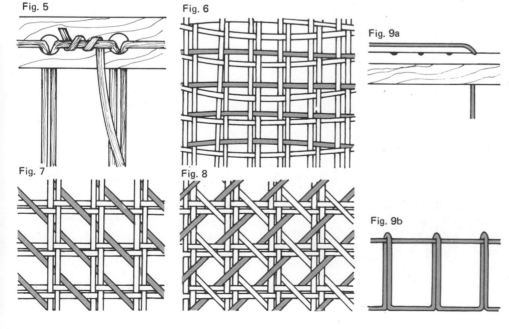

corner, then return to the starting hole, and use another length of cane to complete the other half of the seat.

If you make a mistake, unpick it carefully. If the unpicked cane is not dirty or split, soak it until pliable and use it again.

Step 6

The complementary diagonal cane to Step 5, beginning in the opposite back corner. Weave under the horizontals and over the verticals (Fig. 8). This step should lie at right angles to the first diagonals. When completed, finish all hanging ends.

Step 7

The finishing touch – a border of cane using No. 2 and No. 4 canes or No. 2 and No. 6. Take the thicker cane (4 or 6) and trim one end to a point. Insert this cane, called the beading cane, from below into the right front corner hole and lay the other end along the front of the chair over the other holes (Fig. 9a). Insert a No.2 cane through the second hole and secure the loose end as before. Carry the length over and around the beading cane and back through the same holes so that it has formed a loop securing the beading cane (Fig. 9b). Continue until you reach the corner, then cut the beading cane and start a new one for each side.

Fig. 5

Fig. 6

Fig. 9a

Fig. 7

Fig. 8

Fig. 9b

Rush seating (1)

Nowadays rush work is coming back into fashion, as rushes are more readily available and the rustic look becomes increasingly popular. You can often buy bargain secondhand chairs with worn-out rush seats, then re-rush them yourself. If possible, pick a square seat to begin with, as this is the easiest shape to work on.

Rush seating is very hard-wearing. It is made up of three layers – a smooth but hard twisted rush cord which is on the top, with two layers of plain untwisted rush underneath.

Materials
Rushes are water plants that grow in slow-moving rivers or on the edge of shallow lakes. When fully grown, they are two or three metres (yards) long. After they are harvested, they are left to dry for a fortnight or so.

Rush is sold in bolts of about 2kg. (4-5lb.) in weight, and one bolt should be sufficient to rush two chair seats. Select the thickness of rush to suit the size and shape of your chair. To preserve the soft colour, store the rushes in a cool, dark, dry place.

Tools
Very few tools are needed for rush work, and, for most of these, good alternatives can be found around the house. You will need a pair of sharp scissors and a craft knife; soft thin string that will not cut into the rushes; a packing stick, or a piece of thin rounded dowel or a gardening cane; a rush threader, or a curved sacking needle or large-eyed bent threading bodkin, to help pull the last rushes through the work at the end; and an old sheet or large towel, to wrap the wet rushes in.

Stripping off the old seat
Cover the floor with newspapers before you begin. If the chair has side pieces to protect the rushing and avoid wear-and-tear, these must be removed. Do this carefully, easing out the nails that hold them in position. Store these side pieces so that when the seat is complete and dry they can be replaced.

Now gently cut away the old rush from the chair frame, using a sharp craft knife and cutting round the frame. The old rush seat should come away almost in one piece.

Wipe down the chair. Make any necessary repairs to the frame, and treat the wood with woodworm fluid if needed.

Preparing for work
Wet the rushes thoroughly for a few minutes in cold water. The easiest way to do this is to immerse them in cold water in the bath. Make sure that all the rushes get wet including those in the centre of the bundle. Then wrap the rushes in a wet towel for a further three hours to mellow. When the rushes are ready, they should feel soft and almost leathery. If they still feel papery, leave them awhile longer.

Before you begin, there are two more important things to do. First, wipe down each rush with a wet cloth to remove any dirt and expel any air and surplus water. Press it flat as you work, wiping from the thin end down to the thick end.

Second, discard any of the tip of the rush that is too fragile to work with. Holding the tip end of the rush with both hands, give the rush a sharp tug. Discard the broken end and repeat further down the rush, continuing until it no longer breaks and it feels quite firm. Keep the odd pieces that you discard to use as padding at a later stage.

Basic techniques
Always work with two rushes together, although the resulting strand should look like one firm cord. Pair up one thick end with one thin end – the butt with the tip.

Stroke, pull and twist – these are the basic techniques of rushing. Stroke the rushes to flatten them. Pull the rushes to stretch them and make them tight. Twist the rushes to make a firm cord, making only one twist in one spot.

A chair seat is rushed by first attaching two rushes to one side of the frame. They are twisted, pulled and stroked into a loop on either side of one corner, then pulled along to the next corner and looped in the same way. Gradually the rush seat is built up as you work round and round the frame, finishing at the centre.

Joining rushes
To join in new rushes, use a reef knot. Choose a rush of the same thickness so that the work remains even, and try not to join both of the working rushes at the same time. At the beginning, the knots should be tied on the inner layer, so that they will be hidden. Later on, try to tie the rushes together on the bottom layer so that the knot can be turned into the inside.

At the end of the rushing, tie your working rush to the rush on the opposite side underneath the seat. Use a threader to help pull through the final lengths.

On page 177 you will learn the exact procedure for working the rushing.

Rush seating (2)

If you have followed the steps on page 176, you are ready to begin rushing your chair seat. The instructions apply to a normal, square seat, but there are details also of shaped seats and rectangular seats.

Working the corners

Begin by tying two rushes to the left-hand side rail with soft string, leaving several centimetres (a couple of inches) protruding beyond the string. Tie them securely so that the rushes cannot break away.

With the rushes in your right hand, twist them to the right, stroking and pulling at the same time. Wrap the twisted rush cord over and down the front rail next to the left-hand corner, twisting as you pull. Then bring the rushes up, untwisted, through the inside of the frame.

Now, using your left hand, twist the rushes to the left and take the cord over and down the left-hand rail, stroking and pulling as you twist. Bring the cord up through the inside of the frame, still next to the corner, and again untwisted.

Each corner is worked in the same way. The twisting is always done away from the corner, first to the right then to the left. The rushes are always twisted as they are taken down over the rail, and they are always left untwisted as they are brought up through the frame. Remember to stroke and pull as you twist. As you work, move the chair round so that the corner you are working on is always to your right – this will help to give an even look.

After the looping on the left-hand corner is completed, repeat the process on the right-hand front corner, bringing the untwisted rushes from the left-hand corner along the inside of the front rail to the right-hand corner. Twist to the right, taking the cord over the side rail close to the corner. Bring up the cord, untwisted, through the centre of the frame. Then twist the cord to the left and bring it over and down the front rail and, untwisted, up through the inside of the frame.

Pass on in the same way to the right-hand back rail, then the left-hand back rail, and finally back to the front left-hand corner (Fig. 1). Repeat the procedure, working round and round the seat (Fig. 2).

Special hints

As you build up the corners, be careful to maintain right angles. If you don't pull the work firmly enough, the angles will become too sharp and the centre of the

seat will be filled before the outer rails are covered, leaving gaps at the edges. If you pull the work too hard, the angles will be too flat and the rails will be filled before the centre of the seat is, leaving a hole in the middle.

After you have completed about a dozen rounds, you will find that two pockets have formed under each corner of the seat. These pockets must be filled up with oddments of rush, in order to thicken the seat and press the inner layer up against the upper layer to support it. Cut up any odd pieces of rush, as well as the discarded tips, into small lengths. Make sure that they are nearly dry before you use them, or mildew will form. Push these pieces firmly into the pockets with a packing stick. Repeat this procedure after every dozen rounds, doing it one final time just before the underside is closed up.

Do not complete the seat in one session. When the rushes dry out, they will shrink, so leave them to dry, then push the cords firmly together and continue.

At the end of a session, there are two ways to leave the work. Either leave 30 to 40cm. (12 to 15in.) of the old rushes lying loose; then when you begin again, wet these ends for a few minutes to soften them up before working. Or tie the old rushes to the inner untwisted layer; then when you are ready to start again, tie your new rushes in at the same place and continue working in the same direction. Do not stop work with a corner half-worked.

Rushing a shaped seat

Where the chair seat is wider at the front than the back, only the front is worked until the rushed edges of the seat form a square.

To do this, first measure the distance between the corners on the front rail and on the back rail. Divide the difference between these measurements by two, and mark that distance in from each corner on the front rail.

Begin working by tying your two rushes to the left-hand rail. Work round the two front corners only, then tie the rushes to the right-hand rail, cutting off the surplus. Go back to the left-hand rail and start again with fresh rushes, graduating the starting points. Again work both the front corners, graduating the ending points. Repeat the procedure until you reach the marks on the front rail.

Tie in new rushes on the left-hand side, but this time work right round the seat (Fig. 3). Continue as you would for a square seat.

Rushing a rectangular seat

Follow the procedure for a square seat, but when the short side is filled, continue to fill the long side using a figure-of-eight pattern (Fig. 4).

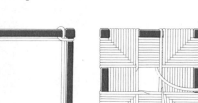
Fig. 1 Fig. 2

Fig. 3

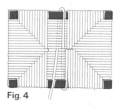
Fig. 4

Mending and filling

A lot can be done for old furniture by careful mending and listed here are several quick tips and hints.

Mending

1. *Joints* that have come apart can be restuck and the traditional glue for this is Scotch glue, which is bought in powder or solid form. This should be heated in a double glue pot and used hot. Joints should be clamped in place while the glue sets. Modern cold PVA adhesives can also be used and have in fact largely superseded the traditional hot glue.

To reinforce broken joints, drill holes in both sections to be joined and insert a piece of dowelling to fit into both holes. Dowelling can be bought in most D.I.Y. shops in assorted sizes. Glue the dowelling and tap into place. Screws should not be used.

2. *Warping of wood* is caused by one side expanding through damp or the other contracting through heat. When this happens, the balance has to be restored and to do this, place the warped wood curved side upwards in the sun with a weight on it while resting the inside curve underneath on a bed of damp rags. Small pieces of warped wood (box lids for example) can be soaked, then clamped in position and allowed to dry naturally.

3. *Drawer runners* often get stiff. To make them run well, clean all the running surfaces and rub them with a candle.

4. *Damaged veneer* can be mended by inserting a razor blade to lift up the damaged piece or alternatively, breaking off the whole damaged part. Using tweezers, dip cotton wool in boiling water, squeeze out with the tweezers and use to clean off the old glue from the back of the veneer and the foundation wood. Dry well and glue back with a cold PVA adhesive. Place a pad of material over the patch, put a weight on it and leave to set. If bits of veneer are missing, it is possible to buy matching veneers from some craft shops.

Filling

At some time during the refurbishing of an old piece of furniture you will come across holes that need filling and cracks which need attention. Plastic wood is fine for the job. Epoxy resin tinted with gouache paints to match the surrounding wood also serves well. Very large holes should be filled by cutting a block of the same type of wood to the shape of the hole, filling in any small gaps left, then sanding. Hints on sanding can be found

on page 164. Open pores in grain can be filled by several layers of French polish, or you can use one of the powder type fillers or plaster, tinted if necessary with a little water colour. Put plaster on with a damp cloth dipped in the powder, quickly rubbing a small area with a circular motion. Before it has time to dry, rub it down. When dry, wipe on a coat of linseed oil. Rub down with fine sandpaper, and wipe clean.

The pine chest

The good pine of this wooden chest was hidden under a film of hard gesso which could not be removed with commercial paint stripper. The chest had, therefore, to be sanded with an electric belt sander as described on page 164. If tackling a job like this, it is better to do it outside, for the dust gets literally everywhere. It took about a day to sand this particular chest.

After sanding, the chest was wiped down with a cloth dipped in white spirit, and holes were filled as already described. The intricate bits were finished by hand sanding. The rusty hinges and lock were polished and after a final sanding the chest was given three coats of matt polyurethane which brought out the glowing colour of the pine. It can be wax polished to give an extra sheen to the wood.

Antiquing furniture

Antiquing is a way of painting wood to give it a soft, mellow, 'antique' look. Frequently used by interior decorators, it can transform an eyesore into a beautiful piece of furniture.

Older wood with an interesting grain looks better than modern items when treated in this way. But the special value of antiqued furniture is that it goes well with both traditional and modern décor. And you can choose a combination of colours that blends with your own colour scheme.

Materials and equipment

The unusual colouring of antiqued wood is achieved by giving it several thin layers of paint, each a different colour. First an oil-based undercoat (in grey, white or cream) is applied, then two pigments. Pigments are available from art shops and craft shops and are the traditional material used for antiquing; but if you have trouble finding them, you could use artist's oil paints instead.

In addition, you will need a tin of yacht varnish, which is available from hardware shops and is thicker and more syrupy than polyurethane varnish; a bottle of turpentine; three glass jars for mixing the glazes and for cleaning brushes; clean cotton rags; and fine sandpaper.

You will also need three paint brushes: a 1.3cm. (½in.) brush for painting the undercoat; an old, ridged brush for applying the glaze; and a new, dry 4cm. (1½in.) brush for smoothing and later varnishing the glaze.

Colours

The pigments used on the chest and picture frame in our photograph are windsor green and burnt umber, but you could use alizarin crimson with burnt umber or cobalt blue; raw sienna with burnt umber; cobalt blue with burnt umber; or green with gold paint.

Don't be afraid to try your own colour combinations, though it's best to try different colours on scraps of wood before starting to antique the piece of furniture. You'll find your technique also improves with practice.

Preparation

Because there are several stages to antiquing, it's best to work in a room in which you can leave the item to dry without its being disturbed. Lay down plenty of newspapers, and wear old clothes.

Remove any handles from the item, and sand it down to produce a good surface for the paint.

If you want to make the antiqued item look even more authentic, you can 'distress' the surface. This consists of adding dents, scratches and worn edges using files, hammers, bricks, chisels, nails, etc.; but it should always be done with restraint!

To prepare the wood for the glaze, apply a light undercoat using the 1.3cm. (½in.) paintbrush. Allow it to dry completely, then sand it lightly with very fine sandpaper. Wipe the surface with a rag soaked in turpentine, and repeat.

Glazing

In a jar, mix 5ml. (1 teaspoon) pigment or oil paint with 30ml. (3 dessertspoons) turpentine. (We used the windsor green pigment.) Mix them well, then add 10ml. (1 dessertspoon) yacht varnish, and mix again.

Dip the old, ridged brush into this glaze and paint over the item to produce a streaky but even effect. Spread the glaze thinly, as it is quite runny.

Now take a clean rag and, starting in the middle, gently wipe a lot of the glaze off, taking more glaze off from the centre than from around the edges.

With the new, dry brush, brush the surface gently, keeping the strokes in one direction only. Continue brushing until the centre is smooth and practically down to the undercoat, and the edges are left with more colour. (The effect is as though the colour has been gradually polished away over the years.)

The glaze tends to dry out fairly quickly. If you are antiquing a large item like a chest, it is advisable to paint only one side at a time, completing the process before beginning another side.

Leave the glaze to dry completely for 24 hours, then mix up the second glaze colour in the same manner and repeat the process. The second colour, which in our photograph was burnt umber, gives a more muted look.

Varnishing

Apply at least three coats of yacht varnish, sanding lightly with very fine sandpaper between coats. If you prefer a dull lustre to a gloss finish, rub down the final coat when it is completely dry with very fine wire wool or a mixture of pumice powder and machine oil.

Other techniques

Experiment to create your own techniques, such as dabbing a crumpled-up cloth over the smoothed glaze.

A technique known as 'pouncing' gives a gentle dotted effect. It is done by dipping a soft, oval brush in the glaze, dabbing out excess glaze on a cloth, then lightly dabbing the brush over the surface.

'Splattering' is done by dipping an old toothbrush into the glaze, then rubbing a pencil along the bristles to splatter the glaze on to the surface.

The art of beadweaving

Beadweaving is a traditional craft of the American Indians, which is now enjoying widespread popularity. It is a satisfying and inexpensive hobby which can be easily taken up and done during spare moments. It is also both creative and useful: you can make up an enormous variety of patterns, and you can design and make jewellery which matches your favourite clothes.

Materials
There is a variety of bead looms on the market, but they need not be elaborate. We recommend the small metal loom, which is inexpensive, strong and light.

The small glass beads needed (seed or rocaille beads) are available from craft shops and come in many different colours. You will also need some special beading needles (available in craft shops and some large stores); polyester thread (strong but fine); and a piece of beeswax or a candle. A needle threader is also an advantage, as beading needles have very small eyes.

Threading the loom
The threads that run lengthwise down the loom are called warp threads; those that run horizontally are the weft threads. You need one more warp that the number of beads for each row (10 warps for 9 beads) as each bead is held between 2 warp threads.

Decide on your pattern and work out the length of the finished work. Cut as many warp threads as you need, allowing 20cm. (8in.) more than the length of the work for finishing and making fastenings. This is very important, as if the threads are too short you will be unable to finish the work properly.

Tie a knot in one end to secure all the threads, and wax them by passing them

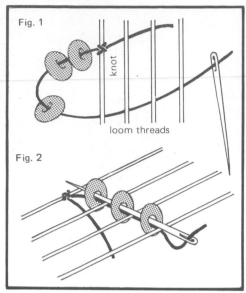

Fig. 1
knot
loom threads

Fig. 2

through the beeswax or candle. Divide the threads roughly in half and put each half round the screw on one of the rollers.

Put each thread in place between the separators at each end, using a beading needle to help you. Tighten the wing screw to stop the roller moving. When all threads are in place loosen the roller and wind the threads on until you can make a knot at the further end, putting this round the second metal screw as before. You must leave a length of warp thread at each end for finishing, so wind on about 10cm. (4in.) of warp thread. Tighten both screws to make the warp taut.

Threading the beads
Put the beads in small shallow tins or plastic boxes so they can be picked up easily and place them on a tray so that you can find any beads which spill.

Thread your beading needle with a long piece of thread and double it. When doubled it should be approximately an arm's length. Pass this weft thread through the wax and knot the end round the left-hand warp thread close to the spiral separator.

Pick up the beads for the first row in a scooping movement and take needle and thread under the warp (Fig. 1), running the beads right down the thread. Use your left-hand index finger to help push each bead up so that it is positioned in the space between two warp threads (Fig. 2).

Take the needle back through the beads, this time securing them from above and drawing the weft through firmly but not too tightly, and you are ready to start the next row. Continue in

the same way, moving the bead rows gently together so that they are kept straight and firm and your work steady and flexible.

Concealing ends
The long tail from the first weft can be tucked in as you go from row to row by catching it in the loop of your thread. Alternatively, thread it through at the end.

To finish off a weft thread, take it back through a couple of bead rows, keeping to the left-hand side of the work, make a slip knot at the edge and continue through a few more beads before cutting it. Never cut off the thread at the edge.

To start a new weft thread, draw the waxed thread through from the right-hand side, and work it through a few rows, make a slip knot to secure it and draw the thread through the left-hand bead on the last row.

When the work nears the top spiral, move the whole piece down by loosening the rollers and winding the work over the wooden roller. A thick piece of paper over the screw will keep the work flat, or it can be moved to the side of the screw and over the roller.

To finish
When the weaving is completed, take it off the loom by loosening the rollers and lay it flat. Cut the warp ends just under the knot and straighten out the threads.

Thread each warp end in turn on to your needle and then thread it back through several rows of loomed work, make a slip knot or weaver's knot, thread it through another few beads and cut it off close to the bead.

If the beads become too tightly packed with thread, take the thread down the work on the outside edge, making a kind of buttonhole stitch, and take it back into the work further down, ending off as before.

Some warp threads, and the last weft thread if it is long enough, can be used to make the fastenings and fringes as described on page 181. Instructions for making the butterfly-patterned choker are given on the same page.

Beadwork choker and bracelet

On this page instructions are given for making the choker and bracelet set illustrated and for the butterfly-patterned choker shown on page 180. The bracelets are made in exactly the same way as the chokers; they are simply shorter.

The geometric pattern is one found in many parts of the world in slightly different forms, and the butterfly pattern was originally part of a needlework design. Both look very attractive when made up, but the geometric pattern is rather easier to work, so if you are a beginner, start with this and leave the butterfly design until you are more practised on the loom.

You will need
Geometric pattern
25g. (1oz.) gold iris beads
25g. (1oz.) turquoise 3-cut beads
25g. (1oz.) black rocaille beads
1 reel polyester thread
Beeswax or candle
Beading loom
1 small wooden bead
Beading needles 10/12
Butterfly pattern
25g. (1oz.) black rocaille beads
25g. (1oz.) pink 3-cut beads
25g. (1oz.) blue 3-cut beads
1 reel polyester cotton thread
Beeswax or candle
1 small wooden bead
Beading needles 10/12

To make up
First read page 180, which explains the technique of bead-weaving. Set up the loom as described, place the beads in suitable containers and you are ready to start. Work the pattern as shown on the diagrams until the work is the required length.

To finish off
A simple way to finish off work is to weave the last weft thread in and out of the remaining warp threads for about 2cm. (¾in.), cutting off any remaining thread. The selvedge made in this way can either be tucked back under the main body of the work and glued on to a piece of material or, preferably, glued between two pieces of soft leather or ribbon binding. In this case a suitable fastening such as a hook and eye is sewn on to the material. If you decide to adopt this method, start your work by making the first selvedge, before threading your beads.

The other method is to work the warp

threads and the last weft thread back into the main body of the work, leaving free only those warp threads which are to be used for fastenings.

How to make the button fastening
Take the thread out between the 5th and 6th beads on the last row, thread on 4 beads, then add a small wooden bead.

Now thread on 4 or 5 beads, to cover half the surface of the wooden bead, take the thread back through the centre of the wooden bead, then add a further 4 or 5 beads in the same way. When the thread is nearly finished, knot it through the beads already on the wooden one, making sure they are secure, and continue to cover the wooden bead using the next warp thread. When the bead is covered add another 4 beads to complete the 'button' and secure it in place between the 5th and 6th beads from the other edge. This makes a small, neat fastening for the choker or bracelet.

Any warp threads which have not been used for the fastening must be threaded back into the finished piece in the usual way.

To make the loop fastening
At the opposite end of the choker or bracelet you will need to make a loop fastening to fit the button. A number of warp threads may be used to make this.

Thread enough beads to go over the button, but not too many or it will slip through. To make sure that the loop is the right length hold the thread tightly and slip the loop over the button. If there are too many beads, unthread some, but if not, secure the thread in the usual way and continue, using as many warp threads as the beads will take. Weave the ends

back into the finished piece, as well as the unused warp threads, and finish in the usual way.

Note
When calculating the length of your choker or bracelet, remember that the button and loop fastening will take up about 1.5cm. (¾in. approximately). This will make a difference to the length of your work.

Right: Geometric pattern
Left: Butterfly pattern

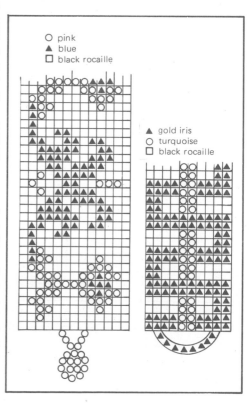

Pearl flower brooch

Jewellery does not have to be bought in a shop and need not be costly. This charming flower brooch, reminiscent of Victorian seed-pearl jewellery, can be made at home using simple and inexpensive materials.

You will need

1 packet small pearl beads (knitting beads are suitable), 5 larger round pearl beads, 3mm. (⅛in.) pearl bugle beads, silver bugle beads (slightly smaller)
A few sequins, pale pink and darker pink
12 small diamanté or silver glass beads
About 4.2m. (14ft.) medium thickness fuse wire
Clear adhesive
Brooch back
Tweezers, small pliers

To make the brooch

Each flower petal is made in the same way. Thread the larger pearl bead on to a length of wire about 35cm. (14in.) long. Slide it to the centre and thread the number of beads for the next row on one end of the wire, then push the other end of the wire through the beads in the opposite direction (Fig. 1). Pull both ends tightly and adjust the position of the beads in relation to those on the previous row. Repeat for each row, following Fig. 2.

Make 5 petals. To avoid the petals spreading out too much each may be joined to its neighbour by a tiny twist of wire between each fourth row from the bottom.

For each stamen cut 7.5cm. (3in.) wire and centre a small diamanté on each. Even the ends and twist the length together. Make 12 stamens and bind all ends together with a short separate length of wire, having all heads together. Place in the centre of the flower, letting them

project for about 2.5cm. (1in.). Bind all ends together.

To make the first leaf spray cut a 35cm. (14in.) length of wire and string a pearl, silver and another pearl bead. Slide them to the centre, bend the wire in half and twist it for 1.3cm. (½in.) (Fig. 3). Thread another 3 beads on one end of the wire, then bend it so that there is a space of about 1.3cm. (½in.) between beads and and wire already twisted. Bend the wire back on itself so that the silver bead is in the centre and twist the two lengths together for another 1.3cm. (½in.), then thread 3 more beads on to the longer wire end and repeat the bending and twisting to make another branch on the other side (Fig. 4). Work 4 leaves on each side of the central one.

The second spray uses 40cm. (16in.) wire and has 4 leaves on one side and 5 on the other; the third uses 50cm. (20in.) wire and has 6 leaves on one side, 5 on the other. Make the fourth spray as the first.

Assemble the flower and leaf sprays and bind all ends tightly together. Cut off most of the ends and use the few remaining ones to secure the flower to the brooch back, adding a little adhesive if necessary. Hold sequins with tweezers and apply a small dab of adhesive to the back of each, glueing them to the centre of the flower. Arrange stamens and leaf sprays.

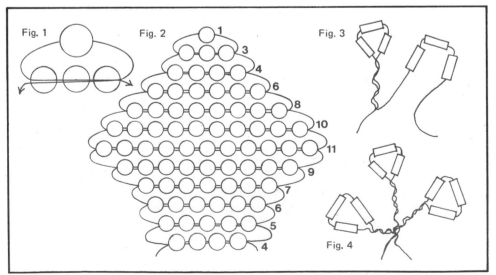

Paper bead necklace

Attractive to look at and fun to make, most of the beads in this necklace are made from rolled wrapping paper and thus cost next to nothing. You can use magazine paper, but gift wrapping is better because the colours are brighter and the pattern can be used to good effect, as the little flowers have been in the necklace illustrated.

The paper beads have been combined with wooden and plastic beads to give a contrast in shape and colour.

You will need
1 sheet of gift wrapping paper
Slim knitting needle, scissors and ruler
Wallpaper paste
Strong coloured thread (fine cord or metallic crochet yarn); 2 large-eyed, long needles
Clear nail varnish, clear adhesive, fine sandpaper
Felt pens or watercolour paint
Necklace clasp
Beads: 14 blue wooden 8mm.; 20 pink wooden 5mm.; 26 yellow wooden 5mm.; 16 white plastic

To make the beads
You will need 35 paper beads for the necklace illustrated and each is made in the same way. Cut a paper strip 45cm. by 2.5cm. (18in. by 1in.) and taper it slightly at each end. Paste along the wrong side leaving the end nearest to you unpasted for about 3cm. (1⅛in.).

Place the tip of a clean knitting needle on the unpasted part and roll the paper over it. Roll the strip, stick the end firmly, slip the bead off the needle. Leave to dry. Wipe the knitting needle clean.

When the beads are dry, rub the ends on fine sandpaper to level them. Colour the ends, then slip the beads back on to the knitting needle and varnish them 2 or 3 times.

To make the necklace
Cut a length of thread about 90cm. (36in.) long. Thread beads as shown in Fig. 1, starting at A, and leaving about 7.5cm. (3in.) of thread hanging at the end. After passing the thread through the clasp ring, come back through the same 4 beads and continue working towards B. When you reach B, thread on the other end of the clasp and then work the thread back through the beads until you reach C. Tie off the thread ends, and dab the knot with a touch of glue.

The central motif is worked on the middle paper bead of the main necklace.

Cut a length of thread 45cm. (18in.) long and thread a needle on both ends. Pass one of the needles through the middle paper bead of the main necklace and slide the thread so that the ends are even. The central motif is worked in 2 stages. Following Fig. 2, thread 1 white plastic bead and 1 paper bead on to each needle, then pass both needles through 1 blue bead. Continue threading, following Fig. 2. To finish the first stage, thread each needle through 1 paper bead and then 1 white plastic bead. Pass both needles through 1 paper bead, from each end, and then take each needle through the white plastic bead again. Your threads should now have crossed and come out at D and E. Fig. 3 shows the completion of the central motif. The thread ends D and E, having picked up 7 beads on each side, top and bottom, pass through the white plastic beads again at F, G and J on one side, and H, I and K on the other. The threads are then taken through the blue beads left and right of the central bead on the main necklace, through 3 or 4 adjacent beads, and then knotted off, cut and glued.

The side motifs are worked on the paper bead to the left and right of the middle paper bead and are joined to the sides of the central motif. Both motifs are made in the same way.

Cut thread 45cm. (18in.) long and thread a needle on both ends. Pass one needle through the paper bead on the main necklace and pull the ends even. Make the first stage in the same way as the central motif, following Fig. 4. When you have crossed threads in the bottom paper bead, the right-hand thread picks up the white plastic bead, then 1 pink and 1 yellow bead and then passes through the beads in the central motif. Pick up 1 pink bead and pass the threads through the white plastic bead and the blue bead of the main necklace. Run the thread end through adjacent beads, knot off. The left-hand thread picks up the white plastic bead, 1 pink, 2 yellow, 1 blue, 2 yellow, 1 pink, through the white plastic bead and through the blue beads of the main necklace. Knot off as before.

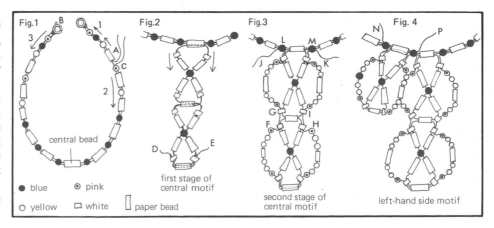

Fig.1

B
3
1
A
C
2
central bead

● blue   ⊙ pink
○ yellow   □ white   ▯ paper bead

Fig.2

D   E
first stage of central motif

Fig.3

J   L   M   K
G   I
F   H
second stage of central motif

Fig.4

N   P
left-hand side motif

Beadwork pendant

This pendant uses a design suggested by an oriental needlework pattern and the shape has been worked out to complement the pattern.

You will need

25g. (1oz.) gold iris or gold rocaille beads
25g (1oz.) black rocaille beads
25g. (1oz.) black bugle beads
Beading loom
Beeswax or candlewax
1 reel polyester thread
Beading needles 10/12

Note

First read page 180, which explains the technique of beadweaving.

Working the weaving

Begin at the bottom of the pattern (Fig. 1) with the gold frame for the birds then continue to work, following the pattern, until you reach the 26th row.

As this pattern is wider than most, you will need to use your hand more to keep the beads in place as you go along. If your needle starts to curve when you are in the middle of a row you may have to take it out and put it back again to complete the row.

To decrease, use one less bead at the beginning and end of the next 5 rows. You will find it easiest to take the thread underneath the work at the point closest to it, leaving the first warp thread free.

To make the vase shape at the top, 2 rows are worked with the same number of beads. One row is then worked with an additional bead at each end, and then 2 more with the same number of beads.

The weaving is now complete and can be removed from the loom.

Finishing off

Each thread at the top of the pendant must be worked back into the main body of the work. Threads left unbeaded where the work was decreased should be worked back into the nearest row.

The fringe

The fringe is made by threading beads on to the warp threads which are left at the bottom.

Starting from the left, thread each warp thread with 27 beads, then take the thread back, skipping the last 3 beads to form a little triangle at the end of the fringe (Fig. 2). Work the end of the thread back into the main piece of work and secure it in the usual way. If you prefer a thinner fringe, take 2 adjacent threads through the same beads thus leaving a space between each row.

The chain

Bugle beads, interspersed with gold ones, are used to make the 'chain' for the pendant.

Measure the right amount of thread for the length you want, double it and secure it to the woven work as if you were starting a new thread.

When it is threaded securely add 6 bugle beads, two gold beads, 6 bugles, 2 gold and so on until you have reached the required length, secure this and start a 2nd chain in the same way, making sure it is exactly the same length.

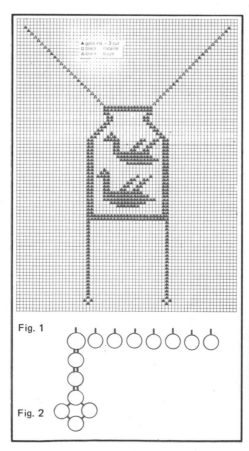

Fig. 1

Fig. 2

Quill work earrings

This jewellery is made using the technique of rolled paper work, or quilling. After the painted paper strips are rolled into shapes they are glued together and set in thin metal hoops. This gives a lovely filigree effect, unusual and quite hard-wearing.

You will need

Good quality paper (something fairly tough, such as watercolour paper, is easiest to handle).
Cocktail stick or very small paintbrush for rolling paper
Tweezers, scissors
Clear household glue
Gold spray paint
1 pair hoop earrings approximately 4cm. (1⅝in.) diameter
8 pearl beads, 6mm. (¼in.) in diameter; 10 smaller pearl beads.
8 head pins; pins

Preparation

Cut 20-25 narrow strips of paper about 3mm. (⅛in.) wide and 5cm. (2in.) long. Be careful to cut very straight; it is helpful to rule pencil lines first. Pin the strips side by side on a board and spray with gold. Turn them over gently with tweezers, repin and spray the other side. They must be pinned in order to stop them from curling up.

The quilling

There are several basic shapes which are used in various combinations in this craft. For these earrings, you need to make the shape known as the S-shape.

Hold the end of one strip of paper to the side of a cocktail stick, and rotate the stick, squeezing the paper on to it. When all the paper is on the stick, it will be in a tight spiral. Allow the spiral to spring open, then secure the end with a dab of glue, and gently ease it off the cocktail stick.

When the glue is dry, pinch the shape to a point at each end so that the pinched ends curl in opposite directions. This forms the basic S-shape.

To make the earrings

Now bead the S-shape into a tulip shape, and glue it into the centre bottom of the earring, as shown in Fig. 1. Quill two further strips of paper in exactly the same way, but the second tulip shape must be longer than the first, and the third longer still, so coil them slightly less tightly. Glue into place as shown in Figs. 2 and 3. Make a closed tulip shape inside the third

(Fig. 4) and glue coils into place. Fill this with a dewdrop and add a tight coil to the top (Fig. 5).

For the drops, thread a pearl on a head pin and cut off the blunt end, leaving a short length. Bend this length into a loop with pliers and hook it over the edge of the earring. (If you do not have head pins, fasten the bead with a short length of thread, making a knot at the bottom so the thread will not pull through.) Glue the small beads between the coils of gold paper (Fig. 6).

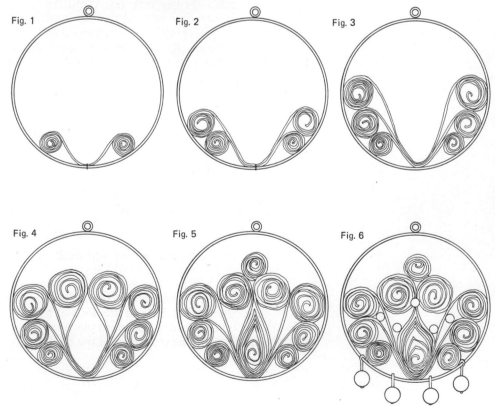

Silver chains

Chains for necklaces, bracelets or anklets are simple to make and attractive to wear. This kind of jewellery can easily be made at home, as the links are made just by cutting short lengths of wire and bending them to shape.

Materials

The pieces illustrated were made from round, silver wire, which is whitish and easy to work. Two metres (two yards) of wire is enough to make a long neck chain. Other suitable metals are copper, which is reddish, and brass, which is yellow. By using combinations of these metals, interesting colour patterns can be produced. All three metals can be polished to give a bright, shiny finish. They can be bought in most craft shops. Round wire, 1mm. in diameter, is suitable for most chains as it is strong enough to retain its shape, but fairly easy to bend. As you become experienced in wire bending, you may like to try heavier wire, say 1.2mm. for a more chunky effect. For extra colour, you can thread some beads on the wire.

You will need small shears for cutting the wire; round-nose pliers for bending it; flour grade glass paper for smoothing edges; grade 4/0 emery polishing paper for removing scratches, and a can of silver polish.

There are many variations of chain links that can be combined to make either plain or lacy chains. The following are those used in the examples illustrated, but you can experiment with your own ideas to make new and original chains.

The single loop link (Fig. 1a)

Snip off 4cm. (1⅝in.) of wire with the shears. Hold the middle of this piece in the round-nose pliers (b). With the fingers, bend the ends of the wire towards each other to form a U-shape (c). Now cross the ends over each other so that a loop is formed (d). Then grip the wire to one end with the pliers and start to wind a ring (e). Stop when the end meets the wire again. Finally use the pliers to bend the ring back until its centre is in line with the straight section of wire (f). Make the loop at the other end in exactly the same way.

Straight connector links (Fig. 2)

Cut a 3cm. (1⅛in.) length of wire. Bend a hook on each end as described above.

The double loop link (Fig. 3a)

Cut off 8cm. (3⅛in.) of wire. First bend a single loop about one third of the way

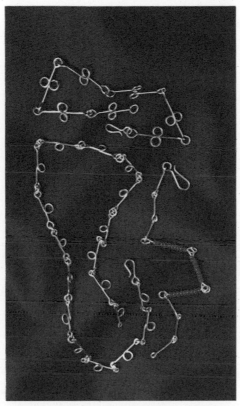

along the wire (b). The next step is to bend another single loop immediately opposite the first one. To do this place one nose of the round-nose pliers in the first loop and the other nose against the crossed-over wire (c). Wind the longer end of wire around the exposed nose of the pliers until the wire can be wound no further around that nose because the other nose is in the way. Move the pliers to the new position shown in (d) and wind the remainder of the loop. Bend the end hooks as described for the single loop (e).

If you want to assemble double loops end to end without using connector links or rings, leave one end hook in the horizontal position and with the pliers twist the other hook into a vertical position (e) to ensure that double hooks lie flat.

Beads

If you would like to add beads to your chain, bend one hook on your wire, slide the bead or beads along the wire, then cut off the wire about 1cm. (⅜in.) beyond the last bead. Bend the hook at the other end to hold the beads in place and to link into the next section of the chain.

The catch or shepherd's crook (Fig. 4)

This hooks into the last loop to secure the chain. Bend an end hook on one end of a piece of wire 3cm. (1⅛in.) long (a). Kink the other end with a pair of pliers (b). Now make a U-shape half way between the end hook and the kink (c).

Assembly and finishing

Arrange the links as you wish. Open the hook or ring *sideways* with the pliers, slide the next link in place then close the hook again.

Remove all sharp ends, burrs of metal or bad marks with the flour paper folded into a small pad. Rub any scratches away with polishing paper folded in the same way. Hammer a small nail into a work bench or other suitable surface. Hook one end of the chain over the nail. Hold the chain taut in one hand and use the other hand to rub briskly up and down the whole length of the chain with silver polish on a cloth. Brighten the work by giving a final rub with a soft cloth.

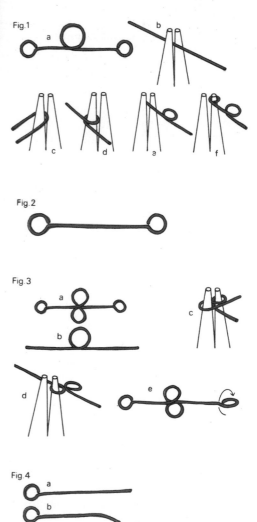

Fig.1

Fig.2

Fig.3

Fig.4

Silver rings

On page 187 we showed you how to make different kinds of links for chain. This page explains how to make rings of various kinds, which gives you a basis for lots of different easy-to-make jewellery.

Materials

The jewellery illustrated is made from silver, but copper or brass is suitable too. The wire for finger rings should be carefully chosen. If it is too thin it will be weak and the ring will buckle, while wire that is too thick will be difficult to bend. To begin with, choose wire about 1.5mm. in diameter. When you have become experienced in wire bending, experiment with different diameters. The smaller rings used in the bracelet are made from round wire 1mm. in diameter, and the ear-rings from round wire 0.8mm. in diameter. In this case the wire is a little thinner so that the hook feels comfortable in the ear. A length of about 8cm. (3⅛in.) of wire will make one finger ring, about 60cm. (23½in.) is enough for a bracelet, and about 20cm. (8in.) for a pair of ear-rings.

As well as the wire, you will need small shears for cutting; round-nose pliers for bending; snipe-nose pliers (2 pairs) for assembling rings; half-round pliers for bending finger rings; and a hammer. Flour-grade glass paper is used for smoothing edges, grade 4/0 emery polishing paper for removing scratches; and silver polish for the final touch.

Small rings

Find a length of steel to act as a former for the rings: a large round nail or a knitting needle will do very well. The diameter of the former you will need depends on the size of the rings you wish to make. A former approximately 3mm. (⅛in.) in diameter is a good size to start with.

Roll a piece of paper tightly twice around the former. This makes the removal of the rings easier. Hold one end of the wire against the former and begin winding the wire firmly around until there are enough turns along it to make all the rings for the chain. Slide the rings and the paper off, and snip the rings off the coil one at a time.

To give greater variety to your rings, you can select different-shaped formers. For instance, you can use a large oval nail to make oval links.

Joining the rings

The ends of the rings clipped from the spiral will be slightly apart. Hold each end of the ring in a pair of snipe-nose

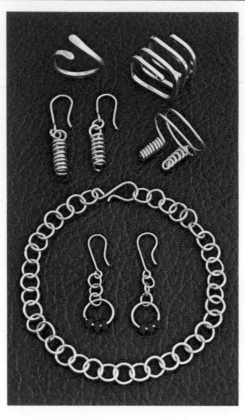

pliers and ease the gap open a little. As far as possible avoid distorting the shape of the ring. Thread another ring into place through the gap, then close this first ring by pushing its ends together with the two pairs of pliers. Continue adding more rings until the chain is the required length.

To join the links, make a shepherd's crook catch as explained on page 187.

Finger rings

To measure your finger size, wind a piece of string around it so that it is a close fit but not too tight, and cut through the string at the point where it crosses the first wind.

Snip off a length of 1.5mm. round wire equal to the length of the string measurement. Support one length of wire on a firm base such as a steel block, and hammer the end flat. This will extend the wire a little. To make the curve on the wire, hammer along one side. This stretches one edge more than the other and so curves the metal.

Hammer the other end in a similar way then curve it in the opposite direction by hammering as before.

When the ends are the shape you require, form the wire into a ring, using the half-round pliers. Move the pliers along the wire, bending only a small section at

a time and making the bends in the wire as smooth as possible.

Square ring

The square ring was made by winding square wire around a former of steel or wood that was especially shaped. Sometimes wire of this thickness is difficult to wind. If so, gently hammer the wire against the former as you wind it.

Spiral ring

This ring is a combination of windings around small and large formers. On one side the spiral of small rings is flattened. This is done by tapping them lightly with a hammer.

There are many combinations of large and small spirals that could be made into finger rings. Experiment with your own ideas and with variations in wire thickness to see how many new and original rings you can develop.

Ear-rings

The hook that goes through a pierced ear is made in a similar way to the shepherd's crook catch. Once you have constructed the hook, there are many interesting dangles you can make. Those illustrated are made from 0.8mm. round wire in the following ways.

Tight spiral. Wind up a tight spiral as described on page 187. Bend the last ring at a slight angle, as this makes a convenient loop for hanging. Join the spiral to the ear hook with a small ring.

Open spiral. Wind a spiral as before. Ease out the rings at each end of the spiral enough to allow access for the snipe-nose pliers. Grip each end ring in the pliers and gently stretch the spiral until you see the effect you want. Make the hanging loop by bending one free end of the spiral back against the wire. Suspend this stretched spiral from an ear hook as before.

Rings with beads. Make a short length of chain by using the methods described. Select your beads and wind the last link to suit the particular beads chosen (a large bead would probably require a larger ring). Slide the beads on to this last ring, and join it into the chain. Suspend the chain from the ear hook as before.

Finish and polish the jewellery as described on page 187.

Papier-mâché jewellery

Make your own bright papier mâché bangles and earrings to match your wardrobe. They are fun and easy, and you can make them appear as chunky or as delicate as you like.

You will need
Newspaper
Tissue paper
Wallpaper paste (a paste that does not contain a fungicide is safer if children will be helping you)
Acrylic or poster paints
Clear household glue
Fine sandpaper
Trimming knife
Clear nail varnish
Earring mounts and rings (for pierced or unpierced ears)
Tin or jar about 8cm. (3in.) in diameter
Dried leaves for trimming
30cm. (12in.) gold braid

Note
If you want really chunky bangles, use a larger tin or jar, remembering that after the papier mâché is added the bangles will be smaller than the jar.

To make the bangles
1. Tear newspaper into long strips, slightly narrower than the finished width of the bangles.
2. In a bowl, make up a small quantity of wallpaper paste in the proportions recommended by the manufacturer.
3. In another bowl, soak the newspaper strips in water for a few minutes, then dip the soaked strips in the paste.
4. Wind the strips around the tin or jar, carefully pressing out any air bubbles. Continue winding until you have six to eight layers, and then leave it to dry in a warm place, such as an airing cupboard or near a radiator. (This can take a day or two, depending on how warm it is.)
5. When it is dry, carefully ease the bangle off the tin or jar. Trim the edges with a trimming knife if necessary.
6. Place a small amount of paste on a plate. Tear the tissue paper into small strips. Paste each piece separately before you use it, without soaking it first. Wind the strips of tissue paper around the newspaper evenly, and leave it to dry.
7. Apply three or four layers of tissue paper, leaving it to dry between each application. When the bangle is the thickness you want, rub it gently with fine sandpaper to get an even surface. Then apply a final layer of tissue paper and leave it to dry.

8. To make the zig-zag bangle, you must shape the bangle before the last two applications of tissue paper. To do this, divide one edge into sections about 4cm. (1½in.) wide, marking the sections with a pencil. Mark the centre of each section about 6mm. (¼in.) from the top edge, and join up the marks to form the zigzag. Cut out the zig-zag shape with a trimming knife. Mark the other edge in the same way, placing the centre point of each section opposite the high point on the other edge. Join up the marks and cut out the shape with the trimming knife. Apply two more layers of tissue paper, sanding the bangle before the last layer is applied.
9. To decorate each of your bangles, paint the entire bangle in the desired colour, applying more than one coat if necessary to obtain a depth of colour. Leave it to dry. Paint on a design – the photograph may give you some ideas. (For a professional look, it is important to make the design even. Dividing the bangle into equal sections with a pencil before you begin painting will help.) Or, instead of painting on a design, try gluing on dried leaves or gold braid. When you have finished decorating the bangle, varnish it with two coats of clear nail varnish and leave it to dry.

To make the earrings
The earrings are made entirely from tissue paper; there is no newspaper base.
1. Tear the tissue paper into very small pieces. Do not soak it. Dab a small amount of the paste on a few pieces of the tissue paper, and mould them in the palms of your hands to make them into the required shape.

2. Take another piece of tissue paper, dab it with paste, and wrap it around the shape. Leave the earring to dry in a warm place.
3. When it is completely dry, rub the earring gently with sandpaper to obtain a smooth surface. If necessary, apply another layer of tissue paper, again leaving it to dry.
4. Paint the entire earring in whatever colour you prefer and leave it to dry.
5. For flat earrings, pierce a small hole in the top of each and insert a ring. For drop earrings, glue on a mount at the top of each.
6. Decorate the earring with more paint or a dried leaf and leave it to dry.
7. Varnish with two coats of clear nail varnish, again leaving it to dry.
8. Attach a hook to the mount or ring, or for leaf earrings glue a screw mount to the back of each.

Threaded bead jewellery

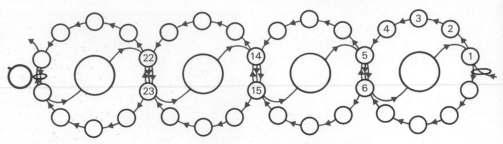

This pretty matching choker and bracelet are made by the bead-threading technique, similar to that explained on page 183. It's very simple, and once you get the hang of it you can make all sorts of different patterns. We have used a combination of blue china beads and pearl beads, but you can use any type or colour you like to match a particular outfit.

The only important thing is the size of the bead to use. The blue beads are the tiny rocaille beads you use for bead weaving. If you're not sure you have the right ones, thread 12 on to a needle – they should measure 2cm. (¾in.) in length. The pearl beads are larger – about 4mm. (3/16in.) in diameter.

You will need
1 pack of china rocaille beads
1 pack of pearl beads, about 4mm. (3/16in.) in diameter
1 loop and eye fastener for each item
1 beading needle
Polyester or nylon thread

To thread the beads
Thread the beading needle with a long length of yarn. Knot the free end of the yarn firmly to the loop part of the fastener.
Make the first 'flower' as follows.

Thread six china beads and one pearl bead, and push them down to the end. Insert the needle back through the first china bead (marked 1 in diagram) and then through the loop of the fastener. Draw yarn tight. Thread four beads on to the yarn, take the needle back through the last two beads before the pearl one (marked 5 and 6 in diagram).

To make the next 'flower', thread five china beads and one pearl bead on to the yarn, take the needle back again through the same two beads as before (5 and 6 in diagram) and draw the yarn tight. Now thread three china beads on to yarn, and take the needle through the two beads before the next pearl bead (14 and 15 in diagram).

Continue in exactly the same way, working each time into the appropriate bead, until the work is 6mm. (¼in.) short of the required length.

To finish, thread four china beads, an eye fastener, one china and one pearl bead on to yarn, take the needle back through the beads marked 22 and 23 in the diagram and draw the yarn tight. Thread three china beads on to the yarn, thread the needle through the china bead and the eye fastener just before the last pearl bead, draw the yarn tight and knot it off securely.

Thread any ends of yarn through the beads to hide them.

By Carol Payton

Beaded butterfly

Fig. 1 (below) for the numbers and colour.
4. To fasten off, thread the ends of the wire back through the previous row and then cut off the excess.
5. Make another upper wing, and then make two lower wings, again following Fig. 1 for colour and order.
6. For the body, cut a piece of wire 45cm. (17¾in.) long and thread black beads in the same way, but do not fasten off the wire when you have threaded the last bead. To make antennae, thread a black bead on the right-hand end of wire 2.5cm. (1in.) from body and thread the wire through this bead several times. Cut off the excess wire, and make the other antenna on the left-hand end.

To complete

Lay the lower and upper wing side by side and lay the other pair of wings on top (as though the wings were closed). With the remaining piece of wire make a line of stitches right across between the first and second beaded rows so that the four wings are securely joined. Now open out the wings. Insert the body into the groove and stitch it into position with the wire. Finally attach the brooch clasp to the underside of the butterfly with wire.

By Carol Payton

This lovely realistic peacock butterfly is made from little china beads threaded onto wire. It can either be worn as a brooch or threaded onto a thick length of wire and used as an unusual and attractive part of a dried flower display.

You will need

China beads: 91 black, 12 light blue, 35 white, 10 yellow and 284 dark maroon
5m. (5½yd.) of 5 amp fuse wire
1 brooch clasp

To make the butterfly

1. Fig. 1 shows the structure of the butterfly and provides a colour key. Make the two upper wings first. Cut a piece of wire 1m. (40in.) long. Hold one end in each hand and thread three maroon beads onto the right-hand end (Fig. 2). Thread the other end of the wire through these beads (Fig. 3). Pull the wire tight so that the beads are held securely in the centre of the wire.
2. Thread another three maroon beads on to the right-hand end of the wire, and thread the other end through them (Fig. 4). Pull the wire tight so that the beads lie above the first row.
3. Continue to thread rows of beads in the same manner. When you reach the sixth row, you will need to thread three black beads and four maroon ones. On the seventh row you must thread one yellow and seven maroon beads. Follow

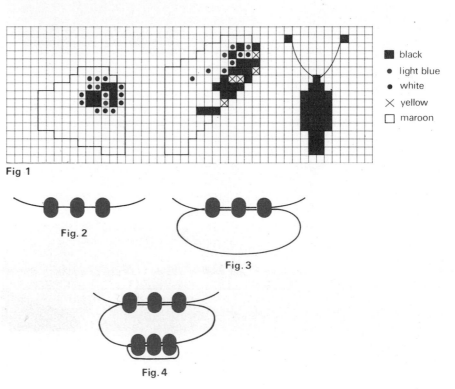

Fig 1

- ■ black
- ● light blue
- ● white
- ✕ yellow
- □ maroon

Fig. 2

Fig. 3

Fig. 4

Resin jewellery

Polyester resin is an ideal material for making jewellery. You can create all sorts of unusual effects, and, for added interest, pretty things like dried flowers or sequins can be embedded in the resin.

The technique of casting with polyester resin is described in detail on page 209. But the basic technique is the same whether you are making chunky bookends or dainty jewellery; the resin is mixed with a catalyst, poured into a mould and left to cure.

Materials and equipment

You will need only small amounts of resin for jewellery making: 220g. (½lb.) is enough for several pendants or earrings. A small bottle of catalyst will be sufficient for a large selection of jewellery. For adding colour to the jewellery, you will need small amounts of coloured resin pigments, which are available from craft shops.

In addition, you will need disposable plastic cups for mixing, wooden stirrers, a special measuring cup, melinex foil for covering the open top surface of the cast, metal polish, tweezers for embedding, a hand drill or epoxy adhesive for attaching the mounts, jewellery fittings such as rings and chains, a suitable mould and a selection of things to embed.

Moulds

A variety of moulds can be used for pendants, earrings, cufflinks, bracelets or rings. Special plastic moulds are available from craft shops, or you can mould plasticene into the desired shape. Plastic bottle lids with the thread removed are also suitable. Or you can create your own shapes by bending 8mm. (⅜in.) copper, brass or aluminium strips into a mould, fastening with epoxy adhesive and placing on a sheet of thin, transparent polyester. Plastic and plasticene do not require waxing first, but the metal strips do require it.

Embedding

Because resin is an ideal medium for embedding, many resin objects are made specially to display a favourite item. There is a wide variety of items that can be embedded in resin jewellery: sequins, buttons, glitter, old watch parts, small beads, broken bits of coloured glass, seeds, a butterfly or dragonfly, a favourite photograph, dried flowers, coins, shells – all can look extremely attractive.

Embedding is not particularly difficult, especially when the cast is as small as

your jewellery will be, but there are a few points to remember.

Air bubbles will spoil the appearance of the cast. To help prevent them, immerse dried flowers in resin and leave to gel before embedding. Never use fresh flowers, for the moisture in them would create air bubbles. When embedding a coin, photograph or other flat object, coat the face with a few drops of resin and catalyst and leave to gel before embedding. Moving the object around with tweezers when it is first embedded will also eliminate some of the air bubbles.

Make sure the item you are embedding is clean and dry and free of dust. Polish coins to a bright shine before embedding. Be prepared for the colour of dried flowers and insects to alter slightly. Vivid colours will remain fairly strong, but there will inevitably be some change.

Don't forget to embed the object face down, since the bottom of the cast will become the front of the jewellery.

Adding colour

Special translucent or opaque resin pigments are available which you can mix with the resin to colour the jewellery. For an unusual streaked effect, cast the resin, then just before it gels drop bits of concentrated pigment into the resin with a cocktail stick.

Casting the resin

Because jewellery is small, the resin and catalyst can be added all at once, rather than in layers, and this will create a smooth, seamfree effect.

However, if you are embedding an object, it is much easier to cast the resin in layers. Cast the first layer about 3mm. (⅛in.) deep, and leave it to cure for two or three hours until it has gelled. Mix up and pour the second layer, then position the item to be embedded in the resin using tweezers. (You can position the object before pouring in the second layer, but you are more likely to get air bubbles.) This second layer should not quite reach the top of the mould. It will shrink slightly as it cures, and when it has gelled you can top up with a thin third layer.

Using too much catalyst will cause the resin to crack, but the smaller the item the more catalyst you have to use. For jewellery, or in fact any item requiring up to 50g. (1¾oz.) resin, you should use 2% catalyst. That means that if you mix up 28g. (1oz.) of resin for your first layer, you will need .56g. catalyst. 20 drops of catalyst equals 1g., so .56g. is 11 drops. Use slightly less catalyst on the subsequent layers, since the first layer will already have generated some heat.

Cover the cast with a piece of melinex foil topped with a sheet of glass, a metal plate or other flat object, and leave to cure overnight. When it is hard and cool, remove the cast from the mould, file or sand away any uneven surfaces, and polish with metal polish.

Using epoxy adhesive, glue a ring to the top of the pendant or earring; or make your own ring with wire. Alternatively you can drill a small hole in the top to attach the ring. Suspend from earring mounts or a long chain. For cufflinks, attach cufflink fittings to the back of the cast with epoxy adhesive.

Copper wire jewellery

This sophisticated copper jewellery can be made with the minimum of special tools. It can be worn as a set or individually, and looks equally stunning with casual daytime clothing or elegant evening wear.

This jewellery is made mostly from copper wire, but silver would be equally suitable. Brass is rather harder and not so flexible as copper, but it could be used for the pendant and ear-rings.

You will need

0.8mm. gauge copper sheet, at least 16cm. (6¼in.) along one length
0.8mm. brass sheet, at least 2.5cm. (1in.) along one length
0.8mm. diameter copper wire (for the pendants and bracelet)
0.5mm. diameter copper wire (for the ear-rings)
Scriber such as a nail or other pointed item
Cabochon cut stones (optional)
Shears; junior hacksaw or piercing saw
Hammer; centre punch; flat needle file
Hand drill and 1mm. drill bit
Snipe-nosed pliers; round-nosed pliers
Epoxy adhesive
Flour grade glass paper
Grade 4/0 emery polishing paper
Silver polish

Notes

Before beginning this jewellery, study page 187, which tells you how to use the pliers to bend wire, and how to finish the jewellery with glass paper, polishing paper and silver polish.

Copper jewellery will of course tarnish, but it can quickly be brightened up by rubbing it gently with wire wool.

Bracelet

With shears, cut a strip from the copper sheet 16 by 1cm. (6¼ by ⅜in.). Using the scriber, mark a line across each end, 1cm. (⅜in.) from the ends. Starting at those points and using the flat needle file, file the sides of the strip to form tapering grooves on each side, 1mm. deep at the marked points (Fig. 1). Neaten the edges by filing, and brighten the copper faces by rubbing with wire wool.

Using the pliers as described on page 187, bend the 0.8mm. copper wire into a right angle 5mm. (¼in.) from the end, and hammer the end flat on a steel block. Position the end alongside one of the marked lines on the copper strip, and begin winding the wire firmly round the strip, covering up the end as you wind

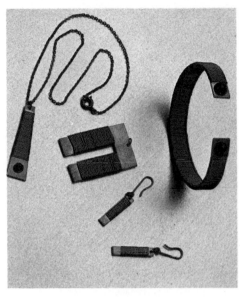

(Fig. 2). Continue winding till you reach the line at the other end, then cut off the wire on the wrong side.

To flatten the wire on to the copper strip, place the bound strip between two pieces of wood and hammer along their length; or tighten the bracelet up in a vice. Secure the end of the wire with adhesive.

To form the oval shape, bend the bound strip with your fingers, curving only a small section at a time. Try the bracelet on and adjust the curve until it is a suitable shape and size.

Finish the bracelet in the same way as on page 187, then glue on cabochon cut stones if desired, using epoxy adhesive.

Copper pendant

Using shears, cut out a rectangle from the copper sheet 4 × 2.5cm. (1⅝ × 1in.). With a junior hacksaw or piercing saw, cut out a slot from the centre 5mm. (¼in.) wide and 3cm. (1⅛in.) long, so that you have an upside-down 'U' shape. Mark lines 5mm. (¼in.) from the ends with the scriber, and file grooves 1mm. deep along all four sides between the lines (Fig. 3). Neaten the edges by filing.

To make a hole for the jump ring, mark a point in the centre of the pendant 2mm. from the top edge. Holding the centre

punch on the mark, tap it once with the hammer, then drill the hole with a hand drill and 1mm. bit.

Bind the 0.8mm. copper wire round one side of the pendant in the same way as for the bracelet, then repeat on the other side. Finish the pendant as above, fix a jump ring through the hole, and hang the pendant from a copper chain.

Copper and brass pendant

With the shears, cut out the shape shown in Fig. 4 from the brass sheet, 4cm. (1⅝in.) long, 5mm. (¼in.) wide at the top edge, and 1cm. (⅜in.) wide at the bottom edge. Mark lines with the scriber 3mm. (⅛in.) from the top edge and 1cm. (⅜in.) from the bottom edge. File grooves 1mm. deep along both sides between the lines, and neaten the edges with the file.

In the centre of the top of the pendant, mark a hole for the jump ring, and drill as for the copper pendant. Bind with the 0.8mm. copper wire as described above, and glue on a cabochon cut stone, if desired, with epoxy adhesive. Finish as above, and attach a jump ring and brass chain.

Ear-rings

From the copper sheet cut out 2 rectangles, each 5mm. × 2.5cm. (¼ × 1in.). Mark lines 2mm. from the tops and 1cm. (⅜in.) from the bottoms. File grooves down each side between the lines; the grooves should be slightly less than 1mm. deep because you will be using thinner wire. File to neaten.

Drill a hole in the centre of the top of each ear-ring, then bind with the 0.5mm. copper wire. Finish, and attach a jump ring and gold sleepers; or make your own in a similar way to the shepherd's crook catch described on page 187.

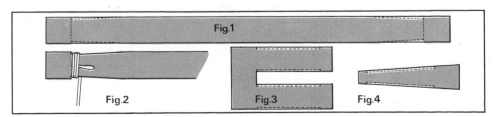

Fig.1

Fig.2

Fig.3

Fig.4

Indian bead necklace

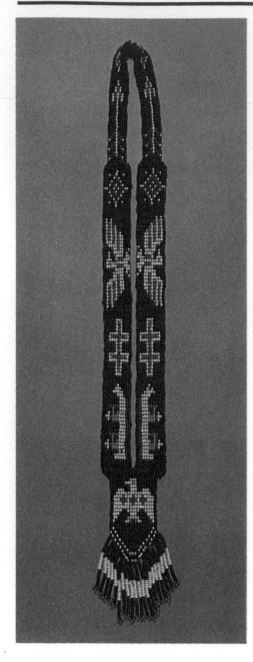

This striking design is adapted from a traditional North American Indian pattern. White eagles and boats are worked on a black background, with red, blue, green and gold beads completing the pattern, and the fringe uses the main colours in the necklace.

If you have not done bead weaving before, first read page 180, which explains the basic method, including how to finish your work and where to obtain the materials that are needed.

You will need
Of rocaille beads: 50g. (2oz.) black,
   25g. (1oz.) white, 15g. (½oz.) blue,
   15g. (½oz.) red, 15g.(½oz.) green,
15g. (½oz.) gold
1 reel polyester thread
Beading loom
Beading needles 10/12
Piece of beeswax or candle

Making the necklace
Work from the diagrams, following the pattern and colour key. Note that the first row (Chart A) starts with three white beads, the second has five and so on. Continue increasing two beads on each row until the ninth row, and then work the pattern until you have reached the 24th row. Increase two beads on each row for the next three rows.

The upper portion of the necklace is worked in two parts of 12 beads each, divided at the centre. To divide, simply take your weft thread through the 12 beads on the left-hand side of the work, then turn and continue the pattern in the usual way. When you need to add a new weft thread, start on the other side of the work, drawing the thread through the main part of the work, and working the pattern up the right side. If you work both sides more or less together in this way the tension will be even and firm.

As the necklace nears the end you must narrow it to fit the neck by removing a bead at each end of the row for two rows. When the beading is complete, the threads no longer in use will be threaded back into the work at the point where they were left. It is easier to complete the work if these spare threads are moved further along the spring separator while working the last section, as otherwise they can become tangled in the weft thread you are working with.

When the weaving is finished, take the necklace off the loom and lay the two ends opposite one another. Knot each warp thread to its pair on the opposite side then thread each one in turn securely through the opposite section of the work.

The fringing
Thread the second warp thread from the left with eight black, eight white, eight black and three gold beads. Take your thread through the last black bead and up to the edge of the loomed work. Gently pull the thread to form a triangle with the gold beads and secure it in the usual way (see page 180). Make sure that the thread is drawn through firmly but not too tightly, so that it falls correctly. If it is too loose the thread will show and if it is too tight it will not hang straight. Now take the second thread from the left, thread it through

the fringe and secure. Repeat process until all threads, except those at each end have been used. The remaining two can either be threaded into the end strands of the fringe, or they can be woven up into the sides of the work.

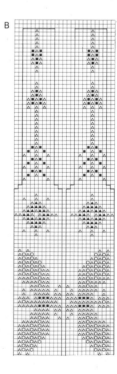

now work from chart B

A

1st row

△ white   ■ red   ● blue
○ gold   ▲ green   □ black

B

Glass jewellery

Pieces of glass found at the seashore are ideal for making beautiful, delicately coloured jewellery. Unlike ordinary glass – which is hard to cut to the right shape and has sharp edges – seashore glass has been literally ground down over the years into smooth lovely shapes and soft colours.

You will need
Selection of glass from seashore or estuary
Epoxy adhesive
Old icing nozzle or cardboard cone
Craft knife
Wet-and-dry glasspaper
Cellophane tape
For the bracelet
Thin-gauge copper sheet (available from large craft shops)
Lid from 200g. (7oz.) jar instant coffee
Strong scissors
Round-nosed pliers
For the multi-coloured pendant
Small metal ring
Chain or leather thong
For the multi-coloured brooch
Brooch back
For the plain pendants
Cone-shaped pendant mounts, wire and beads (sold together at craft shops)

BRACELET
Using scissors, cut a 25 by 4cm. (9⅞ by 1⅝in.) strip of thin-gauge copper sheet. Wipe it with a clean cloth to make sure it is clean and dry and free from grease.

Wrap the copper strip round the coffee-jar lid, overlapping the ends. Glue the ends together with epoxy adhesive, being careful not to stick the copper to the lid. Place two elastic bands or strips of cellophane tape around the outside to hold it in place, and put it somewhere warm to set overnight.

When it has set, remove the elastic bands or cellophane tape, but leave the copper wrapped round the lid so that it won't lose its shape. Select a variety of glass, avoiding large heavy pieces and also pieces which are too long to fit on the curve.

Divide the bracelet into four sections and work on only one at a time. Because epoxy adhesive takes a long time to set, the bracelet would become unmanageable if you attempted to work all the way round at once.

Following the instructions on the adhesive, stick the pieces of glass on the copper one at a time. Fit them together as closely as their shapes will allow, but don't worry about small gaps. Leave a margin of at least 1cm. (⅜in.) between the glass and the edge of the copper. Fix small areas in place temporarily with cellophane tape. When you have filled a quarter of the bracelet, leave it to dry before beginning the next quarter.

When the entire bracelet is complete, leave it to set hard in a warm place for at least 12 hours. Do not remove the cellophane tape until you are sure all the pieces are stuck.

Using sharp scissors, very carefully cut round the shapes, leaving a 5mm. (¼in.) margin of copper. With a craft knife, cut small deep slits along the edges of the copper between each piece of glass. Press the copper margin around the glass with a pair of round-nosed pliers, making sure no sharp areas are left.

Make up a large quantity of the adhesive and carefully fill all the gaps between the pieces of glass. An old icing nozzle is ideal for squirting the adhesive in place (but you won't be able to use it again), or you can make a small cone from cardboard.

Leave the bracelet to harden for a few hours, then scrape off any surplus adhesive with the craft knife. Leave it to dry overnight. Clean the bracelet with wet-and-dry glasspaper, remove the lid, and check that all edges are pressed down well.

MULTI-COLOURED BROOCH AND PENDANT
Choose smaller pieces of glass than for the bracelet, and experiment with different arrangements. You may even be able to create a recognisable subject, like the vase-of-flowers brooch in the photograph.

Stick strips of cellophane tape together to make a square area, and place on a flat surface, sticky side up. Arrange your design on this. Remove each piece and apply glue to the area to be stuck, then replace in position. When all the pieces are glued, fill in small gaps with adhesive, as for the bracelet.

For the pendant, glue on a small metal ring to take the chain or leather thong. Leave the pendant or brooch to dry, then remove cellophane tape, and scrape and sand clean. For the brooch, attach a brooch back.

PLAIN PENDANTS
Sometimes, on the beaches of large estuaries, you will find a well-worn glass bottle stopper, or even a wine-glass stem. These can be topped with cone-shaped silver mounts to make attractive pendants. To make a fitting for a chain or leather thong, bend the length of wire (which comes with the mount) in half, anchoring a small bead (also supplied) at each end. Poke the doubled end of the wire up through the cone, and glue the cone in place with epoxy adhesive.

Happiness necklace

This individual-looking piece of jewellery is based on the Greek 'happiness' necklaces, and is made from small washers. You can use washers made of brass, chrome, alloy or copper according to the effect you want.

This necklace, which follows the traditional design, uses 835/16in. washers (the measurement is the diameter of the hole). You can use fewer, or you can use a different size of washer, but the bigger the hole is in relation to the whole washer, the more attractive the necklace will be. Hardware shops, engineering shops and stockists of door furniture, car spares and bicycle parts all have their own varieties.

You will need
Washers
Chain to match
Fine gauge wire
Round-nosed pliers
Small fine-bladed hacksaw
Piece of dowelling or knitting needle for 'former'

To make the jump rings
The washers are joined with jump-rings. You can buy these in a craft shop but it is quite simple to make your own and quite fun. You must find a long, smooth cylinder, such as a piece of dowel, a wooden spoon handle or a thick knitting needle. The thickness of this cylinder is most important. Place two of the washers on a flat surface, about a centimetre apart. The diameter of the cylinder must be as great as the distance from inside one washer to inside the other washer.

Take your fine gauge wire and wind it around the cylinder. If you have two pairs of pliers, you can hold one end of the wire to the cylinder with one pair and use the other to do the winding, but it is possible to manage with only one pair. When you have wound the wire down the cylinder, in a spiral, take the hacksaw and cut, vertically, down the cylinder. You will have cut through each coil of the spiral and should now have a pile of slightly springy rings. These are your jump rings.

To make the necklace
Now find the centre link of the chain and mark it with a thread or a safety pin. Count three links to the right of the central link, slip a jump ring through this third link and through a washer. You may have to open up the break in the ring by bending it slightly, and then close it again with the pliers. Count three links to the left of centre and join another washer to it. Repeat this right along the chain, joining a washer to every sixth link until you have hung 16 washers on the chain, eight to the right of centre and eight to the left.

Second row: using two jump rings, hang a washer on the first two washers of the first row. Hang the second washer of the second row onto the second and third washers of the first row. Continue along the row and you will use 15 washers.

The third row repeats this pattern, using 14 washers. The fourth and fifth rows have 13 and 12 washers and the sixth row also has 12, each washer being hung simply on to the one above with a single jump ring.

The finished necklace can be polished. If you are a person whose skin is irritated by any of these metals, try coating any piece of metal that touches you with clear nail varnish.

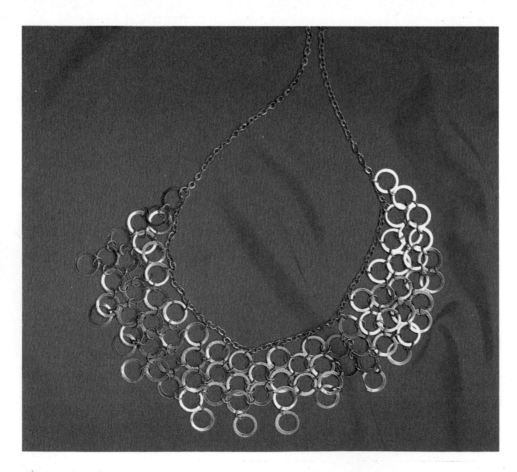

Repoussé fish pendant

This delightful fish, made in three pieces so that it moves when you wear it, is made in a heavy metallic foil. The technique by which the raised design is made is called repoussé, an old technique used for centuries by workers in precious metals. In the case of metals the design was hammered on the reverse side, and the process was a very slow one. Foils are, of course, much softer and so a design can be made quite quickly.

The instructions here relate to the fish, but you can make all manner of different pieces of jewellery, and also decorated boxes, trays and so on, using this fascinating technique. The foil is gold on one side and silver on the other, so you have a choice of metals.

You will need
Heavy metal foil (available from art
   shops)
Thin cardboard
Clear household adhesive
About 30cm. (12in.) silver braid
Modelling tools
Fabric pad (see below)
Silver chain
Black ink or poster paint

The repoussé technique
The design is made by modelling the foil with a tool. Tools used for modelling should be blunt. Thick knitting needles, used ball-point pens or brush handles are all suitable tools. The foil is worked on a pad made by folding fabric (Fig. 2). Trace your design on the wrong side of the foil, reversing it if necessary. Lay the foil on the pad, wrong side up, and work over the design with the tool. Round off some of the hollows with a thicker tool. Turn work to the right side and mark round the raised areas to emphasise them. Continue working on both back and front until the designed shape has been modelled. For variation, lines can be pressed from the front and then marked from the back. Mix black ink or paint with a little toilet soap and rub over the right side of the finished work. Leave until almost dry, rub off excess from the highlights, using a soft cloth. Cut out the shape and mount on a card backing.

To make the fish
Draw the fish shape on to paper, using Fig. 1 as a guide. Our fish is 14cm. (5½in.) long, but you can make it whatever size you like. Cut the pattern into three, for head, body and tail. Lay the paper shapes on the wrong side of the foil and draw round them, leaving 1.3cm. (½in.) extra all round body and tail pieces.

Lay the foil pieces on the fabric pad (Fig. 2), wrong side up, and mark the design with whatever tools you are using. Work over the design as described above, until you have made sufficiently deep indentations, then turn to right side and mark round raised areas.

Cut two card shapes for each piece, using the paper pattern pieces, but this time leaving no margins. Glue these to the backs of the foil shapes. Snip into the foil margins and turn them to the back of the card.

Mix black paint or ink with soap and rub over the mounted foil. When almost dry, rub away from the highlights.

Assemble the pendant as follows. Turn fish segments to wrong side. Cut one piece of braid long enough to go from the top of the tail piece to just above the top of the head and glue at top of tail and top of body, overlapping the pieces slightly. Cut another piece to go from above the top of the head to the middle of the body. Glue at top of body. Cut a short piece for the head and glue to top of head (Fig. 3). Glue the remaining card shapes to backs, sandwiching the braid between the layers of card. Arrange the segments together, overlapping the head and body a little, and stitch braids together at the top. Thread chain through top of braid.

Fig. 1

Fig. 2

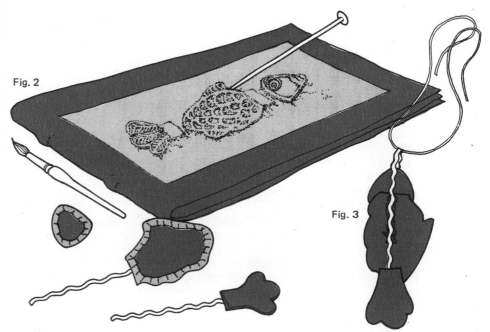

Fig. 3

Polishing pebbles

Most of us have picked up pebbles from the beach or riverside, attracted by their delicate, water-washed colours and to polish them will simply enhance the beauty of the stones' colours. Collect as many pebbles as possible for they can be put to dozens of decorative uses. Some of them are likely to be semi-precious and can be used for jewellery after polishing. Depending on where you look you can find carnelians, chalcedony, agate or jasper, all of which polish beautifully.

Pebbles have to be polished in an electric tumble polisher, which makes use of abrasive grits, polishing powders and water to achieve a smooth finish in a few weeks. Small single barrel tumblers can be bought inexpensively and they are ideal for use at home. It is better to use them in a garage or shed with electric power, as the continuous rumbling can be a little aggravating.

Finding pebbles to polish

Stones suitable for tumbling can be found on beaches, by rivers, mountain streams and in mountainous areas. You may even find some in your own back garden! Most pebbles which are suitable for polishing are composed of quartz and you can test for this using a coin, a penknife and a steel file. If the coin scratches the pebble,

it is too soft to be much use. If the penknife scratches it, it is suitable for polishing with others of the same kind. If the file scratches it, it is very suitable for polishing and if the file does not mark it, it is a very hard mineral and may be an interesting one. You can get a good idea of how a smooth pebble will look when it is polished by dipping it in water.

Local lapidary clubs can give information about the stones you can find in your own locality and enthusiasts can study the subject further by attending courses and going on rock hunting holidays. Observe the basic safety rules when hunting for stones. Take care not to let the tide cut you off and always ask permission before entering private property. If you want the easy life, many rock and craft shops supply raw stones to tumble.

You will need
Tumble polisher
Stones
Coarse grit (no. 80)
Medium fine grit (no. 220)
Fine grit (no. 400)
Water

How to work
Read the manufacturer's instructions carefully before proceeding. The instructions should tell you the right quantities of grit

to use. Stones of mixed sizes can be successfully tumble-polished but no stone should be so large that it almost fills the barrel. Ideally, the stones should be of the same uniform hardness. If you mix hard and soft, the softer ones can get ground away.

Wash the pebbles and stones and place them in the barrel or drum so that it is two thirds to three quarters full. Put in just enough water to cover the stones and add the coarse grit (no. 80). Close the lid firmly and switch on. Undo the barrel each day to release any gases that may have built up during the tumbling, then re-seal the barrel. After about seven to ten days, turn the machine off and look at the stones to see if they are the right shape and smoothness. If not, let the machine run for another day or two. When you are satisfied with the stones, put them in a plastic sieve and wash them well under running water to remove all the grit, letting the water drain into a bowl. This is to stop the sink from getting blocked. Wash out the barrel in the same way. Dispose of the waste in the garden.

Return the washed stones to the barrel. Fill with sufficient water to cover the stones and add the slightly finer grit (no. 220). Run the tumbler again for about seven days. Repeat the washing process, put the stones back in the tumbler and cover with water and fine grit (no. 400). Tumble for a further seven days. Again, repeat the washing process. Return the stones to the barrel and add water and a cupful of detergent powder. Run for 24 hours. Finally, rinse the pebbles under running water and you will see the magnificent results.

Using the polished stones
Using a quick-setting epoxy adhesive, stones can be stuck on to jewellery mountings to make bracelets, necklaces and brooches. To help keep stones and setting steady while the glue sets, fill a small tray with fine sand, press it down firmly and stand the mountings in this. Other ideas for things to make can include lampshades, boxes, bead curtains, key rings, powder compacts – the decorative possibilities are endless once you start on this absorbing hobby.

Gem tree

This beautiful miniature tree, decorated with semi-precious stones, is an attractive ornament and one which can be made quite cheaply. If you have a tumble polisher, you can use stones gathered from the beaches, which are often prettily coloured and marked. If not, many lapidary shops sell polished gem stones at prices within most people's reach. These shops also sell the mountings needed for the stones.

You will need
24-30cm. (12in.) lengths of thick silver-coloured wire (such as 30 amp fuse wire)
Length of fine fuse wire
24 small polished stones
24 bell caps
24 jump rings
48 leaf bails (tiny gold leaves)
Epoxy adhesive
Pair of small pliers
All-purpose filler
A small container
Handful of small polished stones or sand

How to work
Take the 24 lengths of thick silver wire and twist them together with the pliers to form a tree shape with a thick gnarled trunk. From this, branches should gradually peel off on either side of the main trunk. To do this, detach 4 wires at the first branch, then subdivide these into two, which can be further subdivided into single wires. Do this all the way up the tree until no wires are left. You can see clearly from the photograph how this is done. This forms the main trunk and the outline of the tree, so try to arrange it in an attractive shape.

Mix up a stiff mixture of filler and water, and almost fill the pottery container with it. Place the trunk of the tree firmly in the filler. You can use the lid from an aerosol or similar can if there is no pottery container readily available.

Attach each stone to a bell cap using epoxy adhesive so that it hangs downwards. Slip a jump ring through the loop at the top of the bell cap and when the all-purpose filler mixture has set hard, attach to the branches with fine fuse wire, making sure that the join does not show. Attach as many leaf bails as you need to the branches in the same way. To finish off, cover the surface of the container with a sprinkling of small polished stones or sand to hide the filler.

Pendant and brooches

The unusual jewellery in the photograph was all cut out with a piercing saw, an invaluable and relatively inexpensive tool for any serious jewellery maker. Here we show you how to use the saw to make copper or silver brooches and pendants like these.

Materials and tools
The jewellery can be made from 0.8 - 1mm. gauge copper sheet or sterling silver. A piece 10cm. (4in.) square will be enough for six or more items.

Other materials you will need are chain and jump rings for the pendants; brooch backs and epoxy adhesive for the brooches; and double-sided cellophane tape.

As well as a jeweller's piercing saw, you will need suitable blades for the saw. Buy more than one because you are bound to break some blades as you learn to use the saw. The ironmonger will advise you which blade you need for the gauge of metal you are using. As a general rule, the thinner the sheet, the more teeth per centimetre are needed on the blade.

In addition, you'll need a centre punch, a hammer, a hand drill and 1mm. drill bit for making the holes in the pendants; a half-round needle file; and smoothing and polishing equipment as described on page 187.

Finally, you will need to make a wooden peg (Fig. 1) to support the silver or copper sheet while you are sawing and filing it. The approximate dimensions of the peg are shown on the diagram, and it can be fastened to a table or workbench with a G-clamp or screws. The best working position is to sit on a low chair or stool so that your shoulder is level with the V of the wooden peg.

Inserting and tensioning the blade
The cut is made on the downward stroke of a piercing saw. So before you insert the blade, look closely at the teeth on the blade to make sure it is the right way up (Fig. 2). Loosen the wing nut at A in the diagram, insert about 10mm. (4in.) of the blade into the gap and then tighten the wing nut. Next undo the wing nut at C. Set the length of the saw throat to fit the blade, so that the end of the blade projects by about 5mm. (2in.) into the gap at B. Tighten the wing nut at C. This should not need to be adjusted again.

The blade must be tensioned correctly in the saw frame or it will break easily when you turn corners. To tension the blade, hold the saw so that you can push A against the table or against something that will not move. Guide the blade so that the end 10mm. (4in.) can be tightened in the gap at B. The blade should now be taut in the frame.

Using the piercing saw
The saw is used vertically and the work is held with the other hand over the hollow V. Practise sawing straight lines on scrap metal first until you are familiar with the technique.

Hold the saw at 45° to the metal sheet and start sawing gently, then gradually bring it into the vertical position. Don't force the saw or try to push it too much – the sharp blade will cut without force.

Try to use the whole length of the blade and long even strokes. If you need to withdraw the blade, continue the sawing movement, working back towards yourself.

For curves and corners, saw on the spot, at the same time turning the metal; continue sawing as you turn or the blade will break. Remember to hold the work firmly and avoid making any quick movements. To lubricate the blade, rub a candle on it occasionally.

Cutting out the design
Draw or trace your design on to paper and stick with double-sided cellophane tape to the silver or copper sheet. Work right up to the edge of the metal and position the shapes so as to use the material economically. Cut out the shapes as described above. If it is not possible to cut round an outline all at once, withdraw the saw blade and start again at another point.

When you have cut out a shape, hold it vertically against the front of the peg, and true up the edges by filing with the needle file in a horizontal position. Smooth and polish the metal shape as described on page 187. If desired, attach a brooch back with epoxy adhesive.

If you wish to make the shape into a pendant, you will need to make a hole for the jump ring. Centre punch and drill a 1mm. hole. If the shape is not symmetrical, you can find the best place for the hole by holding the shape loosely with pointed tweezers. Mark the point with a felt-tipped pen.

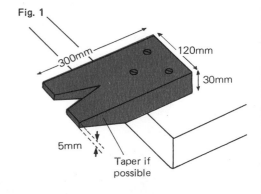

Fig. 1

300mm
120mm
30mm
5mm
Taper if possible

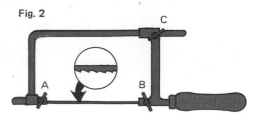

Fig. 2

Perspex jewellery

Perspex is a tough acrylic material that is ideal for making into modernistic jewellery. Because it comes in any number of translucent or opaque colours, as well as clear, there is enormous scope for improvising. Here are some ideas for making pendants, which you could also adapt into other pieces of jewellery.

You will need
Perspex offcuts
Junior hacksaw; coping saw
Medium-grade glass paper
Medium-grade wet-and-dry sandpaper
Fine-grade wet-and-dry sandpaper
Metal polish
Cotton wool; very soft duster
Small g-clamp or vice
Tensol cement or general purpose adhesive
Hand drill with 1mm. or 2mm. bit
Leather thongs

Working with perspex
Perspex usually comes in sheets about the thickness of glass, but unlike glass it can be worked and shaped with ordinary tools. It is an expensive material, but for jewellery you can simply use a few different off-cuts, obtainable from sign manufacturers. Some firms will allow you to rummage through their bins and select what you want, while others sell it by the weight.

Try to get a lot of different colours, both clear and opaque, and also as many small interesting shapes as possible: the less cutting you have to do, the better. Long, thin strips and shapes cut out from letters are especially useful. You will find that most of the offcuts are covered with protective paper. Keep this on as long as you can, with cellophane tape if necessary, because perspex scratches easily. Also, the paper will be handy for marking out your design.

Pieces of perspex can be joined together with special tensol cement, which is obtainable from perspex suppliers. It actually welds the pieces together rather than glueing them – but general-purpose adhesive does the job almost as well.

A shiny, high-quality finish is vital, especially when you are working on a small scale, as with jewellery. This is achieved by sanding the edges with finer and finer abrasives until they shine as much as the surfaces.

Yellow and red pendant
You can make a pendant exactly like the yellow and red one in the photograph, or devise your own variations. Larger versions make unusual headbands, and smaller ones can be used for brooches or badges. (The back of the finished brooch should be roughened, and epoxy adhesive used to attach a brooch pin.)

First draw your design for the bottom layer on the protective paper of a piece of perspex, then cut out the straight edges with a junior hacksaw and the curved edges with a coping saw.

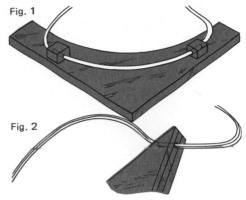

Fig. 1

Fig. 2

Next, sand all the edges with abrasives in the following order: medium glass paper, medium wet-and-dry plus water; fine wet-and-dry plus water; and metal polish applied with cotton wool. Finally, polish with a soft duster.

Mark, cut out, sand and polish the other layers in the same way, then arrange these pieces on the base piece.

Before sticking the pieces together, remove all protective paper from the surfaces to be joined. With a matchstick apply a little tensol or adhesive to each of these surfaces, and work it in. Now bring them together, and clamp in a g-clamp or vice, protecting the outer surfaces (including those still covered with protective paper) with card. Leave for 30 minutes.

Drill 1mm. or 2mm. holes at the two extremities of the base piece, to take the leather thong. Alternatively, drill holes through two separate pieces of perspex, then cut around the holes to form two small squares; stick these to the back of the pendant to take the thong (Fig. 1).

Layered pendants
This 'licorice allsorts' techniques is super for making fun, eye-catching pendants – but you could adapt the technique to make a chunky 'bead' necklace or rings. Simply drill through the finished layers of each 'bead' or ring with a 1.3cm. (½in.) bit, and sand and polish as above (Fig. 2).

To create the layered look, cut out a card template to the desired shape. Keep the shape simple to avoid cutting problems. Draw round the shape on to the protective paper on some clear, coloured and/or smoked pieces of perspex. Cut out all the pieces and stick them together, one by one, with tensol or general purpose adhesive. Try to put contrasting colours next to each other: for example, clear/smoked/coloured/smoked/clear.

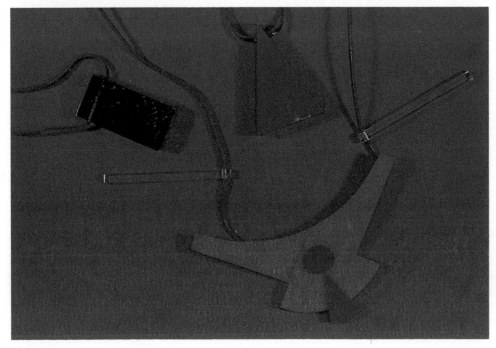

Silver cut pendant

With a piercing saw you can make amazingly intricate jewellery from small pieces of copper or silver. Here we show you how to make an elegant pendant, but before you begin be sure you have mastered the basic technique described on page 200. Also described there is how to make a jeweller's wooden V.

You will need
0.8mm. gauge copper or sterling silver sheet
Matching chain and jump ring
Compass and ruler
Double-sided cellophane tape
Jeweller's wooden V
Small G-clamp
Piercing saw and blades suitable for 0.8mm. sheet metal
Centre punch and hammer; steel block
Hand drill and 0.8mm. drill bit
Small file
Half-round and round needle files
Smoothing and polishing materials as described on page 187.
2 pairs snipe-nosed pliers

Note
Craft shops and model-making shops sell small drill bits that have a thicker shank than usual, making the bit less likely to break during use.

Making the pattern
Using a compass, draw a circle of the desired size on a sheet of paper, then divide the circle into sixteen equal segments with a ruler. Now draw and shade in the areas to be cut away (Fig. 1). Mark the dots shown in the diagram, which indicate where holes are to be drilled.

Attach the paper pattern to the copper or silver sheet with double-sided cellophane tape.

Cutting
Holding the sheet metal horizontally on the wooden V with one hand, saw round the outside circle with the piercing saw. The metal must be held down firmly, for if you allow it to rise up with the saw cut, it will snap the blade. If you prefer, you can use a small G-clamp to clasp the metal to the V, but you will have to loosen it in order to move the metal as the sawing proceeds.

After the outer circle is cut, you will need to centre punch each of the dots on the pattern. Place the circle on a steel block and, holding the centre punch vertically with the pointed end on the centre of the dot, tap the punch firmly once with

the hammer. (Don't hit it too hard or you will bend the metal; and, if you tap it more than once, the punch may move.) Repeat for each hole.

Using a hand drill and a 0.8mm. drill bit, drill through each of the dents made by the centre punch. Do not try to drill without having first centre-punched the holes, for the bit will tend to move around.

You can now saw out each of the inside areas of the design by inserting the blade of the piercing saw through the hole. To do this, open one end of the saw, place the blade in the hole, then tighten and tension the blade as described on page 200.

Saw out the area to be removed (Fig. 2), remembering to continue sawing as you turn corners. Open and remove the blade, repeat the process for each shaded area. Don't worry if you make a mistake – the beauty of this design is that it will look like part of the pattern.

Filing
After all the shaded areas have been sawn out, needle files are used to improve the shapes and smooth the inside edges. A round file is best for the smallest areas, and a half-round file for all other areas.

Hold the pendant vertically against the front of the V so that the area to be filed projects above the wood, then file away excess metal until the edges are smooth.

Use a small hand file to true up the outside edge of the pendant, again holding it vertically against the V. Curve the

file round the pendant as you file, and move the shape round until you get an even edge.

Finishing
Finish and polish the pendant as described on page 187.

To attach the chain, ease the gap on a jump ring open a little with two pairs of snipe-nosed pliers, and insert the ring through the drilled hole left on the outer rim of the pendant. Place the chain inside the jump ring as well, then push the ends of the jump ring together again, using the two pairs of snipe-nosed pliers.

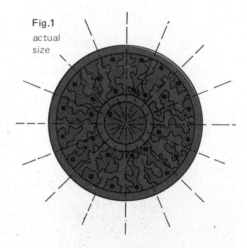

Fig.1
actual size

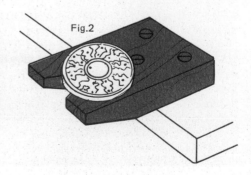

Fig.2

Foil and nail varnish jewellery

You can make pretty pieces of jewellery with thick, double-sided foil decorated with coloured inks and nail varnish. The foil looks like silver (or gold) shining through the clear varnish and the varnish makes the inks swirl in interesting patterns. You can play about for hours getting different effects. This is a technique best suited for large pieces like brooches and pendants because it isn't possible to make accurate, small designs with it. Try it on a larger scale to make a sparkling plaque for the wall, or a mobile for Christmas decorations.

You will need
Thick foil
Clear and coloured nail varnish
Coloured inks
Small tube of clear adhesive
Toothpicks
Ballpoint pen
Length of gold chain
Brooch mounts
Silver paint
Large silver sequins (for the necklace)

How to work
Draw some possible designs on a piece of paper. These designs don't have to be precise because this is not a precise technique. Draw flowing designs based on flowers, plant forms or butterflies or other 'art nouveau' type patterns. When you have a few pleasing designs, draw them on the reverse side of the foil with a ball pen. The lines will show through to the front of the foil, adding decorative raised patterns. Don't cut out the shape yet but leave it on the main sheet of foil.

Go round the main outlines of the pattern you have drawn with a line of clear adhesive and let it dry. This will form 'fields' for the varnish and inks to run into and will keep the colours separate. The glue may bubble a bit but this looks quite pretty when it dries.

Put a few drops of ink into one of the fields, add a drop of clear nail varnish and swirl it round with a toothpick until the area is well covered. Do the same in the next area and so on, using different coloured inks and clear nail varnish. Inks can be mixed to obtain more interesting colours.

For an opaque effect, use pearlised nail varnishes, but use them sparingly for they obliterate the sparkle of the silver. If the nail varnishes are coloured, there is usually no need to add inks unless you want to deepen the colour. When the adhesive, varnish and inks have dried (and the ink will usually take longer than the varnish and glue) cut out the main shapes and trim them as necessary.

Mount the shapes on thick card, painting the edges of the card silver and stick brooch pins to brooches.

For the necklace, use large silver sequins instead of silver foil, as this will give a more even effect. Bore holes when each disc is completed and thread with lengths of gold chain. Then attach to another gold chain.

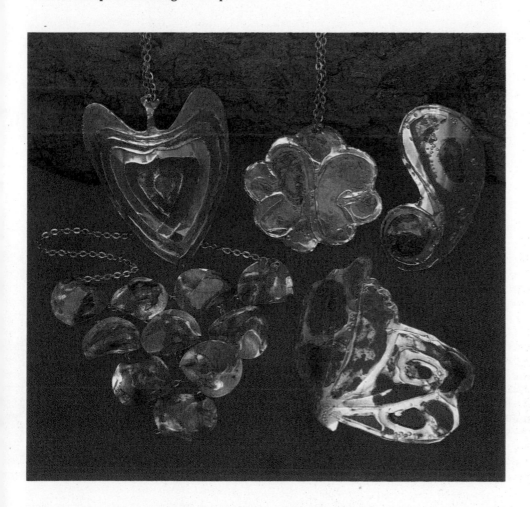

Self-hardening clays

Now that self-hardening clays are available pottery making has become a hobby that everyone can enjoy at home. These clays have a hardener added during their manufacture which allows them to harden without the intense heat needed for ordinary clays. Although articles made from self-hardening clays can never be as durable as fired and glazed pottery, they are hard-wearing enough to satisfy those who would like to try clay-work without having to invest in costly equipment.

When choosing a particular brand, take care to ensure that it contains only natural clay plus hardener. There are products on the market which are not clay based, and the following instructions are not relevant to these.

Obviously people with some pottery-making experience will find working with self-hardening clay easier than those with none, as the basic techniques are the same as for real clays. However these instructions have been devised with the beginner in mind. Also, self-hardening clay can be modelled and carved intuitively, so that an inventive person can achieve individual and exciting results with no experience at all.

Self-hardening clay hardens completely when left uncovered at room temperature for about 3 to 4 days, but becomes firm enough to handle in half a day. The hardening properties begin to take effect as soon as the clay is exposed to air and heat, so that temperature variations can affect the drying process considerably. If the clay becomes too dry while a piece is being made it can be sprayed with water to keep its plasticity, and can be kept in a workable condition from day to day by being wrapped in polythene.

The same applies to storage of this clay before use; as long as it is kept in an airtight container or wrapped in polythene, it can be kept indefinitely. Even when rock hard, it can be reconstituted by breaking it up into small pieces and soaking it in water.

Materials
Self-hardening clay can be worked on any kitchen table that can be easily sponged clean, but you will need a slightly porous surface, such as slate, wood, paper or hessian to place under the clay as a base. A cake-icing stand or pottery modelling stand is an asset, as this enables the work to be turned without disturbing it. Tools are helpful but not strictly neces-

sary. A wire with toggles attached to the ends is useful for cutting the clay, and as you grow more ambitious you may like to buy boxwood modelling tools. Apart from these, the kitchen drawer should provide everything you need – old knives and forks, a rolling pin, skewers – and some wooden sticks of different kinds. All these are useful aids for rolling, cutting and modelling.

Decorating
There are many different ways of decorating finished pieces. Self-hardening clay has light-sensitive properties: when exposed to the light it dries matt black, but if it dries when covered it will be a light grey colour. (This also applies to the inside of objects where the light does not reach.) Interesting contrast effects can be achieved by placing cut out shapes over the clay and removing them when dry. Wax paper stencils are ideal as they are easy to remove, but leaves, grasses, ferns or other natural material give attractive results.

Self-hardening clay can be varnished or sealed with a special glaze to give a

transparent water-resistant finish, and the glaze can itself be burnished or coloured with any sort of paints. Wax crayons can also be used and give an interesting finish. The glaze can also be applied over poster, acrylic or similar paints.

Painted self-hardening clay pottery will not stand up to ordinary washing so it is not recommended for domestic use. It is ideal for decorative vases, boxes, and bowls that do not need to be washed often; these can be cleaned by wiping gently with a damp cloth.

Clay boxes

These lidded boxes have been made from self-hardening clay, a natural clay with a hardener added during its manufacture, which allows it to harden without firing. They are quite simple to make, as they are built from flat slabs of clay. The edges are joined with slip, a 'glue' which is made by mixing clay with water to a thick creamy consistency.

The simplest to make is the square or rectangular box, but more complicated shapes can be attempted with practice. The slab technique can also be used to make round or asymmetrical boxes, which are assembled when the clay is still soft enough to bend, so there is a lot of scope for experimenting.

You will need
Self-hardening clay
Needle stuck in a cork or a craft knife
Large paintbrush
Bowl for mixing slip
Rolling pin and some newspaper
Stiff paper or thin card for templates
Ruler
2 strips of wood 1.5cm. by 1.5cm. (½in. by ½in.), about 45cm. (18in.) long

To make the box
These instructions are for making a box 15cm. long by 10cm. wide and 10cm. deep (6in. by 4in. by 4in.).

Spread some newspaper on the table, and start rolling the lump of clay with the rolling pin, just as you would pastry. Aim to keep the clay of even thickness all over. When you have got it down to about 2.5cm. (1in.) thick, lay the wood strips one each side of the clay and then

go on rolling. The wood strips will make sure that you roll the clay to an even 1.5cm. (½in.) all over (Fig. 1).

Leave the clay for 2 to 3 hours to dry a little. Meanwhile cut templates from the thin card; these are to be used as patterns for cutting out the box pieces. Cut 2 long sides, 15cm. by 10cm. deep (6in. by 4in. deep). Cut 2 short sides 10cm. by 10cm. (4in. by 4in.). Cut a template for the base and the top, 17.5cm. long by 10cm. (7in. by 4in.). The base and top are a bit longer to allow for the thickness of the 1.5cm. (½in.) walls of the box (Fig. 2).

Hold each template down on the clay in turn and cut out the shape with the needle or knife. Next, scratch the surface of the clay on the edges which are to be joined (Fig. 2).

Mix some clay with water to make a thick cream. This is called slip. Brush some of the slip on the scratched edge of the base piece. Press the first wall piece in position. Brush the joining edges of the wall piece and join the next wall. Press edges together. Position all 4 walls in the same way. Ignore any slip which oozes out as it can be scraped away later.

Leave the box to dry, and make the lid. Cut 2 strips of clay 7.5cm. (3in.) long and 6mm. by 6mm. (¼in. by ¼in.) and fix them with slip to the inside of the lid, 1.5cm. (½in.) in from the ends and sides (Fig. 3). Leave to dry. These strips keep the lid from sliding off the box. Scrape any rough places or messy joins when the box and lid have dried completely. The box lid should not be put on to the box until both have dried. Now you are ready to decorate the box.

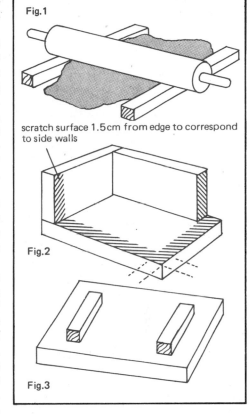

scratch surface 1.5cm from edge to correspond to side walls

Fig.1

Fig.2

Fig.3

Decoration
The decoration of the fish box includes an ornate knob which can be hand-modelled and attached with slip. The knob should not be too heavy or the lid may sag whilst drying. The pattern on the side has been made by applying rolled coils, again attached with slip.

The round box shows how decorations can be made by attaching different materials to the clay when dry. Holes were pierced to allow beading, ribbons, feathers, or anything else suitable to be threaded. The landscape has been painted with acrylics, and applied decoration could also be incorporated here. These boxes are an ideal vehicle for painted patterning – once you make a start further ideas will occur to you.

Papier mâché gift egg

apply pasted scraps of tissue paper over the whole surface, inside and outside the shells; this makes a smoother surface. Lay small pieces over the edges so that they are even and smooth. Leave to dry on the basin.

Finishing the edge
Measure round the edge of one half of the shell and cut a strip of thin card about 9mm. (³⁄₈in.) deep. Glue round the edge of one half as shown in the diagram, butting the ends. Use paper clips to hold the strip while it dries. Give both halves of the finished shell a single coat of white emulsion paint on the outside.

Decorating
The gift egg can be decorated with motifs or designs using either poster colours or modeller's enamels. You might try painting it a bright colour all over, finishing the egg with an edging of gold or a glued strip cut from a silver or gold doily. Decal motifs or transfers could be used as well, or the finished egg could be decorated with beads, sequins, scraps of felt or artificial flowers. A pretty effect can be achieved by pasting small pieces of coloured tissue paper all over the surface.

Children might enjoy a relief painting technique, as follows. Mark lines and spots on the unpainted surface with an end of a wax candle. Then paint or dab water colour on to the egg. Interesting effects can be achieved in this way as the colour will not adhere to the wax. Put tissue paper inside the egg and finish it with a tied satin ribbon.

Papier mâché is an old craftsman's technique and was once used for making coach panels. Paper was mixed with animal glue to form a substance which was hard and waterproof and yet could be shaped easily. Papier mâché is popular again today because it can be used to make many different kinds of attractive objects, and provides a use for old newspapers. There are two basic techniques, layering and moulding. Sometimes both techniques are used in one project, but this gift egg uses only the layering method.

You will need
For a large egg, a melon or an inflated balloon for a mould. For a smaller egg, an orange or a grapefruit can be used.
Quantity of newspaper, basin
White toilet tissue, pencil, fine sandpaper
Paperhanger's paste or flour and water paste
Thin card, sharp knife, cooking oil
White emulsion paint, brush
Glue

Basic technique
Newspaper only should be used for papier mâché, as magazine pages do not absorb paste as easily. Tear newspaper into small 2.5cm. (1in.) squares. Prepare the paste. Rub oil all over the melon mould with your hands, and balance it on a basin to support it. Dip pieces of paper in the paste and remove excess paste with the forefinger and thumb of the other hand. Apply to the surface of the mould. Continue to apply pieces, allowing them to cross each other at every angle. When the surface of the mould is covered leave it to dry (one layer dries quite quickly). Turn the mould up the other way and apply pasted paper to the underside, overlapping pieces at the edges. Continue to apply paper until about 6 layers have been applied and dried. Leave overnight to dry out completely.

Pencil a line round the mould. Cut the mould off along this line. (If you are using a piece of fruit, it will still be quite edible). Lightly sandpaper the cut edges. Now

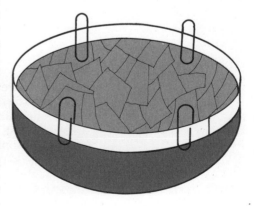

Papier mâché pets

On page 206 we told you how to work paper mâché by the layering method. On this card the pulp method is described.

Papier mâché pulp can be used for all kinds of things for which you would usually use modelling clay. Its advantage is that pulp can be gently baked in an oven and becomes very hard. The surface can be painted with poster colours or modeller's enamels and the pulp will adhere to surfaces which have been covered with the layered paper technique. It is a superb modelling material, but a little time must be taken with the preparation of the pulp.

Materials

1 Soft and absorbent paper; newspaper will do if it is first torn into very small pieces. For small projects, toilet tissue is ideal and makes a smooth pulp.
2 Paste; for economy, flour and water make a good paste. Alternatively, use wallpaper paste.

Flour and water paste

Mix plain flour to a thin paste with cold water. Stir in 1 tablespoon of salt for every 225g. (½lb.) of flour. Cook over a gentle heat, stirring, until the paste begins to thicken, adding warm water as necessary. The paste eventually becomes quite thick and translucent and is then ready for use.

Another method is to mix the flour with cold water, then pour on boiling water, stirring quickly to prevent lumps forming. Stir until the mixture is smooth and translucent.

Making papier mâché

Tear paper into tiny pieces. Put into a bowl. Pour on boiling water. Pour just enough to make the paper wet but not too soggy. Add more later until the paper has absorbed a quantity of water. Squeeze out the water with your hands. Now add paste, a little at a time, kneading the mixture in the hands. It will be a dark grey, unpleasant-looking mixture. When it has the texture of modelling clay it is ready to use.

Modelling figures

The owl and the pussy cat models are made entirely of papier mâché pulp. They are quite small, and can be modelled all in one operation. Make a big ball first, rolling it in the hands. Bang the ball on the table to make it stand, then shape the ball to a cone shape with the fingers. Pinch the ears into shape. Leave to dry

out. You can add small pieces of paper to the surface before painting if you like.

Bigger models need a base of some kind. Small bottles and jars are good and help to shape the figure. You can cover the whole surface of the bottle or jar with pulp so that the bottle stands firmly on its edge or you can use the opening, for instance if you are making a candlestick (see drawing). Prepare the bottle by covering the surface with a layer of pasted paper first and then apply the pulp, a little at a time. Use a spoon handle to help you to shape the pulp.

Painting the model

When the pulp has dried, it is ready for painting, but if you want a smoother surface, paste tiny pieces of tissue paper all over the surface. Paint the model with white emulsion paint first and then paint your design, using poster colours or modeller's enamels.

Garden candle-holder

A candle looks pretty in the garden on a warm summer evening but lasts longer if shielded from the breeze. This holder is made on a 1.5 litre bottle using self-hardening clay and takes three to four days to complete.

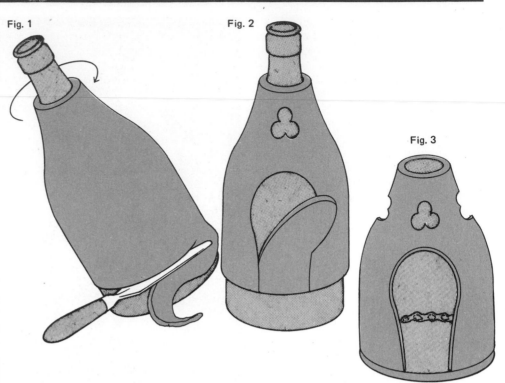

Fig. 1   Fig. 2   Fig. 3

You will need
Self-hardening clay, about 1kg. (2lb.)
1.5 litre bottle
Spatula or palette knife
Modelling tool, rolling pin
Small pastry cutter, cooking oil
Saucer of water
Piece of card
White emulsion and enamel paints

To make
Coat the bottle from neck to base with cooking oil. This acts as a parting agent when the clay has hardened. Cut a piece of clay and seal the remainder in a plastic bag. Roll out the clay with a rolling pin to a thickness of about 6mm. (¼ in.). Wrap the clay gently round the bottle and press lightly to the surface. Continue rolling and wrapping clay until the surface of the bottle is covered from half-way down the neck to about 3.7cm. (1½ in.) from the base. Using both hands, press and smooth the clay on to the bottle turning it round all the time until the clay feels evenly distributed. Cut away surplus clay from the neck and base by resting the bottle at a 45° angle and turning it round while you cut (Fig. 1). From the front cut away a piece of clay to make an opening (Fig. 2). Put the piece in the plastic bag. Press out small decorations round the neck using the pastry cutter. Leave the clay to harden for 2 days.

Making the base
Cut a circle from card the diameter of the bottle plus 1.2cm. (½ in.). Roll out the remaining clay to a thickness of about 1.2cm. (½ in.). Cut a circle using the card as a template. Score round the edge with the tip of a blade where the holder will sit. Moisten the bottom edge of the holder, lift off the bottle and press gently on to the clay base. Using the modelling tool, pull moist clay up from the base to make a good join. Use small pieces of clay and push into the join on the inside (Fig. 3), smoothing out with a damp finger. Allow 2 days more to dry. The surface should be rubbed down with sandpaper if you are painting. The inside can be painted with white emulsion and the outside with coloured enamels. Alternatively, leave the holder in its natural grey colour.

Casting with polyester resin

Polyester resin is an ultra-modern craft material which you can use to make a wide range of beautiful items for the home. Lamp bases, paperweights, sculptures, bookends, jewellery, door knobs – all these look stunning cast in resin.

Materials and equipment

The basis of all clear casting is polyester resin, a type of plastic which is sold by its liquid weight in craft shops. It is always sold along with a catalyst, which makes the resin harden permanently when it is mixed with it.

You can also buy from craft shops the melinex foil which is needed to cover exposed surfaces; plastic moulds of varying shapes and sizes; silicone carbide grit for polishing the cast; a special measuring jug and wooden stirrers.

In addition, you will need an old mixing bowl or paper cups, a craft knife, a file, metal polish or window cleaning spray, and acetone or nail varnish remover.

Working area

Resin casting should always be done in a warm, well-ventilated room. There should not be an open flame in the room, nor should you smoke while working with the resin.

Your work surface should be heat resistant and covered with aluminium foil. Keep all materials away from your eyes and from food. It's best to wear rubber gloves; if you get any on your skin, wash it off immediately with hot water and soap. Remove any spilt resin with acetone or nail varnish remover. If you do spill some, don't use it a second time, and do not throw it away until it is cool.

Always wear old clothing, and use disposable containers for measuring and mixing.

Moulds

As well as the plastic moulds that you can buy, there is any number of suitable objects around your own home; or you can construct the mould yourself.

Glass, glazed china, metal, enamelled tin, glass fibre, acetate sheeting, latex rubber, perspex or polypropylene are all suitable. Some plastics, such as acrylic and polystyrene, should not be used because they would interact chemically with the resin and spoil the cast. To test whether a material is suitable, drop some nail varnish remover or acetone on it: if the material dissolves, you'll know that it shouldn't be used!

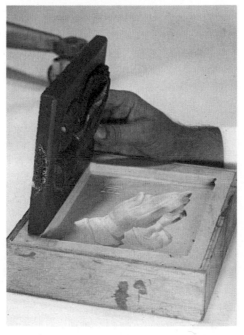

Whatever material you use, the shape of the mould should be such that you can remove the finished cast; obviously a container that was smaller at the top than at the bottom would not be suitable. In the same way, avoid containers with a rim round the top.

Because resin shrinks slightly during the chemical process, it is usually not difficult to remove it from the mould. But to be sure that you can easily remove it, coat the inside of the mould with wax polish. (You can buy special release agents from craft shops if you prefer.) If you have used a mould of latex rubber, acetate sheet or plastic, however, this is not necessary.

Casting the resin

When resin and catalyst are mixed, a chemical reaction causes it to harden gradually, giving off heat in the process. The proportion of catalyst to resin varies with the amount of resin you are using: the more resin, the less catalyst you need. This is the most critical aspect of resin casting, and you must never simply guess at the amount. If you use too much catalyst, your cast will crack; if you use too little, it will not harden properly.

Measure the catalyst very carefully in the special measuring cup. Using a wooden stirrer, mix the resin and catalyst together in an old plastic bowl. You must mix them thoroughly or the cast will not harden evenly; and you must stir slowly or unattractive air bubbles may form.

Pour the mixture into your prepared mould and leave it to harden – 'to cure' is the technical term.

To prevent the top of the cast from becoming tacky from exposure to the air, cover it with a piece of melanex foil. Put a metal plate or piece of glass on top of this and secure it in place with cellophane tape. Alternatively you can leave the surface exposed, then remove the tackiness with acetone or nail varnish. The surface is liable to distort, however, so you would have to file it down flat.

With some very large casts, it is sometimes preferable to pour in the resin and catalyst in two or more layers. This prevents the cast from cracking, which it is inclined to do when the inside of a large solid block becomes too hot. The seams between the layers do show slightly, however, since a second layer is not poured on the first layer until the latter has reached a jelly-like consistency.

The time a cast takes to cure depends on its size and the temperature of the room. When it is no longer giving off heat, it has finished hardening and can be removed from the mould.

Finishing

Many of the moulds made from things found around the home will have unwanted ridges on them. Once the cast has hardened and been removed from the mould, it is similar to wood to work with, and any uneven surfaces can be filed away.

Polishing is one of the most important stages of resin casting. Use a dripping wet cloth, dipped in a paste made of silicone grit and washing-up liquid to lightly polish the cast, then rinse thoroughly with water. Begin with a rough grit and gradually work down to a fine one, then finish off with metal polish or window cleaning spray.

Cornucopia wall plaque

This attractive relief wall plaque is easily made from plastic fruit and provides an attractive focal point for any room décor. Use gold paint as in the photograph, or copper or even gun-metal grey for a completely different look.

You will need
1 piece chipboard approximately 46 by 30cm. (18 by 12in.)
Selection of plastic fruit
Hacksaw or craft knife
Vice (optional)
Glasspaper
Scissors, pencil
Sheet of paper, 46 by 30cm. (18 by 12in.)
Small packet all-purpose filler
Old knife
Light-coloured emulsion paint
Paint brush
Gold or other metallic spray-paint
Hanging fitting

Preparing the fruit
Choose small plastic fruit with interesting textures. The arrangement in the photograph is made from a peach, a pear, an apple, a tangerine and a string of strawberries. Some flowers are added to provide a background.

Place each piece of fruit in a vice, or hold it in your hand, then saw it in half with a hacksaw or craft knife. Foliage can be cut with scissors. Using glasspaper, sand the rough edges of the fruit until smooth.

On the sheet of paper, experiment with different arrangements of the fruit. The cornucopia is a pleasing shape traditionally associated with fruit, but other arrangements may be more suitable for your own selection of fruit. Once you have decided on the design, trace round the fruit with a pencil.

Building up the plaque
Mix up two parts filler to one part water. With an old knife, spread the mixture all over the chipboard to a thickness of about 6mm. (¼in.).

Using your paper pattern as a guide, place the fruit on the chipboard and press each piece into the filler. Leave it to dry overnight.

When the filler is dry, paint the fruit with a light-coloured emulsion paint so that the spray-paint will adhere to it. Leave it to dry for two or three hours.

Before spray-painting the plaque, place newspaper behind and also underneath it; if possible, do the spraying out-of-doors. Spray one coat, then turn the plaque upside-down and spray it again, to coat every bit of it. Be sure to spray the sides as well.

Leave the plaque to dry, and attach a hanging fitting at the back.

Papier-mâché and découpage plate

One of the easiest ways of making papier mâché is to glue layers of newspaper cut into small pieces on to a base, such as a plate, tray or bowl. The paper can then be removed without difficulty when it has set hard. You can make many household items – trays, dishes and so on – in this way very cheaply. When they are decorated with paper cut-outs and varnished, they look most attractive, and though they won't stand up to repeated washings, they can be used as ornaments and as receptacles to hold fruit or odds and ends for many years.

You will need
A large plate to act as a mould
Sheets of newspaper
Adhesive (see Note below)
2.5cm. (1in.) brush
Water-based paint, red or blue
Enamel paint
Wrapping paper or other suitable paper
    with design on it
All-purpose filler
Scissors
Jar for water
Varnish

Note
Adhesive
White PVA adhesive thinned down with a little water is ideal. You can also make a paste by heating flour and water in a pan over a low flame, adding more water and stirring until you have a creamy consistency. This paste will keep for a few days in the refrigerator. Heavy-duty cellulose wallpaper paste can also be used if desired.

Method of working
1. To prevent mess, work on a table top covered with a polythene sheet, or on a plastic table.
2. Cut or tear the newspaper into pieces about 5cm. (2in.) square. Prepare a lot as it is annoying having to stop and cut more in the middle.
3. For the first coat, dampen the squares with water only, as this will enable you to remove the plate easily when the rest of the paper has been stuck on. Lay the dampened pieces all over the plate.
4. For the next coats, brush the squares of paper with glue and stick them down on the plate, covering it entirely, and overlapping the pieces slightly. Smooth out the wrinkles and press well into the curves. When the plate is completely covered, leave to dry in a warm place.
5. When the first layer is quite dry, add a little water-colour paint to the glue and apply another layer of squares. The added colour will enable you to see where one layer of paper begins and the other ends, and thus help you to see that the plate is evenly covered.
6. You can substitute a layer of torn sheeting for one paper layer or add a layer of varnish every now and then, to add strength. Moisten each piece of paper well but don't saturate it, or it will take far too long to dry.
7. If the plate shows signs of warping during the process, weight it at regular points with stones or books.
8. When the plate is dry and firm, trim the rim with a sharp knife and remove it from the mould.
9. The plate must now be sandpapered. It is often quicker to sandpaper with a sanding band on an electric drill attachment, though intricate shapes and curves must be done by hand. Whichever method you use, do not attempt to cut this stage short, but continue until the plate is quite smooth.
10. Mix some filler to a creamy consistency and apply it evenly all over. This gives a smooth final coat.
11. Sand lightly again.
12. Now the plate can be painted with enamel paint. Two coats give a good finish, but be sure to let the first coat dry well before applying the next. Car spray-paints add a metallic lustre.
13. Cut out some patterns from a piece of wrapping paper and stick them on with the PVA adhesive. Varnish with two or three coats of varnish, letting each one dry before applying the next.

Chunky resin bookends

On page 209 you learned the basic techniques of working with polyester resin. As it is quite heavy, resin is ideal for bookends, and here we give you two designs to choose from.

You will need

1 kg. (2lb. 3oz.) clear casting resin
Catalyst
Measuring jug; wooden stirrers
Old plastic mixing bowl
Craft knife
Large box of sand
1 piece melinex foil, 13 × 8cm. (5 × 3in.)
Metal plate or piece of glass
Silicone carbide grit (800 grit and 400 grit)
Washing up liquid
Metal polish or window cleaning spray
For the V-shaped bookend:
1 35 × 50cm. (13 × 20in.) sheet 2mm. (1/16in.)-thick acetate (available from plastics manufacturers)
Scissors; paper; metal ruler; masking tape
Latex adhesive
1 box household candles; paintbrush (optional)
For the rectangular bookend:
Square-cornered milk or juice carton, 2litre (½gal.) plastic squash bottle or similar mould

V-shaped bookend: making the mould

First you must construct a mould out of acetate sheet. Draw up the pattern pieces from the diagrams, label them and cut out the pieces with scissors.

Paste each piece of your paper pattern on to the sheet of acetate with the latex adhesive. If the edges of the acetate are straight, you can position the pattern

pieces even with the edges; if not, leave about 1.3cm. (½in.) extra. Leave about 2.5cm. (1in.) between each pattern piece.

Using the craft knife and a metal ruler, score between the pattern pieces so that the scored line is about 1.3cm. (½in.) from each edge of the pattern pieces. Place each scored line along the edge of the table, and sharply snap it so it breaks cleanly.

You will now have smaller, more manageable pieces of acetate. Again using the metal ruler and craft knife, score exactly along the edges of the paper pieces, snapping the acetate as above.

Assemble all the pieces of acetate so that the mould looks like the bookend in the photograph, sticking the pieces together with masking tape on the outside only. The base of the bookend will be the top of the mould.

It is essential that your mould is absolutely waterproof. Plunge it in water, and seal any leaks with more masking tape. As an extra precaution, melt the contents of a box of household candles in a pan over hot water, and brush the wax all over the outside of the acetate mould.

Once you have prepared your mould, you must provide a support for it that will prevent it from distorting when you pour in the resin. Place some dry sand in a box, position the mould in the sand and pour in more all around it.

V-shaped bookend: casting the resin

For 1kg. (2lb. 3oz.) resin, you should use only ½% catalyst, in other words 5g. (.18oz.), which in the special measuring jug amounts to 5ml. Measure all the required catalyst in the measuring jug, and mix it with the entire amount of resin. Pour it all at once into the prepared mould, covering it with a piece of melinex foil. Top this with a metal plate or a piece of glass.

Leave the cast to harden for about eight hours, or for three hours after it stops giving off heat.

Peel the masking tape off the outside of the mould, then peel off the acetate pieces and the melinex. Leave the cast to harden off for a further 48 hours.

Mix a large spoonful of the 800 grit silicone carbide into a paste with a drop of washing-up liquid. Dip a cloth which is dripping wet into the paste and polish the cast all over lightly and evenly. Rinse thoroughly. Mix the 400 grit in the same way, polish and rinse. Finish off by polishing with window cleaning spray or metal polish.

Rectangular bookend

To make a mould for a plain rectangular bookend, simply cut off the top of an empty square-cornered milk or juice carton with the craft knife, and place the mould in a box, surrounded by dry sand.

For 1kg. (2lb. 3oz.) resin, use ½% catalyst, in other words 5g. (.18oz.), which amounts to 5ml. in the special measuring jug. Because this bookend is a large solid shape, the resin must be added in two stages. Measure out half of it and half of the catalyst, stir slowly and thoroughly, and pour into the mould. Leave the resin for a few hours, or until it is a jelly-like consistency, then measure out the rest of the resin and catalyst, mix and pour in.

Cover the top with a piece of melinex foil, and leave to harden for about eight hours, or for three hours after it stops giving off heat.

Remove the melinex and turn the mould upside down. If you knock it against the table, it will slide out easily. File off any uneven edges, and polish as directed for the V-shaped bookend.

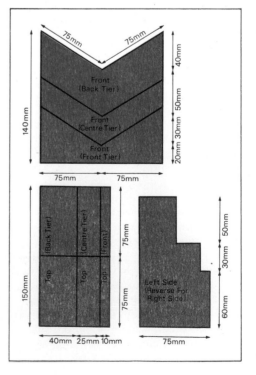

Polystyrene sculpture

How many times have you thrown away some unusual polystyrene packaging and thought what a waste it seemed? In fact this 20th-century material lends itself very well to interesting sculptures of all shapes and sizes. Bright modern colours look especially good on it, and you can make fun decorations for a child's room, such as the one illustrated, as well as more sophisticated sculptures.

Types of polystyrene

Polystyrene can be purchased as blocks, sheets, balls or tiles, and it is also available as ready-formed pieces used in packaging.

Large blocks are generally only available from specialist suppliers, who can supply almost any size and thickness of block. Or they may have some offcuts you can use.

Ready-moulded pieces are much easier to obtain. Electrical appliance shops usually have a variety of discarded containers to choose from. Or you can buy polystyrene coving or tiles from builders' merchants and some D.I.Y. shops. These often contain interesting designs that you can utilise.

There are several grades of polystyrene. Avoid the coarse, open-textured type, as it is difficult to cut properly without sophisticated equipment such as a hot wire tool. Choose the fine-grained type instead.

Remember that polystyrene is a highly inflammable material, so never place it near a naked flame, a heater or a light.

Tools

You don't need expensive tools to make a polystyrene sculpture. Tiles can be cut with a sharp craft knife, and blocks with a hacksaw. Round off small areas with a circular surform, and smooth edges with fine sandpaper.

Materials

A PVA glue should be used for sticking large areas such as whole tiles together, but be prepared for it to take up to a week to dry. Do not use general-purpose glue, for it 'melts' the polystyrene. Rubber-based adhesive is suitable for gluing small areas and will dry relatively quickly. Spread a thin layer on both surfaces and leave it to become tacky before pressing the surfaces together.

Powder paint mixed to a thick creamy consistency is the ideal paint to use. Emulsion paint is also suitable, but do not use cellulose spray paints.

Carving a large block

If you cannot obtain a large block of polystyrene, you can build one up by sticking tiles together. Spread a thin layer of PVA glue on the surface to be joined. Press the tiles together and leave them to dry under a heavy weight for up to a week.

To carve a three-dimensional shape such as an animal out of a large block, draw the outline on all six sides with a felt-tipped pen. With a hacksaw, cut away the large areas that aren't needed. Round off the smaller areas with a circular-shaped surform, and smooth the whole shape over. Finish off with fine sandpaper, and paint the sculpture if desired.

This method of working is very messy and dusty, so cover your work area with newspaper and wear a mask when using the surform and sandpaper.

Because polystyrene is so light, you may want to add a base to the sculpture for stability. You can either glue the sculpture to a large polythene tile, or fix it to a wooden base. Sand and varnish a piece of wood the right size, and drive a nail through it from underneath so that it protrudes at least 4cm. (1⅝in.) above the wood. Coat the nail with glue, position the sculpture on it, and leave to dry.

Sculpting from ready-moulded pieces

To create a sculpture from preformed polystyrene packaging, gather together as many pieces as possible. Experiment with different arrangements to obtain ideas for the sculpture. Many of these shapes suggest space cities, skyscraper towns, and city horizons, and they are also effective as purely abstract sculptures.

The sculpture can be either free-standing or a relief wall panel. You may like to leave it unpainted, as the shadows cast by the high relief areas heighten the effect.

Sculptures from tiles

Polystyrene tiles can be used to create completely free-standing sculptures, such as the jack-in-the-box in the photograph.

For this sculpture, choose three 46cm. (18in.)-square geometrically patterned tiles, one of which has a different pattern from the other two. Cut out six 23cm. (9in.) squares from the two identical tiles. Glue four squares together to form the sides of the box, and when they are dry glue on the base and the lid. Position the lid at an angle so it looks as though the box has just flown open.

From the other tile, cut out Jack and also a shape for his 'spring'. In a small block of polystyrene make a notch that the spring can be wedged into, and glue the block into the base of the box. Wedge the spring in the notch, glueing it in place. Paint the sculpture, using the geometric patterns as a guide, then glue Jack to his spring.

Pottery shop

This charming little shop was made in self-hardening clay, one of the modelling materials which needs no firing. The one we used here comes with a special hardener, which is applied after it has dried, making it quite tough and durable. (You can make it even tougher by baking it in the oven to 200°C, but this is not necessary.) Other self-hardening clays are available which have the hardener added during manufacture (see page 204).

The shop, which is 24cm. (19⅜in.) high, is made by the 'slab' method, in which the clay is rolled out into thin slabs like pastry. The slabs are then cut to size and joined together. The secret of this type of pottery is to let the slabs dry until they are what is known as 'leather hard' (that is, until they can stand up on their own) and then to join them together with plenty of 'slip'. 'Slip' is clay which is almost liquid, about the consistency of thick cream. Dampen the places to be joined, press them together with slip in between, then run more slip down all the seams to make a really good job.

You will need
About 3kg. (6½lb.) self-hardening clay (and hardener if needed)
Kitchen knife; modelling tool
Ruler and set square
Bowl of water
Wood or hardboard working board
Rolling pin
White PVA adhesive (optional)
Poster paints, can of spray varnish

To make the shop
Using the rolling pin, roll out the clay while it is still damp to a thickness of about 5mm. (⅜in.). You can do this on a kitchen work top, as surfaces will wipe clean after use. From the slab of clay you have made, cut out the following rectangles.
Base 14cm. by 10cm. (5½in. by 4in.)
Back of shop, 14cm. by 18cm. (5½in. by 7⅛in.)
Front of shop, 14cm. by 18cm. (5½in. by 7⅛in.)
Sides (cut 2) 9cm. by 24cm. (3½in. by 9⅜in.) See Fig. 1 for shapes
Roof (cut 2) 7.5cm. by 14cm. (3in. by 5½in.) See Fig. 2 for cutting angle
Chimney, about 2.5cm. by 3cm. (1in. by 1⅛in.)

You will not be able to cut out all these pieces from one large slab, so cut out as many as you can and then gather all the left-over pieces together, re-roll them into another slab and cut more pieces, just like pastry cutting.

Stick the sides, the back and the base together with plenty of slip as described above. From the front piece, cut out the holes for the window and door and stick front to sides and base.

Next the roof must be stuck in place. Join the two pieces together first (Fig. 3), cutting the pieces at an angle to get a good join. You will have to shave a sliver off the front and the back pieces where they join the roof in order to get a neat join between the two.

Add the chimney, the blind, the shelf, window ledges and little boxes of fruit and then model a simple figure to stand in the doorway.

Finishing touches
Damp the roof and make indentations with a knife blade to represent tiles. Add a decorated top strip if you like.

Leave the shop to dry in a warm place (on top of a central heating boiler is ideal). When the clay is dry it will be light in tone with no dark patches anywhere. Coat the whole thing with the hardener (if necessary) and allow to dry again. A coat of white PVA adhesive at this stage will help give a smooth surface which is easier to paint, but this is not essential. When completely dry paint with poster paints, referring to the colour illustration, and finally spray with varnish.

Fig. 1
Sides
24cm
18cm
9cm

Fig. 2

Fig. 3

Medieval wall plaque

This three-dimensional wall plaque looks as though it has come straight out of a medieval monastery. In fact, it is made from a mixture of all-purpose filler and salt, which gives an authentic antique look.

You will need
Piece of 2cm. (¾in.)-thick chipboard, size 46cm. by 20cm. (18in. by 8in.)
Sandpaper or file
Paper; pencil
Black water-based felt pen
All-purpose filler
Salt
Compass point or thin nail
Wood dye
Watercolour paints; paint brush

Preparation
First round the corners of the chipboard using a file or sandpaper.

Copy the pattern outline and detail from diagram overleaf on to graph paper to the size as instructed.

Draw over the pattern with a black water-based felt pen. (You can tell whether a felt pen is water-based by dabbing a little on your finger; if it washes off, it is water-based).

Mix a cup of filler with a cup of salt. (A round margarine container is a handy measure.) Add 1 cup of water all at once to the mixture and stir. Add a further ¼ cup gradually, stirring continually until the mixture is of a doughy consistency.

Take the mixture in both hands and shape it into a ball. Toss the ball back and forth in your hands, to make it hold together. Now lay it on the chipboard, spreading it out evenly with the flat of your hand into a roughly oval shape, about 18cm. by 41cm. (7in. by 16in.).

Creating the design
To transfer the design to the filler and salt, place the pattern face down on the dough. Make sure it is centred on the oval shape, then rub over it lightly with your hand for about 15 seconds. Don't allow the pattern to move at all, and don't rub too hard or the ink will run. Carefully peel a tiny portion back to see if the ink has transferred properly; if not, continue rubbing till it does. Remove the pattern.

The carved effect is achieved by modelling the dough during the two hours it takes to harden. To put the figure itself in relief, press the dough down with your fingers from just outside the outline out to the edge of the oval. Now score over all the lines within the outline with a compass point or thin nail. When you have completed the modelling, leave it to dry overnight.

Finishing
To make the filler-and-salt look like old stone, mix up a very watery, dirty-green wash using watercolour paints. It should actually be more like the water you clean your brush in than paint. Paint this wash over all the filler-and-salt.

Now, using a clean paint brush, paint over the figure with clean water. This creates an antique look, causing the paint to fill the cracks and leaving highlights on the relief portions.

Clean up the board all round, then stain it with wood dye. Be careful not to get any stain on the filler-and-salt, because it would rapidly soak it up.

After two or three days, you may notice a white efflorescence on the filler-and-salt. This will eventually darken, imparting an antique look, but if you prefer you can brush it off.

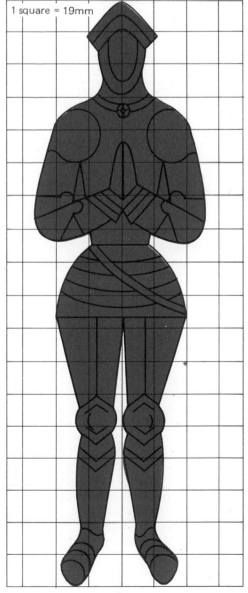

1 square = 19mm

Cocktail stick models

with cocktail sticks in the same way as for the body. Remove the card, and reinforce the underside of each wing with two pairs of trimmed cocktail sticks glued at right angles to the other sticks. Glue the wings to the body, making a support underneath from four trimmed cocktail sticks (Fig. 5).

Trim and glue more cocktail sticks together to form legs and feet, and glue these to the body. Prop up the completed bird until the glue has completely dried, then place him on top of his box. Both bird and box can be varnished if desired with clear or coloured polyurethane.

Very attractive models can be made using nothing but a few containers of cocktail sticks. Here we show you how to make the bird in the photograph, but the same techniques can be used to make other animals, aeroplanes, buildings or abstract geometric shapes.

You will need
3 containers of cocktail sticks
Scissors
Craft knife
Balsa wood glue or strong-purpose glue
Masking tape 1cm. (³⁄₈in.) wide
Small toothpaste carton
Piece of card at least 14.5cm. by 11cm. (5³⁄₄in. by 4¹⁄₂in.)
Clear or coloured polyurethane (optional)

To construct the bird's box
Start with the box, as it is quite straightforward and will help you get used to working with the sticks.

Cut off a 7cm. (2³⁄₄in.) section from a toothpaste carton, with the lid attached. Now cut an additional piece from the carton large enough to make a lid for the open end of the box; keep this piece separate.

Working on an old chopping board, trim off the points of four cocktail sticks with the craft knife, so that each is 7cm. (2³⁄₄in.) long. Glue these to the box to make four upright struts. To complete the framework, cut eight more cocktail sticks to the same length, and glue these to the top and bottom edges (Fig. 1).

Now cut enough cocktail sticks to cover the sides of the box and the lid in an interesting design – some ideas are shown in Fig. 2. The lengths to cut the sticks will vary according to the design. For the diagonal patterns, they should be cut at angles.

Once you have glued all the sticks in position on the box and lid, cut four more sticks and glue them to the underside of the lid (Fig. 3), so that the lid fits snugly and will not slide off.

To make the bird
Draw an outline of the side view of a bird's body on a piece of card, cut it out and place it on a wooden chopping board. Position cocktail sticks side by side on the card, roughly in the same direction as the bird's feathers (Fig. 4). Trim the ends where they meet within the outline, but leave the cocktail sticks protruding beyond the outline. Glue all the sticks to each other – not to the card.

When the glue has dried completely, carefully turn the glued sticks and card over on the chopping board, so that the card is on top. Trim off the ends of the sticks right round the card, using a craft knife held almost parallel to the surface rather than at a very great angle. You will have to press quite hard on the knife, and possibly go over the outline several times before the sticks are cut right through. Now carefully peel the card away from the sticks.

To make the wings, cut out two pieces of card the shape of the wings, and cover

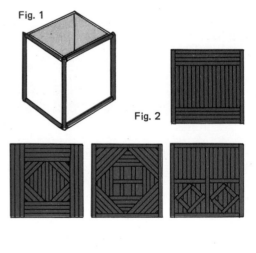

Fig. 1

Fig. 2

Fig. 3

Fig. 4

Fig. 5

wing

supports

body

Heat-treated perspex

All of the items shown in the photograph are made from perspex, which has been curved or twisted into each particular shape. Because it is a thermoplastic material, perspex will bend, stretch and soften when heated, and then hold its new shape permanently when cooled. Yet you don't have to have expensive equipment for heat-treating perspex – it can be done quite safely in your own home.

All perspex objects that are treated in this way need to be cut, sanded and polished before they are heated, so be sure to read page 201 before proceeding. Only the edges of the perspex need to be sanded and polished, as the protective paper must remain on the flat surfaces until the heat treatment.

Oven method
The simplest way of heating perspex is in a gas or electric oven. This method is ideal for 'free form' shaping. Heat the piece of perspex at 120°C. (300°F. or gas mark 2) to bring it to the right temperature for forming. After three minutes, check whether it will bend easily. If not, return it to the oven for another minute or two, then check again. Be sure to wear oven gloves to remove the perspex from the oven.

After heating, bend the perspex to the shape you want (still wearing the oven gloves). Then, holding it firmly in position, submerge it in cold water for about 30 seconds to 'set' the perspex in the new shape.

Heater method
More precise forming is possible if you heat the perspex near a single-element electric fire or a long, wall-mounted bathroom heater. In many ways this is preferable to the oven method, since you have more control over the amount of perspex heated and can therefore achieve either wide or tight bends in the perspex.

It's best to practise this method on an offcut before actually making something, to become familiar with the heating time you will need.

Place the perspex at least 10cm. (4in.) away from the heat. Use bricks, tiles or tin foil to adjust the area exposed, according to how wide a bend you require (Fig. 1 and 2).

After a few minutes, check the perspex to see if it will bend easily. If necessary, heat it for another minute or two, but be very careful not to overheat or it will blister. And, just as for the oven method,

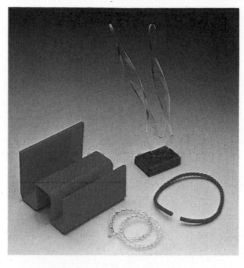

be sure to wear oven gloves when handling the hot perspex.

When you have attained the required shape, submerge it in cold water as for the oven method.

Free-formed sculpture
An abstract sculpture such as the one in the photograph can be made by the oven method. Cut, sand and polish the edges of one or more strips of perspex. Remove the protective paper and heat one of the strips in the oven.

When it will bend easily, twist the strip round quickly into the desired shape, wearing oven gloves. Dip it in cold water, then repeat for the other strip(s). Cut slots in a wooden base and glue the strips into the slots with general purpose adhesive. Polish with a soft duster.

Letter rack
The blue letter rack in the photograph is made by the heater method. Sand and polish the edges of an offcut 60cm. by 15cm. (23⅝in. by 5⅞in.). Then, using a felt-tip pen and set-square, mark on the edges where you will want the bends.

Remove the protective paper and place the perspex near the heat, leaving just

enough perspex exposed to make a tight bend. When it is soft enough, form the bend, then submerge in cold water. Repeat for the other bends until the shape is completed. Polish the letter rack with a soft duster.

Twist jewellery
The twist jewellery shown in the photograph is made from long, thin strips of perspex, using the heater method. Sand and polish the edges, then heat a strip and twist it into a spiral shape. Keeping it taut, with the perspex still hot, form the twisted length round a cylindrical container. Dip the container plus perspex in cold water, and finally polish the jewellery with a soft duster.

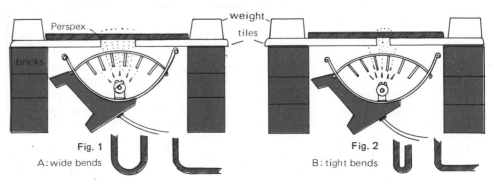

Fig. 1
A: wide bends

Fig. 2
B: tight bends

Building and using a kiln

With an old tin dustbin or some house bricks, you can make a kiln for firing pottery in your own back garden. The same technique is used by potters of third-world countries, who use pits dug in the ground or clay enclosures covered with brushwood and leaves.

The kiln is made by filling a dustbin or brick enclosure with sawdust, then clay pots are placed inside. After the sawdust is set alight, it will smoulder for up to 36 hours, baking the pots to a hard, smooth finish. The pots come out black, or mottled black and brown, because of their close contact with the flames, and burnishing them prior to firing will produce a beautiful ebony-like finish.

Setting up the kiln
The kiln can be made from either an old tin dustbin or bricks. The main advantage of a brick kiln is that you can build ledges to hold metal-grille shelves; this is especially useful for firing larger pots.

Choose a site for the kiln which is not too near the house, as initially there will be quite a lot of smoke. It is also a good idea to light the kiln after dark.

To make a kiln from a metal dustbin, punch about eight holes in the lid to let the air in and let the smoke out. (An old dustbin may already have a few small holes in the bottom, but this does not matter.) Stand the dustbin on some bricks, as the base will get hot and could scorch whatever it is standing on.

To make a kiln from bricks, you will need about 140 ordinary household bricks. Place a paving slab on a level piece of ground, and build up a square,

hollow chimney shape by laying the bricks one on top of another; no mortar is needed. For the sawdust to burn slowly enough, the bricks should be fairly close-fitting, but any large gaps can be filled with wet clay. If you want to include a shelf made out of a metal grille, build brick ledges on two walls to support the shelf. The finished kiln should be about 46cm. (18in.) square on the inside, and about 107cm. (3ft. 6in.) high. Top it with a metal dustbin lid or a sheet of corrugated iron. (Holes are not punched in the lid for a brick kiln, as the bricks themselves will let in enough air and allow the smoke to escape).

Whether you use a dustbin or bricks, you will need about 13kg. (28lb.) of sawdust, the amount depending upon the size of the kiln. Sawdust can usually be obtained free from building contractors specialising in foundry work, but you'll need to take along several strong polythene sacks in which to carry it.

Pots for firing
Red clay is the best clay for sawdust firing, as it is smooth and is ideal for burnishing. Other clays can be used but these may contain sand and grog, which will not burnish well.

Simply shaped objects are best for sawdust firing. Pots can be made by pinching out clay in the thumb-pot fashion. Small wheel-thrown shapes also fire well, as do coiled and modelled figures.

Do not make the pots thinner than 1cm. (3⁄8in.) or they will crack. Also, make sure that they are of a fairly even thickness throughout, because a sudden change of thickness in one piece can cause it to crack. For enclosed hollow forms, be sure to make a small hole to let the air out, or they will explode during firing.

Burnishing
The technique of burnishing has been used throughout the ages by potters with no access to glaze. When the surface of the unfired pot is semi-hard, it is rubbed with a smooth object such as the back of a spoon to compress the particles of clay. The result is a smooth, shiny surface, which makes the pots tougher and more watertight. Although you do not have to burnish sawdust-fired pots, it gives a beautiful and unusual finish.

Loading the kiln
Fill the bottom of the kiln with sawdust to a depth of 10cm. (4in.). Place the pots, which should be completely dry, on this

layer, leaving about 6cm. (2⁄8in.) between the outside pots and the edges of the kiln. Begin with the largest and heaviest pots, and leave about 4cm. (1⁵⁄8in.) between each pot.

Fill bowls and other open shapes with sawdust, and cover all the pots with a 6cm. (2³⁄8in.) layer of sawdust. Repeat with more layers of pots and sawdust until the kiln is almost full, finishing with at least 8cm. (3in.) of sawdust at the top. If you don't have enough pots to fill the kiln, fill it up with sawdust.

Firing
Place some twists of newspaper on the sawdust, then sprinkle some more sawdust on top. Light the newspaper, and when the sawdust is burning well, cover the kiln with the lid.

No more sawdust is needed. The sawdust will continue to smoulder for up to 36 hours, reaching a temperature of 600°C/1112°F. After about 12 hours, you can peep inside. Any pots lying on top, away from the smouldering sawdust, are finished and can be removed with tongs or oven gloves. When the sawdust has finally burnt away, carefully remove all the pots, which may still be hot.

Burnished pots should be buffed gently with a soft cloth when they are cool. Unburnished pots can be wiped clean or scrubbed to reveal the brown surface; or you can coat them with a few layers of boot polish for a shiny bronze look.

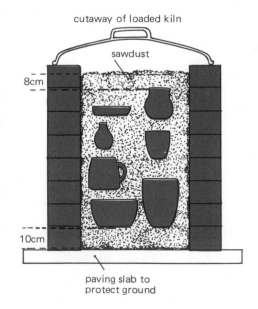

cutaway of loaded kiln

sawdust

8cm

10cm

paving slab to protect ground

Pottery to fire at home

Page 218 explained the basic technique of sawdust-firing pottery in a kiln made from a metal dustbin or household bricks. Here we show you how to make pottery suitable for this type of kiln using the thumb-pot method.

You will need
Red clay (available from large craft shops or local potteries)
Paint brush
Small objects such as matchsticks, pencil or needle for texturing the surface
Teaspoon

Basic thumb-pot technique
Thumb pots are one of the easiest and most effective ways to make a small pot, and both the bird whistles and the pebble pots in the photograph were made from them. No expensive equipment is required – just your hands. The secret is always to keep the clay in both hands, and not be tempted to shape it on the table with one hand. Closing your eyes and just feeling the thickness of the clay will help.

To make a thumb pot
Take a piece of soft clay the size of a small tangerine and roll it around in the palms of your hands to make a sphere.

Holding the ball in the palm of your left hand (or in your right hand if you are left-handed), push your left thumb well into the centre of the ball, leaving just 1cm. (⅜in.) of the top of your thumb out of the clay.

Now slowly turn the pot round on your thumb, using your index fingers to pinch the clay evenly as you turn. Concentrate on the bottom of the pot first, and try to achieve an even thickness of 1cm. (⅜in.) throughout – this will probably take a little practice.

Don't overwork the clay, as the heat from your hands will cause some of the water in the clay to evaporate, cracking the surface. If this does happen, check that your clay is not too hard, or try dampening your hands.

When the bottom of the pot is thinned out, begin to pinch out the top slowly and carefully (Fig. 1). Don't pinch the rim too thin or it will crack.

Making a bird whistle
To make a bird shape, moisten the rim of a thumb pot with water and press it together, trapping air inside the pot (Fig. 2). Smooth over the join. Squeeze one end gently into the shape of a bird's head,

then do the same for the tail, adding more clay if necessary (Fig. 3).

With your fingers, very gently smooth over the whole shape so it is absolutely free from lumps and bumps. This is especially important if you intend to burnish the pots. Make sure that the top of the tail is flat and is wide enough for a small slit.

Add a small amount of clay for the beak, using a paint brush and water to join it to the bird (Fig. 4). Roll out a strip of clay, cut it straight, then bend it round to make a hollow cylinder. Using water and the paint brush, join this to the base of the bird. Add two small balls of clay for the eyes, again using water to fix them.

To create the wings and feathers, press the ends of matchsticks, pencils or other small objects into the clay. It's a good idea to try out different effects on some spare clay first.

Using a matchstick, make a small slit in the top of the tail. Blow across the slit to test the noise, and adjust the slit as necessary. If desired, you can also cut a small

circular hole in the base of the bird (Fig. 5). By covering and uncovering the hole with your finger, you can alter the sound of the whistle.

Making a pebble pot
Using two pieces of clay, each the size of a small tangerine, make two thumb pots. Score the rim of each, moisten and press them together. Smooth over the join so that it does not show at all, adding more clay if necessary.

Gently shape and roll the pot in the palms of your hands, flattening it slightly until you achieve the desired shape. Using your fingers, carefully smooth out any lumps and bumps. Make a small hole in the pot to let the air out when it is being fired.

Burnishing and firing
If you want to burnish a pot before firing it, leave it till it is 'leather hard' – a consistency rather like cheddar cheese. When you think it is ready, test the surface by rubbing it with the surface of your fingernail; it should quickly become shiny. If the clay comes off on your nail, it is still too damp. If it has gone a lighter colour, then it is too dry and you will have to fire it without burnishing it. Do not attempt to dampen the clay.

A teaspoon is ideal for burnishing. Rub the clay firmly with the outside of the bowl of the spoon until the surface is shiny and tough.

Make sure that all pots are absolutely dry before firing them. If you are in any doubt, bake them overnight in a cool oven with the door open before placing them in the kiln.

Set up your kiln, place the pots inside with sawdust all round them, then fire and finish, as directed on page 218.

After firing, you may care to scratch a pattern on to the surface of the pot with a needle, creating an attractive contrast between smooth shiny areas and matt, textured areas.

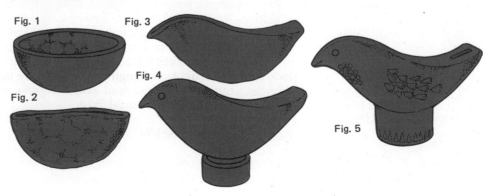

Fig. 1
Fig. 2
Fig. 3
Fig. 4
Fig. 5

Carving from breeze blocks

Thermalite breeze blocks are an excellent material to use for imitation 'stone' carving. Softer and more workable than stone, they can be chiselled, surformed and sanded to make exciting sculptures, both realistic and abstract. You are not even limited by the size of the thermalite blocks, for you can design your sculpture around several blocks and then stick the carved pieces together.

Materials and tools

Thermalite is available as 15cm. (6in.) or 10cm. (4in.) blocks from builders' merchants.

To carve it you will need the following tools: a wooden chisel and a mallet, or a metal chisel and a hammer; a hacksaw and several coarse blades; straight, curved and round surform tools; coarse sandpaper and a pen knife.

You will also need a a piece of chalk, a stiff paint brush, epoxy resin (optional), spray paint (optional), and a protective mask or handkerchief.

Thermalite block carving can be dusty, so it is advisable to work either outside or in a work room where the dust will not matter, and to keep a water spray handy. It also helps to brush the sculpture with water every few minutes when chiselling, surforming and sanding.

Designing

Whether you decide to carve a realistic sculpture or an abstract one, choose a chunky shape without any long extremities. The blocks are fairly brittle, so, for example, a crouching or sitting rabbit with its ears down would be more suitable than a hopping rabbit with legs, ears and head extended.

If you are tackling a realistic subject like, say, the family pet, draw or photograph it from several angles.

When you know what your sculpture will look like from both sides, front, back, top and bottom, outline the shape with chalk on all six sides of the block (Fig. 1).

Carving

The first step in carving is to simplify the curved outline of your subject into straight lines. Draw these lines on the block so that they come close to the curved outline without touching it. (Fig. 1).

Now saw along the straight lines with a hacksaw (Fig. 2). It's better simply to brace the thermalite block against something while sawing, than to clamp it tightly in a vice or G-clamp.

Using a chisel and a mallet or hammer, chisel out the exact shape from the thermalite (Fig. 3). Take particular care with any parts that protrude, such as a tail,

Fig.1

Fig.2

Fig.3

ends of ears, paws, etc. Do not chisel more than a centimetre (half an inch) at a time. Check the shape frequently against your photographs or drawings, since you will gradually be obliterating your chalk outlines.

Once you have chiselled out a crude version of the shape, smooth over the major curves with your surform tools, moving your arm in the same shape as the curve you are aiming for. You may surform in any direction over these curves – but take care not to surform off any details.

Now use a pen knife to carve out the details, such as the ears, eyes, legs, paws and tail.

Finishing

Sand the entire sculpture with coarse sandpaper, then brush it with a stiff brush to remove dust.

You can leave the carving just as it is, which will make it resemble a stone carving, or you can apply spray metal paint. If you want a smoother, less textured surface, apply epoxy resin mixture first, and leave to dry for 24 hours before you spray paint it.

As you become more familiar with the technique, you may want to tackle a large carving, using a number of blocks. The blocks are carved individually then glued together at the end, with a mixture of one part epoxy resin mixture to three parts dry thermalite sawdust. (Use the dust created when sawing the thermalite with a hacksaw.)

Wire sculpture

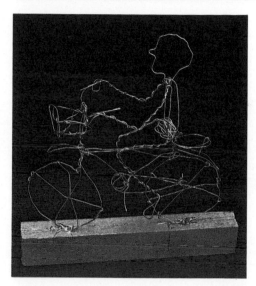

This dramatic, modernistic model is made from ordinary florist's wire. Inexpensive and very easy to obtain, it is also easy to work with and can be spray-painted to any colour.

Here we show you how to create a model of a man riding a bicycle, but you can create all sorts of different motifs once you have mastered the basic technique. They make excellent gifts, because you can choose a favourite pastime or hobby as the subject – for example, an old steam engine, a racing car, a horse and cart, a golfer, a jogger, a motorbike or a hang glider.

You will need
About 10 30cm. (12in.) lengths of
    florist's wire
Tin snips or wire cutters
Round-nosed pliers
Block of softwood; bradawl; epoxy
    adhesive
Spray paint (optional)
Polyurethane

Technique
The technique of wire modelling is based on simplifying the motif down to its basic elements, rather like a cartoon.

Tin snips or wire cutters are used to cut the wire, which comes in 30cm. (12in.) lengths, and round-nosed pliers are used to twist it. Extra twists and thicknesses should be used wherever you want to accentuate the shape.

Bicycle
Begin with the wheels. Bend one length of wire into a circle 6cm. (2½in.) in diameter, and twist the ends together. Cut three 8cm. (3in.) pieces of wire and twist

the ends round the rim of the wheel to form spokes. Make the other wheel in the same way.

For the handlebars, cut a length of wire in half and form it into a 'C' shape, looping the ends over.

Attach the handlebars to the front wheel with a length of wire: bend it back and forth a few times between wheel and handlebars, then take it back to the back wheel, twisting it to attach it to the top of the rim. This forms the lower part of the crossbar (Fig. 1).

To make the saddle, bend a length of wire round into a triangle, then take it straight down to the back wheel and twist it round the top of the rim. Bring it back up to below the saddle, and bend the rest of it into the shape of a carrying platform (Fig. 2).

For the upper part of the crossbar, twist the end of a length of wire round the wire below the handlebars. Bring it back to the carrying platform and twist it round. Now take it back to the beginning, forming a V-shape, and twist to attach (Fig. 2).

To make the chain guard, twist the end of a length of wire round the meeting point of the back spokes. Take it across to the 'V', attach with a 1cm. (⅜in.) loop, then take it back to the spokes and attach (Fig. 3).

Twist and bend a length of wire into a basket shape, attaching it to the handle-

bars (Fig. 3). Bend another length of wire in half, and twist this doubled piece round and round the wire between handlebars and wheel. Allow the doubled-over end to curve out over the wheel, forming the fender (Fig. 4).

Finally, cut a 6cm. (2½in.) length of wire and bend it into an upside-down 'V', with the ends turned up. Twist it in place at the bottom of the 'V' to form the pedals (Fig. 4).

Rider and base
For the rider's head, cut half a length of wire and bend it into a profile and neck. The arms are made from a length of wire looped at both ends, with another length twisted round it. The legs are the same. For the torso, twist a length of wire round, and join the head, arms and legs to it (Fig. 5).

Loop one of the handlebars through the rider's hand, and the pedals through his feet, then slot him on to the saddle.

For the base, cut a piece of wood about 2cm. (¾in.) longer than the bike, 5cm. (2in.) wide and 5cm. (2in.) thick. Using a bradawl, score a small slit for each wheel. Stick the wheels in position with epoxy adhesive, prop the model up, and leave to dry in a warm place for 24 hours.

Varnish the base with polyurethane, or spray the entire model and base with metallic or enamel paint.

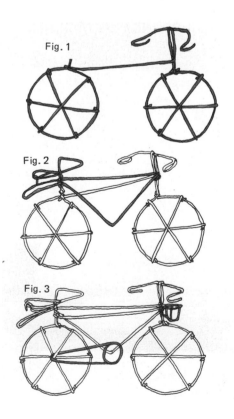

Fig. 1

Fig. 2

Fig. 3

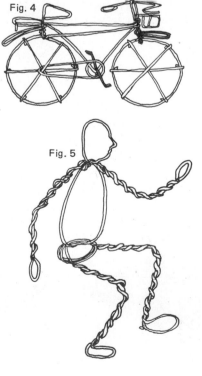

Fig. 4

Fig. 5

Chess pieces

It is quite simple to make one or more delightful chess sets like this for your friends, using one of the sets of flexible rubber moulds that are available from many craft shops and moulding powder. This powder sets very hard but is fine enough to reproduce the beautiful detail that makes these little figures so attractive. There are several variations of these chess sets, and you can get sets with a medieval, Victorian or other themes.

You will need
A set of chess moulds
2 1-kg (2.2lb.) packs of moulding
  powder
Water
Paints
Jam jars
Kitchen knife
All-purpose filler (optional)

How to work
The best place to work is in the kitchen, on a worktop that will wipe clean. Dampen the moulds before filling them but do not allow any globules or drops of water to form inside, as this could spoil the casting. Suspend the moulds inside the jam jars, supporting them with a cardboard collar if necessary. (The cardboard centre of a kitchen roll also serves as an excellent holder.)

For those unacquainted with the game of chess, you will need for each player; 8 pawns, 2 knights, 2 castles, 2 bishops, 1 Queen and 1 King. One set is black and the other white.

Mix up the moulding powder. This has to be done in a ratio of three parts powder to one part water by volume. A simple way of finding out how much you need is to take an egg cup and fill all the moulds about ¾ full with water, counting how many egg cups you use as you go along. For each egg cupful of water used, you will need three egg cupfuls of moulding powder. When filling the egg cup with powder, level it off with a knife and don't try to compress it at all. Pour all the water from the moulds into a mixing bowl and add two thirds of the powder, sprinkling it evenly on the surface of the water until it is absorbed. Don't stir the mixture at this stage but leave it a full two minutes to soak, because if all the moulding powder is added at once, it is impossible to mix.

After a couple of minutes, sprinkle the remaining third of the powder on to the mixture and then slowly begin to stir in the whole mix, starting from the outer edge of the mix and working inwards. Do not use an electric or mechanical mixer. A correct mix will be stiff and syrupy but will pour easily.

Pour the mixture into the moulds. To get rid of air bubbles and to obtain fine detail, carefully vibrate by hand the mix in the mould at the same time flexing the outside of the mould, paying attention to any projections in the mould where the air bubbles are likely to lodge. If you fill right up to the brim of the casting, it will make a firm support for the mould but this plinth will have to be removed later. Leave to set for twenty to forty-five minutes. To test the set, scratch the base of the casting with a finger nail. When the casting is sufficiently hard, moisten the outside of the rubber mould with washing-up liquid. This will help the rubber to roll back on itself as the mould is removed by stripping it from the casting. If you take the casting out of the mould before it has set hard enough, it will break as you remove the mould. Cut away the plinth with a knife and sandpaper the base smooth and level. If you leave this task until the casting is very hard it will have to be sawn off.

Dry completely in an airing cupboard or on a radiator shelf. If placed in an oven, the temperature should not exceed 40°C/104°F.

Finishing
You can fill in any tiny air bubble holes with all-purpose filler, smoothing off with fine sandpaper. Paint half the set ivory or white and the other half black, either with water colours which are then varnished or with enamel paints. Don't paint too thickly or you will lose the fine modelling. You can 'antique' the ivory or white sets by painting them with a little burnt umber oil paint and turps. When the paint has reached all the crevices, wash off the surplus with clean turps on a rag. Allow to dry, then varnish.

Plaster relief plaque

You can make all sorts of interesting relief wall plaques from ordinary white plaster of Paris. Cast in a homemade clay mould and coloured with paint or boot polish, they are surprisingly professional-looking. The motif can be based on a favourite hobby, your own name, or perhaps an event you would like to commemorate.

You will need
Plaster of Paris
Smooth grey or buff earthenware clay (or plasticine, though this is more difficult to handle)
Wooden board, 2.5cm. (1in.) larger all round than the relief plaque
Thick card; cellophane tape
Knife; ruler; pencil; screwdriver (optional)
Soft brush; rubber gloves; cardboard box
Plastic container; short length of wire
Spray paint; or watercolour paints, varnish and brush; or black or brown boot polish, cloth and old toothbrush

Planning the design
Because plaster of Paris is fairly heavy, you should limit the size of your plaque to about 46cm. (18in.) square or less. The thickness of the plaque should ideally be between 2 and 4cm. (¾ and 1½in.).

The relief design on the plaster comes from the design you inscribe in the clay mould. A good way of creating the design is to collect together such household items as buttons, pen tops, matchsticks, children's printing sets, or shells, then experiment with different arrangements on a small piece of clay before you begin work. If you prefer, you could copy a design from a book, for example on art, animals or perhaps heraldry.

Making the clay mould
Once you have planned the design, you can transfer it to the clay mould. First knead the clay gently by pushing it down in the centre, then bringing it gently towards you and pushing down again. The action is rather like kneading bread, but you are not actually folding the clay over.

Continue kneading for three minutes, then roll the clay out on the wooden board until it is slightly larger than the size you need and about 2.5cm. (1in.) thick. Place a ruler along the edges, and cut away the surplus clay with a knife. Then, with a pencil, draw a line all the way round, 1.5cm. (⅝in.) in from the edge – the design will not extend into this margin.

You may find that the clay is too soft to work with at first, so if necessary leave it to harden before you proceed.

Draw your design on to the clay with a pencil. If you are taking it from a book, you can first trace off the design on to tracing paper, then transfer it to the clay by pricking through the outline into the clay with a pin, and joining up the pin holes with a pencil. If you are using household objects, press them straight into the clay.

Remember that the deepest marks you make will be the highest points on the plaster cast. And if you use any lettering in the design, write it out like a mirror image.

Leave the clay till it becomes 'leather hard' – about the consistency of hard cheese. Then use a knife to carve away the outside margin so that it is much lower than the rest of the relief.

If you want to, you can carve a design into this margin to form a decorated frame. You can also accentuate the rest of the design by carving out selected lines with the sharp end of a small screwdriver.

When you have finished, brush away any loose bits of clay with a soft brush.

To keep the plaster in the mould, you need to make a wall around it. Cut four strips of thick card, each 6cm. (2⅜in.) wide – two should be the same length as the length of the mould, and two the same length as the width of the mould.

Stick them together with cellophane tape so that they are resting on the board next to the clay mould. Seal up all the corners and the joins between the card and the board with extra clay, making absolutely sure there are no gaps that the plaster could leak out through.

Plaster casting
You have to be well organised when casting plaster because the plaster sets very quickly. Assemble all your materials and tools before beginning to cast. Place the clay and baseboard on a sheet of newspaper.

Fill a plastic container with about as much water as the space you will be casting. Be sure to leave enough space at the top of the container for adding the plaster.

Sprinkle the plaster quickly and evenly into the water in the container until an 'island' forms in the middle, then plunge your hands in and mix thoroughly. The plaster should be the consistency of double cream. If it is too thin, add some more plaster quickly. Don't allow it to become too thick, however, or it will not fill the mould properly; it's better to have it too thin than too thick. And do work quickly, for once the plaster starts to set, it's too late to add more water.

While the plaster is still creamy, pour it into the mould to the desired depth. Gently tap around the mould to release any air bubbles that are trapped.

Bend a short length of wire into a loop and press it into the back to form a hanging point.

If you have any plaster left, do not pour it down the sink! Pour it into an old box immediately, and clean out the container with newspaper before washing it.

After a few minutes the plastic will begin to feel warm, as a result of the chemical reaction that makes it set hard. You can safely remove the card and clay mould from the cast after about two hours. If some clay adheres, wipe it off with a damp sponge. Before decorating the cast, leave it in a warm place at least three days, till it sets really hard.

Decorating
You can colour the plaster cast with watercolour paints, followed by varnish to protect the colours. Or, for an attractive, even colouring, you can spray paint it. Alternatively, you can attain an unusual bronzed effect – and bring out the textures and highlights – with several coats of black or brown boot polish. Polish with a cloth between coats, and use an old toothbrush to get the polish into the crevices. If you polish really thoroughly after the last coat, the finish will be quite permanent.

223

Bowl of flowers

ten petals will be needed for each rose.
6. Make some pointed leaves and make vein marks by pressing a pin sideways on the leaf.
7. You will need five petals for the primroses. Crimp at the edge with a pin to make a heart shape. Use a small centre circle and prick as for the anemonies.

To finish
Let the bowl of flowers dry thoroughly in a warm but not too hot place for a day or two. Paint the piece. Leave to dry then give one or two coats of varnish.

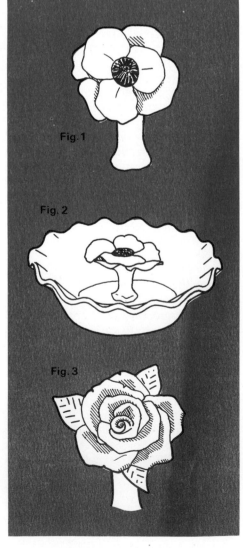

Fig. 1

Fig. 2

Fig. 3

This pretty bowl of flowers is made from self-hardening clay. (See page 204 for information about this type of clay.) It will take about an evening to make and must be done in one session because of the clay drying out. The flowers are made one at a time and pressed into place as they are made starting with the flowers which are at the centre.

You will need
1 pack self-hardening clay
Dish for mould
Knife
Pin
Rolling pin
Board to work on
Poster paints and brush
Varnish and brush
Paper tissue

To make the bowl
1. Find a suitable dish and roll out a slab of clay about 3mm. (⅛in.) thick and the diameter of the dish. The dish used in the picture was about 16cm. (6¼in.) diameter.
2. Place the dish upside-down on the clay and cut the clay to shape.

3. Turn the dish the right way up and put a paper tissue inside to prevent the clay from sticking.
4. Place the clay carefully in the dish shaping it to the mould.
5. Curve the edges up in order to make a frilly edge.

To make the flowers
1. The centre anemone shown in Fig. 1 is made first. Roll a small ball for the centre. Make the petals by pressing a small ball of clay between thumb and forefinger, gradually pinching it out so that the edges become wafer thin.
2. Wrap four petals around the centre ball.
3. Make another layer of four larger petals, and also join these around. As petals build up, more clay protrudes underneath the flower which make a good pillar for joining the flower to the bowl (Fig. 2).
4. Make pin pricks in the black centre of the flowers.
5. The roses, (Fig. 3) are made from petal shapes rolled into a rosebud centre with other petals wrapped around it. About

Macramé

Macramé, the craft of knotting to create ornamental effects, has been practised for about 2000 years, although no one knows where it came from, and it is possible that its origins date back much further. Macramé looks complicated, but in fact it is all based on a few simple knots, on which endless variations can be made. No special training or artistic ability is needed to produce original and creative work, and both adults and children can enjoy the craft. The materials needed to start are few and relatively inexpensive.

Fig. 1 Horizontal clove hitch, often referred to as a cording knot. These knots follow the direction of the horizontal leader.
Fig. 2 Diagonal clove hitch. The leader is placed over the strings to produce a diagonal line of cording.
Fig. 3 Square knot or flat knot.
Fig. 4 Half knot.
Fig. 5 Overhand knot.
Fig. 6 Lark's head

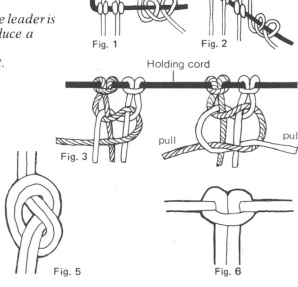

Materials

The first requirement is a board. Most craft shops sell a fibre board on which the top surface is marked with squares for easy measurement. This board is quite adequate, but it will last longer if the cellophane covering is left on and the whole board covered with transparent adhesive book covering. You will also need 5cm. (2in.) T pins, the long steel pins used to fix the string to the board. These are sold in packets.

A tremendous range of string is available, but the best material to start with is the white cotton parcel string sold in stationery shops. This knots firmly and is easy to work with. It can also be dyed successfully with cold dyes before use; this makes it very soft. Parcel string is ideal for bags, belts and plant holders. Jute, a rougher yarn available in its natural brown and in an attractive range of colours, is also much used for casual bags, wall hangings and plant holders, but is not suitable for smaller items. Rayon yarn, much finer and very soft to use, is excellent for bottle covers, chokers, belts, fringes, lampshades and bags. However, it is not recommended for beginners as it is slightly elastic. Lurex thread, a fine shiny yarn, is ideal for delicate, intricate work such as evening collars, chokers and bags. Rug wool and dishcloth cotton can also be used for certain types of knotting.

The wooden or ceramic beads often incorporated with string in macramé work can be purchased in most hobby shops or craft departments.

Macramé terms

The leader, sometimes called the knot bearer, is the string which leads the others in the direction you wish to take. The holding cord is the cord on which the working threads are mounted. A sinnet is a chain of knots which are worked one under the other.

Designing

Once you have learned the knots and followed a pattern through, you will see how easy it is to create your own designs. Either draw a sketch of your work on squared paper or just start working, making up a pattern as you go along. Anything you don't like can easily be undone and reknotted.

Macramé bag

This attractively patterned bag is strong, hardwearing and washable. It looks difficult to make, but in fact the intricate pattern is produced by using only three of the basic macramé knots, so it is a good project to begin with. The completed bag will measure about 35.5cm. (14in.) square.

You will need
251 metres (275 yards) parcel string
Macramé board
T pins
Large-eyed raffia needle for sewing sides together

First read page 225, which explains the basic knots. The abbreviations are: FK – flat knot; HK – half knot. Cords are numbered so that cord 1 is always the left-hand cord of the group being worked.

To make up
Both sides are made in the same way. Cut 4 cords 4m. (13ft.4in.) long and 26 cords 3.65m. (12ft.) long. Set these on to a holding cord 56cm. (22in.) long, using lark's head knots. Place the longer cords at each end of the row.

1st pattern panel a Cut a piece of string 56cm. (22in.) long and work a row of horizontal cording across all cords.
b Work a sinnet of 6FK on first 4 cords.
c Work on the next 10 cords. With cord 5 as a leader slanting to the left work diagonal cording over cords 4, 3, 2, 1. With cord 6 as a leader slanting to the right work diagonal cording over cords 7, 8, 9, 10. Using cords 2 and 9 work 1 FK over cords 3 to 8. Using cords 1 and 10 as leaders work diagonal cording to complete base of diamond. d On next 4 cords work a spiral of 10 HK. e On next 12 cords, using cord 6 as a leader to the left and cord 7 as a leader to the right, work 3 rows of diagonal cording in each direction. Repeat e. Repeat d. Repeat c. Repeat b. Repeat a.

2nd pattern panel On the first 16 cords *work a sinnet of 3 FK on each group of 4 cords. Work 1 FK on cords 3, 4, 5, 6, then on 7, 8, 9, 10 then 11, 12, 13, 14. On the same 16 strings work from * 4 times, then repeat the 3 FK sinnet row again. Work from * again using the 16 cords on the right of the bag. Return to the centre 28 cords. Work 1 FK on each group of 4 cords. Work 1 FK on cords 3, 4, 5, 6 then on 7, 8, 9, 10. Thread cord 1 through the space between 3rd and 4th FKs on left-hand panel. Work 1 FK on 3, 4, 5, 6. Work 1 FK on 1, 2, 3, 4. Take cord 14 as a leader slanting to the left and work diagonal cording over cords 13 to 1, threading cord 1 between 6th and 7th FKs of left-hand panel before cording it. Work 2 more rows of diagonal cording using cord 14 as a leader each time. Using cords 15 to 28 work right-hand side of diamond top to correspond with left. On centre 12 cords: a Work 1 FK on cords 5, 6, 7, 8. b Work 1 FK on 3, 4, 5, 6, then on 7, 8, 9, 10. c Work 1 F on 1, 2, 3, 4, then on 5, 6, 7, 8, then on 9, 10, 11, 12. Repeat b. Repeat a, incorporating cords 4 and 9 into FK. Repeat b. Repeat c. Repeat a. On the 8 cords to the left of the central panel work a spiral of 10 HK on cords 5, 6, 7, 8. Work a spiral of 6 HK on cords 2, 3, 4. Thread cord 1 through space between 9th and 10th FKs on left-hand panel. Repeat the 2 spirals on the 8 cords to the right of the central panel. Work diagonal cording and FKs to complete the base of the central panel (see photograph).

3rd pattern panel Repeat 1st pattern panel reversing direction of cording in c (see photograph).

4th pattern panel On each group of 4 cords work 1 overhand knot. Work a row of horizontal cording over all cords.

Handle and sides Cut cords 13 metres (40ft.) long. Double the cords and pin to board. Leave 15cm. (6in.) of string free for fringe. Work 38 FK; 20 HK; 10 FK; 20 HK; 10 FK; 20 HK; 20 FK (lengthen or shorten the handle by adjusting this number); 20 HK; 10 FK; 20 HK; 10 FK; 20 HK; 38 FK.

To finish
Stitch or tie ends of horizontal cording rows into the back of work. Place wrong sides of bag together and stitch 38 FK sinnet in place to form sides of bag. Divide the cords along the lower edge into groups of 8, 4 from the back and 4 from the front. Work 3 FK on each group, firmly joining front and back together. For a neater finish knot 4 cords from the ends of bag together and push to the inside before working end FK. Trim fringe.

Macramé wall plaque

If you enjoy macramé but don't know quite what to make, try this wall-plaque. You can mount a mirror in the middle, or a photograph, or a dried flower arrangement, as shown in the illustration. It's quite simple to do, so if you've never done macramé before, you could make this your first project.

You will need
25m. (27yd.) nylon macramé cord
18cm. (7in.) diameter wooden ring
15cm. (6in.) round of felt in preferred colour
General-purpose adhesive
Dried flowers, photograph or mirror about 15cm. (6in.) in diameter
Macramé board and T-pins (optional)

Note
If you have no macramé board, use a piece of plastic foam about 30cm. by 25cm. by 6cm. (12in. by 9in. by 2½in.) covered with fabric. Glass-headed pins or steel dressmaking pins can be used instead of T-pins to pin the work down. A macramé board and T-pins, however, are easier to work with.

The basic macramé knots are given on page 225. A diagram of the reversed lark's head mount is below.

Abbreviations
SK = square knot; LH = lark's head knot; RLHM = reversed lark's head mounting; HC = horizontal cord; HK = half knot

To make up
1. Cut the cord into the following lengths: 1 length 297cm. (117in.); 3 lengths 229cm. (90in.); 4 lengths 160cm. (63in.); 2 lengths 336cm. (144in.). It is best to divide lengths by melting with a flame; if yarn is cut with scissors tie a knot at both ends immediately.
2. Pin the 297cm. (117in.) length and the 3 229cm. (90in.) lengths out as shown in Fig. 2. Starting from pin, work 7 LH with longest length over other 3 to the left, and then 7 to the right to form circle.
3. With outside lengths work 4 SK over all other cords.
4. Divide lengths into 2 groups of 4 and work 5 SK on each group.
5. RHLM 4 lengths 160cm. (63in.) at top of ring to fill 3cm. (1¼in.) space.
6. HC left-sided group of 4 threads (those previously square knotted) to left of centre 8 lengths, and HC right-sided group to right of centre.
7. Pull all cords tightly to base of ring and

HC onto it. (It is easier to start in centre and work out to each side.)
8. Pin centre of a 366cm. (144in.) length behind ring immediately to left of top group of corded lengths and with it half knot (to make a twisted knot) over ring to cover left side. In all 64 half knots are worked and after every 6th knot work is twisted over to left and commenced again, knotting with the lengths at right side.
9. As 7 but at right side of ring.
10. Divide lengths into 5 groups of 4 and work 2 SK on centre group, 2½ SK on group to left and group to right of centre, and 3 SK on each outside group.
11. Omit 2 lengths at each side and work 2 SK on 4 groups of 4.
12. Continue to omit 2 further lengths from each end of every row until 3 more rows have been worked.
13. On centre 4 lengths tie a spiral knot 20cm. (8in.) from last SK. Tie a spiral knot on all other lengths on a level with centre group.
14. Burn off ends close to spiral knot.
15. Glue felt to cardboard.
16. Glue chosen centre onto felt, and glue the whole on to the cords at the centre of the ring.

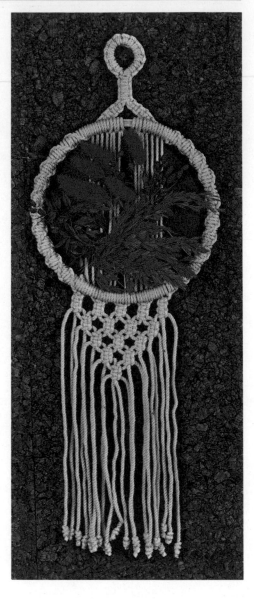

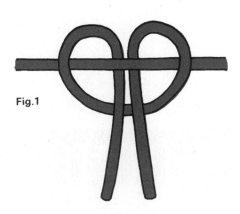

Fig.1

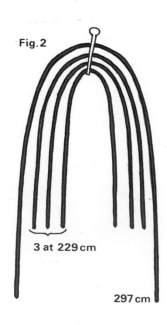

Fig.2

3 at 229 cm

297 cm

Macramé jewellery

Macramé jewellery can make an inexpensive and attractive addition to your wardrobe and, since there is such a wide variety of colours and types of cords, beads and buttons available, you also have the advantage of being able to complement something you already have.

You will need
For the biscuit-coloured choker
12m. (12 yd.) narrow silk braid
4 gilt buttons, about 1cm. (³⁄₈in.) in diameter.
For the white necklace
1 hank tubular rayon
36 pink wooden beads, about 6mm. (¹⁄₄in.) in diameter.

Note
If you have not done macramé before, first read page 225, which shows you how to do the basic knots.

To make the choker
Cut braid into 4 lengths of 3m. (3 yd.). Fold all 4 in half and secure loops to a firm point. With any cord as leader, work horizontal cording (Fig. 1) across all the others.

With the first cord on the left work diagonal cording (Fig. 2) from left to right over the next three cords. Then with the last cord on the right, work diagonal cording from right to left over the next three cords. Repeat this again immediately underneath.

With the centre two cords work an overhand knot (Fig. 3), thread a round gilt button on to one of these two and secure in place with another overhand knot. With one of the centre two cords as leader work diagonal cording with the next three cords from right to left with a second row immediately below. Then with the other centre cord work diagonal cording from left to right with the three

cords on the right with a second row immediately below.

Weave the three working cords from the left under and over the three from the right so that they change places for the next two rows of diagonal cording.

With the first cord from the left work diagonal cording over next 3 cords from left to right and again immediately below. With last cord on the right over the next 3 cords work diagonal cording from right to left plus another row immediately below.

Continue to work in this way till all 4 buttons have been used. Work last diagonals of cording under button, then one row of horizontal cording to finish. Work an overhand knot over all the cords, cut them to the desired length, and finally knot the ends.

To make the white necklace
Cut 2 holding threads of 60cm. (23⁵⁄₈in.) and 18 threads of 75cm. (29¹⁄₂in.). Double holding threads and pin to working surface. Double each of the other 18 threads and mount in centre of holding cords (Fig. 4) with larks heads. Tie flat knot on each group of 4 threads (9 knots). Continue as follows:

1 Leave 3 threads hanging (string a bead on to next 2 threads, leave 2 threads hanging) 8 times, leave 1 thread hanging.
2 Leave 2 threads hanging, work 2 flat knots on following 8 groups of 4 threads, leave 2 threads hanging.
3 Leave 5 threads hanging (string a bead on to next 2 threads, leave 2 threads hanging) 7 times, leave 3 threads hanging.
4 Leave 4 threads hanging, work 2 flat knots on following 7 groups of 4 threads, leave 4 hanging.

Continue in this way having 1 less bead on every alternate row until there is only 1 bead. Work 2 flat knots under this single bead. Trim all the threads in a straight line.

To complete
Cut 2 threads each 150cm. (59in.). Double and mount 1 at either side of centre part on 1st and last threads. Having shorter threads in centre work a sinnet of half knots until there is 7.5cm. (6in.) left unworked on centre threads. Work blackberry ball on left-hand group of threads. To do this, work 3 flat knots one after another on all 4 cords. Using a blunt needle thread the 2 centre cords from front to back through the work above the centre of first knot. Pull up until a ball is formed. The next flat knot worked underneath holds the ball in place. On right-hand group of threads leave space of about 2.5cm., work 1 flat knot over all threads. Trim threads evenly.

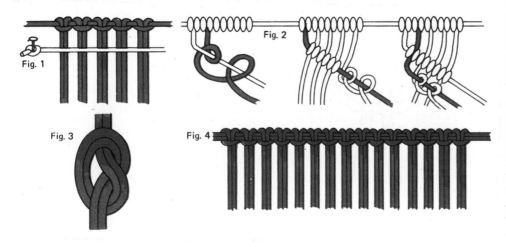

Fig. 1

Fig. 2

Fig. 3

Fig. 4

Macramé lampshade

The craft of macramé can be used to make a stunning lampshade for your home. The lampshade shown here uses the knots shown on page 225, together with three additional knots, which are illustrated here.

You will need

Drum-shaped lampshade frame, 18cm. (7in.) high, with 25cm. (10in.) base and 23cm. (9in.) top
1 can cream-coloured spray car body paint
4 50m. (55yd.) hanks soft cotton twine, 3mm. (⅛in.) thick
24 green wooden beads, 12 × 21mm. (½ × ¾in.) with 5mm. (¼in.) holes
6 green grooved wooden beads, 29mm. (1⅛in.) long, with 9mm. (⅜in.) holes

Abbreviations

HK = half knot; FK = flat knot (or square knot).

Preparation

1. Spray paint the lampshade frame, following the instructions on the can, and leave it to dry overnight.
2. Cut the following cords: 6 'A' cords 240cm. (94½in.) long; 36 'B' cords 220cm. (86½in.) long; 36 'C' cords 220cm. (86½in.) long; 1 holding cord 84cm. (33in.) long; 12 'D' cords 180cm. (70¾in.) long.

Setting cords on the frame

1. Fold each A cord in half and tie a flower knot (Fig. 1). Fasten 1 cord at the top of each strut with clove hitch knots. Work 3FK around each strut, using the strut to replace core threads.
2. Fold B cords in half and tie a flower

knot at the centre of each cord.
3. Fold C cords in half and tie them to the top ring of the frame with reversed lark's head knots (Fig. 2), placing 6 doubled cords in each panel.
4. Tie a B cord to the top of the frame with horizontal clove hitches so that half of the cord is knotted at each side of a C cord (Fig. 3).

Top border

Divide the cords into pairs. Work 2 single knotted chains (Fig. 4) on each pair all round the frame, ignoring the A cords. Tie all cords to the holding cord with horizontal clove hitches, including A cords. Tie the ends of the holding cord together on the inside of the work.

Working the panels

All six panels are alike. Instructions are given for working *one panel*, but it is easier to work each step right around the frame, rather than to complete panels in order.
1. From here on work FK around the struts with the pairs of A cords. Do this as the knotting progresses, remembering that after every 3 knots the panel cords at either side should be looped around the A cords to secure the work.
2. Divide cords into 6 groups of 4 cords. Work 4HK, 1FK on the first group. Repeat across row.
3. Loop one D cord through an A cord at each side and adjust each to give 2 even cords 90cm. (35⅜in.) long. Number panel cords 1-28 from left to right and divide into groups of 4. Work 4HK, 1FK on cords 1-4, 5-8, 9-12. Work 1FK on cords 13-16. Then work 4HK, 1FK on remaining 3 groups of cords.
4. Thread a small bead on to cords 2 and 27. Work 4HK, 1FK, on cords 3-6, 23-26. Work 1FK on cords 1-4 and 25-28.
5. With cord 14 as leader, work diagonal cording to the left over 13 cords.
6. With cord 15 as leader, work diagonal cording to the right over 13 cords.
7. Re-number cords from left to right. Cross cords 14 and 15 over each other. Using these cords as leaders, cord diagonally to left and right under previous row, knotting on the leaders from the first row of cording at the end of each second row.
8. With cords 11, 12, 17 and 18 tie 1FK around cords 13-16.
9. Thread a large bead on cords 13-16. Repeat step 8.
10. The pattern is now reversed to complete the panel. Cord diagonally into the centre with cords 1 and 28 as leaders.

Knot cord 28 on to cord 1.
11. Re-number cords 1-28 and repeat step 10, this time ending by knotting cord 1 on to cord 28.
12. Work 1FK on cords 1-4, 11-14, 15-18, and 25-28.
13. On cords 3-6 and 23-26 work 1FK, 4HK.
14. On cords 7-10 and 19-22 work 1FK, 3HK.
15. Thread a small bead on cords 2 and 27 and secure with 1FK on cords 1-4 and 25-28.
16. Tie all cords tightly to bottom ring with clove hitches.
17. Tie an overhand knot over pairs of cords all round the frame. Cut fringe to an even 8cm. (3⅛in.) and fray the cut ends. Darn in loose ends of holding cord to complete the lampshade.

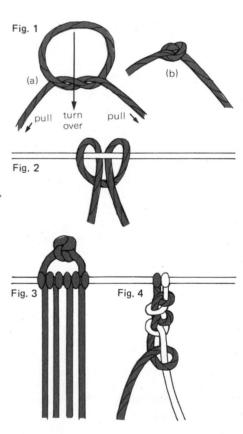

Fig. 1. Flower knot. Tie as shown on the left and pull tight. Turn knot over as on the right, and repeat.
Fig. 2. Reversed lark's head.
Fig. 3. Flower knot is secured at either side of C cord.
Fig. 4. Single knotted chain. Loop the left cord around the right, then loop the right cord around the left, to make one single knotted chain.

Macramé disco bag

You can make this super little macramé disco bag in any of several colours. The rayon cord gives it a special, elegant look that is ideal for evening wear.

The completed bag will measure 21.5cm. by 10cm. (8½in. by 4in.).

You will need
86m. (94yd. or 3 hanks) tubular rayon cord
29 red wooden beads, about 8mm. (⅜in.) in diameter, with holes large enough to take two strands of cord
2 lengths 60cm. (23⅝in.) of string or thin twine
Lining fabric to match beads, 24cm. by 37cm. (9⅜in. by 14½in.)
Sewing thread to match lining
18cm. (7in.) zip to match lining
Macramé board; T-pins
Small length of nylon thread or fine wire
Small tube all-purpose glue

First read page 225, which shows the basic knots.

To make wrist strap and top edge of bag
1. From tubular rayon cord cut two 4m. (157in.) lengths and two 2m. (79in.) lengths.
2. With all 4 cords level at one end, measure along for 42cm. (16½in.) and tie a temporary overhand knot.
3. Pin knot to board. (Pin through the centre of the knot, not through the cord. As the cord is of a fine knitted construction, the pins would cause breakages and runs.) Using the long cords as knotting cords, tie 88 flat knots, tying them very firmly to prevent the cord from slipping.
4. To form the wrist strap, fold the knotted strip in half, untie the overhand knot, and divide the eight cords into two equal groups, using two cords from each group (i.e. two cords from each end of the knotted strip per group).
5. Tie 25 flat knots on each group. Tie an overhand knot over all eight cords. Leave 8cm. (3in.) for a tassel and cut off surplus.
6. Cut 88 lengths of tubular rayon cord, each 86cm. (34in.) long. Using a large-eyed blunt needle, thread a cord through each of the 88 flat knots on the top edge of the bag (Fig. 1). Adjust each cord so that the ends are level.
7. Fold the bag top in half with the wrist strap on the left-hand side and pin to macramé board.

To work the beaded border
1. Pin one length of string across the board over all cords and just under the wrist strap to act as a holding cord. Tie all the tubular rayon cords on to the holding cord with horizontal clove hitches. The knots should be tight and close together. Each horizontal clove hitch should lie below one of the flat knots. If you have trouble fitting the knots into the allotted space, tie only half of them – those on alternate threads – then the adjacent horizontal clove hitch will secure the unfinished knots. Fasten off the ends of the string at the back of the work. Glue or darn the ends in place when the bag is completed.
2. Divide the cords into 29 groups of six cords each. There will be two cords left over and these should be incorporated into any two of the flat knots as extra core threads. On each group of six cords, work one flat knot on the first four cords and pass the other two cords through one of the beads. Use the piece of wire or nylon as a 'needle' to help thread the second cord through each bead.
3. Fasten all cords on to the second length of string as in step 1.
4. Divide cords into groups of 4 threads and work 2 flat knots on each group all round the bag, tying knots very firmly. When working this section of the bag, pin the work over the corner of the macramé board, turning the board over as you work. This will allow the bag to spread at the base, forming a better shape.
5. Re-group cords, taking 2 cords from each group of 4, and work 2 flat knots on each group all round the bag.
6. Repeat steps 3 and 4 three more times.
7. Work 2 rounds of single alternating flat knots.

To fasten off
1. Turn the bag inside out and tie a row of

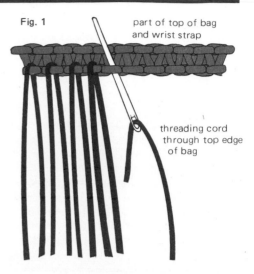

Fig. 1   part of top of bag and wrist strap

threading cord through top edge of bag

flat knots along the bottom of the bag over groups of 4 cords, taking 2 cords from the bag front and 2 from the bag back for each knot. Tie the knots as tightly as possible.
2. Glue these knots generously, making sure the glue does not spread through to the right side of the bag.
3. When dry, cut off surplus cord 12mm. (½in.) from the knots. Glue the ends of the cords to the base of the bag.

To line
1. Fold the lining in half, right sides together, across the width and sew up the two sides. Turn to the right side and press. Turn in raw edges along the top and sew together.
2. Fold the lining in half once more across the width, and sew the sides again, close to the edges.
3. Sew the zip into the opening and catch stitch the lining to the inside of the bag just below the top edging of flat knots.

Macramé pot hangers

Once you have mastered the basic technique of macramé, explained on page 225, you can begin to design pretty pot holders for your indoor and outdoor plants.

The basic principle is simple; for a heavily knotted pot hanger, allow 8 times the required finished length of cords. If lengths of unknotted string are a feature of the design, the amount of cord needed could be halved. Four supporting strands or bars are generally sufficient (although you can have more). After the 4 bars are completed, the holding net is worked.

Square knots and variations on them are the best type for supporting heavy bowls and plants. A wooden or brass ring is needed for the hanger.

You will need
Basic design
Brass or wooden ring
Thick parcel string
Large wooden beads

Method
Slip the ring on to a hook and then work from it. Cut 8 cords 3.20m. (9ft. 8in.) long. Thread one end of each cord through the ring and pull the ends level. (You now have 16 cords.) With 2 cords from each side, make 1 square knot over all cords (see page 225 for knots).

Thread the bead on to the centre 8 cords. Push it up close to the knots.

With the 4 cords from each side, work square knots over the centre 8.

Divide cords into 4 groups of 4. Work on each group as follows to make bars. * Leave a space of 6cm. (2½in.) and then work 1 square knot on the 2 centre cords, and then 1 more square knot.

Leave a space of 9cm. (4½in.) and take the centre 2 cords to the outside and work 1 square knot. On the 2 centre cords work 1 overhand knot close to the square knot. Below, work another square knot. * Repeat from * to * twice more. (4 sets of knots on each bar.)

Holding net
Leave space of 5cm. (2in.) below last knot. Redivide groups of cords, taking 2 and 2 from each to make new groups of 4. Work 1 square knot, 1 overhand knot, 1 square knot.

Leave 5cm. (2in.) space. Take any cord as leader and work 1 row of cording.

Next work 1 more row of cording. Cut cord ends to length desired to make tassel. Knot ends.

Miniature macramé jewellery

Macramé must be one of the most versatile crafts there is. Here it is used to make dainty, brightly coloured jewellery from coloured beads and cotton. One of the necklaces is even based on a macramé plant pot hanger – only this one is in miniature, and boasts a little bead 'pot' and tiny bead 'flowers'.

You will need
Macramé board
General-purpose adhesive
For the rainbow choker and bracelet
15m. (16½ yd.) No. 3 mercerised crochet cotton
58 coloured beads about 6mm. (¼ in.) in diameter, with holes large enough to take 2 knotting cords
2 6mm. (¼ in.) bolt ring style necklace fasteners
For the plant hanger necklace and matching flower earrings:
27m. (29½ yd.) No. 20 mercerised black crochet cotton
Small seed beads for 6 flowers (you will need 7 or 8 of one colour plus 1 in a contrasting colour per flower)
Green sewing cotton
Small pieces of fine and thick fuse wire
6mm. (¼ in.) bolt ring necklace fastener plus 3 extra jump rings
16mm. (⅝ in.) glass or pottery bead
Pair of ear wires

Note
Before you begin, be sure to read page 225, which explains the knots used. The abbreviations are: FK – flat knot; HK – half knot.

Rainbow choker – 37cm. (14½ in.) long
1. Cut 2 cords each 4m. (13ft. 1½ in.) long and 1 cord 2m. (6ft. 6¾ in.) long.
2. Pass the short cord through the small ring joined to the side of the bolt ring fastener and fold the cord in half. These are the centre or core cords. Pin the fastener to a macramé board.
3. Fold the 4m. (13ft. 1½ in.) knotting cords in half and use them to tie three flat knots around the doubled (core) cords, immediately below the fold. This saves passing the cords through the ring and creating an ugly join.
4. Pass each pair of knotting cords through a bead, and tie four flat knots.
5. Repeat step 4 eighteen times.
6. Pass the core threads through the separate jump ring fastener (the other half of the clasp), and tie two more flat knots. Fold these down on to the back of the previous two flat knots and glue in place. Cut off surplus cord.

Rainbow bracelet
The finished bracelet will be 18cm. (7in.) long. It is made in the same way as the necklace but using cords that are half the necklace lengths. Step 5 is worked nine times only.

Plant hanger necklace – 48cm. (19in.) long
Steps **1**, **2** and **3** are as for the rainbow choker.
4. Tie 4 FK. *Tie 28 HK, 6 FK**.
5. Repeat step 4 from * to ** 8 times.
6. As step 6 of the rainbow choker.
7. For 'plant hanger' cut six cords, each 2m. (6ft. 6¾ in.) long.
8. At a point 46cm. (18in.) from one set of ends, work 8 FK. Pass cords through spare jump ring. Fold knotted portion in half over jump ring to form hanging loop of 'planter'. Pin work to macramé board.
9. Separate cords into three equal groups, each containing two long and two short cords. On each group work 2cm. (¾ in.) of HK, 1cm. (⅜ in.) FK and 2cm. (¾ in.) HK.
10. To make a cradle for the bead 'pot', drop down 8mm. (5/16in.) on one group of cords and tie 1 FK with two cords from this group and two cords from the adjacent group. Repeat around the hanger.
11. Repeat step 10.
12. Tie all cords together just below last round of flat knots with an overhand knot, or work a wrapping using a separate length of cord. Leave a 4cm. (1⅝ in.) long tassel and cut off surplus cords.
13. Glue pottery or glass bead 'pot' in position with general-purpose adhesive, and fasten a jump ring to one or two cords at the centre of the necklace.
14. For each flower, thread seven or eight beads on fine fuse wire. Join into a circle by passing one end of wire through the first bead, then thread on the centre bead until bead is in the centre of the flower. Pass wire around outer circle of wire and twist free ends of wire together to make a stem.
15. Cover stem wires by working half knots or buttonhole loops in green sewing cotton over them.
16. For the leaves, work flat knots over lengths of thicker fuse wire. Use green sewing or crochet cotton. Bend wire into leaf shapes.
17. Glue stem and leaf wires in the top of the pottery or glass bead.

Flower earrings – 4cm. (1⅝ in.) long
1. Cut two 1m. (39⅜ in.) cords for each earring. Fold cords in half over a jump ring and work 4 FK, 14 HK.
2. Thread four seed beads on each knotting thread and a contrasting bead on the two cord threads.
3. Tie 1 FK. Tie all cords together with an overhead knot. Cut off ends, leave 2cm. (¾ in.) for a tassel.

Basketry (1)

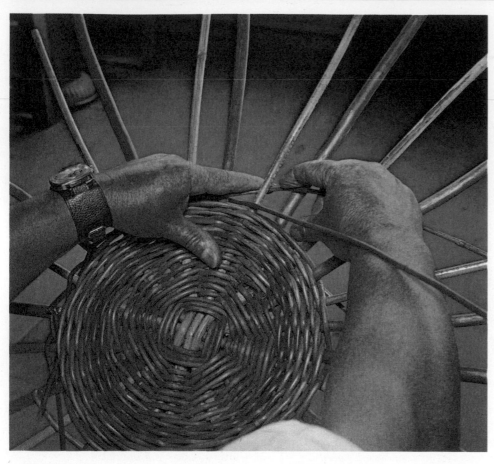

(4in.) pieces of stick or thick cane into the holes to form a ring of pegs. See that they are firmly wedged in and protrude about 2cm. (¾in.) below the board. These sticks represent the stakes, or ribs, of the basket, and you can try out the different weaves on them until you have become accustomed to the technique. Before you can begin to make any kind of basket you must learn some simple techniques. There are several different ones involved in the craft, but here we explain just the basic one needed to make the mats illustrated on page 236. This is called pairing. On pages 235 and 237 we show you some further techniques and give you another basket to make.

Pairing

This is a weave using 2 pieces of cane, which are then referred to as weavers. Bend a piece of cane roughly about the middle, loop it round one of the pegs on your practice board and bring both ends to the front. This gives you 2 weaving canes (weavers), a left-hand one and a right-hand one. Take the left-hand one and pass it in front of the next peg on the right, over the top of the right-hand weaver, behind the next stake, back to the front, and so on all the way round (Fig. 1).

Now repeat this process with the other weaver, which is now the left-hand one, and then with the first again. Continue until you have run out of cane. To join in a new piece, wait till the end is in front, pull the end of the old piece back with your left thumb and insert the new cane beside it (Fig. 2). The rows of weaving will hold the ends in place, and they can be trimmed later.

This method is nearly always used for round and oval bases. If you have any trouble, remember that the rule is 'in front of one and behind one'.

Basketry is a very ancient craft indeed, and has been practised by almost every civilisation we know of. It is a pleasant and relaxing craft, and one of the most practical, as you can make a wide variety of different articles for use.

Materials

Many different materials can be used for basketry, but here we are covering cane, which is most commonly used. Cane comes from the rattan family, a long creeper which grows in south-east Asia. It is processed in factories and sold in easy-to-manage lengths. It comes in various thicknesses, from size 000 (1mm.) to thick cane used for handles, about 10mm. in diameter. Cane is sold in 500g. bundles.

To start basketry you will need a few basic tools. They are not expensive and some can even be home made. Side cutters, for cutting the cane, are used by professionals, but garden shears, wire cutters or florist's scissors will do as long as they are really sharp. A sharp piercing tool is used for splitting the cane or for forming a channel in the weaving to insert extra canes. You can use a basket-maker's bodkin, an old screwdriver ground to a point or even a No. 8 knitting needle. A very sharp knife, such as a craft knife, with disposable blades is essential, and a tape measure or rule.

Before starting to work, the cane must be prepared for use by soaking for a few minutes in hot water. Allow about 20 minutes for thick canes, 10 for medium and just a dip for very fine. If it dries while you are working, just soak it again.

Techniques

If you are a complete beginner it is a good idea to make yourself a practice board from a piece of pegboard. Push 10cm.

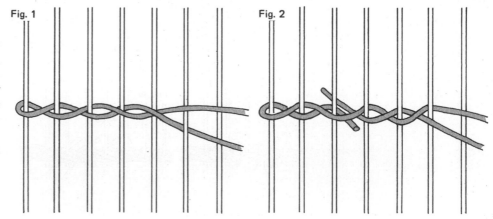

Fig. 1

Fig. 2

Basketry (2)

On page 234 we explained the first technique for basket making. Here we cover the second technique, which is called waling. Waling is a raised strengthening band which is usually put on at the top and the bottom edges of a basket. Three or more weaving canes can be used, but this page illustrates three-cane wale.

Method

Insert three weavers into three consecutive spaces in between the stakes. (If you are using a practice board, as described on page 234, use a size of cane that is easy to bend and no thicker than No. 6.) Mark the stake to the left of the first one with a piece of string or wool (Fig. 1). Now take the weaver on the left, pass it in front of two stakes, over the top of the other two weavers, behind the next one, and back to the front (Fig. 1). Repeat all the way round, using the weaver that lies on the left each time so that each weaver is used in turn. Work until you reach the space before the marked stake, but do not pass it. At this point on every round a step-up·is made to avoid a clumsy jump in the work.

To do this, take the right-hand weaver instead of the left-hand one, pass in front of two stakes and behind one, then the middle one in front of two and behind one, and then the left one in front of one and behind one (Fig. 2a, b, c). Your weavers should now lie in the same spaces that you started in, ready to start ·the next round.

Join in when necessary by pulling back the short end and inserting a new weaver beside it. The old end will lie to the front and the new end will be inside the basket. Avoid joining in near the step-up or the work will become muddled

and bumpy. Go back a few spaces if necessary.

To finish off the waling, get to the point where you would normally begin the step-up, that is, just before the marked stake. Cut off the weavers about 30cm. (12in.) away from the waling. Then use the left-hand weaver once more, passing

it in front of two stakes and behind one. This weaver is now finished with. Now take the next one on the left and pass it in front of two and behind one, but on its way to the front, tuck it under the top weaver of the previous round (Fig. 3a). Now take the next (and last) weaver on the left and pass it in front of two stakes and behind one, but on its way to the front pass it under the top two weavers of the round underneath (Fig. 3b). As you weave try to keep a good shape to your basket. It will help if you remember, every time a weaver goes round the front of a stake, to hold that stake with the thumb and forefinger of the left hand. Also you should try to hold the stakes in the position that you will want them to finish in. For example, pull them well out for a basket that is to flow out, keep them almost erect for a straight-sided basket, or push inwards if you want the basket to be bow-shaped.

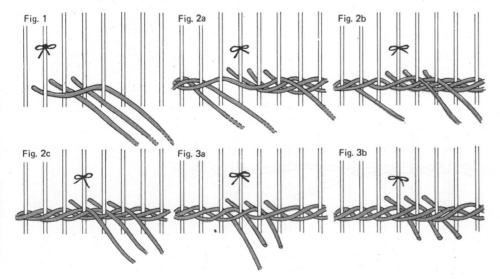

Fig. 1   Fig. 2a   Fig. 2b

Fig. 2c   Fig. 3a   Fig. 3b

Cane table mats

and then tuck them to the back behind the 5th pair. Say to yourself 'behind one, in front of one, behind one, in front of one and tuck it in'. Repeat with each pair of stakes in turn all the way round the mat. The last ones will weave in and out of stakes that are already bent down. Don't be put off by this but try to make sure that each pair follows in its own correct channel and doesn't cross over any of the others. When you are satisfied that they are all correct, trim the ends close to the work, but not so short that they slip back to the front of the mat.

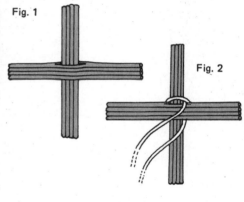

Fig. 1

Fig. 2

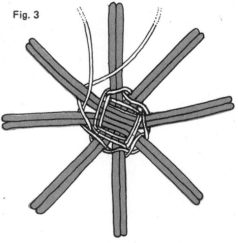

Fig. 3

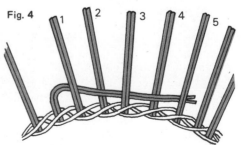

Fig. 4

These table mats are ideal for a first basketry project. They are quite simple, and are inexpensive. You can dye them to match the colour of your dining room or keep them in the natural cane shade to tone in with all colours.

You will need
14g. (½oz.) No. 8 cane for the base sticks
28g. (1oz.) No. 3 cane for the weaving
28g. (1oz.) No. 5 cane for the border
Bodkin or other pointed instrument
Cutters

First read page 234, which explains the basic methods.

To make each mat
Prepare the cane by soaking it in hot water: 5 minutes for the No. 3 cane, 10 minutes for the Nos. 5 and 8 canes. Cut 8 pieces of No. 8 cane 17.5cm. (7in.) long to form the base sticks. Pierce 4 of them in the centre with the bodkin and thread the other 4 through the split, so that it forms one cross (Fig. 1).

Bend a strand of No. 3 cane round one arm of the cross and bring both ends to the front. You are now ready to start pairing (see page 234). Put on 2 rounds of pairing, keeping the base sticks together in their groups of 4 (Fig. 2). You will have to give the work a quarter turn round each time you pair on these two rounds.

On the third round divide the base sticks into pairs and continue to weave round them in this position for a further 3 rounds (see Fig. 3). Now divide all the sticks all out to singles and continue to pair until the work measures about 16cm. (6in.) across. Tuck one of the weaving canes under one strand of the row below to keep the weaving secure. Trim the ends of the weavers, and cut off all ends of base sticks that protrude beyond the weaving.

The trac border
Cut 32 border stakes of prepared No. 5 cane each 30cm. (12in.) long, and point them at one end. Insert the pointed end of each one into the weaving, one on each side of each base stick. Use the bodkin to help form a channel in the weaving and try to push them as far as possible into the centre. The border stakes are woven in pairs. Bend each pair down to the right, 2.5cm. (1in.) above the weaving (Fig. 4). Pass them behind the next pair to the right, in front of the 2nd pair, behind the 3rd pair, in front of the 4th pair

Fruit basket

This attractive basket can be used as a container for fruit, bread rolls, biscuits, or almost any kind of dry food. It is strong and practical and yet looks very elegant.

You will need
15g. (½oz.) No. 8 cane
25g. (1oz.) No. 3 cane
50g. (2oz.) No. 7 or 8 cane
50g. (2oz.) No. 5 cane
Side cutters (or strong kitchen scissors or secateurs)
Sharp piercing tool, such as a bodkin, awl or 4mm. (No. 8) knitting needle
Round-nosed pliers

Note
If you have not done basketry before, first read pages 234-5, which explain the first techniques.

Starting the basket
Prepare the cane by soaking it in hot water for about 10 minutes. Cut 8 base sticks from No. 8 cane, each 23cm. (9in.) long. Make the base as follows. Pierce 4 of the base sticks in the centres with the bodkin and thread the other 4 through the split, so that they form a cross. Bend a strand of No. 3 cane round one arm of the cross and bring both ends to the front. Put on 2 rounds of pairing, keeping the base sticks together in their groups of 4.

On the third round divide the base sticks into pairs and continue to weave round them in this position for a further 3 rounds. Now divide out all the sticks

to singles and continue to pair until the work measures about 19cm. (7½in.) across. Tuck one of the weaving canes under one strand of the row below to keep the weaving secure. Trim the ends of the weavers, and cut off all ends of base sticks that protrude beyond the weaving.

Cut 32 side stakes 43cm. (17in.) long from No. 7 or 8 cane. Point one end of each one and insert the pointed ends into the base, one on each side of each base stick. Use the piercing tool to help form the channels for these side stakes to go right into the centre of the weaving. Nip each of these stakes close to the base so that they will bend up easily and without cracking. Tie them together at the top to form a basket shape (Fig. 1).

Now you use a technique called 'upsett' to change the direction of the basket from going out to going up. This sets the shape of your siding, so take care. Waling is nearly always used as the weaver for the sides. Insert 3 weavers of No. 5 cane into the base weaving against 3 consecutive stakes. You now have 3 weavers ready to start your waling. Wale for 8 rounds. It is very important to keep the first round of the waling close to the base weaving. Try also to keep a good round shape with the thumb and the forefinger of the left hand. Allow the basket to flow very slightly outwards. Cut 32 bye stakes 36cm. (14⅛in.) long from No. 7 or 8 cane, point one end and insert them into the waling beside and to the right of each

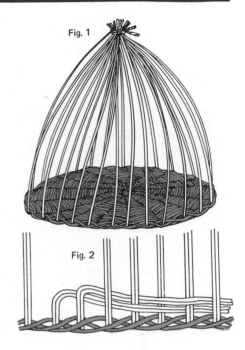

Fig. 1

Fig. 2

side stake. These bye stakes serve two purposes; they add strength to the basket and make the border more decorative. Put on a trac border (see page 236) by bending one pair of stakes down to the right about 5cm. (2in.) above the waling. pass them behind two pairs, in front of two pairs, behind the next two, in front of the next two and then tuck them into the inside of the basket (Fig. 2).

Hints on working
Here are some tips which may help you to achieve a very even and attractive border.
1. Make sure that each pair of stakes is bent down to exactly the same height as the previous pair.
2. Once a stake is bent down it becomes a weaver and must do all the work of going in and out.
3. At the end of the border the bent-down stakes will pass in and out of stakes that have already been bent down. Make sure that they keep in their correct tracs (channels) and do not cross over any other.
4. Check that the border is the same height all the way round. If not, pull down any stakes that are too high.
5. Trim the ends carefully: not too short so that they slip back to the outside of the basket and not too long so that they catch on the contents of the basket. Cut them with a good diagonal cut so that they lie snugly against their own last stake.

Bags of string

This is a handy shopper that's quick and simple to make. Knitted from sisal, just ordinary heavy-duty parcel string, on large needles, it can be made in either the natural string colour or dyed to your own favourite colours. The size, too, can be adapted to suit your own requirements – large enough to carry the groceries or just big enough to carry a few things to work. The bag shown here is 36cm. (14in.) long by 33cm. (13in.) wide.

You will need
5   250g balls of sisal
Pair of wooden handles, overall width 33cm.
Pair of size 1 knitting needles
2 tins cold water dye (we used pink and violet)
2 sachets cold dye fix
Bucket
Stick or garden cane
Cellophane tape
Safety pins

To dye the string
Wind the string into a large hank over the back of an upright chair. Tie the hank loosely at intervals to keep the string together, and remove from the chair.

Mix one of the dye colours in accordance with the manufacturer's instructions and pour into the bucket. Slip the hank on to the stick and place it over the bucket so that the bottom of the string is in the dye. Add enough cold water to cover approximately a quarter of the hank. After 30 minutes add more cold water so that just under half the hank is immersed in the dye and leave for a further 30 minutes. This will produce deep and lighter shades of the same colour. Rinse thoroughly until the water runs clear and dye the remainder of the string in the same way using the second dye colour. When dry, rewind the string into a ball.

To knit the bag
Cast on 26 stitches and plain knit (garter stitch) for 120 rows or until work measures 72cm. (28½in.) in length, slipping the first stitch in each row. Join on new lengths of string at the beginning of a row and weave in the ends.

You can make the bag longer if you wish but it should only be as wide as the overall width of the handles. Cast off.

Making up the bag
Fold the knitted length in half with the wrong side outside and hold together at the top with two large safety pins. Cut two 50cm. (19½in.) lengths of string (one for each side of the bag) and cover one end of each to a depth of 2cm. (¾in.) with cellophane tape to make a 'needle'. Starting at the fold, bind together the edges of the bag, pushing the 'needle' through the loops formed by the slipped stitches. If necessary, loosen the loops with a knitting needle. Leave an 8cm. (3in.) gusset opening on both sides at the top of the bag, but continue to push the binding string through the loops on the front of the bag only, right to the top, to strengthen the edges and weave the end of the binding string into the body of the bag before cutting off the excess. Remove the pins and turn the bag the right way round.

Cut two 107cm. (42in.) lengths of string, tape ends as before to make 'needles' and 'oversew' the handles on to the bag, lining up the edges of the handles with the edges of the bag. Use a fresh length of string for each handle, starting and finishing by knotting the string to the knitting to secure the handles in position, and again, if necessary, loosening the knitting with a knitting needle. Run the string down through the gusset edge-loops on the back of the bag (as you did for the front) and finish off by weaving in the ends on the inside of the bag.

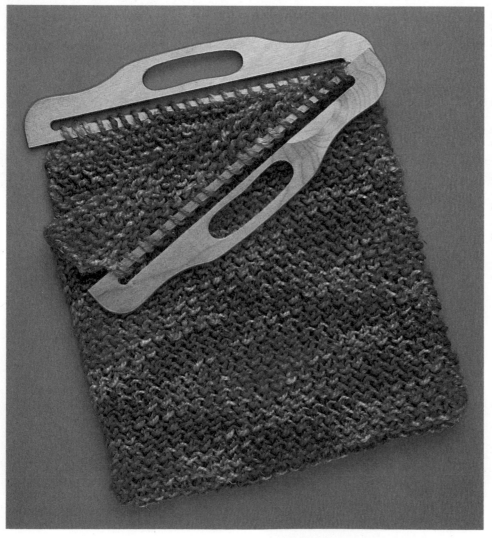

Netting a bag

Very few tools are required for net making. The only essential one is the netting needle onto which the thread is wound. The gauge or meshing stick can be any smooth flat object such as a wooden or plastic ruler or trimmed and smoothed wood. It must be wider than the needle so that the filled needle can be easily threaded through the mesh, and should be half the desired width of the hole in the net. For a larger mesh the fingers can be used, but it takes practice.

Any kind of cord or twine can be used for net making; the choice is governed by what the net is to be used for. Cotton string, jute or hemp cords are best suited for ball bags and shopping bags.

One main knot is used in net making: the sheet bend or weaver's knot, which joins the meshes together. New cords are added by knotting them in with a reef knot. For most bags netting is worked in continuous rounds. Purse nets, hammocks, goal nets and very fine lace netting is worked in squares by travelling from left to right and turning the work over to start the new row.

Work should be anchored to a steady point such as a chair back in front of you.

First practise the knots on a straight piece of netting using fairly thick string. Start by making a foundation loop and fix it to your working point. Fill your needle with as much string as it will comfortably hold. Knot the tail end to your loop and place your meshing stick behind your working cord with the top touching the loop. Hold this firmly in place with the left hand, bring the working cord over the gauge through the foundation loop from the back (Fig. 1a), and make a loop to the left (1b). Take the cord across in front of the foundation loop, around, behind and across in front through its own loop (1c). Keeping the work firmly in position, tighten the knot downwards (1d), making sure the knot is properly round the foundation loop and has not dropped below.

Continue to make more meshes in this way, keeping the meshing stick firmly in place till the end of the row. Then slip it out, turn the work and begin again. Always make sure the meshing stick is close to the knot to keep an even gauged net.

Each of these loops made is half a full mesh. On this size of work the meshing stick is kept in place till the end of the row, but for larger pieces or continuous rounds, a few meshes at a time can be slipped off. However, always keep some on the gauge close to the working point to keep the work even.

Circular netting for shopping bags is worked in much the same way but the rows are continuous and it is useful to mark the beginning of the rounds with a different coloured thread.

To make the shopping bag
Cut a 40cm. (16in.) length of cord and make a slip loop. Anchor it to your working point. Thread your needle with as

much cord as it will hold and, using your gauge, tie 12 loops into the slip loop (Fig. 2).

Work two continuous rounds of netting. At this point you may have to slip off one or two meshes; later you will be able to work more at a time. On the third round increase by working twice into the first and every following 3rd mesh (now 16 meshes). Work two more continuous rounds of netting, then increase in the same way by working twice into every 4th mesh.

To give a good sized bag work 3 continuous rounds and increase again. The number of times you increase is governed by how wide and deep you need your bag. The string bag illustrated has 2 increasing rounds followed by 4 plain rounds.

To make the handles
The meshing stick is not wide enough for making the handle. Use a book and instead of working in rounds work the mesh from one side, under the book to the other side (Fig. 3). Divide these long loops into two groups and bind them at the centre to make the handles. Any joins in the cord should be in the middle so that they can be covered by the binding.

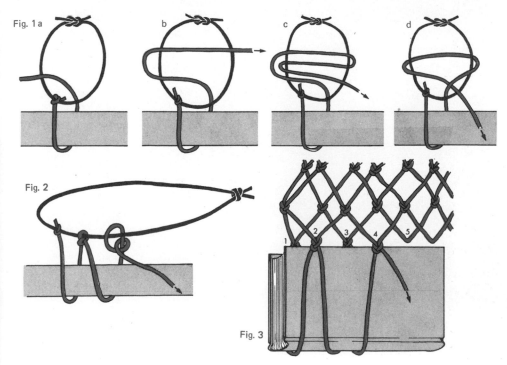

Fig. 1a   b   c   d

Fig. 2

Fig. 3

String and raffia baskets

In the days before everything was made of plastic, Italian white wine came in raffia baskets like this one. It wasn't just for decoration – the raffia was soaked in water to keep the wine cool. But whether practical or purely decorative, such baskets certainly add a touch of charm to bottles, flowerpots or even glasses. They are made by coiling thick string round and round to form a shape. Raffia is used to cover the string and stitch it into position. The baskets are neither expensive nor difficult.

You will need

1 hank of raffia (obtainable from a florist shop)
1 ball of thick string
1 tapestry needle

Note

Raffia is a natural fibre, so every length will vary in width. To obtain a uniform texture choose pieces that are fairly thick and use them single; if you have to use the thinner pieces, use them double.

To make the base

Thread the tapestry needle with a length of raffia. Begin work at the centre of the base.
1. Cover the first 3cm. (1¼in.) of the string with the end of the raffia by wrapping it round and round (Fig. 1). Coil up the raffia-covered string in a clockwise direction to form a tight circle (Fig. 2).
2. To stitch into position, insert the needle through the centre hole, draw the raffia through, make a long stitch over two rounds (Fig. 3), wrap the raffia once round the string. Repeat this step seven times more (Fig. 4), making eight long stitches altogether.
3. Wrap the raffia once round the string, make a long stitch under the round below between the next two long stitches, wrap the raffia once round the string, make a long stitch under the round below between the same two long stitches. Repeat this step seven times more, making 16 long stitches altogether.
4. Wrap the raffia once round the string, make a long stitch under the round below between the next two long stitches. Repeat this twice, wrap the raffia round the string once, make a long stitch under the round below between the same two long stitches. Now repeat this whole step seven more times more, making 24 long stitches altogether.
Continue working rounds, increasing the number of long stitches worked by

eight on every round until the base is one round larger than the base of the bottle or flower pot.

To make the sides

1. Coil the string round the base on top of the last round made, then stitch into position by wrapping raffia once round string, make a long stitch under the round below between the next two long stitches. Continue in the same way all round (see Fig. 5).
2. Continue to coil round and round until the sides are the required height. Try the bottle or flowerpot in the basket from time to time to check that the sides are the required shape. (No increasings have been worked up the sides.)

To finish

Cut the string 100cm. (39in.) from the basket. Wrap the raffia round the next 10cm. (4in.) of string, and loop the covered string to form a large ring. Make a long stitch under the round below between the next 2 long stitches, wrap raffia once round string. Repeat this four times. Wrap raffia round the next 10cm. (4in.) of string, loop the covered string to form a circle the same size as the last, thread it through the ring just made (Fig. 6). Re-

peat this to the end, threading the last loop of the round through the beginning loop as well to join up the round. Finish by making a long stitch under the round below between the next two long stitches, and wrapping raffia once round the string. Repeat this four times, and then fasten off. Cut off excess string and raffia.

By Carol Payton

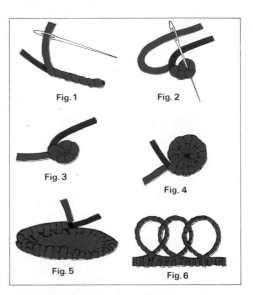

Fig. 1   Fig. 2   Fig. 3   Fig. 4   Fig. 5   Fig. 6

Cover it with string

short piece of string into loops and glue into position. Hold in place with dressmaker's pins pushed through the string at right angles until the adhesive dries.

To make the desk tidy
1. Cut one of the cardboard tubes in half with a sharp knife.
2. Draw three circles round the base of a tube on to thin card. Draw a larger circle round each of these, approximately 2.5cm. (1in.) from the original circle, and cut out around this outer line.
3. Snip round the card from the outer edge to just inside the inner circle at 2cm. ($\frac{1}{2}$in.) intervals and fold these 'fringed' edges upright at right angles to the flat circle.
4. Spread adhesive around the bottom inside edge of each tube and push one of the circular cut-outs ('fringed' edges up) into the top of the tube through to the bottom to form a solid base. Press the cut card firmly against the inside of the tubes with a pencil.
5. Wind the dyed string around the tubes, keeping it in place with a dab of adhesive, and splice the ends as described above.
6. Glue the two small tubes to the sides of the larger tube and tie round with string to hold them in position until the adhesive dries.
7. When dry, as an extra finishing touch, the insides of the tubes can be painted to match, using poster paint or whatever you have handy.

Don't throw your rubbish away; put it to good use! Turn those empty yoghurt pots, coffee jars and toilet roll tubes into decorative herb pots, flower pots, vases and desk tidies. The objects in the photograph are covered in dyed sisal, giving the effect of an expensive multi-tone hessian. They make ideal presents and fund raisers, and are fun to make too.

You will need
3 250g balls sisal
2 cold water dyes for each colour combination, or one if a plain colour is wanted
2 packets cold dye fix
Sturdy plastic containers and glass jars
Bucket, cane or stick
Small tube clear adhesive
2 toilet roll tubes
Piece thin card

The dyeing
The following instructions are for the variegated colours. If you want a plain colour, simply steep the sisal in the dye, following the manufacturer's instructions.
1. Wind the string into three skeins round the back of an upright chair and tie loosely at intervals.
2. Mix the first dye, following the manufacturer's instructions, and pour into the bucket.
3. Slip the skeins on to a cane or stick and lay them across the top of the bucket so that only the bottom section of the string is in the dye.
4. Leave for one hour then rinse to remove excess dye and dye the remainder of the partially coloured skeins in your chosen contrast colour.
5. Rinse well and hang to drip dry.

To make the vases and flower pots
1. Wash the containers and jars in hot water to remove labels and any vestiges of food or grease. Wipe dry.
2. Remove the loose ties from the string (make sure it is quite dry) and wind it into three separate balls.
3. To cover each pot or jar, turn it upside down and, starting where the sides join the base, spread a little adhesive on to the surface.
4. Splice the edges of the string by cutting across diagonally following the twist of the fibres. This will make them lie flush to the surface and give a neater start.
5. Wind the string around the sides of the container, using the adhesive sparingly and pushing the bound string together as you work. At the half-way mark, turn the container the right way up and continue as before to the rim or lip.
6. Splice the string as before when joining on another length, for example when insetting the plain orange band on the coffee-jar vase, and use the same method for finishing.
7. For a little extra decoration, twist a

Synthetic raffia flower spray

This delightful synthetic raffia flower spray makes an attractive trimming for a straw bag like the one in the photograph – or you could use it to decorate a straw hat. It would also look stunning mounted on a cork tile and framed.

Synthetic raffia is made in a continuous length and an even width. Available from most craft shops, it comes in various bright colours, so you could make the flowers in whatever colour you prefer.

You will need
1 hank green synthetic raffia
1 hank red synthetic raffia (or a colour of your choice)
4cm. (1½in.) wide double-sided cellophane tape
Small piece thin card
4m. (4yd.) fine wire such as fuse wire
46cm. (18in.) medium-thick wire (available from craft shops)
3 8mm. (5/16in.) green wooden beads
Bunch of yellow stamens (available from craft shops)

To make the petals
Each petal is made from two layers of synthetic raffia, cut to shape and stuck together, with a wire inserted between the layers.

Using the full-size diagram of a petal in Fig. 1, cut out a pattern from thin card.

Carefully open out the red synthetic raffia to its full width, and stick the double-sided cellophane tape to it at right angles. Cut off the tape and the surplus synthetic raffia, leaving a small piece of synthetic raffia completely backed with cellophane tape.

Cut an 8cm. (3in.) length of fine wire. Peel off the protective backing from the cellophane tape on the synthetic raffia and lay the length of wire across the centre. Cover with another piece of red synthetic raffia again cutting off the surplus.

Lay the card pattern on this double layer of synthetic raffia so that the wire goes right through the middle (Fig. 2). Holding it in place, cut round the outside of the pattern.

Make 14 more petals in the same way.

To make the flower heads
Cut an 8cm. (3in.) length of fine wire and pass it through the hole of a green bead. Bend it back to form a tight loop around the bead, twisting the ends together.

Arrange half a dozen or so stamens around the bead, and wire these in place. Now arrange five petals around the bead

and stamens, and wire them in place.

Make two more flower heads in the same way.

To finish the spray
Cut out a large leaf and a small leaf from thin card, using Fig. 1 as a guide.

Use these patterns to make four large leaves and eight small leaves from the green synthetic raffia in the same way as for the petals.

Arrange two small leaves below a large leaf, and twist the three wires together. Repeat three more times.

Cut two 10cm. (4in.) lengths and one 25cm. (10in.) length of stem wire. Wire a flower head to each length, with a leaf spray below.

Now twist the two shorter lengths of stem wire on to the longer length. One should be about halfway down the wire, and the other about 2.5cm. (1in.) above it. Compare your flower spray with the photograph to make sure it looks realistic.

Dampen a 2m. (2yd.) length of the green synthetic raffia. Open it out and use it to bind the stem wires. The fine leaf wires should be left uncovered.

Shape the petals and leaves with your fingers, and sew the finished spray to the basket with green synthetic raffia.

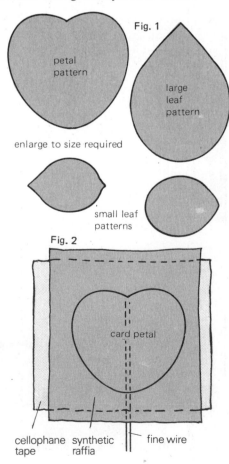

Fig. 1
petal pattern
large leaf pattern
enlarge to size required
small leaf patterns
Fig. 2
card petal
cellophane tape   synthetic raffia   fine wire

Plaited flower basket

Raffia baskets make pretty containers for dried flowers or, for a party table, fill them with sweets or small biscuits. If the basket is worked to fit over a plastic container such as a margarine pot, the basket will hold fresh flowers in water. You can use natural gardener's raffia or coloured synthetic raffia. The basket illustrated has been woven from natural raffia with one strand of 3mm-wide ribbon included for a sparkle of colour. You could also use knitting yarn or coloured string.

You will need
1 bundle of natural raffia or 3 bundles of synthetic raffia
Needle and strong thread to match raffia
Narrow 3mm-wide satin ribbon
Plastic food pot

To make the basket
Make long plaits of raffia and ribbon to make plaits about 1.3cm. (½in.) thick. Experiment with varying numbers of strands until you get a flat plait of this thickness. Keep the plait fairly loosely woven – if it is too tight you will not be able to sew through the strands. Bind the ends of the plaits to prevent them from unravelling.

Stand the pot to be covered on a sheet

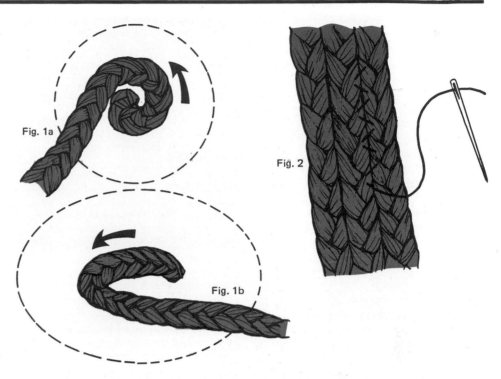

Fig. 1a

Fig. 1b

Fig. 2

of paper and draw around the base. If the pot is round, fold one end of the plait as in Fig. 1a. If it is an oval pot, fold the plait as in Fig. 1b. Pin the fold and thread the needle. Tie a knot in the end. Using a

large catching stitch (Fig. 2) sew the two rows of the plait together. Fold round to make row three and continue catching together the plaits. Keep the stitched plait as flat as possible. It should not have any tendency to 'bowl'. When the stitched raffia 'mat' is slightly larger than the drawn shape you are ready to begin the sides.

Hold the next plait row at right angles to the base and pin the plait all round. Make your stitches from the edge of the base to the middle of the plait and pull quite tightly so that the plait stays at right angles.

Work two rows and then try the base on the pot. The pot begins to slope outwards and you will need to adjust the next row to develop the shape of the basket. Each row now will use more plait as you go around. Keep the outward slopes as even as you can. Keep trying the basket on the pot to check the accuracy of your work.

When you reach the top of the plastic pot, work one more round and then trim off the remaining raffia plait leaving about 2.5cm. (1in.). Bind the end and take the end down inside the basket and oversew it to the inside.

To finish off the basket you can either make a plaited handle and sew the bound ends to the outside of the basket or you can simply work buttonhole stitch round the top edge using two strands of raffia in a blunt needle.

Cane shopping basket

This shopping basket is the most advanced basketry in this book, so do not attempt it as a first piece. To refresh your memory on basic techniques, refer to pages 234-235.

You will need
230g. (½lb.) of No. 12 cane
460g. (1lb.) of No. 5 cane
Small amount of seagrass
Two lengths of handle cane 89cm. (35in.) long
4 handle markers (short pieces of handle cane) approx. 20cm. (8in.) long
A pair of side cutters or scissors
A bodkin
Round nosed pliers

To make the basket
First prepare the cane by soaking it in hot water until it is soft and pliable. Take the No. 12 cane and cut the base sticks. Three of them are 41cm. (16in.) long and ten of them are 26cm. (10in.) long. Pierce the 26cm. (10in.) long sticks in the centre and push the three 41cm. (16in.) sticks through. As this is an oval base the sticks are spread out like a fish bone, as in Fig. 1. (There are two together at each end.)

Bend a soft length of No. 5 cane in half. Loop it round one end of the base and pair for two rounds. Then divide the ends into singles on the third round, continue to pair the base for six rounds. In order to prevent the base from twisting, reverse pairing is used for the next six rows and vice versa. Reverse pairing is taking the same weavers to the back of the work and worked in the same way as pairing but brought to the front and taken to the back. Continue to pair and reverse pair until the base is finished and measures 38cm. (15in.) by 22cm. (8½in.).

Cut 35 side stakes from No.12 cane 64cm. (25in.) long. Point the ends that will go into the base and push them in as far as you can and space them out as in Fig. 2, so the ends have two sticks, one either side (with the exception of one). The straight sides also have one. Squeeze these close to the base with the pliers, bend up and tie the stakes. You should have an odd number of stakes.

Put on the 'upsett' referred to on page 237, which is six rows of waling in No. 5 cane; all the stakes are woven separately. In other words, the end pairs of stakes are divided. After four rows untie the stakes. After six rows, finish off waling and cut off the weavers.

Cut 35 bye stakes of No. 12 cane 19cm. (7½in.) long and push these down into

the waling beside the stakes to the right of them. Take a length of No.5 and start randing (in front of one and behind one). Keep the stakes and bye stakes together in pairs, and rand up the side of the basket with 10cm. (4in.) of randing (Fig. 3). To join randing put both ends on the inside of the basket (also shown in Fig. 3).

After randing, the handle markers, which are temporary, must go in to make space for the handles later. Point the ends of the handle markers so they can be pushed down beside a stake into the randing as far as possible, two markers each side are pushed in as in Fig. 4.

With three weavers of No.5 put on one round of waling. Finish off, then with seagrass, rand for 11 rounds. Three rows

of waling is put on with three strands of No.5 then it is ready for the border.

To make the border
Soak the border stakes and then, leaving the handle markers, cut off all the bye stakes.

The border is a six rod border. Start anywhere by taking down the first stake behind the second then take the second behind the third and so on until six stakes are down. Next, take the first stake in front of these and the seventh stake behind the eighth and out to the front and bring the seventh stake down beside it as in Fig. 5. Continue with the second stake in front of eight behind the ninth and out to the front and bring the eighth stake down beside it. Continue in this manner until the border is completed.

To finish the border continue to thread the left stake behind the first one and out to the front. The next left stake goes under the first and the second and out to the front, the next left stake under the second and out to the front behind the third, and so on until all the canes are threaded one by one in place. Trim off the protruding stakes neatly.

To fix the handles
The handle is called a rope handle. First point the two handles at both ends with a sharp knife. Pull out the handle markers and push the handles in their place. Push them in tightly so that the highest point of the handle is 38cm. (15in.) from the bottom. Make sure the handles are both the same length.

Cut ten lengths of No.5 cane 97cm. (38in.) long and push these down five on each side of the handle. Starting at one side, twist the five strands around the handle to the right to reach the other side, six times in all, and lay the loose ends in the basket as in Fig. 6. Do the same the other side. Fill the gap by inserting five shorter canes 71cm. (28in.) long. Push two of the shorter canes down on one side, three the other and fill the gap. Bring all the ends out to the front under the waling as in Fig. 7. Now weave the 'filling in' canes in and out of the waling.

Take one of the five remaining canes and cross it around the back of the handle, then return it to the front and tuck it under the waling as in Fig. 8. Repeat with the four remaining canes in order so that all the canes are on the inside of the basket. Weave the ends one by one into the waling.

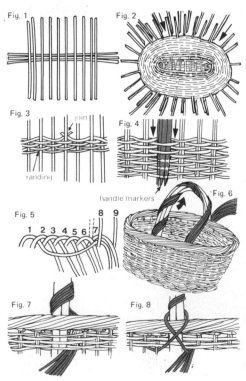

Sisal mats

Quick and easy to make, these chunky placemats, made from dyed sisal (rough parcel string), are the ideal accompaniment to the modern lines of today's tableware. The blended-colour effect is produced by a technique known as 'space-dying', which is very easy and produces lovely effects. We used two cold water dyes, blue and green, but you can use any combination you like.

You will need
(For a set of four 20cm. (8in.) mats)
1 500g. ball of sisal
2 cold water dyes
2 sachets cold dye fix
Reel of matching strong thread
Bucket
Stick or garden cane
Needle
Dressmaker's pins
Small tube of clear adhesive

Space dyeing
1. Cut the string into three separate skeins of 16m. (17½yd.), wind each around a straight-backed chair and tie loosely at intervals.
2. Mix the first dye colour following the manufacturer's instructions and pour it into the bucket.
3. Slip the string on to a garden cane or stick and suspend it over the bucket so that only the bottom halves of the skeins are in the dye. If necessary add more cold water to raise the dye to the correct level.
4. Leave for one hour, then rinse thoroughly to remove excess dye.
5. Mix the second dye and colour the rest of the string in the same way. Rinse until the water runs clear, and drip-dry.

To make the mats
1. When the string is completely dry, undo the loose ties, wind string into three balls and plait into four 3m. (3yd.) lengths, knotting the ends together at the beginning and end of each plait. As you plait the colours will combine to form a decorative random pattern. Use one plaited length for each mat.

2. To form each mat, undo one of the knots, work the ends into the plait and bind round with matching strong thread.
3. Cut off the excess string above the thread; a dab of clear adhesive will prevent it fraying.
4. Keeping the plait flat, coil it into a 5cm. (2in.) diameter circle, holding the string in place with dressmaker's pins pushed through the sides of the plait at intervals (see diagram). Take care not to coil the plait too tight as this will cause the mat to buckle.
5. Sew the coiled rows of plaited string together with strong thread, again pushing the needle through the sides of the plait. Remove the pins as you sew.
6. Repeat this sequence at 5cm. (2in.) intervals until the mat measures 20cm. (8in.) across the centre.
7. Undo the end knot and work the three separate strands of string back through the plait to the underside of the mat.
8. Stitch into position, dab with adhesive and trim off the excess string.
9. If necessary press the finished mats with a steam iron (or hot iron and damp cloth) to keep them flat.

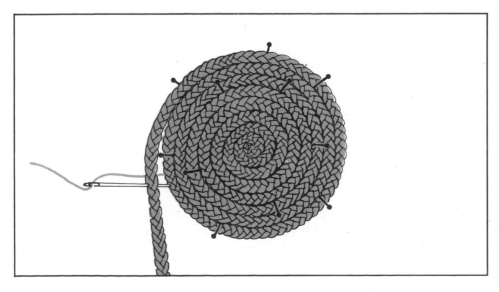

Suede and clothing leather

Soft clothing leather, the kind used for jackets, skirts, trousers and so on, is processed in a different way from the leather which is used for the harder items such as saddlery, belts, shoes and briefcases.

Much clothing leather is made from the skins of sheep. This can be made up into grain leather or suede depending on whether the outside hair surface or the inner flesh side is chosen for the right side of the finished product (suede is the inside and leather the outside). Other animal skins are also used for clothing leathers; suede made from pig skins and from 'split' cow hide are particularly popular. Split hide, as the name implies, is hide which has been divided into several layers to produce supple suede of an even thickness throughout. It has the additional advantage of having a larger surface area.

Cutting
Select the least blemished area of the skin for the most prominent pattern section – leather, unlike fabrics, will seldom be perfect all over. Avoid any thin or hard areas around the edges of the skin as they can distort seams and wear unevenly. Patterns should not be pinned to the leather but weighted down on the wrong side and the outline drawn in with a ballpoint or felt-tip pen on the surface of the leather. Tailor's tacks should not be used. Cut out shapes with very sharp scissors, or for straight lines use a steel ruler or straight-edge and a sharp crafts' knife – this gives a very accurate edge.

Joining with adhesives
Where two suede surfaces are to be stuck together a latex fabric adhesive should be used. Either spread the adhesive on one surface only and stick it in place whilst the adhesive is still wet, or apply adhesive to both layers, leave it till it is almost dry and then press the layers firmly together.

This type of adhesive is not suitable for joining grain leather surfaces as it will not penetrate the smooth surface of the leather. For these you must use clear household adhesive, following the instructions on the tube. Always use adhesives sparingly, as if you apply too much they may ooze out of joins and spoil the surface of the work.

Joining by sewing
It is not practical to use pins to hold layers of leather together for sewing as they will mark the surface and can distort the seams. One way of solving this problem is to use spring-type clothes pins or bulldog paper clips. Adhesive tape can sometimes be used on the wrong side of the leather and removed after sewing. For curved or otherwise difficult seams the leather can be 'stab' stitched within the seam allowance: use a glover's needle and make fairly small stitches. This will prevent one layer of leather from 'creeping' on the other. A glover's needle has a triangular point which is sharpened into blades for cutting easily through the leather.

Most domestic sewing machines will cope with leather provided it is not too thick and you are not attempting to stitch through too many layers at once. Special leather needles can be obtained from sewing-machine shops: these have a spear-shaped blade instead of a round point. When starting or finishing off a line of stitching using this type of needle do not reverse the machine to strengthen the ends of the seam as the blade would cut through the existing stitches. Instead, knot the ends of the thread together firmly on the wrong side of the work. If you intend to sew a lot of leather and suede a special machine foot (available to fit most sewing machines) is a good investment. These incorporate a roller which helps the leather to pass under the needle instead of clinging to the smooth underside of a normal machine foot.

Buttons
To sew buttons on by hand first pierce holes in the leather corresponding to those in the buttons with a glover's needle, then use an ordinary needle to stitch through the holes. It is a good idea to place a smaller button on the inside of the garment to give firm anchorage.

Suppliers
Whole sheep skins – suede and leather – can be bought by post from many suppliers, who can supply cuttings of the colours and types of leather available and their price lists.

Bags of offcuts are offered for sale by several clothing firms who advertise in magazines. Offcuts are a good buy for patchwork and other small items, but the quality is variable.

Suede and leather belt

Suede has been used for the main body of this belt, and the appliqué decoration is made up from leather squares in different colours from a bag of offcuts. These were first stuck in place and then stitched around the edges with two long lines of straight stitching in a zig-zag fashion. The stitching not only holds the edges of the squares in place, it also strengthens and stiffens the belt.

You will need
A strip of suede 12cm. (5in.) wide and 25cm. (10in.) longer than your waist measurement
Scraps of leather or suede in contrasting colours
Latex or clear adhesive
Thread to match the main colour of the belt
A spear-pointed (leather) machine needle
A 6cm. (2½in.) belt buckle
Eyelets and an eyelet tool
Metal ruler and crafts' knife

Note
A latex based fabric adhesive can be used on suede, but if you wish to use shiny grain leather for the background of the belt instead of suede, you will need a clear household adhesive for the appliquéed pieces.

To make the belt
Using a ruler and sharp scissors trim both long sides of the main belt strip so that they are straight and parallel. On the wrong side, rule a central line from one end of the strip to the other, using a ballpoint or felt-tipped pen. Spread the reverse side of the strip evenly with latex adhesive, then turn in each side edge to the ruled line and press it down firmly. Take the belt by both ends with the reverse (seamed) side downwards and pull it several times over the edge of a table or other flat surface to flatten it. Choose the best-looking end and trim it to a diagonal point using a metal ruler and a sharp crafts' knife.

The appliqué
Make a 4cm. (1½in.) square template from stiff cardboard, taking care to make the corners true right angles (see page 9 for method). If the scraps of leather or suede are crumpled, iron them on the wrong side with a medium hot iron. Use the template and a felt-tipped or ballpoint pen to mark out the squares on the wrong side in the thinnest parts of the

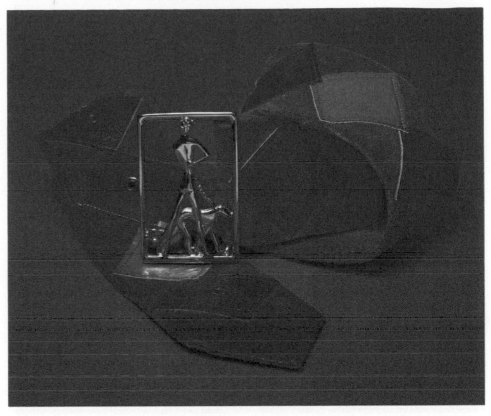

leather or suede. You will need approximately 16 squares on a 90cm. (36in.) long belt. Cut out the squares, using sharp scissors or a crafts' knife and metal ruler.

Place them diagonally on the right, (unseamed), side of the doubled belt in a pleasing colour arrangement. Overlap the central corners of each square by about 6mm. (¼in.) and leave about 4cm. (1⅝in.) between the pointed end of the belt and the central point of the first square. Starting at the shaped end, remove each square in turn, lightly coat the reverse side with adhesive and replace it on the belt. Take care not to get any adhesive on the surrounding areas of suede as it is extremely difficult to remove.

Stitching
Starting at the unshaped end of the belt, and using a medium-sized straight machine stitch, sew down the edges of all the squares. Stitch diagonally from one side of the belt to the other in a zig-zag pattern, taking in the side of two of the squares in each direction. When you get to the shaped end continue stitching to the cut edge, then pivot and stitch to the point of the belt end. Stitch another line to anchor the opposite sides of all the squares in the same way.

To attach the buckle
Punch a hole about 4cm. (1⅝in.) from the unshaped end of the belt and thread the buckle on – the prong goes through the hole. Stick the turned-back end of the belt in place behind the buckle with adhesive. Insert eyelets in the centres of the first few squares as desired following the instructions on the eyelet pack.

Hand sewing leather

On page 246 we told you about working with suede and the soft leather used for clothing. Here we deal with the leather used for bags, wallets and belts, which is processed in a way which makes it firm and fairly stiff.

The best way to stitch these leathers (unless you have a heavy duty sewing machine) is by hand. This is not as difficult as it sounds provided you buy one or two essential tools for the job.

Equipment

You will need the following equipment. A sharp knife for cutting out, essential to give a good clean edge. Unless you are planning to do a great deal of leatherwork a crafts' knife with replaceable blades is quite adequate. Scissors tend to bruise edges and spoil the appearance so they are not used on anything where the finished edges will show. A good steel ruler or straight edge is also a must. For marking the stitch lines you will need a bone folder (a smooth tool made of bone), and a stitch marker. There are two main types of stitch marker. One is rather like a dressmaker's tracing wheel, a small spiked wheel on a handle which is pushed along the seam line. The other kind is like a small flat fork with several prongs and is used with a small hammer or mallet. The number stamped on the marker indicates the number of stitches to the inch. This type of stitch marker is often called a pricking iron in tool catalogues. For making the stitching holes you need a diamond awl, and if you want to make leather belts, you will have to buy a leather punch, which will allow you to make clean and accurate holes of whichever size you need for the prong of the buckle to go through. The sewing itself is done with button thread and harness needles. These have blunt, rounded points which prevent them from splitting the opposite thread.

Choosing the leather

This is very much a matter of learning by experience, but here are some points to bear in mind. Leather is sold by the square foot so the price varies from skin to skin. Unless you can use the offcuts on another project choose the smallest piece of leather which will fit your patterns. Take these along with you when you buy. Thickness and texture must be related to the size and shape of the finished item and the leather should be the same thickness throughout. Avoid skins with too many flaws or an uneven colour.

Method of working

Patterns and templates should be made for all shapes and drawn on the wrong side of the leather with a ball-point pen before cutting out. Plan your layout to avoid flaws or thin patches.

When the pieces are cut, some of the thickness on the edges must be pared away before sewing. This is called skiving, and it is done to reduce bulk on the seams so that they are more manageable. You can buy a special skiving knife, which is like a wide, curved-bladed chisel. This takes a little while to master, however, and has to be sharpened frequently on an oilstone, so for the beginner the crafts' knife with replaceable blades is the best choice. Choose blades with a curved cutting edge and renew them as soon as they begin to dull. Place the leather wrong side up on a smooth hard surface (a small sheet of thick glass is ideal). Arrange it so that the edge to be skived is away from you. Hold the leather down firmly with one hand and cut away from you with the other hand. Slide the knife smoothly out to the very edge of the leather. For most purposes the edge is skived in a straight, tapered line, but in some cases where the leather is folded back on itself the skiving is stepped down at the seam line and then tapered out to the edge. This is rather more difficult to do and requires some practice to get right.

The next stage is making the stitch lines. First use the bone folder to press a groove along the seam lines. This not only serves as a guide for the stitch marker;

it also makes a shallow trough for the stitches to lie in and this reduces wear on them. Now mark the stitches with either kind of stitch marker, but do not attempt to make the holes with the marker; this is done with the awl at the next stage.

When the stitching line has been marked the section can be assembled for sewing. Leather cannot of course be tacked to hold pieces together for sewing so they are either glued together or tied with short lengths of thread as follows. Pierce through the marked stitches at intervals with the awl and tie the sections together. The tying threads are removed as you get to them whilst sewing the seams. Now pierce all the stitch holes with the very sharp-bladed point of the awl, taking care to keep the angle of each stitch consistent.

The strongest and neatest form of seam is saddle stitching, which is done with two needles on one length of thread. One needle is passed through the first hole, and the thread is drawn to equal lengths on each side of the leather. Then a needle is held in each hand and both are passed through the next hole in opposite directions. The thread is pulled through firmly with both hands. The seam is continued in this way to the end and then worked in reverse for a few stitches for extra strength. Waxing the thread with beeswax helps it to slide through the leather and also strengthens it.

Sewing is done in a clamp so that you have both hands free for the two needles. This can be made from two pieces of hardboard and two bulldog clips. The boards should be held firmly between the knees while you sew (see colour illustration above).

Leather wallet and fob

A hand-made wallet is a very acceptable and long lasting gift and is not hard for a beginner to make.

Note

Although this is not a difficult project, you must be sure you have mastered the skill of skiving or paring away the thickness of the leather. Read page 248 and practise skiving offcuts until you are sure you can do it. One slip of the knife could ruin the whole project.

You will need

About .18sq.m. (2sq.ft.) of calf or
    pigskin
Clear household adhesive
Matching button thread; 2 harness
    needles
Beeswax
Metal ruler or straight edge; set square
Sharp crafts' knife with curved blade
Skiving knife (optional)
Bone folder
Stitch marker size 10; hammer or mallet
Diamond awl
2 bulldog clips; hardboard

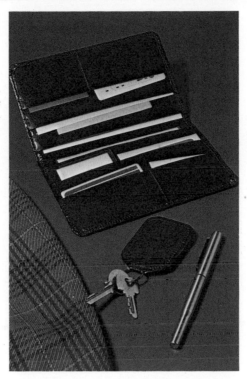

To make the wallet

Avoiding any flaws in the leather, mark out the following shapes on the wrong side of the leather, using ruler and set square. One rectangle 24cm. by 19cm. (19½in. by 7½in.) for the main outer cover; 2 rectangles 7.5cm. by 17.5cm. (3in. by 6⅞in.); 3 rectangles 5cm. by 17.5cm. (2in. by 6⅞in.). Take one of the smallest pieces and carefully skive the wrong side of each long edge until paper thin, tapering from about 1cm. (⅜in.) from the edge. Mark the centre point on the wrong side of each long edge of the main cover piece and position the skived rectangle across the centre. Glue it in place, wrong sides together, to form the centre lining of the wallet.

Round off all four corners of the main piece with the crafts' knife, using a coin as a template. Now rule a line on the wrong side of the leather 1cm. (⅜in.) from the edge using a smaller coin for the corners. Skive these edges, not in a straight taper like the lining, but stepping-down at the line and then tapering out to a paper thin edge.

Round off two corners on one long side of each remaining rectangle, using a coin, then skive this long edge and both short ends of each one. Take one of the smallest shapes and glue it, wrong side down, on the right side of one of the second largest, matching rounded cor-

ners. Measure in 10cm. (4in.) from the left-hand edge and rule a line with the bone folder across the lower pocket at right-angles to the top and bottom edges. Stitch-mark this line, pierce the stitch holes with the awl and saddle-stitch the two layers together. Do the same with the other two similar-sized sections. Place one of the double sections on the right side of each of the remaining rectangles, matching the lower rounded corners, and stick them together around the sides and base. When the adhesive has had time to set, place one pocket section on each end of the wrong side of the main wallet shape, leaving an equal margin of skived edge showing all around. Stick them in place around lower and side edges. Using the adhesive sparingly, turn in the skived edges of the pockets and stick them down. At the corners neatly pleat the skived leather into about seven or eight equal sized pleats. Working on the outside of the wallet and using the ruler and bone folder mark a line about 3mm. (⅛in.) from all edges, rounding the corners to match. Stitch mark along this line, then pierce the stitch holes with the awl and saddle-stitch around the entire wallet with waxed thread.

To make the key fob

Decide on a shape with one narrow, straight edge. Cut this out from folded paper, placing the fold to the straight edge. Open out the paper pattern and mark the shape on to the wrong side of one of the offcuts from the wallet. Cut the shape out with a crafts' knife and skive all the edges on the wrong side until they are half the original thickness. Fold the shape with wrong sides inside, placing a key ring in the fold. Stick the layers together. Mark a line about 3mm. (⅛in.) from the edges around the fob and below the line of the ring. Stitch-mark on this line, then saddle stitch the fob to match the wallet.

Suede waistcoat

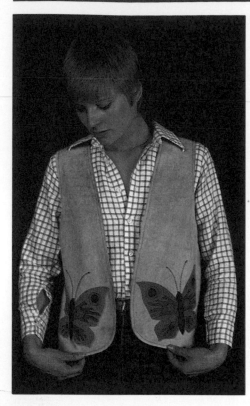

This waistcoat is an ideal garment for a beginner to make, because it is loose fitting, with no linings or facings to deal with. The butterfly motif is a little more complicated, as the inner wing shapes have to be stitched in place around the edges, but this is done before placing the motif on the waistcoat, so you are in no danger of spoiling the garment if your stitching is not perfect. If you feel that the motif is too difficult, a simpler one can be substituted, or you can leave it out altogether.

Before starting the project be sure to read page 246, which gives basic sewing instructions.

You will need

Two suede skins, each at least 7 sq.ft.
Matching thread
Latex fabric adhesive
Scraps of contrast-coloured suede
Matching sewing thread
Sewing machine fitted with a leather needle and if possible a roller foot.
Sharp scissors; ballpoint pen; squared paper for patterns

To make the waistcoat

1. Draw up two patterns of both main waistcoat shapes on squared paper, following Fig. 1. Reverse one of each, and label them right and left side.
2. Place one skin face down on a table and arrange the two back pattern sections on it, avoiding flaws if possible. Weight the patterns down and draw around them with a ballpoint pen.
3. Cut out the shapes with sharp scissors.
4. Cut out the two front shapes from the other skin in the same way.
5. Stitch the two front darts and fold down towards the base on the inside.
6. Sew together sides, shoulders and centre back with 1.2cm. (½in.) seams, matching notches.
7. Fold all the seams open and stick them down flat with adhesive. Turn in 2cm. (¾in.) around the edges of the arm-holes, clipping into the curves and trimming away the ends of the seam allowances to a depth of 2cm. (¾in.).
8. Stick down hem, using adhesive sparingly. Turn in and stick a similar turning around the outer edges of the waistcoat, trimming away the seam allowance and clipping small wedge shapes from the curved front edge.
9. Working on the right side of the garment, top-stitch with matching thread around the edges of the waistcoat about 5mm. (¼in.) from the fold.

The motif

1. Following Fig. 2, make a pattern of the main wing shapes from folded paper.
2. Unfold paper pattern and cut out two butterfly shapes from contrast suede.
3. Trim away the outer section and use the centre part to cut out the inner shapes from suede of another colour.
4. Cut out the spots and the body shapes from two further colours.
5. Stick all the inner details (but not the body sections) onto the main wing shapes, using adhesive sparingly.
6. Stitch around the edges of all these inner details to anchor them firmly to the wings.
7. Place one butterfly on each waistcoat front as shown in the photograph and glue, then stitch them in place around the edges.
8. Glue and then stitch a body shape in the centre of each butterfly, then stitch in the antennae shapes as shown in the photograph.

Fig. 2

One square = 2.5 cm

fold

BODY

Fig. 1

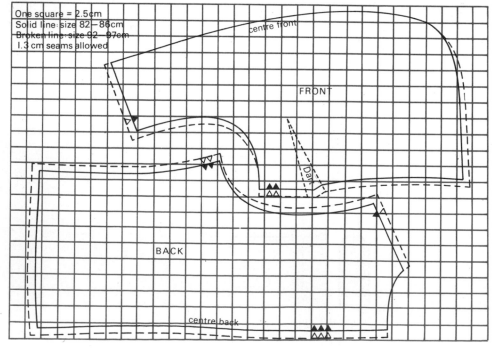

One square = 2.5 cm
Solid line: size 82–86cm
Broken line: size 92–97cm
1.3 cm seams allowed

centre front

FRONT

Dart

BACK

centre back

Leather shoulder bag

This good-looking leather bag is roomy enough for everyday items but not too big and bulky. It is very simply made as it is thonged, not stitched, so you don't have to pare down the leather.

Note
We do not give the exact amount of leather needed, as skins vary considerably in size. The main piece is 63cm. by 26cm. (25in. by 10¼in.) and the shoulder strap is 91cm. (36in.) long, so you will need a piece about 90cm. by 35cm. (36in. by 14in.) Take the pattern with you if you are buying leather locally.

You will need
Leather; leather thonging
Leather punch
Thin cardboard
Crafts' knife or leather knife
Steel rule
General-purpose glue

The pattern
Make templates from cardboard, using the diagram (Fig. 1) and measurements given. The easiest way for the main piece and side pieces is to draw all the corners square as shown by the dotted lines and trim afterwards. Round off the bottom corners and slope off the top end and flap. Fold the patterns in half lengthways to make sure both halves match.

Plate the templates on the wrong side of the leather, weight them down, and draw round them very carefully with a ballpoint pen. Cut out with the knife – never try to use scissors for leather. Use the steel rule for all straight edges.

Making the bag
Fig. 2 shows the placing of the holes through which the thonging is to pass. Measure and mark the holes on main piece, shoulder strap, front bar and side pieces exactly as shown, keeping them 6mm. (¼in.) from the edges and 1.2cm. (½in.) apart. Set the leather punch to the right size of hole for the thonging to pass through (try this out on a spare piece) and punch the holes. When you have made the holes in the front bar, mark through these holes with a pencil. Remove bar and punch holes in the bag front by rolling up the leather until the

punch reaches the holes you've marked.

The thonging is used just like thread; knot the end to start work, and knot it again to finish. Thong on the bar first, sewing each end to the bag with a cross stitch. Place the pocket inside the main piece, with right side to wrong side, matching top edges. Mark through punch holes on main piece, remove pocket and punch the corresponding holes.

Glue a strip on the bottom of the pocket not more than 3cm. (1⅛in.) wide and stick to main piece, aligning tops. Thong on side piece to bag as follows. Tie knot, thread from the wrong side of side piece, through the second hole down. Take the thong up to the first hole, going through three thicknesses (side, pocket and bag) to the bag front. Bring the thong down to the second hole, and again through three thicknesses. Continue with ordinary running stitch all round side piece, finishing with a knot behind. Join the other side piece in the same way.

For the tassel, fringe one edge of the 7cm. (2¾in.) square, roll up and secure with glue. Punch one hole right through the roll and tie the tassel to the flap centre, winding the thonging several times around the tassel top.

Thong each end of the shoulder strap to a side piece with cross-stitch.

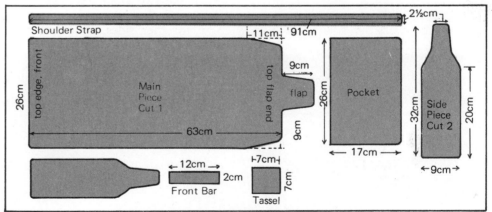

Fig. 1

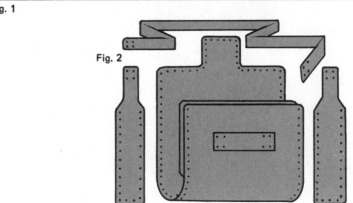

Fig. 2

Patchwork suede bag

This bag is sewn on to one of the frames you can buy in department stores, so you can make it any size you like, using our basic instructions. The patchwork section is stuck on a lightweight fabric backing and then machine stitched together using a zig-zag stitch. This avoids bulky turnings and allows the suede to lie flat. The generous gusset is inserted with a normal seam.

You will need

Scraps of different coloured suede
A piece of fine lawn fabric 29cm. by 14cm. (11½in. by 5½in.) to back the suede
Matching sewing thread
A piece of lining fabric 30cm. by 25cm. (12in. by 10in.)
A snap-fastening bag frame 11cm. wide and 5cm. high at sides (4½in. by 2in.)
Swing-needle sewing machine fitted with a leather needle and roller foot
A fine glover's needle
Latex fabric adhesive

To cut out

Make a pattern of the gusset shape (Fig. 1) and use this to cut out two gussets from two pieces of suede of the same colour. Put these aside for later use. From different coloured suedes cut out five 4cm. (1½in.) squares, four 5cm. (2in.) squares and twelve rectangles 5cm. by 4cm. (2in. by 1½in.). From the lining fabric cut a rectangle 29cm. by 14cm. (11½in. by 5½in.) and two gusset shapes.

The patchwork

Fold the rectangle of fine lawn in half lengthways and crease the fold. Unfold the fabric and place it flat on the table. Using the centre fold as a guide, place the patchwork shapes, following Fig. 2 for the arrangement of squares and rectangles. Remove the patches from the fabric and place them on the table in the chosen sequence. Now you stick the patches down. Start with the central line of squares and the two end rectangles. Lightly coat the reverse of each one with adhesive and stick to the fabric, using the central crease as a guide and butting the edges firmly together. Stick the remaining patches in place to completely cover the fabric rectangle.

Attach a leather needle and a roller foot to your machine and thread it with toning thread. Set the stitch to a wide, fairly close zig-zag and stitch the patches together along all the joins, working right across the whole rectangle each time. When the stitching is complete, trim outer edges straight.

Putting in the gussets

With the right sides of the suede together, place one gusset base as shown in Fig. 2. Using adhesive sparingly, stick the 6mm. (¼in.) seam allowance of the gusset base to the patchwork. Now, using a straight machine stitch, sew the two together to within 6mm. (¼in.) of each end with a 6mm. (¼in.) seam. Join the other gusset base to the opposite side of the rectangle in the same way. Clip into the seam allowance of the patchwork between the seamed patch and the ones at either side to a depth of 6mm. (¼in.), then pivot the edge of the patchwork at this clip and stick the side of the gusset to the side of the patchwork as before. Stitch together. Repeat for second gusset. Trim all gusset seams to 3mm. (⅛in.).

The lining

Make up the lining in the same way as the main part of the bag. With wrong sides together, insert it into the bag and stick the top edges of each together, using adhesive sparingly. Trim edges straight and level and zig-zag stitch them together all around. Insert the top edge of the bag into the slot provided in the frame, arranging the patchwork area centrally across the front and back and the gussets at the hinged sides. Put a few stitches through the holes to hold frame in position, and then, using a fine glover's needle and machine thread, slip-stitch the bag to the frame through the holes provided, removing the temporary stitches as you get to them. Fasten off the ends of the thread very securely.

Fig. 1

10 cm

14 cm

5 cm

Fig. 2

base

Suede drawstring bag

This is a very simple bag to make from offcuts of suede plus a remnant of pretty lining fabric. The double drawstrings close the bag securely enough to be thief-proof, and they are long enough for a shoulder strap.

You will need
4 pieces of suede 23cm. by 20cm. (9in. by 8in.), 2 dark green, 2 blue
Circle of dark green suede 17cm. (7in.) in diameter
Fine lawn: 2 strips 9cm. by 23cm. (3½in. by 9in.), 2 strips 27cm. by 2cm. (10½in. by ¾in.)
Latex fabric adhesive
Matching thread
Lining fabric 70cm. by 25cm. (17in. by 10in.)
Circle of stiff card 14cm. (5½in.) in diameter
2 pieces of ribbon or cord 80cm. (30in.) in length
Swing-needle sewing machine with a leather needle and roller foot
4 large sail eyelets
Sail eyelet punch; hammer
Squared paper

1. Make paper patterns of sections A and B (Fig. 1). With the wrong side of the felt upwards, place pattern A on the pieces of green suede and pattern B on the pieces of blue suede. Weight them down, draw round the patterns, marking the eyelet positions, and cut out with sharp scissors.
2. Take one green shape and one blue shape and one of the wide strips of lawn. Using adhesive sparingly, paste the shaded areas (Fig. 2) on the wrong sides of each piece. Place the lawn over the pasted green suede and smooth it down. Turn over to the right side and press the blue suede on to the remaining lawn, butting the edges of the suede closely together. Repeat for the blue piece. Using a zig-zag stitch, machine stitch the two suedes together along the butted edges, pivoting the stitching at the angles.
3. Insert the sail eyelets where marked, following the manufacturer's instructions.
4. Join the two bag sections together at one side seam, pasting the suede on to the narrow strip of lawn as previously. Zig-zag stitch the seam. Repeat for the second side seam.
5. With right sides facing, stitch the two short ends of the lining together with a 1.3cm. (½in.) seam. Press the seams open.
6. With wrong sides facing, insert the lining in the bag, placing the seam to one of the bag side seams. Using adhesive very sparingly, stick the lining to the bag around the lower edges, then stick the top edge of the lining 1.3cm. (½in.) below the top edge of the bag.
7. Turn over a 1.3cm. (½in.) wide hem around the top of the bag, stick down and top stitch in place.
8. Using a straight machine stitch, sew two rows of stitching around the bag to enclose the eyelets and make a channel for the cords.
9. Fold the circle of dark green suede into four to find the quarter points and mark these on the wrong side with ball-point pen. Find the four quarter points of the base of the bag in the same way.
10. With the bag inside out and right sides together, insert the circle into the base of the bag and secure at the four quarter points with a little adhesive. Gently ease the remaining edges of the circle into place and secure sparingly with adhesive.
11. Using a straight machine stitch, join the two sections together with a 1.3cm. (½in.) seam. Trim the seam to within 6mm. of the stitching line.
12. Run a gathering thread around the edges of the lining circle. Place this face down on the table and centre the circle of card on it. Draw up the gathers to enclose the card, secure the ends of the thread and paste generously with adhesive all over the wrong side of cards and fabric.

13. Centre the circle of lined card on to the base with wrong sides together. Press firmly in place, taking care to avoid the seam around the base. When the adhesive has set, turn the bag right side out and pull it into shape around the edges of the card.
14. Use a bodkin to thread one length of cord through the stitched channel right around the bag so each end comes out at an eyelet at either side of a seam. Knot the ends of the cord together. Thread the other cord around the channel from the eyelets at the opposite seam.

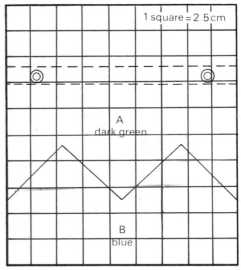

1 square = 2.5 cm

A
dark green

B
blue

Fig.1   Fig. 2

253

Embossing leather

One of the most creative and satisfying aspects of leather craft is the embossing and carving of designs on to leather. Most people start with embossing, and then move on to carving (page 255).

Only vegetable-tanned leather is suitable for embossing; this is normally beige in colour and absorbs water readily. Test your sample by dampening a corner and then pressing your thumb nail into it. If the nail leaves a permanent mark, the leather is suitable for tooling.

Tooling leather is sold by leather merchants and craft shops by the square foot but the most convenient way for the beginner to purchase it, is to buy pre-cut leather shapes. These are available for items like wallets, belts, coasters and table mats.

You will also need a set of design stamps. Buy one of the reinforced nylon type – these are far cheaper than the metal equivalent.

Cut your leather into the shape you require and punch any thonging or rivet holes. With a kit, this will already have been done for you. Then make several paper copies of the shape and work out your design stamps and pressing them on to the paper. The most interesting designs can be made by using a limited number of stamps in a regular manner. The most common beginner's mistake is to over-decorate and to use too many different stamp heads. Limit yourself to three for your first attempts.

When the design has been settled you can begin work on the leather itself. You will need a light wooden or plastic mallet for hitting the stamps, a firm working surface capable of taking the pounding, a sponge and a plastic bowl for water. A wooden or plastic rule is also useful. Do not use metal for fear of damaging the leather.

Use the sponge to moisten the leather thoroughly. The water darkens the leather temporarily. When it begins to lighten again after a minute or two you can begin.

Hold the embossing stamp vertically in a position required by the design (if you cut your own leather you can try this on an offcut) and give it a sharp tap with the mallet. Then move to the next position. The impression created should be clear and fairly deep. Do not hit in the same place twice if the first one was not strong enough – this just blurs the image.

When the design is finished allow the leather to dry before dyeing it with an alcohol-based dye. Shoe stains are suitable but craft shops have special tooling brands. Using a rag from an old tee-shirt (it's lint free), wipe the dye lightly over the leather surface so that impressions escape and are thus picked out. You can have fun with different dye colours as the picture shows. An artist's paint brush can be used to apply dye in the depressions. Dyeing is more important than actual embossing in making your project look good so play around with lots of different approaches. Felt pens can be used for picking out limited areas.

After dyeing, the final stage is to seal the leather with a clear wax polish before assembling the project. This stops damp gradually lifting your design.

Carving leather

Leather-carving is an extension of the leather embossing we dealt with on page 254. Actually, carving is something of a misnomer as it creates an image of gouging the leather away with a chisel, whereas, in fact, the leather is compressed into shape with stamping and modelling tools. The only cutting is done with the swivel knife which is used as you would a pencil in a sketch to delineate the main features of your design.

For a lot of people leather-carving is a more interesting craft than painting--for you do not have to draw to be able to do it well. Most leather-carvers get their designs from the design manuals supplied with their tool kits or from books on wood-carving or Celtic art. Finding attractive designs from here and there is one of the excitements of the craft!

When you have found a design which you think would go well on the bag or belt you are decorating, trace it off on to tracing paper. Then, having cut out your tooling leather or bought a ready-cut kit place the tracing paper over the moistened leather and, using a stylus such as a ballpen which has run out of ink, press the main lines of the design through the paper into the leather.

The next step requires a swivel knife. Again, we recommend the nylon type as they are just as good but much cheaper than the metal ones. They are available packed in sets with carving stamps.

Cut along the lines of your design as pressed into the leather with the stylus, taking care not to press so hard that you cut more than half through the moistened leather. Using the carving stamps in your set, develop the depth and texture of your design. For example, if you are carving a flower, the background is usually depressed to make the flower stand out by using a background stamp which is tapped all around the cut edges of the flower. Then other tools are used to shape the petals, leaves and so on. The instructions in your tool set will tell you all you need to know.

When the carving is complete, the article is dyed and polished as described on page 254.

swivel knife